# On Money and Credit in Europe

# On Money and Credit in Europe

## The Selected Essays of Martin M.G. Fase

Martin M.G. Fase

Executive Deputy Director of
De Nederlandsche Bank, Amsterdam and
Professor of Monetary Economics, University of Amsterdam,
The Netherlands

**Edward Elgar**

Cheltenham, UK · Northampton, MA, USA

Published by
Edward Elgar Publishing Limited
8 Lansdown Place
Cheltenham
Glos GL50 2HU
UK

Edward Elgar Publishing, Inc.
6 Market Street
Northampton
Massachusetts 01060
USA

A catalogue record for this book
is available from the British Library

**Library of Congress Cataloguing in Publication Data**

Fase, M.M.G., 1937–
On money and credit in Europe: the selected essays of Martin M.G. Fase.
Includes index.
1. Demand for money—Europe. 2. Demand for money—Europe—Mathematical models. 3. Monetary policy—Europe. 4. Finance—Europe. I. Title.
HG226.5.F37 1998
332.4'94—dc21 98-13922
CIP

ISBN 1 85898 885 3

Printed and bound in Great Britain by Biddles Ltd, Guildford and King's Lynn

# Contents

PART TWO: MONETARY DISAGGREGATION: ASSET DEMAND, BANK CREDIT, NOTES AND COINS

# List of Figures

# List of Tables

# Acknowledgements

The research reported in this book has benefited from the intellectual input from many colleagues with whom I have cooperated over the years. This is reflected in the papers, many of which are co-authored. I thank my former colleagues J.B. Kuné, F.A.G. den Butter, W.C. Boeschoten and C.C.A. Winder, who have been my co-authors but have at the time also provided me with valuable comments on my single-authored papers. I am indebted to them for their cooperation in the past and for allowing me to republish the fruits of our past scholarly work. I also wish to thank the publishers for their permission to include the published articles as chapters in this book. Last but not least I wish to thank C.K. Folkertsma, F.R. Stork, R.B.M. Vet, as well as Marianne Brouwer, Gita Gajapersad, Mariëtta Bakker-van den Bol and Vera Roos, who are all of the Econometric and Special Studies Department of De Nederlandsche Bank, for their indispensable help in editing this book.

# Introduction

Ever since I studied economics in Amsterdam I have been fascinated by empirical econometrics and economic history as means to gain a better understanding of the economic world. For a range of years the main focus of my empirical research has been on monetary econometrics. This field attempts to understand money, its working and measurement. An important topic in this area of research is the empirical examination of the demand for money. Laidler (1982), in his provocative and stimulating essays on monetarism, considered the demand for money as the theoretical core and a key feature of monetarism as it had developed in the 1950s and 1960s and had become prominent in the monetary debate, at least in continental Europe, from the 1970s onwards. I do not want to quarrel about the question whether or not the demand for money should be viewed as fundamentally Keynesian but would emphasize that it was Milton Friedman (1956) who asserted that the demand for money was an empirically stable relationship with a few measurable arguments. As such Friedman's conviction became a testable hypothesis which was at the heart of monetary debates in the last two decades or so. This was in sharp contrast to the debate following the Report of the Radcliffe Committee on the workings of the monetary system in Britain. Published in 1959 it was dominating that part of the monetary debate of the 1960s and totally ignored monetary empirics, as has been noted by e.g. Walters (1970) in his assessment and *post mortem* of the Radcliffe report. Perhaps, the explanation for this remarkable historical fact is that this important report was, to paraphrase Laidler, largely based on the proposition that demand for money is non-existing as a stable relationship. Thus, as a matter of fact, empirical money demand studies and research on its stability have been the subjects of considerable monetary research since the 1970s. This produced both new empirical evidence and, perhaps more important, novel insights, challenging research strategies, fruitful techniques of data analysis and innovative econometric tools. Apart from this, the monetary questions of the day such as the most appropriate manner to measure money, the optimal boundary between notes and coins or the moneyness of various financial assets have been of great importance to monetary research.

Obviously, these types of problem have not attracted the attention of mainstream monetary economists. However, this does not necessarily imply that they are of lesser importance; on the contrary. Perhaps it only means that we have to recognize the fact that there is high-brow and low-brow monetary economics. Perhaps aggregated and disaggregated monetary problems offer a more suitable label. The 14 chapters in this monograph provide an illustration of this development.

The papers collected in this book cover a period of over two decades of empirical monetary research and have been organized in two groups. The first group is in Part One and consists of eight chapters on aggregate money demand and monetary aggregation in The Netherlands, other European countries and the main other OECD countries. The emphasis is particularly on the evolution in money demand modelling with a focus on the stability issue. An important conclusion, which perhaps conflicts with the monetarist doctrine and with the convictions of those monetary policy makers who have a strong preference for monetary targeting, is that the demand for money is very often unstable but that this instability is dependent on the size of the domestic economy considered. The rationale behind this may be that what matters is not only the demand for money, but also the supply. As is well-known, we measure only the intersection of demand and supply curves and often this simple truth is totally neglected. However, this observation is important because it may imply that perhaps instability on the demand side may be compensated by a similar instability on the supply side as far as the supply is not completely under control of the monetary authorities.

The overwhelming theme of Part One of this book is the aggregate demand for money, which I consider the heart of empirical monetary econometrics over the last three decades or so. Although the eight chapters in Part One differ in many respects, they also share many important features. The first is the steady state specification chosen for the demand for money equation. In five of the eight chapters income, short- and long-term interest rates and inflation are included as the most important explanatory variables for the demand of nominal and real money balances. One chapter, however, considers financial wealth as an additional explanatory variable, showing substantial wealth elasticities which, with the income elasticity, surprisingly add up to one. The implication of this result is that the velocity of money also depends on wealth rather than on income and interest rates alone. This conclusion is supported by other recent research of Fase and Winder (1997) for the EU and is very promising for an understanding of the substantial growth of the money stock over the last decade and seems to moderate the volatility of the monetary picture in the long-run. A second common feature of the eight chapters of Part One is the inclusion of the business cycle indicator to model short-run money demand. I believe this is an important novelty of the money demand research presented here. The main reason for including a cyclical indicator is that it permits allowance to be made for hoarding and dishoarding of money. Another interpretation may be to consider it as a proxy for the substitution process of financial and real assets. Whatever interpretation is adopted, it is, without doubt, a typically short-run phenomenon. Allowance for short-run disequilibria is a third common feature of the chapters in Part One. However, the modelling of it shows a particular evolution over time and this is reflected in the various chapters. In the beginning short-run disequilibrium was modelled either by the partial adjustment mechanism and the cyclical indicator or more general dynamic specifications, very often inspired by the Box–Jenkins time series models. Later on, however, our modelling became more general following the general to specific methodology in econometric modelling. Thus, cointegration and error-correction methodology were applied, systematically distinguishing between short-run and equilibrium demand for money. As a result our cyclical indicator appears only in the short-run dynamics of the money demand equations. The fourth common feature of the chapters of Part One is the search for stability, which in my view has been the basic reason for the important statistical innovations in this area of research. As a matter of fact, the money demand research reported in these chapters illustrates that very often stability increases with the sophistication of statistical methodology and the size of the economic area considered. This perhaps means that money demand instability is an artefact due to misspecification and lack of control or endogeneity of the money supply. The fifth common element of the chapters in Part One is that initially a linear or simple sum monetary aggregate is considered which, however, is abandoned in the later chapters. Simple sum monetary aggregation implies the assumption of perfect substitutability of one unit of any component for one unit of any other component constituting the aggregate. This is a strong assumption and, as Barnett (1997) has argued again and again over many years, a basic source of instability. Following Barnett's (1997) high road Chapters 7 and 8 focus on nonlinear monetary aggregation. The two chapters offer a detailed examination of Europe-wide Divisia monetary aggregates to estimate money demand. Divisia aggregates are used to solve the difficult problem of aggregation across countries as well as to sort out transaction money and the moneyness of the components of financial wealth.

In important details the chapters in Part One also differ. Most prominent are the differences in modelling the dynamics of money demand.

Our approach reflects very much the evolution over time with initially the partial adjustment, Koyck-lags and Almon-lags as the most prominent econometric tools to emphasize the general time series modelling as the common econometric approach. Very often but not invariably adaptive expectations rather than rational expectations are used to model the unobservable expectations. As to the data very often we allow for seasonal variation, while a diversity of geographical areas are examined with emphasis on The Netherlands, other European Union members but Europe-wide money demand is also considered.

Part Two contains six chapters on a variety of money demand issues, such as money demand systems, financial portfolio models and the modelling of demand for either bank-notes or coins. The latter are of particular practical importance to the bank-note or coin producers who have to plan future production capacity for printing notes and minting coins. One chapter in Part Two concerns the demand for bank credit, very often considered to mirror the money supply, with special emphasis on the difficult issue of observing the loan rate.

The six chapters of Part Two are much more diverse than those of Part One but share their importance for practical monetary matters. The common feature of the Parts One and Two is, however, that the research reported is unbashedly empirical and focused on purely monetary matters.

Chapter 9 presents an example of the system-wide approach to money demand by considering several financial assets with money as a particular financial asset. This chapter is set up in the Brainard–Tobin tradition with logical and economic constraints on the model parameters due to the fact that all financial assets considered add up to total financial wealth. The estimated model permits assessment of the substitutability among assets, which is the base for monetary aggregation to be linear or not. The mirror image of money or several financial assets are outstanding loans. Bank loans and the measurement of the macroeconomic lending rate are the focus of Chapter 10. Using a multivariate regression model and an errors-in-variables framework, the loan demand equation is estimated for The Netherlands. This system of equations is used to evaluate the power of the discount rate window in controlling the money supply by the banking system. Bank-notes are the topic of Chapters 11 to 13. Chapter 11 considers payment habits on the basis of a rather unique sample survey carried out for The Netherlands. It reveals that the way we pay matters but also that the payment pattern of Dutch households was fairly stable over the years, with cash payments accounting for almost 80% in terms of numbers and 40% in terms of value. A similar estimate has been found for American households. Moreover, the need for currency depends very much on the way people pay with cash. Chapter 12 focuses on large bank-notes in The Netherlands, again on the basis of sample surveys showing that large bank-notes are mainly used as a means of hoarding but hardly in normal economic transactions. Perhaps an important implication of this finding is that issuing large notes by the future European Central Bank should be reconsidered. Chapter 13 is on forecasting the denominational mix of bank-notes in circulation, which is of particular importance for central banks as producers and suppliers of huge quantities of bank-notes to meet the public demand. Similarly, Chapter 14 considers forecasting the need for coins, again by denomination. The denominational mix of notes and coins is seldom discussed in the monetary literature and greatly neglected in monetary economics. Nevertheless, as pointed out by Manski and Goldin (1987), the combination of bank-notes and coins of different nominal values adds up to currency in circulation and is part of the fine structure of a monetary economy as is the denomination-specific demand for currency. The two forecasting exercises for notes and coins are of particular interest to those who want to reflect on such mundane matters as the future need for notes and coins for the imminent European Economic and Monetary Union with its single currency called Euro.

The research style throughout all chapters in this book has been to examine monetary data. These data cover money, financial assets, notes, coins and bank loans for The Netherlands, other single European countries and Europe as a whole. A common feature is the statistical methodology used and the geographical area covered by the data. These monetary data, the focus and the geographical area justify the title of this collection of essays. My hope is that by reading the 14 chapters of this volume the reader will obtain a feeling for the macro- and micro-microeconomic intricacies of money. Moreover, I hope that the efforts made by the reader of this book will provide him or her with a better appreciation of monetary research pursued at a central bank of a small European country and not the least with the evolution in one important area of monetary macroeconomics. Perhaps, and hopefully, this will lead to a better understanding of how money functions, providing a stimulus for new research in the new European EMU, possibly the main institutional change of the twentieth century.

PART ONE

# Aggregate Money Demand

*Since empirical work on the demand for money is a dramatic growth industry, additional evidence on the empirical issues is accumulating rapidly and we may confidently expect a still further convergence of answers.*

Friedman (1969, p. 143)

*Die Stabilität der Umlaufsgeschwindigkeit ist somit identisch mit der Stabilität der Geldnachfrage, wobei eine stabile Umlaufsgeschwindigkeit dann nicht mehr eine konstante Umlaufsgeschwindigkeit bedeutet, sondern lediglich einen stabilen Zusammenhang zwischen der Umlaufsgeschwindigkeit und den Parametern der Geldnachfragefunktion.*

Bofinger, Reischle, and Schächter (1996, p. 249)

*Faut-il préférer une politique d'agrégats monétaires ou de taux d'intérêt? L'option entre les politiques de quantités et de taux resulte au départ de la volonté de ne pas, en les combinant, 'surdéterminer' le système* [ ... ]

Boissieu (1978, p. 1658)

# 1. Price and Income Expectations and the Demand for Money, Some Quarterly Evidence for The Netherlands, 1952–1971

## 1.1 INTRODUCTION

Since the end of the thirties, when Brown (1938, 1939), published the first statistical studies of the demand for money, there have been so many empirical investigations in this field that today it is virtually impossible to have an overview of the results. It is clear that the investigations differ considerably as regards the specification as well as the empirical results. As to the methods used several mainstreams may be distinguished. First, the majority of the investigations emphasize the demand for money rather than the supply. The supply, then, is assumed – implicitly in most times – to be autonomous, that is independent of the explanatory variables in the demand function. By doing so there are no longer theoretical objections to postulating an isolated demand for money function. The second mainstream is characterized by the choice of the set of explanatory variables. Various authors, including Gilbert (1953) and Teigen (1970), have pointed out the evolution in the theories on this issue. In the classical quantity theory the demand for money is treated mainly as demand for transactions balances. The elasticity of the rate of interest is assumed to be zero while income elasticity is implicitly fixed at unity. It need hardly be said that this approach leaves no room for statistical verification at all. The orthodox Keynesian view not only differs from this approach, but it also distinguishes between transactions demand and speculative demand, *i.e.* cash balances held in anticipation of a decrease of stock exchange prices of – or higher yields on – less liquid assets, such as bonds, for avoiding capital losses. Taken this way, the aggregate demand for transactions and speculative balances

Based on M.M.G. Fase and J.B. Kuné (1974) 'De vraag naar liquiditeiten in Nederland, 1952–1971', *De Economist*, **122**, 326–356.

depends on income and long-term interest rates. This view is reflected in the above-mentioned studies by Brown.

Further theoretical developments consisted mainly in refinements of the above basic themes. First there is the extension by Baumol and Tobin that also the transactions balances are sensitive to the interest rate on account of the opportunity cost of holding cash balances reflected by *e.g.* the yield on time deposits or on easily negotiable assets. Then there is the extension of the model by introducing wealth as an explanatory variable into the demand function. The arguments in support of this variable differ. There is the very formal view, expressed by Friedman and others, that the demand for money is just one single equation in a whole range of demand equations for financial and real assets. In the same way as the budget restriction causes the household's income to be introduced as an explanatory variable into the demand function for consumer goods, so is the wealth restriction a justification for introducing wealth as an explanatory variable into the demand for money function. However, wealth is sometimes introduced because the Keynesian concept of an individual who holds not more than two assets (cash balances and bonds) was judged too simplistic, although statistical elaborations on this point usually work with a kind of permanent income as a short cut to aggregate wealth.

Of the basic principles, the development of which has been outlined in the short retrospect above, the most valuable elements have been incorporated in our own study of the demand for money in The Netherlands on which this chapter reports.

The next section summarizes the studies made so far with regard to The Netherlands. The most important conclusion to be drawn from it is that, although interesting results have been obtained, enough problems remain to justify further research. Section 1.3 outlines the theoretical framework used in the present study. The statistical results are presented in Sections 1.4 and 1.5. They show the income elasticity to be considerably smaller than unity and the interest rate elasticity to be fairly low. The price elasticity yielded by our investigation corresponds very well to the results obtained by others. It also appears that if the period of observation 1952:I–1971:IV is divided into sub-periods the demand function is reasonably stable. In Section 1.6 some of the results are compared with those taken from a number of recent studies for other countries also based on quarterly data.

## 1.2 Earlier Studies of the Demand for Money in The Netherlands

Up till now only a small number of investigations of the demand for money in The Netherlands have been published. Dierick (1967) endeavoured to explain the liquidity ratio from the rate of interest, whereas Stevers (1963) studied the inverse relationship when he explained the rate of interest from the liquidity ratio. Both authors used the liquidity preference theory as a starting point and based their empirical estimates on quarterly figures or on annual figures aggregated from quarterly data. Nieuwenburg (1969) based his work on cross-section data for 1960 and he estimated money demand functions for individual households. Stevers' equation has been re-estimated for a different sample period by Nieuwenburg and Koeman (1969). Finally, it was Adekunle (1968), and in a somewhat wider context also Korteweg (1973a, 1973b), who presented demand for money estimates based on annual figures.[1]

All the above studies differ not only in the data used, but also in the methods applied. The broad variations in model specification and data base usage warrant closer scrutiny before we present the results of our own investigation.

From the work of each of the authors mentioned above who used time series, the most relevant demand function, written in our own notation, is shown in Table 1.1. It also shows the period of observation and the coefficient of determination (adjusted for degrees of freedom), while *t*-statistics have been added in parentheses.

The summary shows first of all that the specifications used are rather different, but that the goodness of fit measured by $R^2$ is on the whole very satisfactory. Both Dierick and Stevers assume a hyperbolic relationship between the rate of interest and the liquidity ratio, the latter taking the rate of interest as the dependent variable. But for a single equation which, moreover, yields a high coefficient of determination, there is little or no objection to a reversal of the relationship. That is not to say that this reversal is allowed from a theoretical point of view. The equation of Stevers is a reduced-form equation, whereas the one of Dierick is a structural equation. Korteweg takes a linear regression equation to explain the liquidity ratio, whereas Adekunle assumes a logarithmic linear relationship between the demand for money (narrowly defined) and, among other things, the rate of interest. The result obtained by

[1] The studies by Bakhoven (1971), Beld (1968) and Driehuis (1972) also contain interest rate and demand for money equations. Although they resemble Stevers' equation they are less suitable for isolated consideration. The work by Cramer and Reekers (1972), an analysis of the money stock by holder, may be left out here.

*Table 1.1: Some previous studies on the demand for money in The Netherlands*

| Study | Estimated equation | Sample period | $\bar{R}^2$ |
|---|---|---|---|
| Stevers (1963) | $\underset{}{r_t} = 5.079 + \underset{(4.29)}{0.030}\frac{1}{l_t - 0.385} - \underset{(5.58)}{3.783c_t} + \underset{(5.81)}{0.636\bar{r}_t}$ | 1949–1960 | 0.94 |
| Dierick (1967) | $l_t = 16.340 + \underset{(7.02)}{3.32}\frac{10}{r_t} + \underset{(10.0)}{1.35}\frac{10}{c_t} + \underset{(7.61)}{0.78b_t}$ | 1951:I–1966:IV | 0.92 |
| Adekunle (1968) | $\ln m_t = \underset{(8.81)}{-1.632} - \underset{(4.40)}{0.340}\ln r_t + \underset{(11.32)}{0.591}\ln y_t - \underset{(1.50)}{0.599}\Delta\ln p_t$ | 1951–1962 | 0.90 |
| Nieuwenburg and Koeman (1969) | $r_t = 5.027 + \underset{(7.34)}{0.235}\frac{1}{l_t - 0.3} - \underset{(2.58)}{2.836c_t} + \underset{(0.60)}{0.110\bar{r}_t}$ | 1949–1966 | 0.93 |
| Korteweg (1973b) | $l_t = \underset{(10.70)}{33.89} - \underset{(7.64)}{2.05r_t} - \underset{(0.84)}{0.08}\Delta\ln p_t + \underset{(8.27)}{0.70}\frac{Tax_{t-1}}{Y_t} - \underset{(0.91)}{0.90l_{t-1}}$ | 1952–1971 | 0.99 |

*Notes:* $t$-values in parentheses; symbols are explained in the main text.

Nieuwenburg and Koeman is a re-estimate – with slight differences and for a somewhat longer period – of the relationship studied by Stevers. One of the differences is that Stevers considers the actual liquidity ratio in deviation from the as normal regarded value of 38.5%; Nieuwenburg and Koeman chose a value of 30% because the actual liquidity ratio had fallen below 38.5% since Stevers made his study, which should be taken into account to avoid implausible implications as to the rate of interest. Another aspect in which the regression equations show large differences are the variables themselves. The liquidity ratio $l_t$ is defined by the total amount of broadly defined money as a percentage of net national income. Differences arise when these concepts are specified in greater detail. Stevers uses the total amount of broadly defined money adjusted for excessive tax assessments. Dierick considers also broadly defined money but includes saving balances because of his empirical findings. On the other hand he introduces $b_t$, current tax assessments as a percentage of net national income, as an additional explanatory variable. Korteweg, entirely in line with his particular approach, defines the liquidity ratio as the ratio of narrowly defined money and gross consumer expenditure. Also Adekunle uses only narrowly defined money, $m_t$, adjusted for price. The interest variable used, $r_t$, almost invariably represents the interest rate on long-term government bonds.

Stevers – and Nieuwenburg and Koeman follow his example – moreover introduces what he called a normal rate of interest, $\bar{r}_t$, an average of interest rates in the past. It is doubtful whether this makes much difference, for the changes in the various rates of interest show great interdependence (see e.g. Fase (1973)). Another point to be noted is that only Adekunle introduces income, $y_t$, as an independent variable. Interesting among the other variables is the business cycle indicator, $c_t$, included by Stevers and Dierick. The relative change in prices, $\Delta \ln p_t$, used in the regression equations of both Adekunle and Korteweg may also be regarded as a business cycle indicator, but it should be emphasized that the authors themselves do not give that interpretation. Finally, Korteweg includes as an independent variable, but not on very convincing grounds, the tax assessments lagged one year, $Tax_{t-1}$, expressed as a percentage of consumer expenditure at current prices, $Y_t$ in his equation. As we shall show later, this procedure has significant consequences for the implied income elasticity of the demand for money.

The above studies provide information on income and interest rate elasticities. The values yielded for the interest rate elasticity show fairly wide divergences. Stevers obtained an elasticity of about $-3.0$, Nieuwenburg and Koeman $-1.15$, Dierick $-0.17$ and Adekunle $-0.34$. From Korteweg's study an interest rate elasticity of $-0.18$ may be derived (all, except Adekunle's, calculated in the mean). When interpreting these results it should be kept in mind that the definitions of money used by the various authors range from narrow (Adekunle and Korteweg) to broad (the other authors). It is surprising, therefore, that Dierick and Korteweg found roughly the same interest rate elasticity. Another point to be noted is the very high elasticity found by both Stevers and Nieuwenburg and Koeman; these results remain remarkable even if the sensitivity of the interest rate elasticity to the point chosen on the curve is taken into account. Interesting results were also obtained for the income elasticity. It may be shown that Stevers, Dierick (if we ignore the latter's $b_t$ variable), and Nieuwenburg and Koeman all assume a unity value for the income elasticity of the demand for money. Korteweg also works with an implied income elasticity but allows it to differ from 1 because he has included the current tax assessments as an independent variable; he thus finds the quite plausible value of 0.77 (calculated in the mean). It is only Adekunle who uses an estimate, roughly 0.6.

At this point it is worth while to make a comparison with some of the results obtained by Nieuwenburg (1969) when he analysed a sample drawn from individual households. For narrowly defined money he found an income elasticity (taken in the mean) of 3.26, and for broadly defined money, i.e. narrowly defined money plus interest-bearing deposits such as time and savings deposits, 2.28. It should be observed, however, that it is quite usual for corresponding behavioural parameters to be higher in cross-sections than in time series.[2]

The above summary of Netherlands' studies shows that there are large differences in results and also that a number of questions are still to be answered.[3] In the next section we shall endeavour to answer some of these questions by presenting estimates of the interest rate, income and price elasticities. Another point we shall investigate is the degree in which our estimates are sensitive to changes in the sample period chosen. This may provide some insight into the stability of the demand for money function. We shall use quarterly figures relating to sub-periods from the whole period of observation.

---

[2] See for instance Aigner and Simon (1970).

[3] It may be asked whether Tinbergen's pre-war investigation of the demand for money for bank credit (Tinbergen 1937) should not be included. We do not think it should, bank credit being the inverse of the demand for money.

## 1.3 Specification of the Demand for Money Function

Many investigations of the demand for money postulate a demand function which, in addition to interest rate, income and (sometimes) price variable, includes the lagged money demand as an independent variable (see, for instance, Chow (1966) and Korteweg (1973b)). To simplify the interpretation of the parameters of such equations it is necessary to state explicitly the structure on which the equations are based. To do so for our present investigation is the major aim of this section. A practical difficulty may be rendered by the fact that different structures sometimes yield the same final equations, which makes it impossible to recognize the model selected. Sometimes also, the specification chosen distorts the results (see for instance Waud (1968)). In our formulation the concept of adaptive expectations has been combined with the concept of partial adjustment and in that respect our study resembles those of Feige (1967), Laidler and Parkin (1970) and Villanueva (1971a), to mention a few authors.

First, we have assumed the public's desired money balances in the period $t$, $m_t^*$, to be determined by expected income in the same period $y_t^*$, the rate of interest $r_t$, and the general price level $p_t$, the last two measured in the middle of the period of observation $t$. The variable $c_t$ has been included as a business cycle indicator.

We already noted the inclusion of the last variable in the studies by Stevers and Dierick. Arguments for its inclusion may be derived from Kessler (1958) who discusses changes in economic activity and their monetary implications. He makes out a case for an increased liquidity preference – desired money balances in our language – as a consequence of a slow down in the economy and generated by speculative and precautionary motives. As an independent variable the price variable allows us to ascertain whether the nominal money balances change in accordance with price changes. As may be seen from the survey published by Feige and Pearce (1972), authors in this respect often assume a unity price elasticity of the demand for money. Only a few authors, among them Price (1972) and Grandmont (1973), test this assumption. We shall do the same. As already shown, interest rate and income are common variables in the demand for money function. However, expected income and desired money balances are non-observable.

To begin with we postulate the following logarithmic-linear relationship between desired money balances and the independent variables:

$$m_t^* = \alpha_0 + \alpha_1 y_t^* + \alpha_2 r_t + \alpha_3 p_t + \alpha_4 c_t \qquad (1.1)$$

where each variable is in logarithmic form.[4]

As already noted, expected income and desired money balances are variables that cannot be observed. We therefore assume expected income to adjust whenever actual income appears to deviate from the last foregoing expectation and the adjustment to take place in accordance with the adaptive expectations model.[5] It follows that

$$y_t^* - y_{t-1}^* = \lambda(y_t - y_{t-1}^*) \tag{1.2}$$

where $y_t$ and $y_t^*$ are the logarithms of income and expected income in the period $t$ , with $0 < \lambda \leq 1$. Because (1.2) is linear in its logarithms, $\lambda$ may be interpreted as the income elasticity of expected income. From repeated substitution of (1.2) it can be derived that $y_t^*$ is a linear function of the present income and all incomes in the past with an exponentially distributed lag, so that $y_t^* = \lambda \sum_{i=0}^{\infty} (1-\lambda)^i y_{t-i}$.

For the money balances held, $m_t$, it has been assumed that

$$m_t = m_{t-1} + \theta(m_t^* - m_{t-1}) \tag{1.3}$$

where $0 < \theta \leq 1$. Equation (1.3) expresses that the logarithm of actual money balances in the period $t$, $m_t$, will move only part of the way from the starting position, $m_{t-1}$, to the optimal position $m_t^*$.

Finally, we assume the supply of money to be autonomous and to be absorbed by the desired money balances in the period of observation.

Substitution of equations (1.1) to (1.3) yields

$$\begin{aligned} m_t = {} & \alpha_0\lambda\theta + [(1-\lambda) + (1-\theta)]m_{t-1} - [(1-\lambda)(1-\theta)]m_{t-2} \\ & + \alpha_1\lambda\theta y_t + \alpha_2\theta r_t - \alpha_2(1-\lambda)\theta r_{t-1} + \alpha_3\theta p_t \\ & - \alpha_3(1-\lambda)\theta p_{t-1} + \alpha_4\theta c_t - \alpha_4(1-\lambda)\theta c_{t-1}. \end{aligned} \tag{1.4}$$

Equation (1.4), the reduced form of the model described above, is a general formulation which contains three interesting special cases.

Equation (1.4) is achieved by combining the adaptive expectations and the partial adjustment model. In our notation, therefore, $0 < \lambda$, $\theta < 1$. A special case of (1.4) arises when $\theta = 1$ (with $0 < \lambda < 1$), or, in other words, by assuming actual money balances to equal desired money

[4] The specifications generally used are linear or logarithmic linear. We prefer the latter because they yield elasticities directly, and also because they emerge from Zarembka's investigation for the United States (Zarembka 1968) as the most suitable.

[5] Formulation (1.2) is intuitively less appealing than at other times in the literature used formula $y_t^* - y_{t-1}^* = \lambda(y_{t-1} - y_{t-1}^*)$, as this formula can be used as an appropriate forecasting scheme. Nevertheless, we prefer (1.2), because this one yields a more general regression equation. In addition we are not concerned with a forecasting scheme but with a suitable determination of expected income.

balances but maintaining the hypothesis of adaptive expectations. The demand for money function then becomes

$$m_t = \alpha_0\lambda + (1-\lambda)m_{t-1} + \alpha_1\lambda y_t + \alpha_2 r_t - \alpha_2(1-\lambda)r_{t-1} + \alpha_3 p_t - \alpha_3(1-\lambda)p_{t-1} + \alpha_4 c_t - \alpha_4(1-\lambda)c_{t-1} \qquad (1.4')$$

A second special case of (1.4) occurs if the hypothesis of adaptive expectations is abandoned while the concept of partial adjustment of actual to desired money balances is maintained, i.e. by specifying $\lambda = 1$ and $0 < \theta < 1$. This yields

$$m_t = \alpha_0\theta + (1-\theta)m_{t-1} + \alpha_1\theta y_t + \alpha_2\theta r_t + \alpha_3\theta p_t + \alpha_4\theta c_t \qquad (1.4'')$$

The most simple special case occurs by assuming expectations to be static ($\lambda = 1$) and adjustments to be immediate ($\theta = 1$). The demand for money function is then

$$m_t = \alpha_0 + \alpha_1 y_t + \alpha_2 r_t + \alpha_3 p_t + \alpha_4 c_t \qquad (1.4''')$$

By the above procedure we obtain four alternative specifications of the demand for money which may be tested empirically. Before doing so we shall consider three problems that are raised by the above equations.

First, it appears that equation (1.4) contains more coefficients than structural parameters. This means that the relationship is over-identified. Below, this problem has been eliminated by testing several *a priori* values of $\lambda$, so that (1.4) can be rewritten as

$$m_t - (1-\lambda)m_{t-1} = \alpha_0\theta\lambda + (1-\theta)[m_{t-1} - (1-\lambda)m_{t-2}] + \alpha_1\theta\lambda y_t + \alpha_2\theta[r_t - (1-\lambda)r_{t-1}] + \alpha_3\theta[p_t - (1-\lambda)p_{t-1}] + \alpha_4\theta[c_t - (1-\lambda)c_{t-1}] \qquad (1.5)$$

where for each $\lambda$ we construct a synthetic variable.[6] The alternative to this procedure is to apply least-squares under nonlinear constraints. For simplicity's sake this method has not been employed.

The second problem is the disturbance term. In the above formulation they are added when the equations (1.4) have been derived; if

[6] As $\lambda$ and $\theta$ are symmetrical, *a priori* values might equally well have been assigned to $\theta$. In cases like the one represented by equation (1.4) it is not always possible, therefore, to distinguish between the adaptive expectations model and the partial adjustment model. Owing to the introduction of the explanatory variables $p_t$, $r_t$ and $c_t$ the problem does not occur in the present investigation. See also Waud (1968). The estimation procedure suggested may be regarded as a conditional maximum likelihood estimate, in which the maximum likelihood function is being maximized for a number of predetermined and feasible values of $\lambda$. From the ML-estimators thus obtained the best is then selected.

there is any autocorrelation it will certainly show up. As long as no autocorrelation is apparent the small sample estimates are unbiased in spite of the fact that $m$ is autoregressive (*cf.* Goldberger (1964, pp. 272 *et seq.*)).

Finally, serious difficulties will arise if autocorrelation would also show up in the disturbance term, as this would mean that the ordinary least-squares estimators are not consistent.

It is possible to include a time variable in the regression equation to express changes in institutional arrangements and social habits. In fact this has been done already by discerning desired and actual cash balances. Most of our regression equations are difference equations, of which the solution for $m_t$ is a timepath. This is not the case however for equation (1.4‴). Therefore we have experimented with a time variable in (1.4‴). The results were unsatisfactory. Therefore we continued without any time variable.

## 1.4 Data and Results

The four regression equations formulated above were initially estimated with quarterly data for the whole sample period 1952:I to 1971:IV. Most of the data are taken from existing sources; in a single instance they are calculated expressly for our investigation, though based on published data. With the exception of interest rates all observations are seasonally adjusted.

Money stock data are based on the broad concept of money as defined by De Nederlandsche Bank [7] and represent quarterly averages. Income is based on gross national expenditure in the relevant quarters in fixed prices (1963 = 100). Interest rates are quarterly averages of the yields on 18 long-term government bond loans. The price variable is the GNP price deflator in the relevant quarter (1963 = 100). The business cycle

[7] The money stock, broadly defined, as used in the present investigation, is the concept of 'total domestic liquid assets' as defined by De Nederlandsche Bank. It consists of 'primary' and 'secondary' liquid assets. Primary liquid assets comprise notes and coin, and demand deposits at banks and giro institutions held by other than public authorities and money creating institutions. Secondary liquid assets comprise claims on public authorities and money creating institutions held by the general public. The claims on public authorities are Treasury bills, Treasury notes, tax certificates, reconstruction bonds, short-term loans, and balances at the Treasury; also call loans, short-term loans, and advances to local authorities and short-term claims of various descriptions on the Bank for Netherlands Municipalities and The Netherlands Polder Boards Bank. The claims on money creating institutions comprise time deposits, call loans, foreign exchange balances of residents and liquid savings. See De Nederlandsche Bank, Annual Report for 1972, Statistical Annex, pp. 18–19, Table 3.1, Explanatory Note.

indicator is the quarterly average of the male labour reserve expressed as a percentage of the male labour force excluding self-employed.

The period of observation encompasses 80 quarters, which yields sufficient observations for the regression calculations to be repeated for a number of sub-periods. Two such repetitions were performed. First, the full period was divided in a somewhat arbitrary way into two sub-periods: 1952:I–1960:I and 1960:II–1971:IV. Second, a more fundamental division was made consisting of three sub-periods, each of which – taking the registered male labour reserve and the number of unfilled vacancies as indicators – encompasses one full period of the trade cycle: viz. 1952:I–1958:IV, 1959:I–1967:IV and 1968:I–1971:IV, respectively covering 28, 36 and 16 quarterly observations.

First the equations (1.4‴) and (1.4″) were estimated. Table 1.2 shows the results; $t$-values have been given in parentheses. The $R^2$-statistics are adjusted for degrees of freedom. The first estimate yields the (a) results which show a high degree of autocorrelation. Re-estimation, based on the assumption that the residuals follow a first-order autoregressive scheme, yields the equations (b), which – at least in this respect – are satisfactory.[8] It is also satisfactory that all regression coefficients have the expected signs. Less satisfactory are the low $t$-values for some of the coefficients. The estimates for the various sub-periods present much the same picture, although the coefficients, particularly those of the price variable, change rather erratically from sub-period to sub-period. As this result has no economic meaning we shall not deal with it in further detail.

For this reason we have continued by investigating the more complicated relationships (1.4′) and (1.4). The most satisfactory of the results have been reported in Table 1.3; $t$-values have again been given in parentheses. For a proper interpretation of the data in Table 1.3 it should be remembered that, to simplify the calculations, *a priori* values for $\lambda$ have been used in both equations. Therefore equation (1.5) has been rewritten as

$$m'_t = \alpha_0\theta\lambda + (1-\theta)m'_{t-1} + \alpha_1\theta\lambda y_t + \alpha_2\theta r'_t + \alpha_3\theta p'_t + \alpha_4\theta c'_t \qquad (1.5')$$

where $m'_t = m_t - (1-\lambda)m_{1-t}$. The same formula applies to $r'_t$, $p'_t$ and $c'_t$. The heuristic calculation of $\lambda$ did not yield sufficiently clear results to justify the selection of any particular value for $\lambda$ as we always obtained high values for $\bar{R}^2$. Another indication is sometimes provided by the Durbin–Watson statistic (DW), while very low values for $\lambda$ imply

[8] In testing for the optimal autocorrelation coefficient $\rho$ the scanning method was used. It was applied to the range $-0.95 \leq \rho \leq 0.95$ with intervals of 0.1. For a justification of this procedure see Dhrymes (1971) and others.

*Table 1.2: Regression results for equations (1.4‴) and (1.4″); 1952:I–1971:IV*

| | | |
|---|---|---|
| (1.4‴) (a) | $m_t$ | $= -1.11 + 0.72y_t - 0.14r_t + 1.05p_t + 0.08c_t$ |
| | | (3.47) (5.47) (2.33) (5.98) (5.53) |
| | | $\text{DW} = 0.23 \quad R^2 = 0.99$ |
| (b) | $m_t$ | $= -0.73 + 0.67y_t - 0.05r_t + 0.94p_t + 0.07c_t$ |
| | | (2.37) (7.13) (0.87) (8.00) (4.03) |
| | | $\text{DW} = 1.52 \quad R^2 = 0.92$ |
| (1.4″) (a) | $m_t$ | $= -0.16 + 0.05y_t - 0.02r_t + 0.06p_t + 0.02c_t + 0.96m_{t-1}$ |
| | | (1.78) (1.20) (1.25) (1.11) (3.75) (33.17) |
| | | $\text{DW} = 1.28 \quad R^2 = 0.99$ |
| (b) | $m_t$ | $= -2.79 + 0.11y_t - 0.03r_t + 0.09p_t + 0.02c_t + 0.91m_{t-1}$ |
| | | (2.19) (1.96) (1.27) (1.23) (3.36) (20.23) |
| | | $\text{DW} = 1.98 \quad R^2 = 0.99$ |

rather implausible adjustment speeds. The various $\lambda$-values for which the results have been shown in Table 1.3 are therefore only a selection from the calculations actually performed.

For equation (1.4′), the (a) results show that the coefficient of $y_t$, i.e. the short-run income elasticity, decreases when $\lambda$ decreases. It is easily shown that the long-run income elasticity moves in the opposite direction. For the present case the other elasticities are similar to the regression coefficients. The interest rate elasticity is practically constant, while the price elasticity decreases in accordance with $\lambda$. The coefficient of the business cycle indicator remains remarkably constant for the various values of $\lambda$. The results also show unsatisfactory values for the DW-statistic, which persist when the equations are re-estimated for subperiods. In view of the autocorrelation found in (1.4′), the equation was re-estimated on the assumption of the residuals of (a) following a first-order autoregressive scheme. The results were entered under (b). Note that for the scanning procedure used the results are very sensitive to the autocorrelation coefficient selected. The selection has been based on the adjusted $R^2$ and DW-statistics. As to the regression coefficients, the picture of (1.4′) (a) is repeated, although in absolute terms the interest rate elasticity is now considerably lower. The price elasticity is also much lower and therefore less plausible.

It was impossible to select a value for $\lambda$ on the strength of the estimates obtained. This was one of the main reasons for estimating re-

*Table 1.3: The main regression results for equation (1.4) and (1.4′), 1952:I–1971:IV*

| | $\lambda$ | Estimates | DW | $\bar{R}^2$ |
|---|---|---|---|---|
| Equation (1.4′) | | | | |
| (a) | 0.9 | $m'_t = -10.76 + 0.67y_t - 0.14r'_t + 1.02p'_t + 0.08c'_t$ | 0.25 | 0.99 |
| | | (3.50) (5.47) (2.38) (5.76) (5.60) | | |
| | 0.7 | $m'_t = -9.07 + 0.56y_t - 0.14r'_t + 0.94p'_t + 0.09c'_t$ | 0.31 | 0.99 |
| | | (3.58) (5.60) (2.23) (5.24) (4.50) | | |
| | 0.5 | $m'_t = -7.48 + 0.45y_t - 0.12r'_t + 0.79p'_t + 0.09c'_t$ | 0.39 | 0.99 |
| | | (3.92) (6.11) (1.98) (5.38) (4.38) | | |
| (b) | 0.9 | $m'_t = -7.30 + 0.65y_t - 0.04r'_t + 0.85p'_t + 0.08c'_t$ | 1.46 | 0.91 |
| | | (2.55) (7.55) (0.71) (7.38) (4.31) | | |
| | 0.7 | $m'_t = -8.74 + 0.62y_t - 0.04r'_t + 0.68p'_t + 0.09c'_t$ | 1.54 | 0.93 |
| | | (3.94) (9.08) (0.71) (6.11) (4.83) | | |
| | 0.5 | $m'_t = -8.07 + 0.53y_t - 0.04r'_t + 0.46p'_t + 0.08c'_t$ | 1.65 | 0.90 |
| | | (4.76) (10.77) (0.81) (4.52) (4.78) | | |
| Equation (1.4) | | | | |
| | 0.9 | $m'_t = -1.68 + 0.05y_t - 0.02r'_t + 0.06p'_t + 0.02c'_t$ | 1.40 | 0.99 |
| | | (1.89) (1.33) (1.35) (1.04) (3.20) | | |
| | | $+ 0.96m'_{t-1}$ | | |
| | | (30.90) | | |
| | 0.7 | $m'_t = -1.63 + 0.06y_t - 0.03r'_t + 0.06p'_t + 0.02c'_t$ | 1.70 | 0.99 |
| | | (1.90) (1.49) (1.35) (0.89) (3.60) | | |
| | | $+ 0.95m'_{t-1}$ | | |
| | | (26.28) | | |
| | 0.5 | $m'_t = -1.69 + 0.07y_t - 0.03r'_t + 0.05p'_t + 0.02c'_t$ | 1.95 | 0.99 |
| | | (2.09) (1.86) (1.28) (0.64) (3.29) | | |
| | | $+ 0.92m'_{t-1}$ | | |
| | | (20.86) | | |

gression equation (1.4). The results clearly show that $\lambda$ hardly influences the estimated coefficients, which implies the long-run income elasticity to change markedly with $\lambda$ (see Table 1.4). The values of the DW-statistic indicate the absence of autocorrelation in the residuals. The sub-period results – again not reported in the table – show significant differences from those for the whole period, with the price elasticity again following erratic movements over the various sub-periods. On the whole, the breakdown into sub-periods suggests a lack of stability in the demand function.

We have summarized the results of this section in Table 1.4 in which, in addition, we have to $\lambda$ and $1-\theta$ presented the elasticities with respect to income, interest rate, price and the business cycle indicator. The elasticities are long-run elasticities. The same objections that could be raised against the results in Tables 1.2 and 1.3 hold for those in Table 1.4. An interesting point is that despite the erratic movements in most of the results, the estimates for $1-\theta$ do not show remarkable differences, although there is considerable variation in the estimates for $\theta$ itself. Broadly speaking, however, the results for equation (1.4″) – the special case of (1.4) with $\lambda = 1$ – resemble very well with those for equation (1.4).

The general inference to be drawn from this section is that the equations show large variations in their empirical results, which makes it impossible to come to any definite decision on the numerical values of the elasticities. This holds for the results in the sub-periods as well, where also a particular variation shows up in the price elasticity, probably due to the specification chosen for the price variable. In the next section we shall take a closer look at these problems and the stability of the money demand function.

## 1.5 Further Specification and Estimation

The basis of all our results reported so far was equation (1.1) which assumed desired money balances to be partly determined by the price level in the current period. This implies that in the current period the price elasticity of the expected price is 1. In other words, what we discussed in the preceding section was a special case of the static price expectations. We shall now study the influence of another assumption on the price expectations on our results. We replace equation (1.1) by

$$m_t^* = \alpha_0 + \alpha_1 y_t^* + \alpha_2 r_t + \alpha_3 p_t^* + \alpha_4 c_t \tag{1.6}$$

*Table 1.4: Some selected elasticity coefficients*

| Relationship | Income | Interest rate | Price | Business cycle indicator | $\lambda$ | $1-\theta$ |
|---|---|---|---|---|---|---|
| (1.4‴) (b) | 0.67 | −0.05 | 0.94 | 0.07 | 1.0[a] | 0.0[a] |
| (1.4″) (b) | 1.22 | −0.36 | 1.01 | 0.25 | 1.0[a] | 0.91 |
| (1.4′) (b) | 0.72 | −0.04 | 0.85 | 0.08 | 0.9[a] | 0.0[a] |
| | 0.89 | −0.04 | 0.68 | 0.09 | 0.7[a] | 0.0[a] |
| | 1.06 | −0.04 | 0.46 | 0.08 | 0.5[a] | 0.0[a] |
| (1.4) | 1.38 | −0.55 | 1.38 | 0.37 | 0.9[a] | 0.96 |
| | 1.45 | −0.49 | 1.06 | 0.33 | 0.7[a] | 0.95 |
| | 1.58 | −0.39 | 0.61 | 0.27 | 0.5[a] | 0.92 |

*Note:* [a] means $\lambda$ has been given the indicated value.

where all variables are expressed in logarithmic form. Because the expected price cannot be observed, we postulate – in the same way as we did for the expected income in equation (1.2) – an adaptive expectations model, so that

$$p_t^* - p_{t-1}^* \leq \zeta(p_t - p_{t-1}^*) \tag{1.7}$$

where $0 < \zeta \leq 1$. Because all variables are in logarithms, $\zeta$ is the elasticity with respect to expected price. It is easily demonstrated that the assumption of $\zeta = 1$ yields equation (1.1).

The model discussed in this section consists of the equations (1.6) and (1.7) combined with (1.2) and (1.3). Suitable substitutions (see Appendix 1.A for derivations and the notation used) yield the final equation

$$\tilde{m}_t = \alpha_0\theta\lambda\zeta + (1-\theta)\tilde{m}_{t-1} + \alpha_1\theta\lambda y_t' + \alpha_2\theta\tilde{r}_t + \alpha_3\theta\zeta p_t' + \alpha_4\theta\tilde{c}_t. \tag{1.8}$$

Because (1.8) is over-identified, and particularly in order to simplify the estimation process, we have used *a priori* values for $\lambda$ and $\zeta$. The observations in (1.8) are therefore synthetic and functions of $\lambda$ and $\zeta$ (see the Appendix 1.A and, *mutatis mutandis*, footnote 5).

A somewhat simpler case occurs by selecting $\theta = 1$, that is by assuming observed balances always equal desired balances. The demand for money function then becomes

$$\tilde{m}_t = \alpha_0\lambda\zeta + \alpha_1\lambda y_t' + \alpha_2\tilde{r}_t + \alpha_3\zeta p_t' + \alpha_4\tilde{c}_t. \tag{1.8'}$$

The coefficients of the variables in (1.8) and (1.8′) are composite and may be taken to represent short-run elasticities and the $\alpha$ as long-run elasticities (see Appendix 1.A). The relationship between short- and long-run elasticities is entirely determined by the values of $\theta$, $\lambda$ and $\zeta$, that is by the speed at which desired or expected values adjust to realizations.

The regression equations (1.8′) and (1.8) have been estimated for the same data as used for equation (1.4). We again faced the difficulty that the maximization of $\bar{R}^2$ did not yield unique values for $\lambda$ and $\zeta$. Within the class of the parameters $\lambda$ and $\zeta$, which may be judged to be optimal parameters in this respect, the long-run price elasticity has been used as a second selection criterion because there are economic justifications for the expectation that the price elasticity will be roughly equal to unity. On these considerations, and also in view of the results for the sub-periods (to be discussed later), we have finally chosen for $\lambda = \zeta = 0.5$. The results are presented in Table 1.5. In parentheses $t$-values have been reported. For equation (1.8) a number of results of equal plausibility are shown in Appendix 1.B.

Because (1.8′) yields a low value for the DW-statistic, it has been re-estimated on the assumption of the disturbance term following a first-order autoregressive scheme. The results are entered under (b) in Table 1.5.

As mentioned before, no unique regression results were obtained for (1.8), though most of the results are within a fairly narrow range. The estimates for $1 - \theta$ show considerable dispersion (see table in Appendix 1.B). Note that the DW-statistics are very satisfactory throughout. Taken across the various sub-periods, the price elasticity of equation (1.8) is closer to unity than that of equation (1.8′) (b). We therefore prefer equation (1.8) to equation (1.8′) (b).

An interesting point is whether the regression equation is stable over time. For (1.8) this has been investigated by dividing the reference period into two parts and applying the Chow-test to the equality between the regression coefficients. This yielded an $F$-value of 0.627 with 6 and 65 degrees of freedom. Equivalent results were obtained for other values of $\lambda$ and $\zeta$ (see Appendix 1.B). The results warrant the conclusion that the demand for money function may be considered stable.

The problem may also be approached in a different way by making separate estimates for each of the three trade cycles in the period of observation. For equation (1.8) the results are reported in Table 1.6.

The table shows considerable differences between the coefficients. Note particularly the wrong sign with the interest rate coefficient for the period 1968:I–1971:IV. The elasticities are summarized in Table 1.7.

*Table 1.5: The main regression results for equations (1.8′) and (1.8), 1952:I–1971:IV, with $\lambda = \zeta = 0.5$*

$$(1.8')\ \text{(a)}\ \tilde{m}'_t = \underset{(2.70)}{-2.40} + \underset{(4.87)}{0.34y'_t} - \underset{(1.93)}{0.10\tilde{r}_t} + \underset{(6.02)}{0.52p'_t} + \underset{(3.88)}{0.06\tilde{c}_t}$$
$$\text{DW} = 0.79 \quad R^2 = 0.98$$

$$\text{(b)}\ \tilde{m}'_t = \underset{(2.83)}{-2.14} + \underset{(6.07)}{0.33y'_t} - \underset{(1.63)}{0.07\tilde{r}_t} + \underset{(7.92)}{0.53p'_t} + \underset{(3.41)}{0.05\tilde{c}_t}$$
$$\text{DW} = 2.08 \quad R^2 = 0.94$$

$$(1.8)\quad \tilde{m}'_t = \underset{(2.06)}{-1.28} + \underset{(2.43)}{0.13y'_t} - \underset{(1.62)}{0.06\tilde{r}_t} + \underset{(2.19)}{0.16p'_t} + \underset{(2.73)}{0.03\tilde{c}_t} + \underset{(8.70)}{0.70\tilde{m}_{t-1}}$$
$$\text{DW} = 2.32 \quad R^2 = 0.99$$

*Table 1.6: Regressions results for equation (1.8) for the indicated sub-periods, with $\lambda = \zeta = 0.5$*

1952:I–1958:IV

$$\tilde{m}'_t = \underset{(0.19)}{-0.37} + \underset{(1.50)}{0.17y'_t} - \underset{(0.76)}{0.08\tilde{r}_t} + \underset{(1.27)}{0.21p'_t} + \underset{(2.23)}{0.07\tilde{c}_t} + \underset{(2.37)}{0.47\tilde{m}_{t-1}}$$
$$\text{DW} = 2.09 \quad R^2 = 0.72$$

1959:I–1967:IV

$$\tilde{m}'_t = \underset{(0.68)}{-0.60} + \underset{(1.80)}{0.14y'_t} - \underset{(1.80)}{0.09\tilde{r}_t} + \underset{(2.10)}{0.28p'_t} + \underset{(1.36)}{0.02\tilde{c}_t} + \underset{(3.09)}{0.51\tilde{m}_{t-1}}$$
$$\text{DW} = 2.18 \quad R^2 = 0.97$$

1968:I–1971:IV

$$\tilde{m}'_t = \underset{(0.52)}{-1.42} + \underset{(1.33)}{0.26y'_t} + \underset{(0.90)}{0.05\tilde{r}_t} + \underset{(1.61)}{0.31p'_t} + \underset{(1.16)}{0.04\tilde{c}_t} + \underset{(0.72)}{0.27\tilde{m}_{t-1}}$$
$$\text{DW} = 2.21 \quad R^2 = 0.95$$

*Table 1.7: Elasticities from equation (1.8) for the whole period and for the sub-periods, with $\lambda = \zeta = 0.5$*

| Period | Income | Interest rate | Price | Business cycle indicator | $1-\theta$ |
|---|---|---|---|---|---|
| 1952:I–1971:IV | 0.85 | −0.20 | 1.05 | 0.10 | 0.70 |
| 1952:I–1958:IV | 0.64 | −0.15 | 0.80 | 0.13 | 0.47 |
| 1959:I–1967:IV | 0.55 | −0.18 | 1.15 | 0.04 | 0.51 |
| 1968:I–1971:IV | 0.70 | +0.07 | 0.86 | 0.05 | 0.27 |

It is significant that for the whole period the income elasticity is 0.85, while for each of the three trade cycles it is lower. Similar results are obtained for other combinations of $\lambda$ and $\zeta$. However, in all cases the income elasticity is smaller than unity. This justifies the conclusion that income is not only a scale variable, but that *ceteris paribus* an increase in income leads to a relatively lower increase in the demand for money. Apart from the implausible value of +0.07 [9], the interest rate elasticity ranges from −0.15 to −0.20. The price elasticity varies slightly over the sub-periods. The elasticity with respect to the business cycle indicator has the expected sign, which means that desired money balances increase when economic activity declines. In other words, the components of the money stock on which our investigation is based are influenced by other motives than the transactions motive alone. These might include the desired accumulation of money balances on speculative motives (investment, spending in general) or on precautionary motives (*cf.* Kessler (1958, Chapter 7)). Finally, it should be noted that the values for $1-\theta$ are considerably lower than in earlier cases. This implies a more important role played by the adjustment mechanism. The discrepancies between $1-\theta$ values for the various sub-periods suggest a markedly higher speed of adjustment of actual to desired money balances for the last trade cycle considered.

[9] It is an interesting question why the interest elasticity in the last business cycle differs so much from the previous ones. It is possible that the inflationary component of the interest rate has become more important, so that part of the (positive) influence of the price variable has been absorbed by the interest rate. It is not easy to test this supposition, because the real interest rate cannot be determined uniquely. See Fase (1972) for instance for the relationship between interest rate and inflation.

*Table 1.8: Adaption schedule of $m_t$ to $y_t$, $p_t$ and $r_t$*

| Time | $\Delta y_t$ and $\Delta p_t$ | $\Delta r_t$ |
|---|---|---|
| $t$ | 0.15 | 0.30 |
| $t+1$ | 0.33 | 0.51 |
| $t+2$ | 0.49 | 0.66 |
| $t+3$ | 0.63 | 0.76 |
| $t+4$ | 0.73 | 0.83 |
| $t+5$ | 0.90 | 0.98 |

## 1.6 Speed of Adjustment and Forecasts of the Money Stock

In this section we report about two experiments indicated by our results. First we have investigated for equation (1.8) the speed with which money balances adjust to a given change in $y_t$, $p_t$ and $r_t$. The results are reported in Table 1.8. Because of $\lambda = \zeta$ the adaption schedules of $m_t$ to $y_t$ and $p_t$ are the same. Five quarters after a given change in $y_t$ or $p_t$ took place $m_t$ has adjusted its equilibrium value for 90%; as regards to $r_t$, this amounts to 98%. So our results imply a rather high speed of adjustment of money balances to their equilibrium value.

Second, we investigated the forecasting ability of equation (1.8) for 1972 and 1973. We predicted $m_t$, first using only historical values, second using a dynamic method in which the lagged values of the dependent variable in the equation are generated by the equation itself. The predicted values of $m_t$ appear respectively in columns 1 and 2 of Table 1.9. Column 3 shows the realizations.

The corresponding RMSEs in millions of guilders are 51.91 and 99.44, indicating that the predictive power is not too bad.

## 1.7 Comparison With Other OECD Countries

The outcome of our investigation is a long-run income elasticity of 0.8 to 0.9 and a long-run interest rate elasticity of about −0.20. Money – the dependent variable – was broadly defined because this is the most relevant variable for monetary policy in The Netherlands. It is

*Table 1.9: Realized and predicted values of $m_t$ (millions of Dutch guilders)*

| Quarter | | Prediction (1) | (2) | Realization (3) |
|---|---|---|---|---|
| 1972 | I | 45 750 | 45 750 | 42 750 |
| | II | 42 550 | 47 800 | 44 400 |
| | III | 46 850 | 49 750 | 45 650 |
| | IV | 46 900 | 51 300 | 47 250 |
| 1973 | I | 49 200 | 52 750 | 49 000 |
| | II | 50 850 | 54 100 | 51 650 |
| | III | 53 850 | 55 100 | 53 050 |
| | IV | 54 350 | 56 200 | 56 850 |

interesting to compare our results with those for a number of other countries.

Table 1.10 below summarizes the most important studies carried out for 10 European countries, Australia, Canada and Japan. Excluded are the important contributions for the United States and the developing countries.[10] Furthermore we confined ourselves to time series analyses of the demand for money, based on quarterly data. Table 1.10 lists the most important features of the reported studies. It appears that, on the whole, two definitions are used to characterize the money variables: broad money and narrow money. Cotula for Italy, Crouch for England and Mattfeldt for Western Germany disaggregate into components, like notes and coin, demand deposits and time deposits. Price and also Hacche in their analyses for England allow for different money-holders. It is interesting to note that Teigen in his study of Norway extends the definition of money to include unutilized credit lines.[11] At particular details, however, money definitions differ from country to country. In some studies the money stock – and the other explanatory variables – are taken in constant prices. In nearly all studies income is represented either

[10] For the developing countries the reader is referred to e.g. Adekunle (1968), Silveira (1973) or Banerjee (1973). Interesting summaries, particularly of studies for the United States, are given by Frazer (1967), Goodhart (1970), Laidler (1969), Nieuwenburg (1969) and Walters (1970). Very interesting, not least because of its methodology, is the summary by Feige and Pearce (1972) and the study of Goldfeld (1973).

[11] In The Netherlands, unutilized credit lines are not counted as part of the money stock. Cramer and Reekers (1972, p. 90) estimate them at *f* 9 billion as at the end of March 1971. It is noteworthy in this respect that as early as the twenties Holtrop (1928) advocated the inclusion of unutilized credit lines into the money stock.

by gross national product (GNP) or by gross domestic product (GDP). Only a few studies use other aggregates, like gross national expenditure (GNE). It should be kept in mind, however, that if one postulates a logarithmic-linear relationship between real money balances and real income, this assumption implies that the price elasticity of the demand for nominal money is assumed to be equal to unity. Only Price for the United Kingdom, Grandmont for France and Fase and Kuné for The Netherlands give explicit estimates of the price elasticity. Grandmont attaches, as we do, great weight to equations based on an estimated price elasticity of unity. In our study for The Netherlands we found a price elasticity close to unity.

A large number of the studies takes into account the possibility of short-term disequilibria, or, in other words, the possibility that the actual demand for money differs from the desired money holdings. This idea leads to a particular specification of the demand for money equations since the partial adjustment mechanism determines the underlying structure. Others introduce the concept of adaptive expectation with respect to one or more of the explanatory variables. A few authors combine both concepts, like Villanueva for Japan, Laidler and Parkin for England, Grandmont for France and Fase and Kuné for The Netherlands.

In case of a dynamic structure it is meaningful to distinguish between short- and long-run elasticities. Where appropriate the elasticities shown in Table 1.10 are long-run elasticities. The table shows that the income elasticities are often smaller than unity, irrespective of the money definition that has been used. Some of Price's estimates are exceptionally high but, in all fairness, it should be noted that he presents his results with ample reservations. Grandmont's income elasticities are also fairly high; they approach Friedman's well-known estimate of 1.81 (see Friedman (1969, p. 126)), an estimate, incidentally, was also found by Price in one case. However, we do not believe this similarity to be very significant. Another point to be noted is that many authors find a higher income elasticity with broad money than with narrow money. For Italy a similar situation occurs with notes, coins and deposits, which, according to our conjecture, may be due to the particular tax regime which seems to favour deposits. Our own income elasticity of 0.85 for The Netherlands lies somewhere in the middle.

The interest rate elasticities vary somewhat between countries. We see that in most of the cases the interest rate elasticity is also higher with broad money than with narrow money. The interest rate variables used are rather varied and show more subtle differences than the simple distinction between long- and short-term suggests. Some authors, like Clinton, Teigen and Villanueva (for Belgium) test the stability of their

*Table 1.10: Summary of empirical studies of the demand for money (quarterly data)*

| Country | Author | Period of observation | Concept of money | Income variable | Interest rate | Income elasticity | Interest elasticity | Price elasticity[a]) |
|---|---|---|---|---|---|---|---|---|
| Australia | Jüttner and | 1952:I–1972:III | broad[b]) | GNP[b]) | short | 0.89 á 1.01 | −0.17 á − 0.31 | * |
| | Tuckwell (1974) | | broad[b]) | GNP[b]) | long | 0.92 á 0.97 | −0.28 á − 0.50 | * |
| Austria | Fürst, Schebeck, | 1954:I–1966:IV | narrow | GNP | long | 0.91 á 0.96 | −0.18 á − 0.36 | – |
| | and Schulz (1970) | | broad | GNP | long | 0.92 á 1.46 | −0.18 á − 0.43 | – |
| Belgium | Papers (1974) | not reported | narrow[b]) | industr. prod.[b]) | short | 0.85 | −0.09 | * |
| | Villanueva | 1957:I–1969:IV | narrow[b]) | GNP[b]) | short | 0.75 | −0.04 | * |
| | (1971b) | | narrow[b]) | GNP[b]) | long | 0.71 | −0.15 | * |
| | | | broad[b]) | GNP[b]) | short | 1.03 | −0.04 | * |
| | | | broad[b]) | GNP[b]) | long | 0.95 | −0.04 | * |
| Canada | Clinton (1973) | 1955:I–1970:IV | narrow[b]) | GNE[b]) | short | 0.74 á 0.85 | −0.18 á − 0.30 | * |
| | | | narrow[b]) | GNE[b]) | long | 1.04 | −0.51 | * |
| | | | broad[b]) | GNE[b]) | short | 0.82 á 0.98 | −0.30 á − 0.66 | * |
| | | | broad[b]) | GNE[b]) | long | 0.78 á 1.20 | −0.79 á − 1.03 | * |
| | Smith and | 1955:I–1967:IV | narrow[b]) | GNE[b]) | short | 0.61 á 0.64 | −0.04 á − 0.07 | * |
| | Winder (1971) | | narrow[b]) | GNE[b]) | long | 0.51 á 0.65 | −0.07 á − 0.19 | * |
| | | | broad[b]) | GNE[b]) | short | 0.83 á 0.94 | −0.001 á − 0.05 | * |
| | | | broad[b]) | GNE[b]) | long | 0.66 á 0.92 | −0.004 á − 0.03 | * |
| | Haulman (1972) | 1947:I–1968:IV | narrow | GNP | short | 2.11 | −0.63 | – |
| Germany | Hamburger (1973) | 1963:I–1970:IV | narrow | GNP | short | 0.93 | −0.09 | – |
| | | | narrow | GNP | long | 0.98 | −0.35 | – |
| | König (1968) | 1957:I–1966:IV | narrow | GNP | short | 0.96 á 0.98 | −0.15 á − 0.18 | – |
| | Mattfeldt (1974) | 1950:I–1967:IV | (demand deposits) | GNP | short | 1.02 | −0.14 | – |
| | | | broad | GNP | short | 0.97 á 1.09 | [g]) | – |
| | Roskamp and | 1953:I–1965:IV | narrow | GNP | short | 1.02 | −0.07 | – |
| | Laumas (1969) | | broad | GNP | short | 1.35 | −0.08 | – |
| | Westphal (1970) | 1959:I–1967:IV | narrow | GNP | short | 0.99 á 1.05 | −0.10 á − 0.12 | – |

| | | | | | | | | |
|---|---|---|---|---|---|---|---|---|
| England | Crouch (1967) | 1954:II–1965:II | (demand deposits) | nat. income | long | 1.02 | −0.88 | – |
| | | | demand deposits + time deposits | nat. income | long | 1.08 | −0.48 | – |
| | Fisher (1968) | 1955:I–1967:II | narrow | dispos. pers. income | short | 0.54 á 0.56 | −0.09 á − 0.11 | – |
| | | | narrow | pers. income | long | 0.66 á 0.68 | −0.31 á − 0.36 | – |
| | | | broad | pers. income | short | 0.69 á 0.71 | −0.003 á − 0.004 | – |
| | | | broad | pers. income | long | 0.74 | −0.09 á − 0.12 | – |
| | Goodhart (1970) | 1955:III–1969:III | narrow | GDP | short | 1.25 | −1.05 | – |
| | | | narrow | GDP | long | 1.09 | −0.80 | – |
| | | 1963:III–1969:III | broad | GDP | short | 0.77 á 1.41 | −0.09 á − 0.21 | – |
| | | | broad | GDP | long | 1.09 á 1.55 | −0.35 á 0.51 | – |
| | Hamburger (1973) | 1963:II–1971:II | narrow | GDP | short | 0.77 | −0.15 | – |
| | | | narrow | GDP | long | 0.85 | −0.24 | – |
| | Laidler and Parkin (1970) | 1956:II–1967:VI | broad[b][c] | GNP[b][c] | short | 0.61 á 1.08 | −0.01 á − 0.16 | – |
| | Price (1972) | 1956:I–1969:III | narrow | GDP | short | −2.38[d] | −9.52[d] | 17.33[d] |
| | | | narrow | GDP | long | 0.42 á 0.84 | −0.12 á − 0.86 | 0.34 á 1.79 |
| | | 1964:I–1970:IV | broad | GDP | short | 1.00 á 2.47 | −0.03 á − 0.44 | −0.00 á 0.90 |
| | | | broad | GDP | long | 0.55 á 1.81 | −0.03 á − 1.46 | 0.06 á 2.31 |
| | | | narrow[e] | GDP | long | 2.29 | −0.30 | 0.90 |
| | | | narrow[f] | industr. prod. | short | 2.27 | −0.36 | 0.41 |
| | Hacche (1974) | 1963:IV–1971:III | narrow[b] | GNE | both | 0.39 | −0.08 (short) −0.18 (long) | * |
| | | | broad[b] | GNE | short | 0.45 | −0.09 | * |
| | | | broad[b][e] | GNE | long | 0.93 | −0.07 | * |
| | | | broad[b][f] | dispos. pers. | both | 0.51 | −0.07 (short) | * |
| | | | | income | | | −0.20 (long) | – |

| Country | Author | Period of observation | Concept of money | Income variable | Interest rate | Income elasticity | Interest elasticity | Price elasticity[a]) |
|---|---|---|---|---|---|---|---|---|
| Finland | Leponiemi (1966) | 1952:I–1962:I | broad | GDP | none | 1.19 | – | – |
| France | Grandmont (1973) | 1960:I–1971:IV | narrow | GDP[b]) | short | 1.66 á 1.84 | −0.19 á − 0,21 | 0.72 á 1.0 |
| | | | broad | | short | 1.18 | −0.39 | 1.0 |
| | Mélitz (1972) | 1959:I–1970:IV | narrow[b])[c]) | GDP[b])[c]) | long | 0.65 á 0.70 | −0.21 | * |
| Italy | Cotula (1970) | 1958:I–1967:IV | coins | labour income | long | 0.44 | −0.26 | – |
| | | | deposits | gross nat. income | long:short | 0.80 | −0.29 | – |
| Japan | Villanueva (1972) | 1958:I–1971:I | narrow | GNE | short | 1.01 | −0.34 | – |
| | | | broad | GNE | short | 1.92 | −0.08 | – |
| The Nether- | Dierick (1967) | 1951:I–1966:IV | broad | net. nat. income | long | 1[h]) | −0.17 | 1[h]) |
| lands | Fase and Kuné (1974a) | 1952:I–1971:IV | broad | GNE | long | 0.80 á 0.99 | −0.16 á − 0.25 | 0.97 á 1.06 |
| Norway | Teigen (1971) | 1959:I–1969:IV | broad[b]) | GDP[b]) | none | 0.91 | – | * |
| Switzerland | Schelbert-Syfrig (1967) | 1947:I–1963:II | narrow | net nat. product | short | 0.86 á 0.90 | −0.18 á 0.76 | – |

*Notes:*

[a]) * means that the price elasticity of the demand for nominal money is implicitly unity, when real income is included.

[b]) In fixed prices.

[c]) Per capita.

[d]) This result has no serious meaning.

[e]) Held by private households.

[f]) Held by firms.

[g]) Statistically not different from zero.

[h]) Implicity.

estimates over the various sub-periods, while Hamburger investigates for Germany the predictive power of his demand function. Most of the results of the stability tests are satisfactory, although for Norway Teigen finds a tendency for the income elasticity to increase with time. Our own analyses of the stability of the demand for money in The Netherlands are in line with these findings. Finally a few remarks on the methods used are in order. With the exception of Leponiemi for Finland, Crouch for England and Haulman for Canada, all authors study a single demand for money function. This procedure may introduce simultaneity biases as far as the supply of money is endogenous and dependent on the explanatory variables in the demand function. However, the results obtained by Leponiemi, Crouch and Haulman show only slight differences between simple least-squares estimates and estimates taking into account simultaneity. Another point concerns the use of seasonally adjusted data. All authors, except Crouch and Mélitz in all but one case, take seasonal variation into account by using seasonally adjusted data or by introducing dummy variables. In our investigation of the demand for money in The Netherlands we did not find much difference between the two methods although from a statistical point of view we believe the use of dummy variables superior to the use of mechanically adjusted data. More important, however, is that we found the regression results change considerably if any form of seasonal adjustment of the data is omitted.

## 1.8 Summary and Conclusions

In our investigation we estimated the demand for money in The Netherlands from quarterly data for the period 1952:I–1971:IV. In doing so we formulated a number of assumptions for the adjustment of disequilibria. We also assumed the nominal supply of money to be exogenous. The demand for money was observed from the broadly defined money stock because that is a variable of strategic importance for monetary policy.

Six different logarithmic linear regression equations were estimated, five of them were special cases of the most general one. The most general equation yielded the most satisfactory results – an income elasticity of 0.85 and an interest rate elasticity of −0.20. The demand for money also appeared to be negatively related to the state of economic activity. Finally, there were statistical indications for the demand for money function in The Netherlands to be reasonably stable.

The income elasticity obtained is markedly smaller than 1. We remark that changes in payment habits and institutional arrangements during the period considered are implicitly taken into account by the specification used. Money can therefore not be considered as a luxury good. This may become clear when we realize that there are several motives, like the transactions motive, the speculative motive and the precautionary motive, for holding money. This means that income is not just a scale variable, but that an increase in income corresponds to a lower increase in money balances. This conclusion contradicts all but one of the results so far obtained for The Netherlands but is very much in accordance with findings for other countries. A further point worth mentioning is the close correspondence between the interest rate elasticity as found by us and the figures found by both Dierick and Korteweg for The Netherlands.

## APPENDIX 1.A SOME DERIVATIONS AND NOTATIONS

The model used in Section 1.5 is:

$$m_t^* = \alpha_0 + \alpha_1 y_t^* + \alpha_2 r_t + \alpha_3 p_t^* + \alpha_4 c_t \tag{1.A.1}$$

$$y_t^* - y_{t-1}^* = \lambda(y_t - y_{t-1}^*) \text{ or } y_t^* = \frac{\lambda}{1-(1-\lambda)B} y_t \tag{1.A.2}$$

$$p_t^* - p_{t-1}^* = \zeta(p_t - p_{t-1}^*) \text{ or } p_t^* = \frac{\zeta}{1-(1-\zeta)B} p_t \tag{1.A.3}$$

$$m_t = m_{t-1} + \theta(m_t^* - m_{t-1}) \text{ or } m_t = \frac{\theta}{1-(1-\theta)B} m_t^* \tag{1.A.4}$$

where, all variables being expressed as logarithm, the coefficients represent elasticities. The meaning of the symbols is the same as in the text. $B$ is a lag operator.

Substitution of (1.A.2), (1.A.3) and (1.A.4) in (1.A.1) yields

$$\begin{aligned} m_t = {} & \alpha_0\theta\lambda\zeta + \alpha_1\theta\lambda\{y_t - (1-\zeta)y_{t-1}\} + \alpha_2\theta\{r_t - (2-\lambda-\zeta)r_{t-1} \\ & + (1-\lambda)(1-\zeta)r_{t-2}\} + \alpha_3\theta\zeta\{p_t - (1-\lambda)p_{t-1}\} \\ & + \alpha_4\theta\{c_t - (2-\lambda-\zeta)c_{t-1} + (1-\lambda)(1-\zeta)c_{t-2}\} \\ & + (1-\theta+2-\lambda-\zeta)m_{t-1} - \{(1-\theta)(2-\lambda-\zeta) \\ & + (1-\lambda)(1-\zeta)\}m_{t-2} + (1-\theta)(1-\lambda)(1-\zeta)m_{t-3} \end{aligned} \tag{1.A.5}$$

Rewriting $m_t - (2-\lambda-\zeta)m_{t-1} + (1-\lambda)(1-\zeta)m_{t-2} = \tilde{m}_t$, etc. yields

$$\begin{aligned} \tilde{m}_t = {} & \alpha_0\theta\lambda\zeta + (1-\theta)\tilde{m}_{t-1} + \alpha_1\theta\lambda y_t' + \alpha_2\theta\tilde{r}_t + \alpha_3\theta\zeta p_t' \\ & + \alpha_4\theta\tilde{c}_t \end{aligned} \tag{1.A.6}$$

The variables marked with an accent or a tilde are synthetic variables and defined as

$$\begin{aligned} \tilde{m}_t &= m_t - (2-\lambda-\zeta)m_{t-1} + (1-\lambda)(1-\zeta)m_{t-2} \\ \tilde{r}_t &= r_t - (2-\lambda-\zeta)r_{t-1} + (1-\lambda)(1-\zeta)r_{t-2} \\ \tilde{c}_t &= c_t - (2-\lambda-\zeta)c_{t-1} + (1-\lambda)(1-\zeta)c_{t-2} \\ y_t' &= y_t - (1-\zeta)y_{t-1} \\ p_t' &= p_t - (1-\lambda)p_{t-1} \end{aligned}$$

Equation (1.A.6) is equivalent to equation (1.8) presented on page 23 of the text. It is not difficult to see that (1.A.6) with $\zeta = 1$ is identical to equation (1.5′) on page 19.

Long-run elasticity is the elasticity in a situation of equilibrium. That is, in our model, the situation in which there are no longer any discrepancies between desired or expected values and realized values. In other words, $m_t^* = m_t$, $y_t^* = y_t$ and $p_t^* = p_t$. This implies that the $\alpha$ coefficients of equation (1.A.1) may also be regarded as long-run elasticities. The relationship with short-run elasticities follows immediately from equation (1.A.6).

## Appendix 1.B Some Alternative Estimates for Equation (1.8)

In the following Tables 1.B.1 and 1.B.2 we present selected estimates for equation (1.8) for the whole reference period and for the several sub-periods at various combinations of $\lambda$ and $\zeta$. Each sub-period covers one full period of the trade cycle. The results are shown in Table 1.B.1. The corresponding elasticities have been entered in Table 1.B.2. We have investigated whether for these variants too the relations are stable over time. For that purpose we have divided the period of observation in two and, using the Chow-test, tested the regression coefficients for equality. This yielded $F$-values of between 0.60 and 0.69 ($\nu_1 = 6$, $\nu_2 = 65$), which means that the relations may be regarded as stable.

*Table 1.B.1: Regression results of equation (1.8) for the whole observation period and the sub-periods at various combinations of $\lambda$ and $\zeta$*

$\lambda = 0.45 \quad \zeta = 0.45$

1952:I–1971:IV

$$\tilde{m}_t = -1.16 + 0.14y'_t - 0.06\tilde{r}_t + 0.19p'_t + 0.03\tilde{c}_t + 0.61\tilde{m}_{t-1}$$
$$(2.07) \quad (2.61) \quad (1.58) \quad (2.48) \quad (2.67) \quad (6.74)$$

$\mathrm{DW} = 2.29 \quad R^2 = 0.99$

1952:I–1958:IV

$$\tilde{m}_t = 0.16 + 0.15y'_t - 0.07\tilde{r}_t + 0.22p'_t + 0.07\tilde{c}_t + 0.39\tilde{m}_{t-1}$$
$$(0.09) \quad (1.35) \quad (0.63) \quad (1.33) \quad (2.19) \quad (1.84)$$

$\mathrm{DW} = 2.01$ and $R^2 = 0.62$

1959:I–1967:IV

$$\tilde{m}_t = -0.49 + 0.14y'_t - 0.09\tilde{r}_t + 0.29p'_t + 0.02\tilde{c}_t + 0.43\tilde{m}_{t-1}$$
$$(0.61) \quad (1.81) \quad (1.80) \quad (2.30) \quad (1.20) \quad (2.95)$$

$\mathrm{DW} = 2.17$ and $R^2 = 0.96$

*Table 1.B.1: (continued)*

1968:I–1971:IV

$$\tilde{m}_t = -1.11 + 0.26y'_t + 0.04\tilde{r}_t + 0.32p'_t + 0.04\tilde{c}_t + 0.17\tilde{m}_{t-1}$$
$$(0.46)\ (1.40)\quad (0.70)\quad (1.77)\quad (1.16)\quad (0.44)$$
DW = 2.18 and $R^2 = 0.93$

$\lambda = 0.45 \quad \zeta = 0.50$

1952:I–1971:IV

$$\tilde{m}_t = -1.29 + 0.13y'_t - 0.06\tilde{r}_t + 0.17p'_t + 0.03\tilde{c}_t + 0.66\tilde{m}_{t-1}$$
$$(2.15)\ (2.58)\quad (1.56)\quad (2.19)\quad (2.67)\quad (7.75)$$
DW = 2.31 and $R^2 = 0.99$

1952:I–1958:IV

$$\tilde{m}_t = -0.13 + 0.16y'_t - 0.07\tilde{r}_t + 0.21p'_t + 0.07\tilde{c}_t + 0.44\tilde{m}_{t-1}$$
$$(0.07)\ (1.47)\quad (0.67)\quad (1.24)\quad (2.27)\quad (2.16)$$
DW = 2.05 and $R^2 = 0.67$

1959:I–1967:IV

$$\tilde{m}_t = -0.67 + 0.14y'_t - 0.09\tilde{r}_t + 0.28p'_t + 0.02\tilde{c}_t + 0.48\tilde{m}_{t-1}$$
$$(0.78)\ (1.87)\quad (1.78)\quad (2.04)\quad (1.33)\quad (2.88)$$
DW = 2.19 and $R^2 = 0.96$

1968:I–1971:IV

$$\tilde{m}_t = -1.50 + 0.26y'_t + 0.05\tilde{r}_t + 0.31p'_t + 0.04\tilde{c}_t + 0.23\tilde{m}_{t-1}$$
$$(0.56)\ (1.37)\quad (0.81)\quad (1.63)\quad (1.19)\quad (0.59)$$
DW = 2.19 and $R^2 = 0.94$

$\lambda = 0.50 \quad \zeta = 0.55$

1952:I–1971:IV

$$\tilde{m}_t = -1.39 + 0.12y'_t - 0.06\tilde{r}_t + 0.15p'_t + 0.03\tilde{c}_t + 0.74\tilde{m}_{t-1}$$
$$(2.14)\ (2.39)\quad (1.61)\quad (1.97)\quad (2.90)\quad (9.83)$$
DW = 2.33 and $R^2 = 0.99$

1952:I–1958:IV

$$\tilde{m}_t = -0.70 + 0.17y'_t - 0.08\tilde{r}_t + 0.21p'_t + 0.07\tilde{c}_t + 0.51\tilde{m}_{t-1}$$
$$(0.34)\ (1.57)\quad (0.82)\quad (1.21)\quad (2.31)\quad (2.69)$$
DW = 2.13 and $R^2 = 0.76$

1959:I–1967:IV

$$\tilde{m}_t = -0.80 + 0.14y'_t - 0.08\tilde{r}_t + 0.27p'_t + 0.02\tilde{c}_t + 0.55\tilde{m}_{t-1}$$
$$(0.86)\ (1.83)\quad (1.75)\quad (1.89)\quad (1.54)\quad (3.46)$$
DW = 2.19 and $R^2 = 0.98$

*Table 1.B.1: (continued)*

1968:I–1971:IV

$$\tilde{m}_t = -1.79 + 0.25y'_t + 0.06\tilde{r}_t + 0.31p'_t + 0.04\tilde{c}_t + 0.33\tilde{m}_{t-1}$$
(0.60) (1.31) (1.00) (1.48) (1.23) (0.88)

DW = 2.22 and $R^2 = 0.96$

$\lambda = 0.55 \quad \zeta = 0.55$

1952:I–1971:IV

$$\tilde{m}_t = -1.39 + 0.12y'_t - 0.06\tilde{r}_t + 0.14p'_t + 0.03\tilde{c}_t + 0.77\tilde{m}_{t-1}$$
(2.11) (2.25) (1.63) (1.97) (2.70) (10.93)

DW = 2.33 and $R^2 = 0.99$

1952:I–1958:IV

$$\tilde{m}_t = -0.97 + 0.18y'_t - 0.09\tilde{r}_t + 0.21p'_t + 0.07\tilde{c}_t + 0.54\tilde{m}_{t-1}$$
(0.46) (1.58) (0.92) (1.24) (2.24) (2.92)

DW = 2.17 and $R^2 = 0.80$

1959:I–1967:IV

$$\tilde{m}_t = -0.75 + 0.13y'_t - 0.09\tilde{r}_t + 0.27p'_t + 0.02\tilde{c}_t + 0.58\tilde{m}_{t-1}$$
(0.79) (1.77) (1.81) (1.93) (1.58) (3.66)

DW = 2.18 and $R^2 = 0.98$

1968:I–1971:IV

$$\tilde{m}_t = -1.67 + 0.25y'_t + 0.06\tilde{r}_t + 0.30p'_t + 0.04\tilde{c}_t + 0.37\tilde{m}_{t-1}$$
(0.55) (1.27) (1.07) (1.43) (1.17) (1.02)

DW = 2.24 and $R^2 = 0.97$

$\lambda = 0.50 \quad \zeta = 0.60$

1952:I–1971:IV

$$\tilde{m}_t = -1.48 + 0.11y'_t - 0.06\tilde{r}_t + 0.13p'_t + 0.03\tilde{c}_t + 0.77\tilde{m}_{t-1}$$
(2.18) (2.33) (1.63) (1.77) (2.80) (11.00)

DW = 2.33 and $R^2 = 0.99$

1952:I–1958:IV

$$\tilde{m}_t = -1.03 + 0.17y'_t - 0.08\tilde{r}_t + 0.20p'_t + 0.07\tilde{c}_t + 0.55\tilde{m}_{t-1}$$
(0.49) (1.63) (0.88) (1.15) (2.36) (3.04)

DW = 2.16 and $R^2 = 0.80$

1959:I–1967:IV

$$\tilde{m}_t = -0.99 + 0.14y'_t - 0.08\tilde{r}_t + 0.25p'_t + 0.02\tilde{c}_t + 0.59\tilde{m}_{t-1}$$
(1.02) (1.86) (1.72) (1.68) (1.75) (3.78)

DW = 2.19 and $R^2 = 0.98$

*Table 1.B.1: (continued)*

1968:I–1971:IV

$$\tilde{m}_t = -2.14 + 0.25y'_t + 0.06\tilde{r}_t + 0.29p'_t + 0.04\tilde{c}_t + 0.38\tilde{m}_{t-1}$$
$$(0.66) \quad (1.28) \quad (1.07) \quad (1.37) \quad (1.26) \quad (1.03)$$

DW = 2.22 and $R^2 = 0.97$

*Table 1.B.2: Elasticities from equation (1.8) for the whole observation period and sub-periods at various combinations of $\lambda$ and $\zeta$*

| Period | Income | Interest | Price | State of economic activity | $1-\theta$ |
|---|---|---|---|---|---|
| $\lambda = 0.45 \quad \zeta = 0.45$ | | | | | |
| 1952:I–1971:IV | 0.80 | −0.16 | 1.05 | 0.08 | 0.61 |
| 1952:I–1958:IV | 0.55 | −0.11 | 0.80 | 0.11 | 0.39 |
| 1959:I–1967:IV | 0.54 | −0.16 | 1.15 | 0.03 | 0.43 |
| 1968:I–1971:IV | 0.69 | +0.05 | 0.85 | 0.04 | 0.17 |
| $\lambda = 0.45 \quad \zeta = 0.50$ | | | | | |
| 1952:I–1971:IV | 0.87 | −0.18 | 0.99 | 0.09 | 0.66 |
| 1952:I–1958:IV | 0.61 | −0.13 | 0.76 | 0.12 | 0.44 |
| 1959:I–1967:IV | 0.60 | −0.17 | 1.08 | 0.04 | 0.48 |
| 1968:I–1971:IV | 0.74 | +0.06 | 0.81 | 0.05 | 0.23 |
| $\lambda = 0.50 \quad \zeta = 0.55$ | | | | | |
| 1952:I–1971:IV | 0.92 | −0.22 | 1.01 | 0.11 | 0.74 |
| 1952:I–1958:IV | 0.70 | −0.17 | 0.77 | 0.14 | 0.51 |
| 1959:I–1967:IV | 0.61 | −0.19 | 1.09 | 0.05 | 0.55 |
| 1968:I–1971:IV | 0.75 | +0.08 | 0.82 | 0.06 | 0.33 |
| $\lambda = 0.55 \quad \zeta = 0.55$ | | | | | |
| 1952:I–1971:IV | 0.91 | −0.24 | 1.06 | 0.12 | 0.77 |
| 1952:I–1958:IV | 0.72 | −0.19 | 0.82 | 0.14 | 0.54 |
| 1959:I–1967:IV | 0.57 | −0.20 | 1.16 | 0.05 | 0.58 |
| 1968:I–1971:IV | 0.72 | +0.09 | 0.86 | 0.06 | 0.37 |
| $\lambda = 0.50 \quad \zeta = 0.60$ | | | | | |
| 1952:I–1971:IV | 0.99 | −0.25 | 0.97 | 0.12 | 0.77 |
| 1952:I–1958:IV | 0.77 | −0.19 | 0.76 | 0.15 | 0.55 |
| 1959:I–1967:IV | 0.68 | −0.20 | 1.02 | 0.05 | 0.59 |
| 1968:I–1971:IV | 0.80 | +0.10 | 0.79 | 0.06 | 0.38 |

# 2. The Demand for Money in the EU Countries

## 2.1 INTRODUCTION

This chapter focuses on the demand for money in the EU countries. The relationship between money balances and their determinants has been studied extensively during the last decade, and several surveys portray the state of affairs for single countries (see, e.g., Boorman (1972), Fase and Kuné (1975), Goodhart (1975), Laidler (1977)). There is ready agreement on the view that the knowledge of the demand for money function is important for the formulation of an appropriate monetary policy. Or as Boorman (1972, pp. 250–251) remarks:

> The stability of the money demand function, together with a capacity on the part of the monetary authority to influence closely the stock of assets corresponding to the theoretical concept of money employed in that function would seem to be necessary conditions for the successful implementation of monetary policy.

A recent descriptive note published by the OECD (1977) indicates that the liquidity concepts applied in the various countries differ, particularly when a broader measure of the money stock is taken. This as well as differences in the particular specification of the demand for money function makes it difficult to compare the estimates among countries.

These difficulties would hopefully be attenuated if a common methodology were adopted in the estimation of the demand for money function for a set of countries. The present chapter purports to do so. This enables us to discover whether there is evidence for a convergence of empirical results, while differences in the estimates obtained must be related to monetary behaviour in the various countries.

---

Reprinted from *Journal of Monetary Economics*, **8**(2) (September 1981), F.A.G. den Butter and M.M.G. Fase, 'The demand for money in EEC countries', 201–230, ©1981 with kind permission from Elsevier Science-NL, Sara Burgherhartstraat 25, 1055 KV Amsterdam, The Netherlands.

Since we started this research at least three studies in the same vein have appeared. Canarella and Roseman (1978) using annual data covering 1957–1972, provide estimates of the narrowly defined demand for money in 10 continental European countries and Ireland. On the basis of a common specification they found income elasticities of around one in all the countries considered. Their interest elasticities and speeds of adjustment, however, vary substantially among countries. The estimated equilibrium interest elasticities are between −0.05 and −0.30. The adjustment coefficients also vary, indicating an average lag of between 1.2 and 1.9 years in bringing money balances to their equilibrium level.

In addition to stability Al-Khuri and Nsouli (1978) also examine the speed of adjustment of actual to desired money stock among six major industrialized countries, using quarterly data, which in most cases cover the period 1960–1976. The reported estimates for both M1 and M2 indicate that with two exceptions the speeds of adjustment for narrow money are not significantly different. When broad money is used the differences are more marked. Both the UK and Germany have slower speeds of adjustment than the other countries studied. As these estimates result from differencing of the original equation, one should be aware of the fact that this procedure may affect the estimated adjustment speeds.

The question of stability emerges, among other things, also in a study of Boughton (1979). Boughton, using quarterly data for 1960–1976, presents estimates obtained for narrow and broad definitions of money in the major OECD countries. His estimated income elasticities for M1 cluster around unity but are uniformly greater than unity when the broad definition is used. The interest elasticities for M1 are significant and range from −0.06 to −0.55. This pattern does not differ importantly for the demand functions of M2. A notable but, in view of an earlier study of one of us on the interdependence of interest rates (see Fase (1973)) not surprising finding is that the interest elasticities do not alter substantially when short interest rates are replaced by long interest rates. As to stability, the study reveals stable demand functions for broad money while instability dominates for M1 demands.

This analysis departs from the studies mentioned above in at least five important respects. First, it starts from a common economic framework for the eight EU countries considered, which allows for shifts from non-money assets to M2 and vice versa. The importance of this has been recognized by, e.g., Goldfeld (1976) or by Heller and Khan (1979) in their attempt to incorporate the term structure of interest rates in the demand for money function. Second, special attention is given to the dynamic structure of the statistical model, which seems warranted in order to draw meaningful conclusions on the speed of adjustment. This view is supported by recent comments on studies of the demand for money by Hendry and Mizon (1978) and Plosser and Schwert (1978) pointing out the importance of properly specified dynamics of the model, while misspecification due to the modelling of the adjustment lags is also indicated in papers by Laidler (1980) and White (1978). Moreover our modelling of adjustment behaviour goes beyond a simple Koyck-lag, which in view of its restrictive character may be open to criticism. Third, the study is really novel in that it is entirely based on a uniform set of quarterly data collected for this analysis. Fourth, and this is another novelty, the study contains careful examination of the residuals. Finally we investigate the stability of the estimated equations by testing their ability to predict the future course of the money demand in the eight countries considered.

The rest of the chapter is laid out as follows. Section 2.2 discusses the economic framework and statistical methodology underlying this chapter. Section 2.3 describes the data drawn from the countries examined. The estimation results are given in Section 2.4. In Section 2.5 the interpretation of the results is carried further by a closer consideration of the residuals and forecasts of the money stock in the countries considered. In Section 2.6 the conclusions are drawn.

## 2.2 Specification and Methodology

We postulate the desired nominal demand for broad money, $\mathrm{M2}^*$, to depend on expected real income $y^*$, the expected price level $p^*$, the expected long-term interest rate $r^*$, the expected change in the price level $p'^*$, and the expected level of economic activity $c^*$. Thus we get

$$\mathrm{M2}^* = f(\overset{+}{y^*}, \overset{+}{p^*}, \overset{-}{r^*}, \overset{-}{p'^*}, c^*) \tag{2.1}$$

with expected signs of the partial derivatives as indicated. With the exception of the business cycle, the arguments of (2.1) are convential and spelled out extensively in the literature. Therefore we do not need to repeat them again. In order to account for cyclical variation in desired money balances – since precautionary motives encourage people to keep larger balances when the level of economic activity slows down – we include the quantity $c^*$ in equation (2.1) (see also Fase and Kuné (1974b)). A theoretical justification for this variable may be provided also by arguing that there is substitutability between money or liquidities and commodities, with our cyclical indicator as a simple proxy for the latter. There are several ways of measuring economic activity, and therefore the expected sign of the derivative $\partial f/\partial c$ is determined by this measurement.

The general question may be raised whether one can estimate a demand for money function without also specifying a supply function. Of course, there is a consensus of opinion among monetary economists that theoretically the supply side matters. However, there is also a lot of evidence in the literature going back to the early work of Brunner and Meltzer (1964) or Teigen (1964) that in practice neglecting the supply side does not matter much. Recent research by Laidler (1980) on the exogeneity of the money supply and its implications for the appropriate estimation of the demand for money function suggests that this still seems to stand.

Without much loss of generality we assume (2.1) to be approximately linear in logarithms. Then

$$\ln \mathrm{M}2_t^* = \alpha_0 + \alpha_1 \ln y_t^* + \alpha_2 \ln p_t^* + \alpha_3 \ln r_t^* + \alpha_4 \ln p_t'^* + \alpha_5 \ln c_t^*. \quad (2.2)$$

The problem with equation (2.2) is that the quantities are not observable. Therefore we need to relate them to an observed time series in order to obtain an estimable function. If we assume each variable of (2.2) to be generated by a linear difference equation of past values, then (2.2) could be parsimoniously represented by the general multiple regression or, to borrow the terminology of Box and Jenkins (1970), the transfer function model

$$\begin{aligned} \delta(B) \ln \mathrm{M}2_t = \alpha_0 &+ \alpha_1\omega_1(B)B^{d_1} \ln y_t + \alpha_2\omega_2(B)B^{d_2} \ln p_t \\ &+ \alpha_3\omega_3(B)B^{d_3} \ln r_t + \alpha_4\omega_4(B)B^{d_4} \ln p_t' \\ &+ \alpha_5\omega_5(B)B^{d_5} \ln c_t + \theta(B)a_t, \end{aligned} \quad (2.3)$$

where $\delta(B)$, $\omega_i(B) - i = 1, 2, 3, 4, 5 -$ and $\theta(B)$ are scalar polynomials in the backward shift operator $B$, so that $\delta(B) = 1 - \delta_1 B - \delta_2 B^2 - \ldots \delta_r B^r$, $\omega(B) = 1 - \omega_{i1}B - \omega_{i2}B^2 - \ldots - \omega_{is_i}B^{s_i}$ and $\theta(B) = 1 - \theta_1 B - \theta_2 B^2 - \ldots - \theta_q B^q$; the $d_i$ are integers with $d_i > 0$; and the $a_t$ are stochastically independent random disturbances or white noise. Equivalently (2.3) could be rewritten as

$$\ln \mathrm{M}2 = \alpha_0' + \sum_{i=1}^{5} \frac{\alpha_i\omega_i(B)}{\delta(B)} \ln x_{i-d_i} + \frac{\theta(B)}{\delta(B)}a, \quad (2.4)$$

where the $x_i$ have the appropriate meaning according to (2.3). Thus the transfer function is represented by the ratio of two polynomials in the lag operator $B$.

Obviously the general formulation (2.4) includes the well-known distributed lag models as special cases. Two examples which have gained popularity particularly among examiners of the demand for money are the partial adjustment and adaptive expectation hypotheses. It can easily be derived that the two hypotheses lead to the following *a priori* specification of the lag polynomials:

$$\delta(B) = (1 - \delta B)/(1 - \delta), \qquad \text{and} \tag{2.5}$$

$$\omega_i(B) = (1 - \omega_i)/(1 - \omega_i B), \qquad i = 1, \ldots, 5, \tag{2.6}$$

respectively. As to the partial adjustment model, we note that $1 - \delta$ is the fixed fraction of the desired adjustment accomplished within one particular time period. Straightforward application of the techniques of time series analyses to the transfer model (2.4) may induce differencing of the variables and the noise part which – apart from the noise part – does not make much economic sense. Therefore in this study we follow another, more heuristic approach by consecutively imposing restrictions on the lag functions $\delta(B)$, $\omega(B)$ and $\theta(B)$. In this way the estimations which we finally selected are partly determined by economic plausibility and partly by the data.

## 2.3 On the Data

As some data required for this analysis were not to be found in published sources, we asked the central banks of the EU countries to provide us with the relevant quarterly series. Our sample period runs from the beginning of the sixties to 1976:IV and we have 1977:I–1978:IV for *ex ante* prediction, with the exception of Denmark and Ireland where data were not available for this entire period. The resulting data file, set up as uniformly as possible, has the following general characteristics:

- M2 nominal M2-data; quarterly averages,
- $Y$ nominal GNP (from Italy, France and the United Kingdom we obtained data on GDP),
- $p$ price deflator GNP (GDP) with 1970 = 100,
- $y$ $Y/p$: real GNP(GDP) in prices of 1970,
- $p'$ $p/p_{-4}$ (hence $\ln p'$ is the rate of inflation),
- $r$ the long-term interest rate; quarterly averages,
- $c$ (a) a detrended index derived from the supplied data on the business cycle indicator, or (b) the percentage of unemployment (following Fase and Kuné (1974b)).

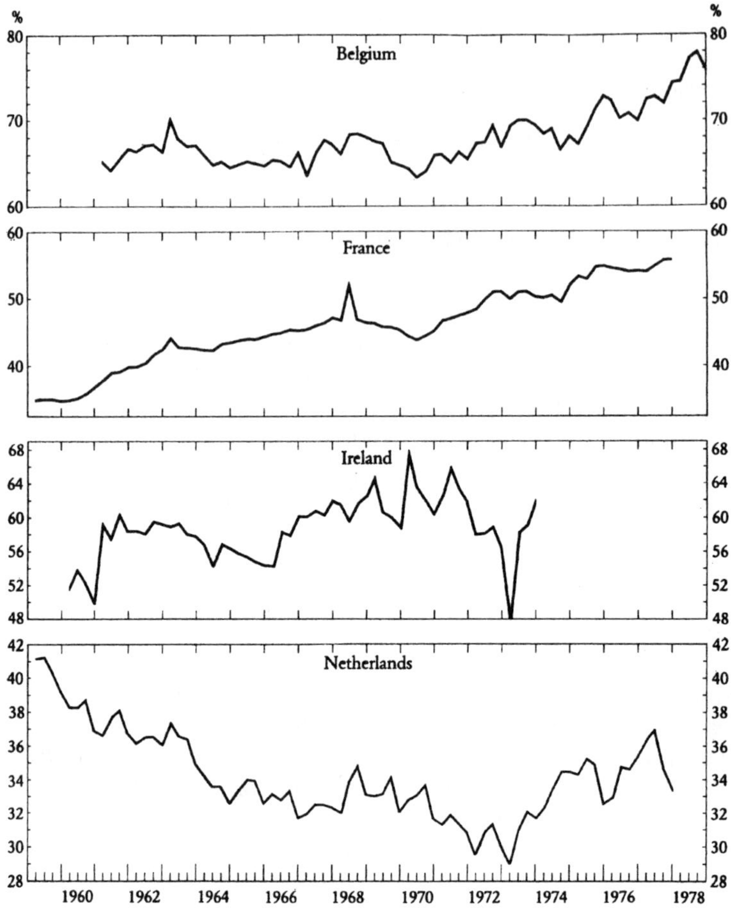


*Figure 2.1: Liquidity ratio in eight EU countries*

In view of our preference for unadjusted data in regression analysis (see Lovell (1963), Thomas and Wallis (1971)), the data on M2 are not seasonally adjusted. However, for some of the explanatory variables unadjusted data could not be obtained. Therefore we use adjusted data for these variables throughout (apart from the interest rates where no seasonality occurs). A description of the data is given in Appendix 2.A.

As the liquidity ratio or the Cambridge $k$, i.e., the ratio of M2 and national income, plays a crucial role in Dutch monetary analysis, we think it is interesting to consider this quantity for the other members of the EU as well. Figure 2.1 shows the time profile of this quantity for all

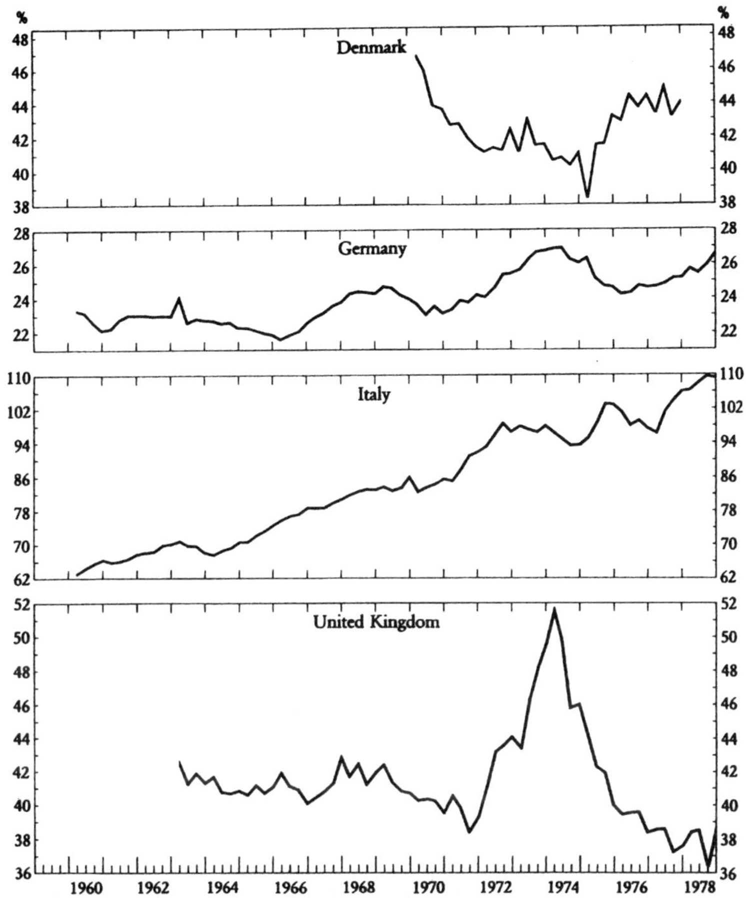


*Figure 2.1: Liquidity ratio in eight EU countries (continued)*

member countries.[1]

The graphs show a wide range for the values of the liquidity ratio in the various countries. This is partly due to the fact that for all countries we use the national M2 concept (M3 in the case of the United Kingdom) rather than the harmonized EU concept, because the majority of the countries was unable to provide us with a harmonized series long enough for estimation. On average the lowest values of the ratio are found in

1 The data on the money stock in the numerator of the ratio depicted in this figure are seasonally adjusted by means of the Census X11 method.

Germany while the highest values occur in Italy. This means that the velocity of the M2 circulation, which is the reciprocal of the liquidity ratio, is high in Germany and low in Italy, where nowadays the stock of M2 even exceeds the GDP yielding a velocity smaller than one.

Both France and Italy show a steadily growing liquidity ratio while the pattern is more complicated in the other countries. Yet, in the majority of the EU countries the average liquidity ratio has increased in the period 1972–1978, compared with the sixties. Figure 2.1 shows a steadily declining liquidity ratio for The Netherlands up to 1972.

## 2.4 Estimation Results

### 2.4.1 Nominal Demand for Money

When applying the techniques of time series analysis to the transfer function model (2.4) no economically plausible results were obtained. Then we proceeded by estimating a function with a more restricted lag structure, *viz.*

$$\ln \mathrm{M2} = \alpha_0' + \frac{\alpha_1 \ln y}{(1-\omega_1 B)} + \frac{\alpha_2 \ln p}{(1-\omega_2 B)} + \frac{\alpha_3 B^{d_3} \ln r}{(1-\omega_3 B)} + \frac{\alpha_4 B^{d_4} \ln p'}{(1-\omega_4 B)} + \frac{\alpha_5 B^{d_5} \ln c}{(1-\omega_5 B)} + u \tag{2.7}$$

In the above specification every explanatory variable may influence the demand for money by means of its own geometrically distributed lag with $1-\omega_i$, as the speed of adjustment. The respective long-run elasticity is calculated as $\alpha_i/(1-\omega_i)$. We recall from Section 2.2 that this lag structure can be interpreted as an adaptive expectations mechanism. However, if $\omega_1 = \omega_2 = \omega_3 = \omega_4 = \omega_5 = \delta$ and if the structure of the disturbances is appropriately specified, specification (2.7) is identical to a specification with partial adjustment of the dependent variable, i.e., to a specification with a Koyck-lag. In that case partial adjustment and adaptive expectations are not distinguishable. It is obvious that without this restriction specification (2.7) allows for a far more complicated lag structure than the simple Koyck-lag. Table 2.1 gives the estimation results for specification (2.7). All equations are estimated with a constant term and three seasonal dummies.

As indicated above, this study considers two alternative cyclical indicators. We constructed the first indicator in such a way that its expected sign is negative while the expected sign of the second indicator, the

*Table 2.1: Estimation results for* $\ln \mathrm{M2} = \alpha_0' + \frac{\alpha_1 \ln y}{(1-\omega_1 B)} + \frac{\alpha_2 \ln p}{(1-\omega_2 B)} + \frac{\alpha_3 \ln r}{(1-\omega_3 B)} + \frac{\alpha_4 \ln p'}{(1-\omega_4 B)} + \frac{\alpha_5 \ln c}{(1-\omega_5 B)} + \text{seasonals} + u$

| | | Real income ($y$) | | | Price deflator ($p$) | | | Interest rate ($r$) | | | Inflation ($p'$) | | | Cyclical indicator ($c$)[b] | | | |
|---|---|---|---|---|---|---|---|---|---|---|---|---|---|---|---|---|---|
| Country | Sample period | $\alpha_1$ | $\omega_1$ | Long-run elasticity | $\alpha_2$ | $\omega_2$ | Long-run elasticity | $\alpha_3$ | $\omega_3$ | Long-run elasticity | $\alpha_4$ | $\omega_4$ | Long-run elasticity | $\alpha_5$ | $\omega_5$ | Long-run elasticity | Box–Pierce $\bar{\chi}^2_{12}$ test statistic[c] |
| Belgium | 1961:IV–1976:IV | 0.71 | 0.25 | 0.95 | 1.33 | – | 1.33 | −0.20 | 0.55 | −0.44 | −0.28 | – | −0.28 | 0.007+ | 0.88+ | 0.055+ | 13.0 |
| | | (7.69) | (4.40) | | (17.79) | | | (6.40) | (6.08) | | (2.12) | | | (1.73) | (8.47) | | |
| Denmark[c] | 1971:I–1976:IV | 0.38 | 0.51 | 0.77 | 0.63 | 0.51 | 1.29 | −0.10 | 0.52 | −0.20 | −0.52 | 0.51 | −1.07 | – | – | – | 18.4 |
| | | (1.73) | (2.96) | | (3.22) | (2.96) | | (2.12) | (2.96) | | (1.84) | (2.96) | | | | | |
| France | 1960:IV–1976:IV | 1.51 | – | 1.51 | 1.13 | – | 1.13 | −0.14 | 0.51 | −0.28 | −0.29[d] | – | −0.29 | −0.85 | – | −0.85 | 81.5 |
| | | (24.24) | | | (16.59) | | | (3.47) | (4.52) | | (1.45) | | | (5.62) | | | |
| Germany | 1960:I–1976:IV | 0.75 | 0.27 | 1.03 | 1.33 | – | 1.33 | −0.18 | 0.28 | −0.25 | – | – | – | 0.023+ | – | 0.023+ | 61.0 |
| | | (6.75) | (3.39) | | (9.54) | | | (2.00) | (0.80) | | | | | (1.34) | | | |
| Ireland | 1963:I–1973:IV | 0.81 | 0.45 | 1.46 | 0.96 | – | 0.96 | – | – | – | −1.28 | – | −1.28 | −0.36 | – | −0.36 | 30.4 |
| | | (5.33) | (5.51) | | (6.19) | | | | | | (2.50) | | | (1.02) | | | |
| Italy | 1962:II–1976:IV | 1.41 | 0.09 | 1.55 | 1.30 | – | 1.30 | −0.27 | – | −0.27 | −0.35 | – | −0.35 | −0.49 | – | −0.49 | 40.0 |
| | | (18.15) | (2.12) | | (31.71) | | | (7.10) | | | (3.05) | | | (3.08) | | | |
| The Netherlands[c] | 1960:I–1976:IV | 0.15 | 0.84 | 0.94 | 0.23 | 0.84 | 1.42 | −0.06 | 0.84 | −0.34 | −0.16 | 0.84 | −0.98 | −0.14 | 0.84 | −0.84 | 24.4 |
| | | (2.34) | (14.81) | | (2.34) | (14.81) | | (2.17) | (14.81) | | (1.37) | (14.81) | | (0.31) | (14.08) | | |
| United Kingdom | 1964:IV–1976:IV | 1.17 | 0.45 | 2.13 | 0.84 | – | 0.84 | −0.13[d] | – | −0.13 | −0.15[d] | – | −0.15 | −0.13 | – | −0.13 | 17.9 |
| | | (6.38) | (5.01) | | (6.04) | | | (1.74) | | | (0.48) | | | (1.37) | | | |

*Notes:*

The figures in parentheses are $t$-statistics.

[a] A + indicates that unemployment is used as a cyclical indicator.

[b] Corrected for downward bias.

[c] A Koyck-lag is used in the estimations.

[d] Lagged three quarters.

percentage of unemployment, is positive. In the regressions we chose the indicator with the best fit, on the understanding that if the outcomes were more or less the same the first indicator would be chosen.

When in the regressions either the coefficient of the interest rate ($\alpha_3$), of inflation ($\alpha_4$), or the coefficients of both cyclical indicators ($\alpha_5$) obtained the wrong sign these variables were lagged up to three quarters. In other words we tried for $i = 3$, 4 or 5: $d_i = 1, 2, 3$. If this still did not yield a coefficient with the correct sign we set $\alpha_3$, $\alpha_4$, or $\alpha_5$ equal to 0 and left the interest rate, the rate of inflation or the cyclical indicator altogether out of our regression equation.

When the value of the denominator parameter of an explanatory variable ($\omega$) turned out not to lie between 0 and 1, or when our iterative estimation procedure did not converge, we set this $\omega$ equal to 0 and hence estimated no geometrically distributed lag for that variable. In the case of Denmark and The Netherlands the regressions yielded more plausible results with a Koyck-lag than unrestricted estimation of (2.7) did. Therefore, for these countries we have set $\omega_1 = \omega_2 = \omega_3 = \omega_4 = \omega_5 = \delta$.

In the last column of Table 2.1 we present the $\chi^2$-distributed values of the portmanteau or Box–Pierce test statistic. With this test the residuals are tested for white noise and these figures may provide us with a more general check on residual correlation than the DW-values usually presented in connection with regression results do.

For Belgium a most satisfactory equation is found. The coefficients of all explanatory variables obtain the expected sign and are significantly different from 0 even though for the coefficient of unemployment as cyclical indicator this is only true at the 10% level. Surprisingly the coefficient of the alternative indicator, the so-called synthetic curve also obtains a positive sign. One would expect these two indicators to be negatively correlated, but they are not. The speed of adjustment with regard to the adaptive expectations appears to be high for real income, somewhat lower for the interest rate and fairly low for the cyclical indicator. The price deflator and the rate of inflation show no clear geometrically distributed lag. We have corrected the break in the M2 series in 1969 (see the Appendix 2.A) by means of a dummy variable which obtains the value of 0.37 ($t$-value: 23.12) in the regression.

As mentioned before, in the case of Denmark inclusion of a Koyck-lag leads to much more economically plausible results than without. It means that by assumption the speed of adjustment is the same for each explanatory variable. We measure an average speed of about one quarter. With the exception of both cyclical indicators, all variables yield the expected sign, and in spite of the few observations we have at our disposal, the coefficients of the price deflator, the long-term interest rate and the rate of inflation differ significantly from 0 at the 10% level.

For France a geometrically distributed lag can only be detected for the interest rate variable where we measure an average speed of adjustment of about one quarter. In this equation all estimated coefficients obtain the expected sign and are, with the exception of the coefficient of inflation, highly significant. A dummy with the value of 0.11 ($t$-value: 4.46) accounts for the revolution of May 1968, when economic activity temporarily dropped, but the money stock remained at its 'normal' level (causing a bump in the liquidity ratio of Figure 2.1).

In Germany, as in The Netherlands (see Fase (1977)) and in the United Kingdom the money stock has been much affected in the seventies by interest rate induced switching between components of M2 and assets that do not form part of M2. This switching can be attributed to the unprecedented high levels and the great variability of short-term interest rates. In order to account for this phenomenon two explanatory variables are added to those of (2.1), namely a short-term interest rate ($\ln r_s$), which is set equal to 0 before 1970, and a dummy variable ($\text{dum}\, r_s$), compensating for this break.[2] This procedure proved successful when re-estimating the Dutch demand for money function of Fase and Kuné (1974b). The estimation results for the three countries in question with respect to the term structure are presented in Table 2.2. All coefficients are significant with the expected sign, i.e., positive for the short-term interest rate and negative for the dummy.[3] Namely when the short-term rate is high compared to the long-term rate, switching takes place from non-money to M2, and vice versa. As for specification (2.7) and the results of Table 2.1, in the German function a distributed lag is estimated for real income and the long-term interest rate. In both cases the adjustment is fast. The influence of unemployment as cyclical indicator is, as expected, positive but not significant and the coefficient of inflation obtains the wrong sign.

In the case of Ireland a distributed lag is taken for real income. The influence of the rate of inflation is apparent, whereas the cyclical indicator obtains the expected positive sign but is not significant. For the interest rate no influence can be found.

For Italy, again, we only have a distributed lag for real income with a very high speed of adjustment. The coefficients of all explanatory variables obtain the expected sign and differ significantly from 0.

The equation for The Netherlands, as with Denmark is estimated

---

[2] $\text{dum}\, r_s = 0$ up to 1969:IV and 1 from 1970:I.

[3] In fact we have considered the effects of switching in all our demand for money functions, but only in the case of these three countries it leads to significant coefficients and to an improvement of our estimation results.

*Table 2.2: Estimation results for the nominal demand for money functions with respect to the term structure*

| Country | Short-term interest rate ($\ln r_s$) | | | Dummy ($\text{dum}\, r_s$) | | |
|---|---|---|---|---|---|---|
| Germany | 0.15 | (7.44) | | −0.30 | (6.12) | |
| The Netherlands[a] | 0.022 | (3.34) | [0.13] | −0.044 | (3.29) | [−0.27] |
| United Kingdom | 0.17 | (3.91) | | −0.35 | (4.05) | |

*Notes:* The figures in parentheses are *t*-statistics.
[a] Long-run elasticities in brackets.

with the same distributed lag for each explanatory variable. The estimated average speed of adjustment amounts to 5 1/4 quarter, which is very low compared to the estimates for the other countries. The coefficients of all explanatory variables have the expected sign and, with the exception of inflation and the cyclical indicator, they are all significant at the 5% level.

Finally, in the equation for the United Kingdom switching has also been taken into account. It improves the regression in the sense that with inclusion of these variables all other explanatory variables obtain the expected sign. On the other hand, the long-run elasticity of real income now comes out at the almost implausible value of 2.13, which makes our results for this country less satisfactory.

### 2.4.2 Real Demand for Money

Theory on the demand for money takes for granted that the demand for nominal balances is proportional to the price level. From this follows logically that the demand for money function should be cast in real terms. In Section 2.4.1 we investigated this matter directly. By estimating the coefficients $\alpha_2$ and $\omega_2$ of the price deflator in specification (2.7) we let the data decide whether the demand for nominal balances varies, *ceteris paribus*, proportional to the price level. From Table 2.1 it appears that, according to our estimations, the long-run price elasticities are significantly larger than unity in Belgium, Germany and Italy. Thus, apart from the fact that the *t*-statistics might be biased upward (see footnote 6), our results for these countries do not support the economic theory which considers the demand for money as demand for real balances. However, it can be argued that this matter should be studied also by assuming the price elasticity in the demand for money function

*Table 2.3: Estimation results for* $\ln \frac{M2}{p} = \alpha_0' + \frac{\alpha_1 \ln y}{(1-\omega_1 B)} + \frac{\alpha_2 \ln p}{(1-\omega_2 B)} + \frac{\alpha_3 \ln r}{(1-\omega_3 B)} + \frac{\alpha_4 \ln p'}{(1-\omega_4 B)} + \frac{\alpha_5 \ln c}{(1-\omega_5 B)} + \text{seasonals} + u$

| | | Real income ($y$) | | | Interest rate ($r$) | | | Inflation ($p'$) | | | Cyclical indicator ($c$)[b] | | | |
|---|---|---|---|---|---|---|---|---|---|---|---|---|---|---|
| Country | Sample period | $\alpha_1$ | $\omega_1$ | Long-run elasticity | $\alpha_3$ | $\omega_3$ | Long-run elasticity | $\alpha_4$ | $\omega_4$ | Long-run elasticity | $\alpha_5$ | $\omega_5$ | Long-run elasticity | Box–Pierce $\bar{\chi}^2_{12}$ test statistic[c] |
| Belgium | 1961:IV–1976:IV | 0.95 | 0.12 | 1.09 | −0.14 | 0.55 | −0.31 | – | – | – | 0.067+ | 0.30+ | 0.095+ | 30.3 |
| | | (16.84) | (2.52) | | (3.71) | (3.41) | | | | | (2.07) | (1.01) | | |
| Denmark[c] | 1971:I–1976:IV | 0.76 | 0.52 | 1.58 | −0.08 | 0.52 | −0.16 | −0.45 | 0.52 | −0.94 | 0.014+ | 0.52+ | 0.028+ | 15.0 |
| | | (3.74) | (3.02) | | (1.42) | (3.02) | | (1.94) | (3.02) | | (2.13) | (3.02) | | |
| France | 1960:1V–1976:IV | 1.61 | – | 1.61 | −0.13 | 0.49 | −0.26 | −0.10[d] | – | −0.10 | −1.05 | – | −1.05 | 102.6 |
| | | (42.64) | | | (3.13) | (3.83) | | (0.58) | | | (9.26) | | | |
| Germany | 1960:I–1976:IV | 1.01 | 0.17 | 1.21 | −0.12 | 0.38 | −0.20 | – | – | – | 0.052+ | – | 0.052+ | 58.8 |
| | | (13.29) | (2.47) | | (1.74) | (1.01) | | | | | (4.70) | | | |
| Ireland | 1963:I–1973:IV | 0.78 | 0.45 | 1.41 | – | – | – | −1.37 | – | −1.37 | −0.33 | – | −0.33 | 33.8 |
| | | (6.99) | (5.42) | | | | | (3.30) | | | (0.99) | | | |
| Italy | 1962:II–1976:IV | 1.68 | 0.06 | 1.78 | −0.12 | – | −0.12 | – | – | – | −0.62 | – | −0.62 | 102.1 |
| | | (17.46) | (1.06) | | (3.32) | | | | | | (2.76) | | | |
| The Netherlands[c] | 1960:I–1976:IV | 0.25 | 0.79 | 1.19 | −0.06 | 0.79 | −0.30 | −0.31 | 0.79 | −1.49 | −0.74 | 0.79 | −3.61 | 13.2 |
| | | (4.92) | (13.39) | | (2.19) | (13.39) | | (3.18) | (13.39) | | (2.97) | (13.39) | | |
| United Kingdom | 1964:IV–1976:IV | 1.14 | 0.39 | 1.89 | −0.18[d] | – | −0.18 | −0.45[d] | – | −0.45 | −0.08 | – | −0.08 | 17.2 |
| | | (5.92) | (3.81) | | (3.12) | | | (2.41) | | | (0.99) | | | |

*Notes:*

The figures in parentheses are $t$-statistics.

[a] A + indicates that unemployment is used as a cyclical indicator.

[b] Corrected for downward bias.

[c] A Koyck-lag is used in the estimations.

[d] Lagged three quarters.

to be equal to unity. The estimated income elasticities with this case are not expected to differ from our earlier estimates, unless misspecification occurs. In order to investigate this we have estimated a specification with the real M2 as dependent variable. In other words, in (2.7) $\alpha_1$ is set *a priori* equal to unity and $\omega_2$ equal to 0.

The estimation results for these real demand for money functions are presented in Table 2.3. Again, the regressions comprise three seasonal dummies and a constant term, which are not shown in the table. The results with respect to switching are given in Table 2.4.

In the equation for Belgium inflation gets the wrong sign, while the speed of adjustment with respect to the unemployment rate increases drastically. The estimate of the Danish long-run income elasticity doubles when the price deflator is left out of the estimations. The unemployment rate as cyclical indicator now obtains the expected sign and differs significantly from 0. In the German equation too, the unemployment rate becomes highly significant. In the case of Italy inflation gets the wrong sign and the estimate of the interest rate elasticity is more than halved but remains significant. It must be noted that, of course, there is a substantial correlation between inflation and long-term interest rates. The Dutch demand for money function improves substantially by setting the price elasticity equal to unity. The coefficients of the rate of inflation and the cyclical indicator become significant even at the 1% level.[4] In the equation for the United Kingdom the measured long-run income elasticity decreased somewhat and the influence of inflation triples. In the case of France and Ireland there are no substantial

[4] In accordance with (2.7) the equations are estimated either with a Koyck-lag (Denmark, The Netherlands) or with a different distributed lag for each explanatory variable (the other countries). By way of experiment for the Dutch real demand for money function estimates are also made with both a Koyck-lag, i.e., partial adjustment, and adaptive expectations for real income. The result for 1960:I–1976:IV is ($t$-values in parentheses; sre = short-run elasticity; lre = long-run elasticity):

| Real income $y$ | | | | Interest rate $r$ | | Inflation $p'$ | | Cyclical indicator $c_1$ | |
|---|---|---|---|---|---|---|---|---|---|
| $\alpha_1$ | $\omega_1$ | sre | lre | sre | lre | sre | lre | sre | lre |
| 0.23<br>(4.52) | 0.19<br>(1.42) | 0.28 | 1.35 | −0.08<br>(2.45) | −0.38 | −0.31<br>(3.21) | −1.49 | −0.67<br>(2.59) | −3.24 |

| Short-term interest rate ($r_s$) | | Dummy (dum $r_s$) | | | Box–Pierce $\bar{\chi}^2_{12}$ test |
|---|---|---|---|---|---|
| sre | lre | sre | lre | Koyck-lag | statistic |
| 0.026 (3.54) | 0.13 | -0.055 (3.44) | -0.26 | 0.79 (13.33) | 13.7 |

This specification of the lag structure makes the measured long-run income elasticity increase from 1.19 to 1.35. We note that Fase and Kuné (1974b), apart from partial adjustment, allowed for adaptive expectations with respect to both real income and the price deflator in their preferred specification of the nominal demand for money function.

*Table 2.4: Estimation results for the real demand for money functions with respect to the term structure*

| Country | Short-term interest rate ($\ln r_s$) | | | Dummy ($\text{dum}\, r_s$) | | |
|---|---|---|---|---|---|---|
| Germany | 0.13 | (6.87) | | −0.23 | (5.79) | |
| The Netherlands[a] | 0.024 | (3.39) | [0.12] | −0.048 | (3.25) | [−0.23] |
| United Kingdom | 0.14 | (4.04) | | −0.28 | (4.42) | |

*Note:* See Table 2.2.

differences between the estimation results of the nominal and the real demand for money function.

All estimates of the long-run elasticity of real income in Table 2.3 are greater than unity. The lowest values are found in the Low Countries and Germany, and with respect to the high elasticities of France and Italy we recall the steadily growing liquidity ratio depicted in Figure 2.1. However, the high value of the income elasticity found for the United Kingdom is exceptional, the more so as the money stock grew proportionally less than income in this country. It is most probable that the United Kingdom's demand for money function lacks stability, especially in the seventies where there is an extraordinary sharp rise of the liquidity ratio in 1972–1974 and an equally sharp decline in 1974–1976 (see Figure 2.1).[5]

The high values of the Box–Pierce test statistic of the last columns of Table 2.1 and 2.3 indicate that, in most equations, the residuals differ significantly from white noise and need further investigation. We will do this for the real demand for money functions in the next section.

[5] The lack of stability becomes apparent when we re-estimate the United Kingdom's real demand for money function for the 1964:IV–1978:IV period ($t$-values in parentheses; lre = long-run elasticity):

| Real income $y$ | | | Interest rate $r_{-3}$ | Inflation $p'_{-3}$ | Cyclical indicator $c_1$: $\alpha_5$ |
|---|---|---|---|---|---|
| $\alpha_1$ | $\omega_1$ | lre | $\alpha_3$ | $\alpha_4$ | |
| 0.88 | 0.13 | 1.02 | −0.16 | −0.22 | −0.05 |
| (2.97) | (0.45) | | (2.42) | (0.96) | (−0.41) |

| Interest rate $r_3$ | Dummy($\text{dum}\, r_s$) | Box–Pierce $\bar{\chi}^2_{12}$ test statistic |
|---|---|---|
| 0.19 (5.16) | −0.31 (4.13) | 53.2 |

By this extension of the sample period with two years the long-run income elasticity falls from 1.89 to 1.02 while the influence of inflation is no longer significant.

## 2.5 Further Analysis of Estimation Results for the Real Demand for Money Functions

### 2.5.1 Analysis of the Residuals

The question of whether the demand for money function is stable is of crucial importance in an empirical study, the more so as we conjecture that the economic turbulence of the last years may have affected the demand for money. Some indication of (in)stability can be gathered from comparison of the estimation results for the nominal and the real demand for money functions. In order to examine this matter further we show in Table 2.5 the standard deviation of the residuals in the estimated equations for the real demand for money, considering the whole sample period and three sub-periods of equal length.

In this table three groups of countries can be distinguished. In the first, consisting of Belgium, France, Germany and The Netherlands the variation of the residuals is of about the same size in all three sub-periods. In the second set including Denmark, Ireland and ltaly, the standard deviations in the first and the last sub-period correspond to each other, but surprisingly, those of the second period obtain a much lower value. The standard deviation of the residuals in the United Kingdom which is in the third group, is much higher in the last sub-period than in the other two sub-periods, again suggesting instability of this function in the seventies.

In order to trace what events could have had a destabilizing effect on the demand for money we present in Table 2.6 the outliers of the residuals of our selected equations with their date of occurence. With the exception of France, where we overestimate the money stock in all quarters of 1970, the number of outliers is surprisingly small considering the fact that for most countries we have about 60 residuals. The majority of the outliers relate to the seventies but from Table 2.6 no single event clearly emerges as having caused a prominent and general shift in the demand for money in the EU. Not even the oil crisis may be mentioned in this respect as around that period an outlier only has been detected for France (1974:II).

At the end of the previous section we concluded that the residuals for most countries differ significantly from white noise. This has led us to construct (according to the procedure described in Box and Jenkins (1970)) ARMA-models for the residuals. In other words we allow $\theta(B)$ in specification (2.3) to be determined by the data without imposing *a priori* restrictions on it. These ARMA-models are not only useful in view of this analysis of the residuals, but are also applied when predicting the

*Table 2.5: Standard deviation of residuals*

| Country | Sample period | Full sample period | First sub-period | Second sub-period | Third sub-period |
|---|---|---|---|---|---|
| Belgium | 1961:IV–1976:IV | 0.016 | 0.010 | 0.016 | 0.016 |
| Denmark | 1971:I–1976:IV | 0.014 | 0.018 | 0.010 | 0.015 |
| France | 1960:IV–1976:IV | 0.019 | 0.016 | 0.021 | 0.017 |
| Germany | 1960:I–1976:IV | 0.026 | 0.023 | 0.026 | 0.026 |
| Ireland | 1963:I–1973:IV | 0.042 | 0.043 | 0.031 | 0.046 |
| Italy | 1962:II–1976:IV | 0.031 | 0.029 | 0.019 | 0.034 |
| The Netherlands | 1960:I–1976:IV | 0.014 | 0.015 | 0.012 | 0.015 |
| United Kingdom | 1964:IV–1976:IV | 0.038 | 0.032 | 0.028 | 0.051 |

*Note:* The standard deviation is calculated without adjusting for the degrees of freedom used in the regression.

*Table 2.6: Outliers of the real demand for money functions*

| Belgium | Denmark | France | Germany | Ireland | The Netherlands | United Kingdom |
|---|---|---|---|---|---|---|
| 1967:I(−) | 1971:IV(−) | 1963:I(+) | 1972:III(+) | 1963:I(−) | 1965:I(+) | 1976:IV(−) |
| 1968:I(−) | | 1970:I/ | | 1970:I(+) | | |
| | | 1970:IV(−) | | | | |
| | | 1974:II(+) | | | | |
| | | 1975:I(+) | | | | |

*Notes:* This table shows the observations where the residual of our demand for money function falls outside the two sigma range; + indicates a positive value of the residual and hence underestimation of the demand for money; − indicates a negative value of the residual and hence overestimation of the demand for money. There is no outlier of the Italian real demand for money function.

money stock.

Table 2.7 shows the ARMA-models transforming the residuals to white noise. In the case of Denmark and The Netherlands we have not estimated an ARMA-model as the residuals of these demand for money functions with a Koyck-lag are already white noise. Seasonal moving average parameters appear in the models for Belgium, Ireland and Italy. It means that in the demand for money functions of these countries the seasonal dummies are too rigid to capture seasonality completely.

According to widely accepted economic theory the demand for money balances should be formulated in stocks. Yet, a number of empirical studies on the demand for money estimates the demand function in first differences instead of levels. Stationarity of the disturbances, which is, as known, a necessary condition for statistical inference in regression analysis, is often alleged as a rationale for it. However, the ARMA-models of Table 2.7 show that in our demand for money functions the residuals are stationary series. Hence, estimating in levels is in our case also statistically justified. Here, differencing may lead to misspecification as argued by Hendry and Mizon (1978).[6]

The stability of a regression equation is commonly assessed by re-estimating that equation for two (or more) sub-periods and applying a Chow-test. Because of nonlinearities and the length of the sample period we were unable to follow this procedure, but re-estimated the ARMA-models of the residuals for two equal sub-periods. The results suggest stability in the case of France, Germany and Italy, and instability in the case of Belgium, Ireland and the United Kingdom.

### 2.5.2 Forecasting the Money Stock

One of the main objectives of this study is to come to a uniform forecasting device for the broadly defined money stock in the EU countries. In order to assess the predictive power of our equations we present in Table 2.8 the root mean square error of the *ex ante* forecasts for 1977 and 1978. In these forecasts we used the realized values of the explanatory variables. Forecasts of the residuals are obtained from the ARMA-models from 1976:IV onwards. Of course the figures of Table 2.8 give but a very limited indication of the predictive power as they cover two years only.

---

6 For those functions where the residuals are no white noise, the $t$-values of the parameter estimates in Table 2.1 and 2.3 may be biased (e.g., see Kiviet (1980)). We have tried to estimate the parameters of the demand for money functions and the ARMA-models jointly, but unfortunately the iteration algorithm either did not converge or converged to implausible parameter values (including values outside the admissible regions for the ARMA-parameters).

*Table 2.7: ARMA-models for the residuals of the real demand for money functions*

| Country | Sample period | Auto-regres-sive para-meters $\phi_1$ | Moving average parameters $\theta_1$ | $\theta_2$ | $\theta_4$ | $\theta_8$ | $\bar{\chi}^2_{12}$ / $\sigma_a$ |
|---|---|---|---|---|---|---|---|
| Belgium | 1961:IV–1976:IV | 0.32 (2.49) | – | – | −0.31 (2.27) | – | 7.2 / 0.015 |
| Denmark | 1971:I–1976-IV | – | – | – | – | – | 15.0 / 0.014 |
| France | 1960:IV–1976:IV | 0.74 (8.37) | – | – | – | – | 8.2 / 0.013 |
| Germany | 1960:I–1976:IV | 0.66 (7.14) | – | – | – | – | 12.7 / 0.020 |
| Ireland | 1963:I–1973:IV | 0.57 (4.99) | – | – | −0.32 (1.83) | – | 10.9 / 0.030 |
| Italy | 1962:II–1976:IV | 0.69 (6.10) | – | −0.24 (1.89) | 0.34 (2.33) | 0.40 (2.93) | 14.0 / 0.018 |
| The Nether-lands | 1960:I–1976:IV | – | – | – | – | – | 13.2 / 0.014 |
| United Kingdom | 1964:IV–1976:IV | – | −0.36 (2.37) | −0.43 (2.79) | – | – | 9.1 / 0.033 |

*Notes:* ARMA-models of the following general form are estimated: $(1 - \Sigma\phi_i B^i)u_t = (1 - \Sigma\theta_i B^i)\alpha_t$ where $u_t$ is the residual and $\alpha_t$ the noise of the ARMA-model; $t$-values are in parentheses; $\bar{\chi}^2_{12}$ is the Box–Pierce test statistic with 12 degrees of freedom (adjusted for downward bias); $\sigma_a$ is the standard deviation of the noise (adjusted for degrees of freedom).

From Table 2.8 we see that in general our equations yield poor predictions for 1977 and 1978. In The Netherlands and the United Kingdom we overestimated the money stock, while M2 grew faster than predicted in Belgium and Italy. The bad performance of the equation for The Netherlands in 1978 is partly due to the fact that in this equation the predicted values of the lagged dependent variable are used and therefore the prediction errors cumulate.

The stability of the demand for money function, which is a necessary condition for predictive power, has extensively been explored by, e.g., Goldfeld (1976) and Laidler (1980). The present analysis is along similar lines as Goldfeld's paper in that it focuses on M2 rather than M1 as is common in many US money demand studies. As Goldfeld's this study attributes considerable importance to modelling the adjustment lags, without ending up with stable demand functions for all countries considered. However, most EU countries are small, fixed, exchange rate open economies in which the money supply is endogeneous. This issue and its implications for the appropriate estimation of the demand for

*Table 2.8: Root mean square error of* ex ante *forecasts of the money stock in 1977:I–1978:IV*

| Period | Belgium (in billions of Bfr) | France (in billions of Ffr) | Germany (in billions of DM) |
|---|---|---|---|
| 1977:I–1977:IV | 32.6 (1.6) | 14.8 (1.6) | 16.8 (5.6) |
| 1978:I–1978:IV | 86.2 (3.7) | 35.6 (3.4) | 13.8 (4.1) |
| 1977:I–1978:IV | 65.2 (2.9) | 27.3 (2.8) | 15.4 (4.9) |
| | Italy (in 1 000 billions of Lire) | The Netherlands (in billions of *f*) | United Kingdom (in billions of £) |
| 1977:I–1977:IV | 11.3 (6.4) | 5.3 (5.7) | 5.0 (10.6) |
| 1978:I–1978:IV | 18.9 (8.6) | 12.1 (12.5) | 3.5 (6.5) |
| 1977:I–1978:IV | 15.6 (7.9) | 9.3 (9.8) | 4.3 (8.5) |

*Note:* In parentheses as a percentage of the average money stock in the relevant year(s).

money has recently been explored by Laidler (1980). In this respect our results seem to indicate that the underlying long-run elasticities of the demand for money functions are more stable than the short-run elasticities and the parameters of the dynamic processes.

## 2.6 Summary and Conclusions

This chapter has attempted to estimate both nominal and real demand for money equations for the old EU countries (except Luxembourg), using a common econometric framework and a uniform data file which is constructed with data supplied to us by the various central banks. This framework allows us to use the same but very general dynamic structure for all countries.

Our empirical estimates show that in the nominal demand for money functions the long-run income elasticities range from 0.77 (Denmark) to 2.13 (United Kingdom). Although we measure a price elasticity significantly greater than unity for Belgium, Germany and ltaly in these functions, we prefer for empirical reasons the results and the real demand for money. Here all estimates of the income elasticity are above unity with the lowest value in Belgium (1.09) and the highest in the United Kingdom (1.89). Confining ourselves to these real demand for money functions, only in the case of Ireland no (negative) influence of the long-term interest rate on the demand for money could be traced. In the other countries long-run interest rate elasticities cluster around −0.20 with the highest value in Belgium (−0.31) and the lowest in Italy (−0.12). The range of the estimated elasticities of inflation is much greater. We found no influence in Belgium, Germany and Italy and very little in France, while the elasticity is greater than unity in Ireland and The Netherlands. The inclusion of a cyclical indicator as an explanatory variable is a novelty of this study. We could assess the cyclical influence on the demand for M2 for all countries, although the estimations for Ireland and the United Kingdom do not differ significantly from 0. As the way of measurement of the cycle varies from country to country, the size of the elasticities cannot be compared among the countries.

We believe that the inclusion of a cyclical indicator may lead to more stable demand functions. To that end we have also accounted for interest rate induced switching in Germany, The Netherlands and the United Kingdom. In order to examine the question of stability we have analysed both the residuals and the predictive power of our equations. According to different criteria our analysis of the residuals suggests stability of the demand for money functions in the majority of the countries. However, the United Kingdom's demand for money function is, in our specification, obviously unstable in the seventies. The predictive performance of the equations for 1977 and 1978 turned out to be poor in comparison with the residual standard errors in the sample period. This may be just bad luck, but it may also indicate that our demand for money functions are not so stable outside the sample period.

An important property of our equations concerns its lag structure, notably in view of the speed of adjustment of actual to desired money balances, and of expected to actual values of the explanatory variables. A specification with partial adjustment appeared to be necessary in order to obtain economically plausible outcomes for Denmark and The Netherlands. For all other countries, however, partial adjustment did not lead to useful results. Therefore we have estimated our equations with either partial adjustment or adaptive expectations, noting that adaptive expectations is identical to partial adjustment when the expectations of the explanatory variables adjust to the actual values with the same speed of adjustment for each variable. Our estimates show a great variety of speeds of adjustment in the case of adaptive expectations, while in the case of partial adjustment the average speed is low in The Netherlands and somewhat higher in Denmark. We noticed that the specification of the lag structure has a considerable impact on the numerical values of the estimated elasticities in the demand for money functions.

As a final comment we mention that in addition to the reported results we have tested two alternative specifications. First we included the rate of interest linearly rather than logarithmic-linearly. Thus we allow the interest rate elasticity of the demand for money to increase with the level of interest. Second, we extended our original specification by adding the (expected) rate of appreciation of the home currency as an explanatory variable, as an expected appreciation may encourage foreigners to hold cash balances of the strong currency country (and vice versa). However these modifications did not improve our results. This is especially surprising in the case of the appreciation variable, as one expects the recent commotion in the foreign exchange markets to be partly responsible for the instability of the demand for money in the seventies. Some of these effects may have been captured by the short-term interest rate variable, which is introduced in our equations for Germany, The Netherlands and the United Kingdom to take account of interest rate induced switching.

## Appendix 2.A On the Data

Some of the data employed in this chapter does not stem from public sources but are provided to us only for the purpose of this demand for money study. This leads us to make the following remarks for the individual countries. In addition we indicate what measure is used for the cyclical indicator.

*Belgium* Up to 1969:III data on M2 are collected from 'Main Economic Indicators'; from 1969:IV we use the new series on M2 provided to us by the National Bank of Belgium; both series are end of quarter figures; $c1$ is the so-called 'synthetic curve' of the National Bank.

*Denmark* $c1$ is constructed by means of the volume of retail sales; data on $c2$ are collected from 'Main Economic Indicators'.

*France* $c1$ is constructed by means of the volume of the gross industrial production.

*Germany* $r_s$ is the interest rate on three month interbank deposits; $c1$ is the index of output in the producing sector, excluding construction and energy industry, with its trend removed.

*Ireland* Yearly figures for $p$ are derived from national income and expenditure data. From these we constructed quarterly figures by means of the so-called Lisman-method (see Boot, Feibes, and Lisman (1967)); $c1$ is the index of capacity utilization.

*Italy* The data on M2 and $r$ are end of quarter figures; $c1$ is the index for the assessment of total order books of industrial farms.

*The Netherlands* $r_s$ is the interest rate on three month loans to local authorities; $c1$ is the utilization rate of labour.

*United Kingdom* For the money stock end of quarter figures of M3 are used; the data on $r$ are also end of quarter figures; $r_s$ is the interest rate on three-month interbank sterling deposits; $c1$ is the C.S.O. measure of the deviations from trend of the percentage of farms reporting below-capacity working to the Confederation of British Industries.

# 3. The Demand for Money in The Netherlands Revisited

## 3.1 INTRODUCTION

The empirical analysis of the demand for money had traditionally formed the main component of monetary econometrics. This prominence is due to its significance for monetary policy analysis and to the existence of a widely accepted theoretical basis. This basis has its roots in both microeconomic and macroeconomic theory. A much discussed part of demand for money analysis relates to the stability of money demand. Stability essentially means the extent to which a statistically satisfactory description using a limited number of explanatory variables can be obtained for the holdings of monetary assets. Stability also means that the fitted function does not show too much variance over different sample periods, and that its predictive power is reasonable. Since the 1970s the lack of stability in demand for money in many countries has been the main motivation behind the ongoing interest in the empirical research of money demand. This has led to important refinements of the analysis, relating to both the theoretical specification and the nature of the data employed.

As for the theoretical specification, considerable progress has been made in the field of model formulation. In particular, greater attention is now paid to the distinction between the short- and long-term demand for money, which traditionally was chiefly modelled by means of the partial adjustment mechanism. In addition, since the well-known criticism by Hendry and Mizon (1978) of a study of the demand for money by the Bank of England, the statistical verification of the assumptions made in the model has been given greater emphasis.

As regards the data of the present study, the demand for money analysis on the basis of aggregated data is backed up by an analysis for households on the one hand and for businesses on the other. Incidenti-

Reprinted from *De Economist*, **138** (1990), M.M.G. Fase and C.C.A. Winder, 'The demand for money in The Netherlands revisited', 276–301, ©1990 with kind permission from Kluwer Academic Publishers.

cally, The Netherlands is almost 20 years behind the United Kingdom in this field.

The present study aims to apply these new developments in the methodology and availability of additional data sources to the analysis of the aggregate money demand in The Netherlands as well as the disaggregated demand for money by the individual sectors. The chapter is organized as follows. Section 3.2 discusses the general dynamic specification of the demand for money function. Section 3.3 discusses the estimated demand functions for M2 and M1. Section 3.4 deals with the estimations of the money demand functions for the households and businesses sector. Section 3.5 is devoted to an evaluation of the estimated demand for money. Finally, Section 3.6 draws a number of conclusions.

## 3.2 Theoretical Framework

The starting point is the traditional demand for money function, in which the desired demand for money is determined by real income, the rate of inflation and the short- and long-term interest rates. If we assume a price elasticity of unity, then the following money demand equation can be postulated:

$$\mathrm{M}/P = \beta y^{\alpha_1} \exp\left(\alpha_2 \dot{p} + \alpha_3 r_k + \alpha_4 r_l\right) \tag{3.1}$$

where M is the desired money stock held in a steady state situation, $P$ is the price index – so that $\mathrm{M}/P$ is the real money stock –, $y$ is real income, $\dot{p}$ is the rate of inflation, $r_k$ the short-term interest rate and $r_l$ the long-term interest rate. The income elasticity is equal to $\alpha_1$. $\alpha_2$ measures the relative change in the demand for money due to a rise in inflation by one percentage point, and $\alpha_3$ and $\alpha_4$ measure the relative changes in the money demand for a one percentage point change in short- and long-term interest rates, respectively. Equation (3.1) describes the relationship between the optimum real or deflated value of the money-holdings on the one hand and the expected value of the determining factors on the other hand, and is as such a description of the long-run steady state relationship. In the chosen set-up, a fundamental distinction is made between the relationship in the steady state situation and the relationship in the short-run. For practical purposes like forecasting, it is also desirable to model deviations from the steady state relationship. This means that, for purposes of estimation, a dynamic formulation of (3.1) must be adopted in which the long-run properties of the demand for money are determined simultaneously with the short-run adjustment processes. To this end, an error-correction mechanism is used in conjunction with the modelling of lags. To describe the short-term dynamics of the demand for money, a cyclical indicator, $q_k$, has also been introduced. This variable represents the tendency for money to be hoarded when the economy is going into recession and for dishoarding in an economic boom. An alternative and perhaps more profound economic interpretation of this variable is to think of it as a proxy for the costs of real assets for which the liquid financial assets are a substitute. Hoarding and dishoarding reflect this substitution process. Be that as it may, it has, however, been assumed that, in the long-run – in other words over the full business cycle – this influence can be ignored. This assumption is the most important difference compared with previous analyses of the demand for money, in which the business cycle was also reflected – albeit weakly – in the long-run equilibrium (see Fase and Kuné (1974a, 1974b), Fase (1979), Butter and Fase (1981)). With respect to long-run equation (3.1), real income $y$ represents the influence of the transaction volume or wealth, while the inflation variable $\dot{p}$ and the two interest rates $r_k$ and $r_l$ determine the composition of the broad money stock. For this, assets of lesser liquidity, such as bonds, are a possible alternative. Thus the purpose of simultaneously including short- and long-term interest rates is also to take into account the influence of the yield curve on the demand for money.

The above leads to the following general model specification of the demand for money:

$$\delta(L)\ln\left(\frac{\mathrm{M}}{P}\right)_t = \alpha + \beta_1(L)\ln y_t + \beta_2(L)\dot{p}_t + \beta_3(L)r_{kt} + \beta_4 r_{lt} + \beta_5(L)\Delta\ln q_{kt}$$

where $\delta(L)$ and $\beta_i(L)$ are polynomials of the lag operator $L$, with $L^n y_t = y_{t-n}$, such that $\beta_i(L) = \beta_{0i} - \beta_{1i}L - \beta_{2i}L^2 - \cdots - \beta_{p_i i}L^{p_i}$ for $i = 1, \ldots, 5$ and $\delta(L) = 1 - \delta_1 L - \delta_2 L^2 - \cdots - \delta_p L^p$ and $p, p_i$ are integers. This equation can be rewritten in the form:

$$\bar{\delta}(L)\Delta\ln\left(\frac{\mathrm{M}}{P}\right)_t = \alpha + \bar{\beta}_1(L)\Delta\ln y_t + \gamma\left(\ln(\mathrm{M}/P)_{t-1} - \pi\ln y_{t-1}\right) + \beta_2(L)\dot{p}_t + \beta_3(L)r_{kt} + \beta_4 r_{lt} + \beta_5(L)\Delta\ln q_{kt} \quad (3.1')$$

where $-\gamma$ is equal to the sum of the coefficients of $\delta(L)$ and $-\gamma\pi$ represents the sum of the coefficients of $\beta_1(L)$. The lag polynomials $\bar{\delta}(L)$ and $\bar{\beta}_1(L)$ are of the order $p - 1$ and $p_1 - 1$. The coefficients of these polynomials are derived from those of $\delta(L)$ and $\beta_1(L)$. The demand for money functions presented in this chapter are special cases of specification (3.1′), which has been used as the basis for the estimations.

The money demand equations specified on the basis of the foregoing were initially estimated using seasonally unadjusted quarterly figures for the period 1959:I–1988:IV. Because the data were not seasonally adjusted, equation (3.1′) was supplemented with three seasonal dummy variables $s_i$. The actual order of the polynomials and thus the maintained empirical demand for money equation has been determined on the basis of the common diagnostic-estimation-verification cycle in the time series estimation practice. An element of this has been careful inspection of residual patterns and testing for significance of the coefficients in the polynomials of the lag operator $L$. Apart from these statistical considerations we also employed economic plausibility of the estimates as a selection device. Thus, of course, we deliberately introduced an element of art into our analysis.

## 3.3 Results for the Aggregate Money Demand

### 3.3.1 The Demand for M2

Proceeding from the postulated steady state formulation (3.1′) we obtained, using ordinary least-squares estimation with quarterly data for 1959:I–1988:IV, the following estimation for the real demand for money M2/$P$. (The real variables are expressed in 1980 prices.)

$$\begin{aligned}
\Delta \ln \left(\frac{\mathrm{M2}}{P}\right) = {} & \underset{(6.41)}{0.5637}\Delta \ln \left(\frac{\mathrm{M2}}{P}\right)_{-4} \\
& - \underset{(2.22)}{0.0655}\left(\ln \left(\frac{\mathrm{M2}}{P}\right)_{-1} - \ln y_{-1}\right) \\
& + \underset{(2.12)}{0.2202}\Delta \ln y - \underset{(8.41)}{0.0103}\dot{p} + \underset{(6.85)}{0.0087}\dot{p}_{-1} \\
& - \underset{(2.36)}{0.0065}(r_l - r_k) + \underset{(2.08)}{0.0055}(r_l - r_k)_{-1} \\
& - \underset{(1.66)}{0.1708}\Delta \ln q_k + \underset{(2.19)}{0.0334} + \underset{(2.12)}{0.0154}s_1 + \underset{(2.14)}{0.0147}s_2 \\
& - \underset{(2.43)}{0.0169}s_3 \qquad (3.2)
\end{aligned}$$

where the $t$-values, adjusted for any heteroscedasticity, are given in parentheses, $\bar{R}^2 = 0.71$, and the standard error of the residuals $SE = 0.0214$. Equation (3.2) implies estimates for the parameters of the steady state function. These are:

$$\alpha_1 = 1; \quad \underset{(2.74)}{\hat{\alpha}_2 = -0.0247} \quad \underset{(0.65)}{\hat{\alpha}_3 = -\hat{\alpha}_4 = 0.0152}$$

According to this estimated demand for money function, the growth in the money stock at constant prices stems from the growth in broad money in the past, the growth in real income, inflation, the differential between long- and short-term interest rates, the relative change in capacity utilization and the error-correction term $\ln(\mathrm{M2}/P)_{-1} - \ln y_{-1}$. This correction mechanism ensures that there is a tendency to equilibrium in case of any departure from the steady state path (3.1). Implicit in this mechanism is the assumption that the coefficients of $\ln(\mathrm{M2}/P)_{-1}$ and $\ln y_{-1}$ are equal, but with opposite signs, which is a testable hypothesis. A likelihood ratio test of this restriction yields $\chi^2(1) = 1.30$, which does not lead to rejection of the null hypothesis. This restriction, which implies a long-run income elasticity of unity, is therefore supported by the estimations obtained. The relative change in capacity utilization $\Delta \ln q_k$ has been included as a determinant in (3.2) instead of the absolute capacity utilization factor $q_k$ in order to nullify the effect of the cyclical variable in the long-run.

The effect of interest rates is modelled in (3.2) by the differential between the capital market and money market rates, since this differential represents the opportunity costs of holding various broad-money assets. It is also an approximation of the gradient of the yield curve. A flatter yield curve leads to lower opportunity costs and therefore to an increase in the demand for M2. A steeper yield curve, on the other hand, leads to a drop in the money demand. Including the interest differential implies the assumption that the two interest rates possess the same coefficient with opposite signs. The likelihood ratio test for this restriction on the interest rate coefficients of $r_l$ and $r_k$ yields an insignificant $\chi^2(2) = 0.076$ statistic and supports our modelling of the yield curve as explanatory variable. As is known, the yield curve gradient may also be viewed as a measure of expected inflation. An expected increase in inflation, according to this interpretation, leads to a steeper yield curve and hence to a drop in the demand for money. If the yield curve is included in the money demand function as the differential between long- and short-term interest rates, the interest rate effect also measures the influence of expected inflation on demand for money. However, in equation (3.2) the inflation effect is also explicitly modelled.

Equation (3.2) has been subjected to an exhaustive misspecification analysis – reported in Fase and Winder (1989) – which leads to the conclusion that the adopted specification is statistically satisfactory.

This is also confirmed by graphical inspection – not shown here – of the discrepancies between actual and fitted pattern of $\ln \mathrm{M2}/P$. The movement in the liquidity ratio over the period 1970–1988 implied by equation (3.2) is represented in Figure 3.1, and shows that the fitted time path coincides rather well with the historical time path, albeit that, from 1987 onwards, there is a systematic discrepancy between the two. This means that, from this point of view, the approach adopted here is less satisfactory and needs closer scrutiny.

Apart from statistical quality, economic plausibility of the estimations obtained offers a yardstick for assessing equation (3.2). The long-term demand elasticities which can be calculated from equation (3.2) are 1 with respect to income; 0.09 with respect to the short-term interest rate; −0.11 with respect to the long-term interest rate; −0.12 with respect to inflation. In view of the results of other studies, these values do not appear unreasonable. The speed with which the equilibrium values are achieved provides a further yardstick. Table 3.1 illustrates that this speed differs substantially among the various determinants.

Table 3.1 shows that an increase in real income of 1% leads to an initial rise of 0.22% in M2 at constant prices. The adjustment to the ultimate increase of 1% however is gradual. After two years, the increase in M2 is around 70% of the total adjustment. An increase in inflation of one percentage point, on the other hand, leads to an immediate drop of 1% in the demand for money. After two years, almost 90% of the adjustment has taken place. An increase in the differential between long- and short-term interest rates immediately leads to a drop of 0.65% in the real demand for money. After two years, however, 90% of the total adjustment of 1.5% has occured. An increase in capacity utilization of 1% leads to an immediate drop in the demand for money of 0.17%. Convergence to the long-term impact of 0, however, is extremely slow.

### 3.3.2 The Demand for M1

In order to place the results obtained so far in a broader perspective, the demand for M1, was also estimated. For the period 1959:I–1988:IV the results obtained are:

$$\begin{aligned}\Delta \ln\left(\frac{\mathrm{M1}}{P}\right) = &\ \underset{(4.42)}{0.2898}\,\Delta \ln(\mathrm{M1}/P)_{-4}\\ &- \underset{(5.19)}{0.3335}\,(\ln(\mathrm{M1}/P)_{-1} - \ln y_{-1})\end{aligned}$$

$$
\begin{aligned}
&+ \underset{(5.63)}{0.6494}\Delta \ln y - \underset{(2.93)}{0.0040}r_k - \underset{(3.73)}{0.0070}\Delta r_k \\
&- \underset{(3.11)}{0.0071}r_l - \underset{(4.61)}{0.0036}\dot{p} - \underset{(3.98)}{0.4453}\Delta \ln q_k \\
&- \underset{(3.36)}{0.1768}\Delta \ln q_{k-1} + \underset{(4.87)}{0.0725} - \underset{(0.40)}{0.0032}s_1 \\
&+ \underset{(3.26)}{0.0277}s_2 - \underset{(1.26)}{0.0113}s_3 \qquad (3.3)
\end{aligned}
$$

where the $t$-values, adjusted for any heteroscedasticity, are given in parentheses, $\bar{R}^2 = 0.86$, and the standard error of the residuals $SE = 0.0196$. Implicit in these estimations are the parameter estimations for the steady state function (3.1) for M1, which are:

$$
\alpha_1 = 1; \quad \hat{\alpha}_2 = \underset{(4.92)}{-0.0107} \quad \hat{\alpha}_3 = \underset{(3.59)}{-0.0121} \quad \hat{\alpha}_4 = \underset{(4.19)}{-0.0212}
$$

Like the estimated equation for M2, the demand equation for M1 was subjected to a misspecification analysis, on the basis of which it can be concluded that the estimated equation is statistically satisfactory (see Fase and Winder (1989)).

As far as the economic interpretation of (3.3) is concerned, an income rise of 1% leads to a similarly large increase in the real money stock. The restriction of an income elasticity equal to unity imposed by the error-correction formulation is confirmed by the value of the likelihood ratio test of 0.26, which follows a $\chi^2(1)$ distribution. An increase in inflation of one percentage point leads to a drop in the real demand for money of 1.07% in the long-run. An increase in short- and long-term interest rates ultimately implies a decrease in the real demand for money of 1.21% and 2.12%, respectively. The influence of capacity utilization is only important in the short-run. However, the demand for narrow money is very much affected by the business cycle. The impact elasticities with respect to inflation, short- and long-term interest rates are $-0.05$, $-0.07$ and $-0.15$, respectively.

The adopted method of modelling the interest rate structure means that a general rise in interest rates mitigates the growth in the money demand via the short-term as well as via the long-term interest rate. With the elasticities found, even modest interest rate changes lead to substantial changes in the money demand. Since this does not appear to be very plausible we have estimated an alternative specification using only short-term interest rates, assuming the near-money is the most obvious alternative for narrow money. This means that the demand for

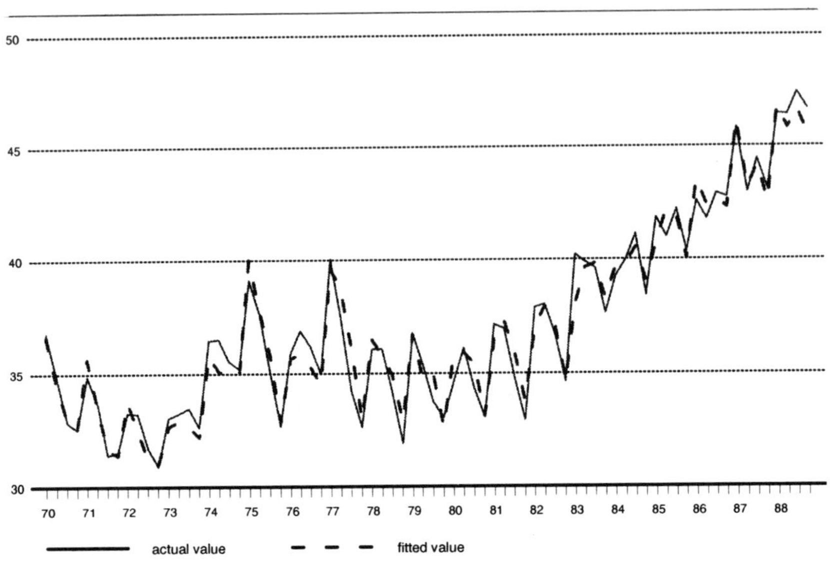


*Figure 3.1: Actual and fitted liquidity ratio, 1970–1988 (in %)*

*Table 3.1: Short-term response of* M2 *(in %) to shocks in the determinants*

| Quarter | Income | Inflation | Interest differential | Cyclical indicator |
|---|---|---|---|---|
| 1 | 0.22 | −1.03 | −0.65 | −0.17 |
| 2 | 0.27 | −1.12 | −0.71 | −0.16 |
| 3 | 0.32 | −1.21 | −0.76 | −0.15 |
| 4 | 0.36 | −1.29 | −0.81 | −0.14 |
| 5 | 0.53 | −1.94 | −1.23 | −0.23 |
| 6 | 0.59 | −2.03 | −1.28 | −0.21 |
| 7 | 0.64 | −2.11 | −1.32 | −0.19 |
| 8 | 0.69 | −2.17 | −1.37 | −0.17 |
| ∞ | 1 | −2.47 | −1.52 | 0 |

*Notes:* The shocks are 1% for income and the cyclical indicator and one percentage point for inflation and interest rates. Therefore, the responses shown for inflation and interest rates have been multiplied by 100.

M1 is determined solely by the short-term interest rate, apart from the other money demand determinants in (3.1).
Estimating this alternative for the sample period 1959:I–1988:IV yields:

$$\begin{aligned}\Delta\ln\left(\frac{\mathrm{M1}}{P}\right) = {} & \underset{(3.97)}{0.3049}\,\Delta\ln(\mathrm{M1}/P)_{-4} - \underset{(5.01)}{0.2096}\,(\ln(\mathrm{M1}/P)_{-1} - \ln y)\\ & - \underset{(3.61)}{0.0051} r_k - \underset{(2.89)}{0.0061}\Delta r_k - \underset{(3.70)}{0.0042}\Delta r_{k-1}\\ & - \underset{(2.13)}{0.0029}\dot{p} - \underset{(2.13)}{0.1153}\Delta\ln q_k + \underset{(5.07)}{0.0431} - \underset{(1.60)}{0.0134} s_1\\ & + \underset{(3.42)}{0.0300} s_2 - \underset{(4.88)}{0.0384} s_3 \end{aligned} \qquad (3.4)$$

where the $t$-values, adjusted for any heteroscedasticity, are given in parentheses, $\bar{R}^2 = 0.84$, and the standard error of the residuals $SE = 0.0211$. We note that equation (3.4) differs from equation (3.2) or (3.3) in that $\ln y$ rather than $\ln y_{-1}$ appears in the error-correction term while the term $\Delta\ln y$ is missing. However, it is easily shown this is not entirely different from the earlier specification. The form of equation (3.4) is obtained by imposing a particular restriction on the parameters of the lag polynomials.[1]

The long-term steady state function underlying equation (3.4) differs from that in equation (3.1) by the absence of the long-term interest rate. It reads as:

$$\mathrm{M1}/P = Ay\exp(\,-\underset{(3.98)}{0.014}\;\dot{p} - \underset{(6.21)}{0.024}\;r_k) \qquad (3.5)$$

where $A$, for the sake of simplicity, is not numerically evaluated and with the derived $t$-values in parentheses. Equation (3.5) means that, in the steady state, a relative rise in real income leads to an equal rise in the real money demand. A rise in inflation of one percentage point implies a drop in the real M1 money stock of 1.4%, and a rise in the interest rate of one percentage point ultimately leads to a drop in the real money stock of 2.4%. A surprising difference compared with the estimated steady state specification for the demand for M2 is that the interest rate effect differs significantly from 0.

Money demand function (3.4) was also subjected to an exhaustive misspecification analysis. The results, which are again given in Fase and

---

[1] More specifically, when in the term $\gamma(\ln(\mathrm{M}/P)_{-1} - \ln y_{-1}) + \bar{\beta}_{11}\Delta\ln y$ we impose $\gamma + \bar{\beta}_{11} = 0$, the term $\gamma(\ln(\mathrm{M}/P)_{-1} - \ln y)$ results. Hence, rather than $\Delta\ln y$ the modified error-correction with $\ln y_{-1}$ being replaced by $\ln y$ does appear as an explantory variable.

Winder (1989), lead to the conclusion that the chosen specification is satisfactory from a statistical point of view. The likelihood ratio test on the restriction on the coefficients of $\ln(\mathrm{M}/P)_{-1}$ and $\ln y$ implied by the error-correction formulation in (3.4) should, strictly speaking, lead to the rejection of the error-correction formulation. However, since equation (3.4) behaves better than the model without this restriction as far as its predictive quality is concerned, equation (3.4) has nevertheless been maintained. In terms of predictive power, specification (3.4) is also suitable for recent years from 1987 onwards.[2] A graphical inspection reveals that the movement of the liquidity ratio implied by equation (3.4) in effect describes the historical movement fairly satisfactorily (Figure 3.2), indicating that the dynamics of our modelling are very important for a description.

It is interesting to take a closer look at the results for M1 and M2, partly because the elasticities in the demand for money according to the narrow and broad money definitions have interesting implications for the elasticity of the demand for near-money – i.e. M2 – M1. The elasticities concerned are set out in Table 3.2.

Table 3.2 shows that, in all cases, the income elasticity is unity. The table also shows that the interest rate and inflation rate elasticity of the demand for near-money in absolute terms is greater than those of the demand for narrow money. This result probably reflects the fact that investment incentives play a relatively more important part in the holding of near-money than in people's behaviour with respect to holding of narrow money. The short-term interest rate elasticities of the demand of M1 and M2 suggest that there is a considerable amount of interest-rate-induced shifting between M1 and near-money assets. From earlier studies by e.g. Fase (1977, 1978b, 1979) as well as from a detailed data analysis, it has been found that this shifting takes place primarily between giro account balances on the one hand and foreign currency balances and time deposits on the other. To illustrate this point, Figure 3.3 shows the movement in the shares of giro account balances compared with foreign currency balances and time deposits in the total money stock for the 1970s and 1980s. There appears to be a strong negative correlation between the two series.[3]

In the 1970s in particular, there was a great deal of shifting between these two assets. Even in the 1980s there was still a significant amount of

---

[2] The equation without the restriction that the coefficients of $\ln(\mathrm{M}1/P)_{-1}$ and $\ln y$ are the opposite of each other – i.e. there is an income elasticity of unity – produces an income elasticity of 0.91. The short-term interest rate and inflation elasticity values are in that case – 0.10 and −0.07, respectively.

[3] For the period 1970–1988, the correlation is −0.88. For the years 1970 and 1980, we get values of −0.81 and −0.91, respectively.

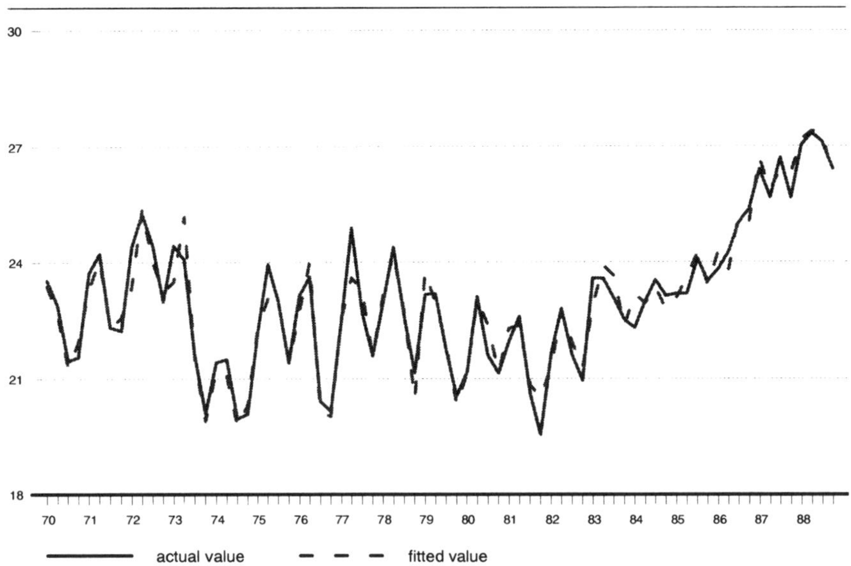


*Figure 3.2: Actual and fitted* M1*-ratio, 1970–1988 (in %)*

*Table 3.2: Long-term elasticities*

| Money definition | Income | Inflation | Short-term interest rate | Long-term interest rate |
|---|---|---|---|---|
| M1 | 1 | −0.07 | −0.13 | – |
| M2 | 1 | −0.12 | 0.09 | −0.11 |
| M2 − M1 | 1 | −0.21 | 0.50 | −0.31 |

*Notes:* By approximation one has, $d \ln \mathrm{M2} = \mathrm{M1}/\mathrm{M2}\, d \ln \mathrm{M1} + (\mathrm{M2} - \mathrm{M1})/\mathrm{M2}\, d \ln(\mathrm{M2} - \mathrm{M1})$. The reported elasticities for near-money have been calculated using the average shares of the narrow and near-money in the total money stock over the sample period, taking $\mathrm{M1}/\mathrm{M2} = 0.65$.

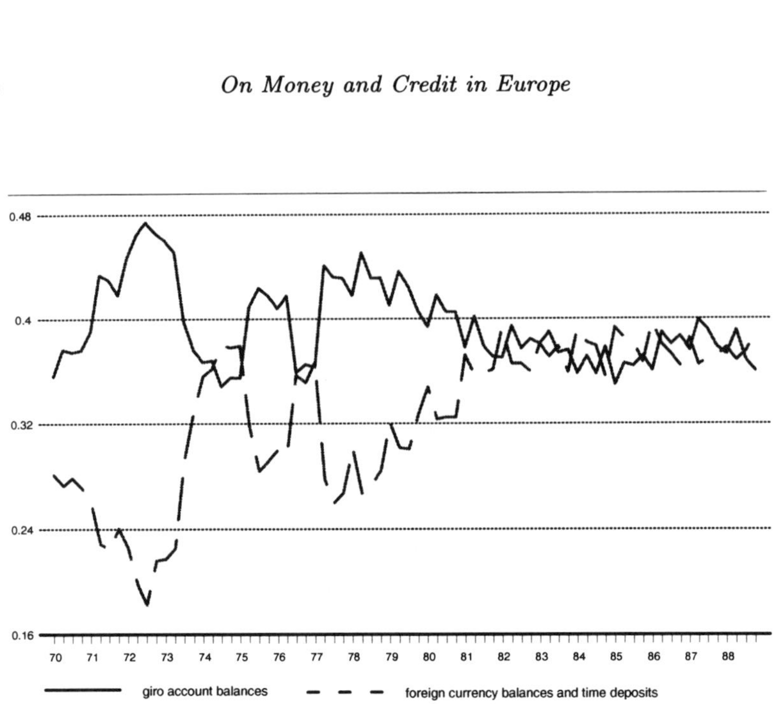


*Figure 3.3: Giro account balances and foreign currency balances and time deposits as a proportion of* M2

substitution, although on a smaller scale. This difference can be largely attributed to the smaller variation in interest rates during the 1980s as well as to the manner of data registration.

The estimation results imply that roughly half of the increase in near-money in response to an increase in short-term interest rates is due to shifting from M1 into near-money assets. The remaining half of the increase is the result of shifting between near-money and assets not included in the definitions of M2.[4] From Table 3.2, it can also be seen that the demand for near-money is more sensitive to inflation than demand for M1. This implies that the inflation elasticity of the share of narrow money in total money stock is positive, namely 0.05, being the difference between the inflation elasticities of M1 and M2. The share of

[4] An increase in the short-term interest rate initiates two substitution processes. On the one hand, narrow money is converted into near-money and, on the other hand, a shift takes place out of assets which are not part of the money stock into near-money. In the first of these substitution processes, the total money stock remains unchanged and, in the second, the narrow-money stock remains the same. By means of the formula $d\ln \mathrm{M2} = \mathrm{M1}/\mathrm{M2}\, d\ln \mathrm{M1} + (\mathrm{M2} - \mathrm{M1})/\mathrm{M2}\, d\ln(\mathrm{M2} - \mathrm{M1})$ the increase in the near-money stock can be calculated for each case, resulting in 0.26 and 0.24, respectively. For the purposes of the calculation, the average shares of the narrow and near-money supplies in the total money stock over the sample period were used.

the near-money assets therefore has a negative inflation elasticity.[5]

As with the demand for M2, the adjustment processes in response to shocks in the determinants have also been analysed for the demand for M1. Table 3.3 shows the effects of a change in the determinants for the first eight quarters. This table again shows that a change in income of 1% leads to an initial rise in M1 of over 0.2%. After one year, over 60% of the total adjustment of 1% has been achieved. A similar response occurs with an inflationary shock of one percentage point. For the short-term interest rate, over 80% of the total adjustment has been completed after four quarters. As expected, and in accordance with earlier work by Fase (1979), the impact on M1 of an increase in capacity utilization is weaker than that on the total money stock M2. As regards all the money demand determinants, convergence to the long-term effects takes place more quickly for M1 than for M2.

## 3.4 Results for the Sectoral Demand for Money

The sectors households and businesses together hold around 95% of the total money in circulation.[6] Over the period 1970–1988, this share varies between 93.5% and 96.8%, and is fairly constant. The remaining share is held by local authorities, insurance companies, pension funds and social insurance funds. In view of the fact that the bulk of the total money stock is held by households and businesses, behavioural equations which adequately describe the demand for money by these sectors also provide a satisfactory description of the total money stock. Moreover, a sectorally disaggregated analysis offers the opportunity of investigating the differences in behaviour of the two sectors. An insight into these differences could be useful for the interpretation of the actual development in the total money stock. A possible instability in the total demand for money in the broad sense could, for example, be traced to instability of the demand in one of these sectors. If the demand for money in each of the sectors, households and businesses, is stable, the total demand for money should be stable too. Approaching the problem from this angle, incidentally, presupposes an identical money

---

5 It is interesting to note that the MORKMON I portfolio model implies a greater sensitivity to inflation for M1. Using data for the period 1970:II–1982:IV, the inflation elasticity for that part of the total money stock which is held in the form of time deposits and foreign currency balances – these assets make up the bulk of near-money – equals 0.012 (see De Nederlandsche Bank (1985)).

6 The data used were taken from the data base compiled for MORKMON II. The data relating to the money-holdings of households and businesses were partly constructed.

demand specification for the two sectors. This has been achieved in the following discussion by taking steady state equation (3.1) as the basis for M 2 and steady state equation (3.5) as the basis for M 1. In practice this means that income for the two sectors is interpreted as a proxy for the level of spending by households and for the size of commercial transactions of the business sector, respectively. Quarterly figures on the money stock held by household and business sectors separately are available from 1970 onwards. For the sake of comparability, the demand equations for aggregate broad and narrow money have been re-estimated on the basis of data for the sample period 1970:I–1988:IV. Comparing the features of each of the three demand for money functions also permits the mutual consistency of the estimation results to be evaluated. The use of this different sample period for the aggregated money demand also provides the opportunity to compare the money demand functions estimated on the basis of data for the period 1959–1988 with estimations for the shorter sample period and to assess the stability of the estimated demand for money functions.

For the income variable in the equations for the total demand for narrow money and for the demand by households alone, it was decided to use net national product at market prices. In the specification for the demand by businesses, the gross added value of businesses at market prices was the scale variable used. The inflation variable and the deflator for the money stock correspond to the price of the scale variable. The lags describe the adjustment processes which occur in case of departures from the steady state path. In order to model the short-term dynamics, the cyclical variable, $q_k$, was also used.

### 3.4.1 The Demand for M 2

The ordinary least-squares estimation of the demand for money by households, $\mathrm{M}2_h/P$, is given by:

$$
\begin{aligned}
\Delta \ln\left(\frac{\mathrm{M}2_h}{P}\right) = \; & \underset{(3.83)}{0.4505}\,\Delta \ln(\mathrm{M}2_h/P)_{-1} \\
& - \underset{(2.45)}{0.0865}\,(\ln(\mathrm{M}2_h/P)_{-1} - \ln y) \; - \underset{(3.53)}{0.0071}\dot{p} \\
& + \underset{(4.08)}{0.0104}\dot{p}_{-1} \; - \underset{(2.40)}{0.0048}\dot{p}_{-2} \; - \underset{(3.28)}{0.0107}\,(r_l - r_k)
\end{aligned}
$$

*Table 3.3: Short-term response of* M1 *(in %) to shocks in the determinants*

| Quarter | Income | Inflation | Interest differential | Cyclical indicator |
|---|---|---|---|---|
| 1 | 0.21 | −0.29 | −1.12 | −0.12 |
| 2 | 0.38 | −0.52 | −1.81 | −0.09 |
| 3 | 0.51 | −0.70 | −1.93 | −0.07 |
| 4 | 0.61 | −0.84 | −2.02 | −0.06 |
| 5 | 0.76 | −1.05 | −2.44 | −0.08 |
| 6 | 0.86 | −1.19 | −2.64 | −0.06 |
| 7 | 0.93 | −1.28 | −2.62 | −0.04 |
| 8 | 0.97 | −1.35 | −2.60 | −0.03 |
| $\infty$ | 1 | −1.37 | −2.43 | 0 |

*Note:* See note in Table 3.1.

$$\begin{aligned} &- \underset{(3.61)}{0.0146}\,(r_l - r_k)_{-1} - \underset{(2.33)}{0.0064}\,(r_l - r_k)_{-2} \\ &- \underset{(1.62)}{0.1848}\Delta \ln q_{k_{-1}} + \underset{(0.05)}{0.0008} - \underset{(0.22)}{0.0025}s_1 \\ &+ \underset{(1.77)}{0.0288}s_2 - \underset{(5.80)}{0.1056}s_3 \end{aligned} \tag{3.6}$$

where the $t$-values, adjusted for any heteroscedasticity, are given in parentheses, $\bar{R}^2 = 0.80$, and the standard error of the residuals $SE = 0.0239$.

The lag structure used in the above equation is somewhat more extensive than that in the equation for the total money demand. The error-correction term $\ln(\mathrm{M}2_h/P)_{-1} - \ln y$ has a greater effect on the growth in the money stock than in (3.2) and is significantly different from 0. We note that the form of the error-correction term used here is the same as in equation (3.4) which was shown to be equivalent to the basic model in equation (3.1′). Since the likelihood ratio test on the restriction imposed by the error-correction mechanism is insignificant we have maintained the hypothesis. With $\chi^2(3) = 4.93$, the hypothesis of modelling of the interest rate structure as the differential between long- and short-term interest rates cannot be rejected.

As far as the sector businesses is concerned, the ordinary least-squares estimation of the demand for money yields:

$$\begin{aligned}\Delta \ln\left(\frac{\mathrm{M}2_b}{P}\right) = \;& \underset{(3.73)}{0.3933\,\Delta \ln(\mathrm{M}2_b/P)_{-4}} \\ & - \underset{(0.22)}{0.0108}\,(\ln(\mathrm{M}2_b/P)_{-1} - \ln y_{-1}) + \underset{(2.46)}{0.3295\,\Delta \ln y} \\ & - \underset{(2.48)}{0.0048\dot{p}} + \underset{(2.20)}{0.0040\dot{p}_{-1}} - \underset{(1.67)}{0.0056\,(r_l - r_k)} \\ & + \underset{(1.67)}{0.0050\,(r_l - r_k)_{-1}} - \underset{(0.81)}{0.1102\,\Delta \ln q_{k-1}} \\ & - \underset{(1.21)}{0.0139} + \underset{(4.98)}{0.0846 s_1} + \underset{(0.58)}{0.0063 s_2} - \underset{(0.28)}{0.0031 s_3} \qquad (3.7)\end{aligned}$$

where the $t$-values, adjusted for any heteroscedasticity, are given in parentheses, $\bar{R}^2 = 0.67$, and the standard error of the residuals $SE = 0.0304$.

The lag structure of equation (3.7) shows strong similarities to that of equation (3.8) for the total money stock to be presented below. The coefficient of the error-correction term $\ln(\mathrm{M}2_b/P)_{-1} - \ln y_{-1}$ is not significant. However, in view of the likelihood ratio tests the inherent restriction as well as the restrictions implicit in modelling the interest rate structure as a differential between long- and short-term interest rates cannot be rejected. More important, perhaps, is the fact that the movement in the liquidity ratio for 1988 implied by (3.7) shows a discrepancy compared with the actual movement. Strikingly enough, a similar picture emerges for the total demand for money. This suggests that the very strong growth in the money stock in 1988 cannot be properly interpreted within the framework of the traditional money demand function. The obvious conclusion, therefore, is that the behaviour of sector businesses seems to be responsible for this since a similar discrepancy is not apparent in the demand for money by households.

To provide a benchmark for the disaggregated demand for money estimations, the aggregate demand for M2 was finally re-estimated for the same sample period as the two sectoral money demand functions. The estimation result is as follows:

$$\begin{aligned}\Delta \ln\left(\frac{\mathrm{M}2}{P}\right) = \;& \underset{(2.89)}{0.3492\,\Delta \ln(\mathrm{M}2/P)_{-4}} - \underset{(0.64)}{0.0271}\,(\ln(\mathrm{M}2/P)_{-1} - \ln y) \\ & - \underset{(4.33)}{0.0076\dot{p}} + \underset{(4.33)}{0.0067\dot{p}_{-1}} - \underset{(2.99)}{0.0095\,(r_l - r_k)}\end{aligned}$$

$$
\begin{aligned}
&+ \underset{(2.99)}{0.0083}\,(r_l - r_k)_{-1} - \underset{(1.86)}{0.1605}\,\Delta \ln q_{k-1} + \underset{(0.45)}{0.0097} \\
&+ \underset{(4.57)}{0.0456}\,s_1 + \underset{(2.77)}{0.0282}\,s_2 - \underset{(1.94)}{0.0200}\,s_3 \qquad (3.8)
\end{aligned}
$$

where the $t$-values, adjusted for any heteroscedasticity, are given in parentheses, $\bar{R}^2 = 0.74$, and the standard error of the residuals $SE = 0.0226$.

The most remarkable difference compared with the demand for money (3.2) for the whole sample period 1959–1988 concerns the error-correction term, which seems to be different but is also much weaker and less significant than in (3.2) for the whole sample period. The difference is only illusory apparent as is easily shown. More important, perhaps, is the fact that the dynamic structure hardly changes with the shorter sample period. The estimations of the parameters and the elasticities implicit in them also reveal a consistent picture. Both features suggest a certain stability as regards the total demand for money.

### 3.4.2 A First Appraisal of the Results for M2

To begin with, Table 3.4 summarizes the estimated long-term parameters for the sample period 1970–1988, as well as those obtained for the sample period 1959–1988, for each of the demand for money equations considered. As indicated before, this long-term relationship reads as:

$$\mathrm{M}/P = Ay^{\alpha_1} \exp\left(\alpha_2 \dot{p} + \alpha_3 r_k + \alpha_4 r_l\right)$$

The economic meaning of the estimations reported in Table 3.4 for 1970–1988 is straightforward and need not be repeated here. More important is that the estimates very often hardly differ statistically from 0. However, we should not ignore that the relevant $t$-values are approximations and therefore less convincing. A more convenient approach to evaluate the results is provided by considering the impact elasticities shown in Table 3.5.

In Table 3.5 the income elasticities are unity for all the estimated functions. The interest rate and inflation rate elasticities for the period 1970–1988 are greater (in absolute terms) than those for the money demand function estimated for the period 1959–1988.[7] This suggests

[7] The interest rate elasticities in the equation for the total money demand for the sample period 1970–1988 show a close correlation with the estimates in MORKMON I. Here the demand for money is modelled simultaneously with the demand for other financial assets according to the portfolio approach, producing long- and short-term interest rate elasticities of −0.29 and 0.30, respectively.

that the interest rate and inflation rate elasticity of the demand for money has increased with the passage of time. This change could be a result of the increased scope for more active cash management, but also of the increased interest and inflation rates in the recent period, which lowers the adjustement costs relative to the feasible gains. Unlike the period 1959–1988, the sample period 1970–1988 shows a much greater interest rate elasticity of the demand for money than the elasticity to inflation and therefore shows the opposite of the results obtained for the whole period.

The estimates for the total demand for money over the two periods differ considerably from each other at first sight. Statistically, however, they lie within each other's 95% confidence intervals. Perhaps more interesting is the result in Table 3.5 showing that the demand for money by businesses shows a much higher elasticity to interest rates and inflation than for households. As already mentioned, this may reflect the greater scope which businesses have for conducting active and systematic cash management. The estimations of the interest rate parameters in the long-term specification for households and businesses, however, lie within each other's 95% confidence intervals. An equal interest rate elasticity would therefore be statistically defensible. The estimation of the inflation rate elasticity of the demand for money by businesses, however, does not lie within the 95% confidence interval of the corresponding estimator in the specification for households. This suggests that the two sectors behave differently when it comes to inflation.

The households and businesses sectors together hold 95% of the total money in circulation. The elasticities of the total demand for money must therefore approximately be equal to a weighted average of the corresponding elasticities of the demand for money by households and businesses. The weightings are the shares of the money-holding of the two sectors. Weighting the estimated elasticities of the demand for money given in Table 3.5 for households and businesses by the respective average values of the share of money held during the sample period yields the elasticities shown in the bottom line. Comparing these values leads to the conclusion that the three demand for M2 functions produce a consistent picture in terms of long-run elasticities.

### 3.4.3 The Demand for M1

The ordinary least-squares estimation for the real demand for narrow money by households, $M1_h/P$, over the sample period 1970:I–1988:IV is

*Table 3.4: Parameter estimates in the long-term steady state function*

| Money definition | $\alpha_1$ | $\hat{\alpha}_2$ | $\hat{\alpha}_3 = -\hat{\alpha}_4$ |
|---|---|---|---|
| M2 | 1 | −0.0340 | 0.0425 |
| | | (1.19) | (0.45) |
| $M2_h$ | 1 | −0.0172 | 0.0288 |
| | | (1.48) | (1.13) |
| $M2_b$ | 1 | −0.0789 | 0.0577 |
| | | (0.35) | (0.15) |
| M2(1959–1988) | 1 | −0.0247 | 0.0152 |
| | | (2.47) | (0.65) |

*Note:* $t$-values in parentheses.

*Table 3.5: Long-term elasticities in the demand for* M2

| Money definition | Income | Inflation | Short-term interest rate | Long-term interest rate |
|---|---|---|---|---|
| M2 | 1 | −0.17 | 0.29 | −0.35 |
| $M2_h$ | 1 | −0.09 | 0.20 | −0.24 |
| $M2_b$ | 1 | −0.39 | 0.40 | −0.47 |
| M2 (1959–1988) | 1 | −0.12 | 0.09 | −0.11 |
| Average of $M2_h$ and $M2_b$ | 0.95 | −0.24 | 0.29 | −0.34 |

as follows:

$$\begin{aligned}
\Delta \ln\left(\frac{\mathrm{M1}_h}{P}\right) = & -\underset{(1.07)}{0.0355}\,(\ln(\mathrm{M1}_h/P)_{-1} - \ln y) - \underset{(2.81)}{0.0021} r_k \\
& + \underset{(1.86)}{0.0022}\Delta r_k - \underset{(3.98)}{0.0056}\Delta r_{k-1} - \underset{(0.50)}{0.0005}\dot{p} \\
& - \underset{(1.87)}{0.0033}\Delta\dot{p} - \underset{(1.92)}{0.1634}\Delta \ln q_{k-1} - \underset{(0.09)}{0.0018} \\
& + \underset{(1.60)}{0.0106} s_1 + \underset{(9.98)}{0.0759} s_2 - \underset{(8.41)}{0.0624} s_3 \qquad (3.9)
\end{aligned}$$

where the $t$-values, adjusted for any heteroscedasticity, are given in parentheses, $\bar{R}^2 = 0.94$, and the standard error of the residuals $SE = 0.0152$.

The empirically determined lag structure in (3.9) differs considerably from that found in the corresponding equation for M2 in which, unlike equation (3.9), the long-term interest rate also appears. The surprising thing is also the very weak influence of the error-correction mechanism, for which the formulation used in (3.4) proved to be most satisfactory. Another novel element is the occurrence of changes of inflation rate. The latter and the particular formulation of the error-correction term also occur with the demand for narrow money by businesses, which for the sample period 1970:I–1988:IV results in:

$$\begin{aligned}
\Delta \ln\left(\frac{\mathrm{M1}_b}{P}\right) = & -\underset{(3.48)}{0.3986}\Delta \ln(\mathrm{M1}_b/P)_{-1} \\
& - \underset{(1.01)}{0.0471}\,(\ln(\mathrm{M1}_b/P)_{-1} - \ln y) \\
& - \underset{(1.43)}{0.0040} r_k - \underset{(5.33)}{0.0180}\Delta r_k \\
& - \underset{(1.58)}{0.0079}\Delta r_{k-1} - \underset{(2.60)}{0.0031}\dot{p} - \underset{(1.77)}{0.0048}\Delta\dot{p} \\
& - \underset{(0.54)}{0.0939}\Delta \ln q_{k-1} - \underset{(0.08)}{0.0028} - \underset{(0.00)}{0.00004}\, s_1 \\
& + \underset{(2.19)}{0.0304}\, s_2 - \underset{(1.28)}{0.0177}\, s_3 \qquad (3.10)
\end{aligned}$$

where the $t$-values, adjusted for any heteroscedasticity are given in parentheses, $\bar{R}^2 = 0.69$, and the standard error of the residuals $SE = 0.0348$. Here, too, the specification found differs considerably from that which is established for the demand for M2 on the part of businesses. The surprising thing in this case is that, unlike the equation for households, the influence of the error-correction term is substantially greater than in the equation for M2.

Finally, the total demand for narrow money, M1/P, was estimated for the period 1970–1988 in order to provide an initial benchmark. The result is:

$$
\begin{aligned}
\Delta \ln\left(\frac{\mathrm{M1}}{P}\right) = & \underset{(3.38)}{-0.3022\Delta \ln(\mathrm{M1}/P)_{-1}} \\
& - \underset{(1.00)}{0.0559}\,(\ln(\mathrm{M1}/P)_{-1} - \ln y_{-1}) + \underset{(4.62)}{0.2953\Delta \ln y} \\
& - \underset{(2.44)}{0.0035 r_k} - \underset{(5.00)}{0.0087\Delta r_k} - \underset{(2.30)}{0.0040\Delta r_{k-1}} \\
& - \underset{(2.10)}{0.0017\dot{p}} - \underset{(2.37)}{0.0032\Delta\dot{p}} \\
& - \underset{(1.35)}{0.1201\Delta \ln q_{k-1}} + \underset{(0.80)}{0.0076} + \underset{(3.99)}{0.0399 s_1} + \underset{(8.24)}{0.0709 s_2} \\
& - \underset{(0.10)}{0.0012 s_3}
\end{aligned}
\qquad (3.11)
$$

where the $t$-values, adjusted for any heteroscedasticity, are given in parentheses, $\bar{R}^2 = 0.91$, and the standard error of the residuals $SE =$ 0.0170.

### 3.4.4 A First Appraisal of the Demand for M1

The above equations by sectoral and aggregate M1 demand have been subjected to an extensive specification analysis (see (Fase and Winder 1989)). This leads to the conclusion that the relationships revealed are statistically satisfactory. In order to assess the economic plausibility of the estimation results, the parameters of the long-term steady state function are calculated and set out in Table 3.6.

Table 3.6 shows that the signs of the calculated parameters are as predicted, but very often not significant. This is a surprising difference compared with the estimations obtained for the aggregate demand for M1 over the period 1959–1988. As stated before the steady state relationship is

$$\mathrm{M1}/P = Ay^{\alpha_1} \exp(\alpha_2 \dot{p} + \alpha_3 r_k).$$

As in the case of M2, the results for the sectors can be used to evaluate their consistency. It should be borne in mind that narrow money is virtually entirely in the hands of households and businesses. The elasticities, which provide the easiest way of making such an evaluation, are shown in Table 3.7.

The first conclusion from Table 3.7 is that the averages of the elasticities for the two sectors match those for the aggregate very closely. The fact that the weighted income elasticity amounts to 0.97 merely reflects the fact that 97% of the M1 stock is in the hands of the household and business sectors. As far as the inflation rate and interest rate elasticitiy of the demand for M1 is concerned, Table 3.7 shows that businesses are more sensitive to inflation and interest rates than households. If we compare the elasticities obtained for the period 1959–1988 with those for 1970–1988, then the difference – apart from income elasticity – is remarkable. This suggests a lack of stability in the demand for M1.

## 3.5 The Assessment of our Estimation Results

To make an assessment of anything, you need to decide what angle you are going to view it from. The present assessment looks at the demand for money from two angles. The first is from an economic viewpoint and mainly concerns the interpretation of the results. The second is an econometric viewpoint and mainly concerns a number of statistical aspects obtained by application of the technique.

*Table 3.6: Parameter estimates in the long-term steady state function*

| Money definition | $\alpha_1$ | $\hat{\alpha}_2$ | $\hat{\alpha}_3$ |
|---|---|---|---|
| M1 | 1 | −0.0309<br>(1.51) | −0.0617<br>(1.39) |
| $M1_h$ | 1 | −0.0134<br>(0.74) | −0.0602<br>(1.02) |
| $M1_b$ | 1 | −0.0856<br>(1.71) | −0.0652<br>(0.98) |
| M1(1959–1988) | 1 | −0.0137<br>(3.98) | −0.0243<br>(6.21) |

*Note:* $t$-values in parentheses.

*Table 3.7: Long-term elasticities in the demand for* M2

| Money definition | Income | Inflation | Short-term interest rate |
|---|---|---|---|
| M1 | 1 | −0.16 | −0.42 |
| $M1_h$ | 1 | −0.07 | −0.41 |
| $M1_b$ | 1 | −0.33 | −0.59 |
| M1 (1959–1988) | 1 | −0.07 | −0.13 |
| Average of $M1_h$ and $M1_b$ | 0.97 | −0.16 | −0.46 |

### 3.5.1 The Economic Viewpoint

The first question which arises with respect to the estimation results is how they compare with those obtained in other money demand studies for The Netherlands. Table 3.8 shows that the income elasticities of unity found in our study – i.e. established on the basis of a specification analysis – correspond reasonably well with those derived from other studies for The Netherlands conducted since 1974; only the income elasticity found in the study by Butter and Fase and in the study by Kuipers and Boertje are obviously different. Presumably this is partly due to the use of a different income concept. The elasticity for long-term interest rates in our study varies strongly with the sample periods employed, but, for the sample period 1970:I–1988:IV, it is reasonably close to the value found in most of the other studies; only in the case of Kuipers and Boertje is the absolute value substantially lower. In the case of Blommestein and Palm, the interest rate elasticity has the wrong sign. The short-term interest rate elasticity in our study agrees reasonably well with that found in the other studies. The picture as regards the inflation rate elasticity, on the other hand, is rather confusing, but this is largely due to the specification of the demand for money equation employed by the various authors. Not included in Table 3.8 is the cyclical indicator as explanatory variable. This is because, in the set-up used for the present study, the effect of the business cycle is taken to be temporary in each case and therefore does not occur in the steady state function to which this evaluation relates. The error-correction formulation distinguishes our research from most of the other money demand studies for The Netherlands known to us: the only exception is the research of Cesar, Haan, and Jacobs. Therefore it has not been reported in Table 3.8.

Apart from the study by Kuipers and Boertje, our study is the only

*Table 3.8: Long-term elasticities in previous studies for The Netherlands*

| Study | Sample period | Money definition | Income | Short-term interest rate | Long-term interest rate | Inflation |
|---|---|---|---|---|---|---|
| Fase and Kuné (1974a) | 1952:I–1971:IV | M2 | 0.85 | – | −0.20 | 1.05[a] |
| Butter and Fase (1981) | 1960:I–1976:IV | M2 | 1.19 | 0.12 | −0.30 | −1.49 |
| Blommestein and Palm (1982) | 1952:I–1971:IV | M2 | 1.00 | – | 0.37 | $-0.95\dot{p}$ |
| Palm (1983) | 1952:I–1979:II | M2 | 1.00 | – | – | $-1.31\dot{p}$ |
| Knoop and Hooijmans (1985) | 1970:I–1984:IV | M2 | 0.97 | 0.05 to −0.07[b] | – | – |
| Taylor (1986) | 1960:I–1978:IV | M2 | 1.00 | 0.02 | −0.23 | $-3.65\dot{p}$ |
| Huijser (1987) | 1959:I–1983:IV | M2 | 0.95 | 0.14 | −0.14 | −0.76 |
| Kuipers and Boertje (1988) | 1964:I–1984:IV | M2 | 0.75 | – | −0.04 | 1.16[a] |
| Cesar, Haan, and Jacobs (1990) | 1971:III–1984:IV | M1 | 0.92 | −0.07 | −0.15 | – |
| The present study | 1959:I–1988:IV | M2 | 1.00 | 0.09 | −0.11 | −0.12 |
| | 1970:I–1988:IV | M2 | 1.00 | 0.29 | −0.35 | −0.17 |
| | 1959:I–1988:IV | M1 | 1.00 | −0.13 | – | −0.07 |
| | 1959:I–1988:IV | M1 | 1.00 | −0.07 | −0.15 | −0.05 |
| | 1970:I–1988:IV | M1 | 1.00 | −0.42 | – | −0.16 |

*Notes:*
[a] Refers to price elasticity.
[b] Interest rate structure modelled by means of an approximation of the interest rates by a quadratic function based on the terms to maturity.

*Table 3.9: Long-term elasticity of the demand for money by households and businesses*

| Study | Sector | Sample period | Income | Short-term interest rate | Long-term interest rate | Inflation | Share of employment income |
|---|---|---|---|---|---|---|---|
| Kuipers and | households I | 1964:I–1984:IV | 0.60 | – | −0.18 | 1.00[a] | – |
| Boertje (1988) | households II | 1964:I–1984:IV | 0.69 | – | −0.18 | 1.13[a] | – |
| Present | M2 households | 1970:I–1988:IV | 1.00 | 0.20 | −0.24 | −0.09 | – |
| study | M1 households | 1970:I–1988:IV | 1.00 | −0.41 | – | −0.07 | – |
| Kuipers and | business I | 1966:I–1984:IV | 1.32 | – | – | 1.12[a] | −1.11 |
| Boertje (1988) | business II | 1966:I–1984:IV | 0.99 | – | – | 1.11[a] | −1.12 |
| Present | M2 business | 1970:I–1988:IV | 1.00 | 0.40 | −0.47 | −0.39 | – |
| study | M1 business | 1970:I–1988:IV | 1.00 | −0.59 | – | −0.33 | – |

*Notes:*
Kuipers and Boertje construct their own data for the money-holdings by households and businesses. They do this in two ways, indicated here by I and II.
[a] Refers to price elasticity.

one in The Netherlands to make estimates of the demand for money on the part of the separate sectors of households and businesses. Table 3.9 presents the results of these two studies together for the sake of comparison. A quick glance at Table 3.9 reveals that the studies are scarcely comparable; the only thing which they have in common is the disaggregation into the household sector on the one hand and the business sector on the other. Kuipers and Boertje consider only M2, which justifies their taking long-term interest rates as the determinant in the case of households. For the demand for money by businesses, they do not use an interest rate variable at all, but introduce the share of labour income in total income instead. As they show, this variable is related to profits. In our analysis of M2, we take into account both short- and long-term interest rates, as well as the inflation rate. The difference compared with the respective results obtained by Kuipers and Boertje is largely due to the fact that, in our study, we are working with deflated amounts of money, which presupposes a price elasticity of unity. When this is borne in mind, the differences between the study of Kuipers and Boertje and ours in this regard are small. For the M1 demand by sector, we only use the short-term interest rate as determinant, an approach which is also found, for example, in the often quoted studies by Goldfeld (1973, 1976). For the aggregate demand for M1, however, we have of course also investigated the influence of long-term interest rates. It is interesting to note that the short-term interest rate elasticity of around −0.60 found by us for the demand for money by businesses corresponds nicely to the elasticity implied in the inventory transaction cash approach of Baumol (1952) or Tobin (1956).

If we compare our results with those obtained, for example, in the United Kingdom – not reported here – a close correspondence of the income elasticity for households relative to M2 is immediately apparent, although the interest rate sensitivity in the UK study is generally much lower. As far as the business sector is concerned, there is a certain amount of correpondence between interest rate and income elasticities, but the estimations obtained for the United Kingdom do not seem to be very robust (see Price (1972), Hacche (1974)).

A totally different aspect concerns the predictive power of our equations. If we restrict ourselves to the prediction of the aggregate demand for M1 and M2 we see that the demand for M1 in particular is highly sensitive to the assumption made with respect to interest rates, while the adjustment to the steady state takes place much more quickly for M1 than for M2. It is found that, for 1989, the equation for M1, which takes into account only the short-term interest rate, describes the actual development much more satisfactorily than that which also includes long-term interest rates. It is for this reason that we preferred the specification which includes only the short-term interest rate. The predictive power of the equation for M2 is also satisfactory up to 1988, but beyond this date it no longer is. In order to shed more light on this unsatisfactory aspect, we have experimented with a somewhat amended demand function in which a wealth variable $W$ is added as an additional explanatory variable.

The analysis including wealth as an additional explanatory variable is not reported here because of its preliminary character. However, it casts a new light on the development of the liquidity ratio during the 1980s. The preliminary findings suggest that the substantial increase of the liquidity ratio in the 1980s is largely due to the sharp increase in financial wealth in the private sector, whereas the development in incomes should in itself have actually led to a slight relative decline. To mention a small detail, we note that an increase in income of 1% implies an initial rise of 0.16% in M2, leading to an ultimate increase of 0.96% in a steady state process. After one year, over 70% of the total adjustment has already occurred. An increase of 1% in wealth produces an immediate increase in M2 in virtually 1%. After this immediate proportional increase, a rearrangement of the portfolio takes place involving all kinds of substitution processes, and this ultimately results in an increase in M2 of 0.36%. This adjustment takes place relatively quickly. After one year, 85% of the total adjustement has occurred (see (Fase and Winder 1989) for details).

### 3.5.2 The Econometric Viewpoint

The present analysis is distinguished from earlier demand for money analyses in that a considerable amount of attention was devoted to the modelling of the dynamics and to a specification analysis. As to the dynamics, an explicit distinction was made between the long-run steady state functions and the incorporation of deviations from the equilibrium path in the short-run. The cyclical indicator as a determinant – a prominent aspect of earlier demand for money studies in The Netherlands – appears in the present set-up only in this short-term context, as does the error-correction mechanism governing the return to equilibrium. Error-correction specifications are closely related to the concepts of integration and cointegration recently introduced into the econometric literature. An evaluation on the basis of cointegration techniques, another feature of this study, reveals that the demand for money functions for the businesses sector can be interpreted as long-term functions. The other demand for money functions, however, come out of the cointegration test in a less convincing manner. The detailed results of the various cointegration and specification tests, together with a concise description of the methodology employed, are reported in Fase and Winder (1989). The equations presented in the above have withstood the scrutiny of the specification analysis including, among other things, tests on residual correlation and a test on predictive failure, so that, from an econometric point of view, the estimation results appear to be fairly robust.

## 3.6 CONCLUSIONS

The present study analyses the aggregate demand for both M1 and M2, as well as the money demand by single sectors, for the sample period 1970:I–1988:IV. Apart from this disaggregation to sector, the present study distinguishes itself from earlier studies by a detailed analysis of the dynamics and by the explicit modelling of deviations of the long-run relationships of the demand for money by means of the error-correction mechanism. As a consequence, there is a clear distinction between the long-run steady state demand and the actual demand for money, in which departures from the equilibrium occur. In our set-up, these discrepancies depend partly on the stage reached in the business cycle and the size of disequilibria.

The principal findings are an income elasticity of the money demand which is equal to unity, regardless of whether we consider narrow or broad money. The elasticities for long- and short-term interest rates in the case of M2 for the period 1970:I–1988:IV are −0.35 and 0.29, respectively. In the case of M1, it is particularly the short-term interest rate which is important. This elasticity varies from around −0.10 for 1959–1988 to −0.40 for 1970–1988. Finally, for both M1 and M2, there is an inflation elasticity, which fluctuates around −0.15. The reported estimates are consistent with the results obtained for the demand for narrow money and the total demand for money by the two sectors considered. Here, too, an income elasticity of unity was found for both households and businesses. It was also found that the interest elasticity in the case of households is roughly half the value found for businesses, regardless of the money definition concerned. For instance, the long-term interest rate elasticity of M2 for households is −0.24 and, for businesses, −0.47. For M1, we get short-term interest rate elasticities of −0.41 and −0.59, respectively. Another surprising finding was that for households the inflation elasticity for both M1 and M2 is around −0.10 and considerably lower than for the business sector, where an inflation elasticity of around −0.35 was found.

The predictive power, and hence the stability of the functions arrived at, appears to be satisfactory, although there is a systematic underestimation in the predictions of M2 for 1988. An explanation appears to be offered by the growth in the financial wealth of the private sector. Our preliminary result for the wealth elasticity is around 0.35, with an income elasticity of 0.96 and an interest rate elasticity which corresponds nicely with that estimated for M2. Therefore the conclusion is that further research should investigate the role of wealth in money demand in particular.

# 4. The Demand for Money in The Netherlands and the Other EU Countries

## 4.1 Introduction

The demand for money is not just the classical issue in monetary econometrics, it also occupies a prominent place in monetary policy analysis. The first is supported by the number of empirical studies on the demand for money, while the second can be seen from, for example, De Nederlandsche Bank's latest Annual Report, for 1991. An interesting question is why the demand for money – by contrast with other monetary phenomena – has always been given so much attention in econometrics. A possible answer is besides the availability of reliable data necessary for estimation purposes, the existence of a reasonably sophisticated theory of the demand for money. This presumption is supported by the history of thought about the demand for money. This history begins with Fisher's quantity theory, which assumes that the magnitude of current transactions determines the demand for money. The ensuing Cambridge variant put forward by, among others, Marshall, Pigou and Robertson refined the theory by paying attention to money as a component of wealth. As a result, it was – at least implicitly – assumed that the famous cash ratio, $k$, central in this cash balance theory, could be dependent on interest rates. A major step forward in the development of ideas about the demand for money, however, was Keynes' analysis of cash-holding behaviour with his three famous motives for holding money balances, resulting in income, bonds rate, and wealth as explanatory variables. The fact that short-term interest rates were not included among the explanatory variables was a purely practical matter as, in Keynes' days, they were to be assumed more or less constant. Friedman, who reformulated Fisher's quantity theory, saw the demand for money

Reprinted from *De Economist*, **141**(4) (1993), M.M.G. Fase and C.C.A. Winder, 'The demand for money in The Netherlands and the other EU countries', 471–496, ©1993 with kind permission from Kluwer Academic Publishers.

notably as a special case of the demand for goods and services. In his approach, the demand for money is in fact one equation plucked from a system of demand equations. Friedman's approach is therefore well in line with the portfolio approach introduced by Tobin. The latter makes explicit allowance for the restrictions ensuing from the fact that total wealth is held in the form of some financial or real asset. In this view, money is the most liquid financial asset in the spectrum of wealth components.

Although the above views can be classified as mainly macroeconomic, a number of more microeconomically based theories on the demand for money were also formulated. These could be distinguished from the macroeconomic ones in that they suggested a specification for the demand for money which contained specific numerical values for the interest rate and income or turnover elasticities. The theories in question were formulated by Baumol and Tobin, and concerned the business sector in particular. They were subsequently supplemented with uncertainty by Whalen, and Miller and Orr, and found their way into the theory of finance.

The main purpose of the present study is to examine the demand for money in the EU disaggregated by country. Thus, this chapter goes into the macroeconomic demand for money in The Netherlands and the other member states of the EU. It builds forth on a study made by Fase and Winder (1990) for The Netherlands. That study focused on the theoretical specification and the statistical model formulation which does justice to typically economic phenomena as disequilibria and frictions as well as on the empirical estimation and economic interpretation. Since the pioneering work of Hendry (1979) and Hendry and Ericsson (1991b), on which we build forth too, more attention is paid to the distinction between the short- and the long-run demand for money. In the traditional demand for money studies, this was modelled notably via the partial adjustment mechanism. Since the well-known criticism by Hendry and Mizon (1978) of the Bank of England's demand for money analysis, the statistical verification of the model assumptions has also come to the fore to a greater extent.

As a result of the progressing European integration, the demand for money in the EU has become the focus of growing attention. The future European central bank, for instance, will need to have insight into the properties of the demand for money in the EU. The present study attempts to contribute to the discussion by looking at the demand for money in the EU. To investigate the differences and similarities between the countries, a common economic framework and methodology is adopted. Also, the definitions of monetary aggregates and the determinants of the demand for money used are as uniform as possible, and the sample period considered is the same for all countries. The study differs from other work in two major respects. In the first place, not just one monetary aggregate is analysed, but three – M1, M2 and M3 – yielding a more complete picture of monetary developments. Additional reasons to consider several monetary aggregates are that the EU member states differ as to what they regard as the central monetary aggregate, and that there has been a shift in monetary analysis in many countries in the course of the 1980s – in reaction to the more irregular developments of the monetary aggregates – as a result of which they have begun to monitor the development of several aggregates. Second, this study looks at developments per country, not at EU aggregates as such. In our opinion, this disaggregated approach allows a much more comprehensive interpretation of the development of the demand for money in the EU than the more commonly used aggregate method.

The present study is organized as follows. On the basis of a graphic analysis, Section 4.2 takes a brief look at the developments of the various monetary aggregates in the 11 EU countries considered. Section 4.3 deals with the general dynamic specification of the demand for money which forms the theoretical foundation for the empirical analysis contained in this chapter. Section 4.4 presents a survey of our estimation results for each of the countries and the monetary aggregates looked into. Section 4.5 contains an assessment of the results obtained, and compares them to similar studies made by others. Finally, Section 4.6 summarizes the main conclusions and policy implications. Details on data and estimation results are given in Fase and Winder (1992), particularly in Appendices I to III.

## 4.2 Development of Money Stock in Member States

In terms of the money supply, the member states of the EU have their own characteristics, which, when reviewed closely suggest great dissimilarities. This can be seen from the charts contained in Figure 4.1, which show, for each of the monetary aggregates, the development of the relevant money stock, expressed as a percentage of GNP, for the period 1971–1989. For reasons of presentation, two groups of countries have been distinguished: the northern member states and the southern ones. The first – group A – is made up of Belgium, Denmark, Germany, Ireland, The Netherlands and the United Kingdom, while the second – group B – comprises France, Greece, Italy, Portugal and Spain. Graphic inspection shows, first of all, that irrespective of the monetary aggregate considered, the countries show considerable differences. Second, the broader the monetary aggregate, the greater the differences. In the third place, during the past decade the ratios concerned seem to have shown a substantial rise in virtually all the northern countries, while the southern countries, with the exception of Greece, offer a comparatively stable picture. Perhaps this different pattern may be explained by restrictions on capital mobility in the southern countries and differences in financial sophistication. Fourth, the ratios in the northern EU countries seem to be lower than those in the southern member states. That holds notably for M1 in the 1970s.

Of the northern EU countries, it is the United Kingdom, Denmark and The Netherlands for which the greatest monetary expansion in the 1980s is recorded. In the United Kingdom in particular the ratios increased substantially. Over the past decade, the M1, M2 and M3 ratios rose from 13%, 29% and 48% at the end of 1980 to 22%, 54% and 81%, respectively, in 1989. That constitutes an average increase of no less than 75%. The M1 ratio has been on the rise notably since 1984, while the ratios for the broad monetary aggregates started to increase in 1981. Figure 4.1 shows that in The Netherlands, too, the increase in the M1 ratio lagged behind that in the other ratios. The M2 and M3 ratios for The Netherlands went up by 44% and 32%, respectively, in the 1980s. At 23%, the increase in the M1 ratio is more modest, but it must be noted that it took place mainly after 1984. In Denmark, the ratios of all monetary aggregates reviewed here began to rise considerably after 1983, whereas they had been almost constant before then. Since 1983, the ratios have increased by, on average, 55%. Monetary developments in Germany have been much more moderate, albeit that a steady monetary expansion occurred there too. Since the early 1970s, the German ratios have risen by about 30%. Belgium and Ireland are characterized by a falling M1 ratio. Ireland's M1 ratio was even nearly halved on the level recorded in the early 1970s. These countries' M2 ratios are, however, relatively stable, albeit that in Belgium a substantial rise is recorded around 1981. During the whole sample period, the M3 ratio is showing an upward tendency.

Of the southern EU countries, it is Italy and Portugal which have the highest ratios. The average ratios for France roughly correspond with those for the northern EU countries. The development of the French ratios is fairly stable, the M1 ratio showing a slight downward tendency, while the M2 ratio has been on the increase in recent years. Italy's M2 and M3 ratios have also been rising over the past few years. Italy's M1 ratio fell sharply in the 1970s, stabilizing at around 35 percentage

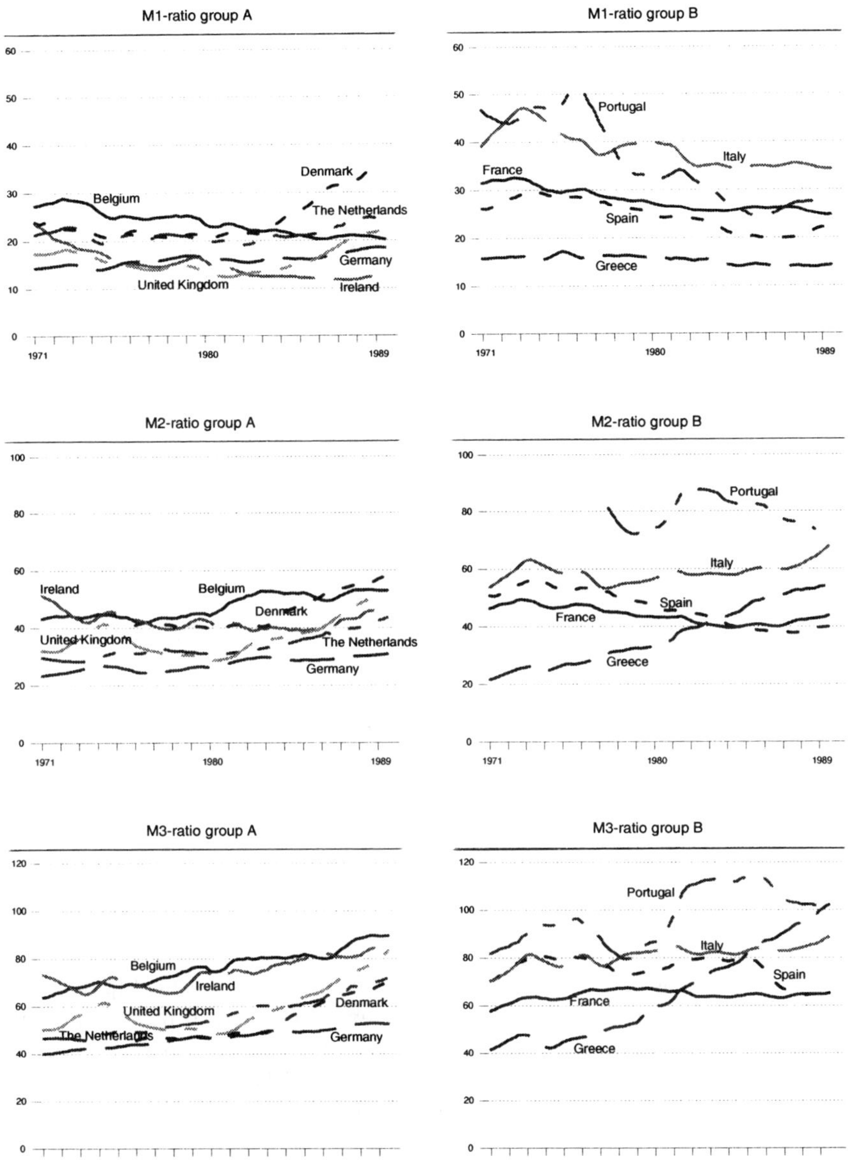


*Figure 4.1: Developments in monetary ratios in The Netherlands and other EU countries*

points since 1981. Spain's M1 and M2 ratios are declining slowly. The development of the M3 ratio is, however, fairly erratic, showing a considerable fall of around 10 percentage points in 1985. A similar decrease occurred for Portugal's M3 ratio. The Portuguese ratios are subject to wide fluctuations. In Greece finally, the M1 ratio is fairly constant. However, the ratios for the broader concepts of money have been undergoing a steady increase since the beginning of the 1970s, the rise of the M3 ratio in particular having been very considerable.

The general picture that emerges from this graphic inspection shows relatively little coherence. Considering the averages of the northern and southern member states – of which the characteristics are summarized in Table 4.1 – yield a change for the better.[1] The most remarkable feature is that with respect to M1 the average for the group of northern countries – group A – is nearly half that of the southern countries, whereas the relative spread in group A is over double that of group B. This considerably greater relative spread for the group A countries appears also for the other monetary aggregates, and reflects the rise in these countries' ratios. The average ratios for the broader monetary aggregates in the southern countries are also substantially higher than in the northern EU countries, albeit that the discrepancies are smaller than in the case of M1. A tentative interpretation could be that, in the southern countries, the portfolio investment alternatives for liquid assets are not as abundant as in the northern member states, so that M2 and M3 are relatively important. The values for secundary and tertiary liquidities reported in Table 4.1 support this interpretation. A more sophisticated analysis, however, can be carried out by considering the analytical framework provided by the theory of the demand for money.

## 4.3 Theoretical Basis

Starting point is the traditional demand for money relationship, according to which the desired demand for money is determined by real income, the rate of inflation, and short- and long-term interest rates. Assuming a price elasticity possibly unequal to one, the following macroeconomic demand for money equation is postulated:

$$\mathrm{M} = AP^{\alpha_1} y^{\alpha_2} \exp\left(\alpha_3 r_k + \alpha_4 r_l + \alpha_5 \dot{p}\right) \tag{4.1}$$

[1] The weights used are the respective shares of the member states' GNP in the EU aggregate in 1989. The percentages are: Belgium 3.16, Denmark 2.16, France 19.78, Germany 25.54, Greece 1.12, Ireland 0.70, Italy 17.87, The Netherlands 4.62, Portugal 0.93, Spain 7.84, United Kingdom 17.28.

*Table 4.1: Average ratios and ratio spreads, 1977–1988*

| Monetary aggregate | | Average | Variation | Spread, as percentages |
|---|---|---|---|---|
| M1 | group A | 17.2 | 5.1 | 29.5 |
| | group B | 29.3 | 4.0 | 13.7 |
| M2 | group A | 33.7 | 11.3 | 33.5 |
| | group B | 49.0 | 3.5 | 7.5 |
| M3 | group A | 55.8 | 16.5 | 29.6 |
| | group B | 74.2 | 3.2 | 4.3 |
| M2 − M1 | group A | 16.5 | 7.4 | 44.9 |
| | group B | 19.7 | 5.7 | 29.2 |
| M3 − M2 | group A | 22.1 | 5.2 | 23.8 |
| | group B | 25.2 | 4.1 | 16.4 |

*Notes:*
The sample period 1977–1988 is the period that all countries, data on the three monetary aggregates are available. M1 − M2 correspond to secondary liquidities and M3−M2 to tertiary liquidities according to the Dutch monetary terminology.

with M the desired money stock in a steady state situation, $P$ the price index – so that M/$P$ is the real money stock –, $y$ real income, $\dot{p}$ the rate of inflation, $r_k$ the short-term interest rate and $r_l$ the long-term interest rate. The price and income elasticities are equal to $\alpha_1$ and $\alpha_2$, respectively; $\alpha_3$ and $\alpha_4$ indicate the relative changes in money demand when short- and long-term interest rates change by one percentage point, while $\alpha_5$ measures the relative change in the demand for money due to a rise in inflation of one percentage point. These coefficients are therefore semi-elasticities. Following, for example, Butter and Fase (1981) and a recent study by Boughton (1991), the usual assumption of a price elasticity of 1 – i.e. price homogeneity of order 1 – is not made *a priori*, but considered as a testable hypothesis. Equation (4.1) describes the relationship between the optimum nominal amount of liquid assets held, on the one hand, and the expected equilibrium value of the explanatory variables, on the other. As such, equation (4.1) is a description of the long-run equilibrium relationship based on an aggregated macroeconomic approach for broad monetary concepts. An alternative route is provided by postulating a systems approach – as in *e.g.* Fase (1978b, 1979) – modelling demand for disaggregated monetary assets. However, in view of the main purpose of our analysis we have preferred the single equation approach embodied in equation (4.1). In the approach chosen, a fundamental distinction is made between the relationship in the steady state and in the short-run. For practical purposes like forecasting, it is desirable to model deviations from the equilibrium relationship. This means that a dynamic formulation of equation (4.1) must be formulated for the estimation process, whereby the long-run properties of the demand for money are determined jointly with the short-run adjustment processes. An error-correction specification was chosen together with the introduction of lags. In accordance with earlier studies performed by us (*cf.* Fase and Kuné( 1974a, 1974b), Fase (1979), Butter and Fase (1981)), a cyclical indicator, *conj*, was used to describe the short-run dynamics of the demand for money. This variable represents the tendency to hoard at times of a recession and the tendency to dishoard in an economic boom. An alternative, and deeper economic interpretation of this variable is to regard it as a proxy for the costs of real assets, for which liquid financial assets form a substitute. Hoarding and dishoarding reflect this substitution process. With respect to the long-run relationship equation (4.1), income represents the influence of the transaction volume or wealth, while the rate of inflation and the two interest rates determine the composition of the monetary aggregate, for which the holding of, for example, less liquid financial assets such as bonds form an alternative. By including simultaneously the short- and long-term interest rate it is also intended to take into account the influence of the yield curve on the demand for money.

The above leads to the following general dynamic specification of the demand for money:

$$\alpha(L)\ln \mathrm{M} = \beta_1(L)\ln P + \beta_2(L)\ln y + \beta_3(L)r_k + \beta_4(L)r_l + \beta_5(L)\dot{p} + \beta_6(L)\ln(conj) \tag{4.2}$$

with $\alpha(L) = 1 - \alpha_1 L - \ldots - \alpha_p L^p$ and $\beta_i(L) = \beta_{io} + \beta_{i1}L + \ldots + \beta_{ip_i}L^{pi}$, with $i = 1, \ldots, 6$. (Of course, the indices $p$ and $pi$ rather than $i$ indicate the number of lags.)

The parameters of $\beta_1(L)$ and $\beta_5(L)$ are not all identified as a result of perfect multicollinearity between the $\ln p$ and $\dot{p}$ (plus lags). This identification problem can be solved by imposing *a priori* restrictions on the polynomials concerned.

One possible method is to consider the real money balances as the dependent variable. This means – in terms of equation (4.2) – that the restrictions $\beta_{10} = 1$ and $\beta_{1i} = -\alpha_i$, for $i = 1, \ldots, p$ are imposed. These $p + 1$ restrictions imply that the long-run price elasticity is equal to 1. This set of restrictions chosen is sufficient, but not necessary to obviate the identification problem, since only $p$ restrictions are needed. In the present study we deliberately chose the $p$ restrictions $\beta_{1i} = -\alpha_i$, $i = 1, \ldots, p$ . Because these restrictions serve for avoiding the identification problem, they are untestable. Thus, equation (4.2) can be rewritten as:

$$\begin{aligned}\alpha(L)\ln(\mathrm{M}/P) = (\beta_{10} - 1)\ln P + \beta_2(L)\ln y + \beta_3(L)r_k \\ + \beta_4(L)r_l + \beta_5(L)\dot{p} + \beta_6(L)\ln(conj) \qquad (4.3)\end{aligned}$$

so that it is no longer assumed *a priori* that the price elasticity equals 1.

In the specification analysis, the following reformulation of equation (4.3) is considered:

$$\begin{aligned}\bar{\alpha}(L)\Delta\ln(\mathrm{M}/P) = (\beta_{10} - 1)\ln P - \alpha(\ln(\mathrm{M}/P)_{-1} - \ln y_{-1}) \\ + (\beta_2 - \alpha)\ln y_{-1} + \beta_3 r_k + \beta_4 r_l + \beta_5\dot{p} \\ + \bar{\beta}_2(L)\Delta\ln y + \bar{\beta}_3(L)\Delta r_k + \bar{\beta}_4(L)\Delta r_l \\ + \bar{\beta}_5(L)\Delta\dot{p} + \bar{\beta}_6(L)\ln(conj) \qquad (4.4)\end{aligned}$$

with $\alpha = 1 - \alpha_1 - \cdots - \alpha_p$, $\beta_i = \beta_{i0} + \cdots + \beta_{ip_i}$, $i = 2, \ldots, 5$, while $\bar{\alpha}(L)$ and $\bar{\beta}_i(L)$, $i = 2, \ldots, 5$ are lag polynomials of order $p-1$ and $p_i - 1$. The parameters of $\bar{\alpha}(L)$ and $\bar{\beta}_i(L)$ are linear combinations of those of $\alpha(L)$ and $\beta_i(L)$, for example, $\bar{\alpha}_i = -\sum_{j=i+1}^{p}\alpha_j$, $i = 1, \ldots, p-1$, with $\bar{\alpha}_i$ the parameters of polynomial $\bar{\alpha}(L)$.

Equation (4.4) served as the general formulation for the estimation and specification analysis. Estimating equation (4.4) instead of equation (4.3) has several advantages. The most important one is that it opens up the possibility to estimate the long-run (semi-)elasticities in a relatively simple way, as they equal the quotient of two estimates. The long-run elasticities are for the short-term interest rate $\beta_3/\alpha$, for the long-term rate $\beta_4/\alpha$, for the rate of inflation $\beta_5/\alpha$ and the income elasticity is $\beta_2/\alpha$. The hypothesis that the income elasticity equals 1 corresponds with the restriction that the coefficient of $\ln y_{-1}$ equals 0. The price elasticity is equal to $(\beta_{10} - 1 + \alpha)/\alpha$. The hypothesis that the price elasticity equals 1 can be tested by assessing the significance of the estimate of the coefficient of $\ln P$. This restriction together with the identification restrictions $\beta_{1i} = -\alpha_i$, $i = 1, \ldots, p$, implies that the polynomial $\beta_1(L) - \alpha(L)$ has a unit root, which is therefore an alternative interpretation of the hypothesis that $\beta_{10} - 1 = 0$. In the sequel, however, we will use the terminology that is related to the economic interpretation of the hypothesis, that the price elasticity equals 1. The second advantage of equation (4.4) over (4.3) is that the multicollinearity problem is mitigated, because many explanatory variables are expressed in first differences. This will improve the precision of the estimates and thus enhance the possibility of making appropriate inferences.

The demand for money function specified above belongs to the class of error-correction models. Formulation (4.4) is in line with the first studies into the demand for money which applied these models, the error-correction term representing the reciprocal of the velocity of circulation of money. However, our formulation (4.4) differs from that used in the more technically oriented cointegration literature put forward by Engle and Granger (1987). In this cointegration approach, the error-correction term is defined as the deviations from the equilibrium relationship (4.1), and hence is given a somewhat different interpretation. Collecting the level terms in (4.4) yields the formulation commonly used in the cointegration literature and shows that real income, the price level as well as the interest rates and inflation are important in the long run. In the present study, the long-run properties are modelled simultaneously with the short-run adjustment processes. This approach differs from the two-step procedure proposed in the cointegration literature, where the long-run equilibrium relationship is estimated first by means of a static regression, and next – conditional on the estimated long-run relationship – the short-run dynamics is determined. It must be noted that if the number of observations were infinite, the two approaches would yield identical results.

## 4.4 Estimation Results

The demand for money equation (4.4) is estimated for the three monetary aggregates M1, M2 and M3 of each of the EU countries over roughly the period 1970–1989. Quarterly seasonally unadjusted data are examined. A description of the data can be found in Fase and Winder (1992). In light of the requirement that the data should be comparable across countries, the definitions are as uniform as possible. Because the data are not seasonally adjusted, and a constant has been added to equation (4.4), three seasonal dummies $s_i$ are included in the estimation equation. Section 4.4.1 begins by discussing some estimation results for Germany and The Netherlands. Section 4.4.2 assesses the empirical results from an economic viewpoint and concerns the interpretation of the results for all EU member countries. Section 4.4.3 goes into the stability of the demand for money and Section 4.4.4 presents a brief evaluation made from a statistical point of view.

### 4.4.1 Results for Germany and The Netherlands

Equation (4.4) has been estimated for 33 monetary aggregates. A complete report of the estimated specifications is given in Fase and Winder (1992). In this section only two of those will be discussed, viz. the M3 equations for Germany and The Netherlands. They were chosen because there is a slight preference to focus on this broad concept of money at present, and also because the two countries are the most interesting from a Dutch viewpoint. It may be noted that the preference for M3 corresponds with the view advocated by, for example, Friedman and the proponents of the portfolio approach, that money is a component of wealth. The estimated specification for Germany (the figures in parentheses being $t$-values) is:

$$\begin{aligned}\Delta \ln(\mathrm{M3}/P) = {} & \underset{(4.829)}{-0.1285}\ (\ln(\mathrm{M3}/P)_{-1} - \ln y) \ \underset{(4.453)}{+0.3761}\ \Delta \ln(\mathrm{M3}/P)_{-4} \\ & \underset{(2.816)}{-\ 0.0050} r_l \ \underset{(2.694)}{+0.0081}\ \Delta r_l \ \underset{(1.776)}{+0.0017}\ r_k \ \underset{(2.099)}{-0.0027}\ \Delta r_k \\ & \underset{(3.804)}{-0.0043}\ \dot{p} \ \underset{(3.598)}{-0.1639}\ \ln(conj) \ \underset{(3.993)}{+0.8757} \ \underset{(5.868)}{+0.0278}\ s_1 \\ & \underset{(0.880)}{+0.0030}\ s_2 \ \underset{(2.373)}{+0.0074}\ s_3\end{aligned}$$

Estimation period: 1971:II–1989:IV, $\bar{R}^2 = 0.7960$ $SE = 0.009$

The corresponding equation for The Netherlands reads as:

$$\begin{aligned}\Delta \ln(\mathrm{M3}/P) = {} & \underset{(2.527)}{-0.0533}\ (\ln(\mathrm{M3}/P)_{-1} - \ln y) \ \underset{(3.906)}{-0.3721}\ \Delta \ln(\mathrm{M3}/P)_{-1} \\ & \underset{(2.527)}{-0.0034}\ \ln P \ \underset{(2.735)}{+0.0025}\ \Delta r_k \ \underset{(2.759)}{-0.0030}\ r_l \\ & \underset{(2.584)}{-0.0042}\ \Delta(r_l - r_k) \ \underset{(2.759)}{-0.0030}\ \dot{p} \ \underset{(0.669)}{-0.0948}\ \Delta \ln(conj)_{-2} \\ & \underset{(1.840)}{+0.0495} \ \underset{(8.910)}{+0.0490}\ s_1 \ \underset{(8.363)}{+0.0592}\ s_2 \ \underset{(1.555)}{+0.0123}\ s_3\end{aligned}$$

Estimation period: 1971:I–1989:IV, $\bar{R}^2 = 0.6544$ $SE = 0.016$

Measured by the $\bar{R}^2$, the fit of the German equation is slightly better than that for the demand for money in The Netherlands. The standard error of the residuals, indicated by $SE$, is also considerably smaller for Germany than for The Netherlands. In contrast to the findings for Germany, the price figures among the explanatory variables in the equation for The Netherlands. This means that the price elasticity for The Netherlands does not equal 1. For both countries, changes in long- and short-term interest rates have a significant influence. For The Netherlands, however, the parameters are subject to the restriction that only changes in the interest rate differential, which is an approximation of the yield curve, have an impact. In Germany the business cycle has a significant influence. For The Netherlands, the cyclical influence – modelled through the change of the cyclical indicator lagged by two quarters – is weaker and not significant. Inclusion of the change of the cyclical indicator instead of the level as an explanatory variable implies a more rapid adjustment of the demand for money: after an initial negative effect, in the following quarter an adjustment in opposite direction takes place. Notice, however, that because of the lags of the money stock in the money demand equations, these adjustments take place gradually.

It is noteworthy that the impact of the error-correction mechanism, i.e. the term $\ln(\mathrm{M3}/P)_{-1} - \ln y$, is over twice as strong in Germany as in The Netherlands. In both equations the error-correction term is significant, which illustrates the importance of including an equilibrating mechanism as an explanatory variable. The error-correction term does not have the traditional form of $\ln(M/P)_{-1} - \ln y_{-1}$, but figures in both equations as $\ln(M/P)_{-1} - \ln y$. This formulation follows if in the equation with explanatory variables $\ln(M/P)_{-1} - \ln y_{-1}$ and $\Delta \ln y$ the restriction is imposed that the corresponding coefficients are each other's opposite. This was suggested by the estimation results obtained from the equation without imposing this restriction. The error-correction terms in the above demand for money equations thus indicate that the equilibrating effect as a result of a deviation of $\ln(M/P)_{-1}$ from its equilibrium value, and the partial effect ensuing from the current income growth are equally large.

In addition to the above restrictions, the demand for money equations also include restrictions imposed on the long-run elasticities. In both countries, the income elasticity is set equal to 1. In Germany the price elasticity is also 1, while the equation for The Netherlands contains a restriction which implies that the price elasticity of $\mathrm{M3} - \mathrm{M1}$ equals 1. Furthermore, in the demand equation for The Netherlands the long-run semi-elasticities with regard to long-term interest rates and inflation are equal. All these restrictions, which are dictated by the unconstrained estimation results, improve the statistical outcomes and form testable hypotheses. As discussed in Section 4.4.4, an evaluation based on $t$-tests leads to the conclusion that the hypothesis that the restrictions are valid need not be rejected.

### 4.4.2 Economic Assessment

An evaluation from an economic viewpoint of the estimated equations for the 11 countries considered is hampered by both the large number of results, and the fact that in the estimated equations long- as well as short-run properties are mixed together. Most important are the results for the equilibrium relationship. In all 33 cases the income elasticity is set *a priori* equal to 1. The long-run elasticities of the price level, interest rates and the rate of inflation have, however, been estimated and have been presented in Table 4.2. The figures in Table 4.2 show wide discrepancies. For most monetary aggregates, the estimates of the price elasticity vary from 0.8 to 1. In general, the broader the monetary aggregate, the higher the price elasticity. With regard to interest rates and the rate of inflation, the elasticities for the various monetary aggregates vary between 0.20 and 0.40. M2 is slightly more sensitive to interest rates and the rate of inflation than the other monetary aggregates. Of greater importance might be that the elasticities of interest rates and the rate of inflation are the product of the estimated semi-elasticity and the average interest rates or rate of inflation. The values contained in Table 4.2 consequently reflect not just the structure of the demand for money relationships in the various member states, but also the differences in the level of interest rates and the rate of inflation. If we look at the parameter estimates presented in Table 4.3, we obtain therefore a more comprehensible picture. Regardless of the monetary aggregate considered, the semi-elasticities for interest rates and the rate of inflation for The Netherlands are higher than those for the other EU member states. The United Kingdom is also characterized by a considerable sensitivity of the demand for money to interest rates and the rate of inflation.[2] In Germany, these elasticities are slightly smaller, albeit still fairly high in comparison to the other EU countries. The interest rate semi-elasticities for M1 have the same size as in The Netherlands. The inflation rate semi-elasticity of M1 in The Netherlands is, however, twice as large as in Germany. For the broader monetary aggregates, the sensitivity to both interest rates and the rate of inflation is substantially smaller in Germany than in The Netherlands. The estimates of interest rate and inflation rate semi-elasticities for France are fairly small, especially for M1. They do, however, differ significantly

---

[2] Large values of the semi-elasticities for the interest rates are also found for the UK by Hendry and Ericsson (1991b). A comparison of the results shows that in both studies the income and price elasticities are equal to 1. For the short-term interest rate and the inflation rate Hendry and Ericsson find semi-elasticities of −0.07 and −0.02, respectively. For the second half of the 1980s Hendry and Ericsson include also a learning adjusted own interest rate, for which a semi-elasticity of 0.07 is found.

*Table 4.2: Long-term elasticities for interest rates, prices, and the rate of inflation*

| | Short-term interest rate | | | Long-term interest rate | | | Rate of inflation | | | Price level | | |
|---|---|---|---|---|---|---|---|---|---|---|---|---|
| | M1 | M2 | M3 | M1 | M2 | M3 | M1 | M2 | M3 | M1 | M2 | M3 |
| Belgium | −0.11 | 0.38 | 0.32 | −0.11 | −0.39 | −0.33 | −0.07 | −0.23 | −0.20 | 0.59 | 1 | 1 |
| Denmark | −0.21 | 0.11 | 0.05 | −0.26 | −0.40 | −0.34 | −0.14 | −0.21 | −0.18 | 1.24 | 1.18 | 1.25 |
| France | −0.04 | | | −0.04 | −0.18 | −0.13 | −0.03 | −0.13 | −0.10 | 0.82 | 0.89 | 0.92 |
| Germany | −0.18 | 0.16 | 0.09 | −0.21 | −0.31 | −0.31 | −0.06 | −0.17 | −0.14 | 1 | 1 | 1 |
| Greece | −0.28 | 0.44 | 0.34 | | | | −0.32 | −0.51 | −0.39 | 1 | 1 | 1.21 |
| Ireland | −0.13 | 0.13 | 0.14 | −0.15 | −0.16 | −0.17 | −0.10 | −0.13 | −0.14 | 0.73 | 0.88 | 1 |
| Italy | −0.15 | | | | −0.16 | −0.13 | −0.11 | −0.16 | −0.12 | 0.87 | 1 | 1 |
| The Netherlands | −0.20 | 0.38 | 0.33 | −0.23 | −0.45 | −0.46 | −0.14 | −0.27 | −0.28 | 0.84 | 0.89 | 0.94 |
| Portugal | −0.16 | 0.16 | 0.18 | −0.17 | −0.16 | −0.19 | −0.17 | −0.19 | −0.22 | 0.85 | 0.94 | 0.95 |
| Spain | −0.13 | 0.10 | 0.29 | −0.13 | −0.10 | −0.10 | −0.12 | −0.09 | −0.09 | 0.83 | 0.75 | 0.79 |
| United Kingdom | −0.27 | 0.42 | 0.36 | −0.30 | −0.47 | −0.41 | −0.25 | −0.39 | −0.34 | 1 | 1 | 1 |

*Table 4.3: Estimated semi-elasticities for interest rates and the rate of inflation*

| | Short-term interest rate, $\alpha_3$ | | | Long-term interest rate, $\alpha_4$ | | | Rate of inflation, $\alpha_5$ | | |
|---|---|---|---|---|---|---|---|---|---|
| | M1 | M2 | M3 | M1 | M2 | M3 | M1 | M2 | M3 |
| Belgium | −0.01 | 0.04 | 0.03 | −0.01 | −0.04 | −0.03 | −0.01 | −0.04 | −0.03 |
| Denmark | −0.02 | 0.01 | 0.00 | −0.02 | −0.03 | −0.02 | −0.02 | −0.03 | −0.02 |
| France | −0.00 | | | −0.00 | −0.02 | −0.01 | −0.00 | −0.02 | −0.01 |
| Germany | −0.03 | 0.02 | 0.01 | −0.03 | −0.04 | −0.04 | −0.02 | −0.04 | −0.03 |
| Greece | −0.02 | 0.03 | 0.03 | | | | −0.02 | −0.03 | −0.03 |
| Ireland | −0.01 | 0.01 | 0.01 | −0.01 | −0.01 | −0.01 | −0.01 | −0.01 | −0.01 |
| Italy | −0.01 | | | | −0.01 | −0.01 | −0.01 | −0.01 | −0.01 |
| The Netherlands | −0.03 | 0.06 | 0.05 | −0.03 | −0.06 | −0.06 | −0.03 | −0.06 | −0.06 |
| Portugal | −0.01 | 0.01 | 0.01 | −0.01 | −0.01 | −0.01 | −0.01 | −0.01 | −0.01 |
| Spain | −0.01 | 0.01 | 0.02 | −0.01 | −0.01 | −0.01 | −0.01 | −0.01 | −0.01 |
| United Kingdom | −0.03 | 0.04 | 0.04 | −0.03 | −0.04 | −0.04 | −0.03 | −0.04 | −0.04 |

*Notes:* For the sake of simplicity all semi-elasticities have been rounded off to two decimals. More precise estimates of the parameters of the long-run relationship as well as the attending $t$-values, which can easily be calculated for the ratio of the two parameter estimates, are reported in Fase and Winder (1992).

from zero. The values for Spain and Italy, too, are relatively small. These outcomes indicate that in the southern EU countries the sensitivity of the demand for money to interest rates and the rate of inflation is smaller than in the northern part of the EU. This constitutes empirical support for the hypothesis put forward in Section 4.2 that the alternatives for liquid assets are more abundant in the northern than in the southern EU countries.

The discussion in Section 4.2 of the development of the monetary ratios in the EU member states showed that the largest monetary expansion was recorded in the United Kingdom, Denmark and The Netherlands. In Denmark this would seem to be related to the size of the price elasticity, for which an estimate of 1.2 was found, irrespective of the monetary aggregate considered. By contrast with the price elasticity, the magnitude of the interest rates and the rate of inflation semi-elasticities corresponds roughly to that in the other EU countries. However, for the United Kingdom and The Netherlands the price elasticity is not higher than 1. For The Netherlands, it is even below 1. However, these countries have the highest semi-elasticities for interest rates and the rate of inflation, so that the conclusion is warranted that the sharp rise in these countries' ratios in the 1980s has to do with the sensitivity to interest rates and the rate of inflation. In three countries – Belgium, Greece and Ireland – diverging developments were recorded for the different monetary aggregates. The fall in the M1 ratios in Belgium and Ireland seems due to the low values of the price elasticity. In the case of Greece, the high price elasticity for M3 would seem responsible for the very substantial rise of its M3 ratio.

Another criterion for assessing the economic plausibility of the estimation results is the mutual consistency of the estimates obtained for the various monetary aggregates. The elasticities found for M1, M2 and M3 can be used to determine the elasticities of the demand for M2−M1, M3−M1 and M3−M2; these must be economically plausible.[3] Table 4.4 presents the long-run elasticities of M2 − M1, M3 − M1 and M3 − M2 implied by the estimated equations.

The values given in Table 4.4 present an economically plausible picture indeed. The analysis distinguishes between two types of interest rates: capital and money market rates. The latter is the return on near-money, but is indicative notably of the interest rate on time deposits. The interest rate on short-term saving deposits is usually strongly correlated with that on time deposits, so that a positive short-term interest

[3] It can easily be verified that $d\ln(\mathrm{M2}) = \omega d\ln(\mathrm{M1}) + (1-\omega)d\ln(\mathrm{M2}-\mathrm{M1})$, with $\omega = \mathrm{M1}/\mathrm{M2}$ and $1-\omega = (\mathrm{M2}-\mathrm{M1})/\mathrm{M2}$. Similar relationships hold for the other assets. In the calculation of the elasticities given in Table 4.4, the sample means of the quotients concerned were used for $\omega$ and $1-\omega$.

rate elasticity for M3 – M2 is in line with the expectations. A negative elasticity need, however, not be implausible if the correlation between the two interest rates is smaller and a rise in short-term interest rates would lead to considerable shifts from savings to time deposits. Obviously the occurrence of such shifts would also depend on the prevailing rules and regulations and the manner of statistical registration (*cf.* Fase 1977, 1978b). Table 4.4 shows that positive values are found for almost all countries. For the other elasticities contained in Table 4.4, the sign is determined unequivocally. All of them have the theoretically plausible sign. This leads to the conclusion that for all countries the elasticities found for M1, M2 and M3 are mutually consistent, and thus gaining in plausibility.

### 4.4.3 Assessment of Stability

An important assessment criterion, both from a policy and economic viewpoint, is the degree of stability of the demand for money. Several methods are used to assess stability: re-estimating the equation for sub-periods or appraising the predictive performance of the estimated relationship. The former, which focuses on the constancy of the estimates, is the most attractive, but cannot be used in this case because the time series would be too short. However, the latter approach also has practical disadvantages. Other approaches to assess stability are recursive estimation of the relevant parameters, the evaluation of the size of the error-correction parameters – which indicate the speed of adjustment in case perturbations arise – and the residual variation. Here we consider the residual variation, which reflects the noise rather than the degree of misspecification, as a measure of stability. The standard error of the residuals for the countries and monetary aggregates considered are shown in Table 4.5.

This table shows that according to our criterion there are wide discrepancies in stability among the different countries and the various monetary aggregates. It is also clear that Germany and France, and to some extent Spain too, have a more stable demand for money than the other countries, irrespective of the monetary aggregate considered. Where M1 is concerned, it is also noteworthy that Greece, Portugal and the United Kingdom have the least stable demand for money. Table 4.5 furthermore shows that in The Netherlands the demand for money is less stable than in Germany. Notice finally that for all countries, the broader the monetary aggregate, the greater the observed stability.

Comparison with the outcomes of other studies is another way of assessing stability. Here we have only compared with Fase and Winder

*Table 4.4: Long-run elasticities for near-money*

| Country | Monetary aggregate | Price | Income | Short-term interest rate | Long-term interest rate | Inflation |
|---|---|---|---|---|---|---|
| Belgium | M2 − M1 | 1.43 | 1 | 0.89 | −0.67 | −0.40 |
| | M3 − M1 | 1.19 | 1 | 0.52 | −0.42 | −0.25 |
| | M3 − M2 | 1 | 1 | 0.21 | −0.22 | −0.13 |
| Denmark | M2 − M1 | 1.12 | 1 | 0.50 | −0.56 | −0.30 |
| | M3 − M1 | 1.26 | 1 | 0.28 | −0.41 | −0.22 |
| | M3 − M2 | 1.60 | 1 | −0.30 | −0.03 | −0.01 |
| France | M2 − M1 | 1 | 1 | 0.07 | −0.43 | −0.31 |
| | M3 − M1 | 1 | 1 | 0.03 | −0.21 | −0.15 |
| | M3 − M2 | 1 | 1 | – | −0.03 | −0.02 |
| Germany | M2 − M1 | 1 | 1 | 0.64 | −0.45 | −0.32 |
| | M3 − M1 | 1 | 1 | 0.22 | −0.36 | −0.18 |
| | M3 − M2 | 1 | 1 | −0.02 | −0.30 | −0.10 |
| Greece | M2 − M1 | 1 | 1 | 1.05 | – | −0.67 |
| | M3 − M1 | 1.28 | 1 | 0.54 | – | −0.42 |
| | M3 − M2 | 1.47 | 1 | 0.22 | – | −0.26 |
| Ireland | M2 − M1 | 0.96 | 1 | 0.28 | −0.17 | −0.15 |
| | M3 − M1 | 1.07 | 1 | 0.21 | −0.17 | −0.15 |
| | M3 − M2 | 1.16 | 1 | 0.15 | −0.17 | −0.14 |
| Italy | M2 − M1 | 1.25 | 1 | 0.27 | −0.47 | −0.25 |
| | M3 − M1 | 1.12 | 1 | 0.13 | −0.24 | −0.13 |
| | M3 − M2 | 1 | 1 | – | −0.02 | −0.02 |
| The Netherlands | M2 − M1 | 1 | 1 | 1.42 | −0.84 | −0.51 |
| | M3 − M1 | 1 | 1 | 0.65 | −0.60 | −0.36 |
| | M3 − M2 | 1 | 1 | 0.25 | −0.47 | −0.28 |
| Portugal | M2 − M1 | 1 | 1 | 0.35 | −0.16 | −0.20 |
| | M3 − M1 | 1 | 1 | 0.33 | −0.19 | −0.24 |
| | M3 − M2 | 1 | 1 | 0.27 | −0.28 | −0.32 |
| Spain | M2 − M1 | 0.67 | 1 | 0.36 | −0.08 | −0.07 |
| | M3 − M1 | 0.77 | 1 | 0.50 | −0.09 | −0.08 |
| | M3 − M2 | 0.85 | 1 | 0.61 | −0.09 | −0.08 |
| United Kingdom | M2 − M1 | 1 | 1 | 0.95 | −0.61 | −0.50 |
| | M3 − M1 | 1 | 1 | 0.60 | −0.45 | −0.37 |
| | M3 − M2 | 1 | 1 | 0.27 | −0.31 | −0.25 |

*Table 4.5: Standard error residuals for the various demand for money equations*

| | M1 | M2 | M3 |
|---|---|---|---|
| Belgium | 0.012 | 0.014 | 0.009 |
| Denmark | 0.020 | 0.015 | 0.013 |
| France | 0.010 | 0.012 | 0.008 |
| Germany | 0.011 | 0.013 | 0.009 |
| Greece | 0.028 | 0.021 | 0.010 |
| Ireland | 0.019 | 0.023 | 0.017 |
| Italy | 0.016 | 0.012 | 0.009 |
| The Netherlands | 0.020 | 0.025 | 0.016 |
| Portugal | 0.026 | 0.015 | 0.012 |
| Spain | 0.012 | 0.013 | 0.010 |
| United Kingdom | 0.026 | 0.028 | 0.020 |

(1990) who – with slightly different definitions for the variables used – estimate error-correction specifications for M1 and M2 in The Netherlands for the period 1970–1988. The long-run elasticities found in Fase and Winder (1990) are given in Table 4.6. Comparing the values from Table 4.6 with those in Table 4.2 shows that the income elasticity equals 1 throughout. A major and remarkable difference is that in the present study the price elasticities are smaller than 1, whereas Fase and Winder assumed a value equal to 1 *a priori*. Another difference is that in the M1 equation, Fase and Winder consider short-term interest rates as the only interest rate variable. In the present study, both long- and short-term interest rates are included in the equation. It is also remarkable that for M1 the algebraic sum of the short- and long-term interest rate elasticities from Table 4.2 are virtually equal to the value for the short-term interest rate elasticity given in Table 4.6.

The inflation rate elasticity of M1 is of a comparable order of magnitude in both studies. In the present study, the inflation rate and interest rate elasticities of the demand for M2 found for The Netherlands are higher than those found by Fase and Winder.

### 4.4.4 Statistical Assessment

With respect to the statistical evaluation of the estimated demand for money relationships – whose outcomes are described in detail in Fase and

*Table 4.6: Long-run elasticities in Fase and Winder (1990)*

| Monetary aggregate | Price | Income | Short-term interest rate | Long-term interest rate | Inflation |
|---|---|---|---|---|---|
| M1 | 1 | 1 | −0.42 | – | −0.16 |
| M2 | 1 | 1 | 0.29 | −0.35 | −0.17 |

Winder (1992) – two questions arise. The first is whether the assumption that there is an equilibrium relationship (4.1) is met, statistically speaking. We applied the testing procedure developed by Hylleberg, Engle, Granger, and Yoo (1990), which, unlike other procedures as e.g. the system approach of Johansen (1991), offers the opportunity to test for the occurrence of seasonal unit roots. The cointegration analysis shows that, for 21 out of the 33 demand for money relationships, the hypothesis of existence of a long-run relationship cannot be rejected. In cases where this hypothesis must be rejected, the test statistics have fairly large values, so that there is a strong tendency towards cointegration.

A second interesting question is whether, according to statistical standards, the restrictions imposed upon the demand for money equations are justified. These restrictions relate to the parameters of the long-run relationship and the parameters describing the short-run adjustment processes. With respect to the long-run parameters, the hypothesis that the income elasticity equals 1 is not rejected in any of the 33 cases, albeit that there are some statistical doubts as to the demand for M3 in Ireland. The restriction that the price elasticity equals 1 does not – insofar as imposed – need to be rejected either. In most cases, testing of the restrictions on the interest rate and the inflation rate semi-elasticities leads to the conclusion that these restrictions too are statistically warranted. The sole cases in which the restrictions are to be rejected concern the demand for M3 in Portugal and the demand for M2 and M3 in the United Kingdom. However, in view of the fact that – from an economic viewpoint – more plausible outcomes are obtained for these countries if the restrictions are imposed, they are nevertheless maintained. Of the restrictions on the short-run parameters, those implied by the formulation of the error-correction term are the most important. Testing of these restrictions yields supportive results. In addition, restrictions are also imposed on the short-run, featuring interest rate and inflation rate effects. Apart from some exceptions, these restrictions do not need to be rejected either.

Finally, it has been examined whether residual autocorrelation is absent. The hypothesis that the residuals are white noise is not rejected for all of the 33 equations.

## 4.5 Comparison with Earlier Research

In principle, there are two ways for analysing the demand for money in the EU: countrywise or for the EU as a whole. This study uses the countrywise approach despite the fact that it is very labour-intensive and time-consuming. However, the advantage of additional information obtained by the geographically disaggregated approach more than outweighs this disadvantage. Moreover, a number of problems relating to the aggregated approach are consequently bypassed. The aggregated approach is based on the assumption that the demand for money is the same for all countries, neglecting the differences per country. In addition, it requires conversion of data expressed in the domestic currency into time series expressed in a common unit. Finally, particular interpretation problems may arise when the aggregated approach is applied.[4]

This section aims at comparing the outcome of our study with that of studies conducted by other researchers, who all use the aggregated approach. Table 4.7 shows the most important results of this comparison as well as the outcome of our study, summarized in average figures.

Bekx and Tullio (1989) only examine the long-run demand for money within the framework of an analysis of the effects of international currency substitution on the Deutsche Mark–US dollar exchange rate. It is estimated on the basis of quarterly figures for the sample period 1978–1986. It is not entirely evident whether their analysis relates to M1 or M2; neither is it clear whether their analysis uses the short- or the long-term interest rate as explanatory variable. In view of the context of their study, we assume, however, that the analysis concerns M1 and the long-term interest rate. Kremers and Lane (1990) re-estimate Bekx and Tullio's equation for the sample period 1978–1987. In contrast to Bekx and Tullio, Kremers and Lane measure currency substitution on the basis of the ECU–dollar exchange rate instead of the differential between the long-term interest rates in the EMS and the

[4] If the demand for money is not identical for all countries, the elasticities of the aggregated demand for money cannot be interpreted unequivocally. Take, for example, two countries A and B. The demand for money in country A is assumed to be more sensitive than in country B. Consequently, the interest rate sensitivity of the total demand for money differs to the extent that changes in the average interest rate are reflected in changes in the interest rate in both countries. This interpretation problem cannot be solved by analysing aggregates on EU level. By contrast, the per country approach enables calculation of the effect on the total demand for money of assumed interest rate changes in the EU countries.

*Table 4.7: Estimation results for demand for money EU*

| Author | Monetary aggregate | Parameters for | | | | | |
|---|---|---|---|---|---|---|---|
| | | price | income | short-term interest rate | long-term interest rate | inflation | currency substitution |
| Present study [a]) | M1 | 0.89 | 1 | −0.02 | −0.01 | −0.01 | – |
| | M2 | 0.96 | 1 | 0.02 | −0.03 | −0.03 | – |
| | M3 | 0.97 | 1 | 0.01 | −0.02 | −0.02 | – |
| Bekx and Tullio (1989) | M1 | 0.42 | 0.91 | – | −0.01 | – | −0.01 |
| Re-estimation Bekx and Tullio | M1 | 1.28 | 0.70 | – | −0.02 | – | −0.11 |
| Kremers and Lane (1990) | M1 | 1 | 1 | −0.01 | – | −0.01 | 0.08 |
| Monticelli and Strauss-Kahn (1992) I | M3 | 1 | 1.33 | −0.01 | – | – | 0.01 |
| Ditto II | M3 | 1 | 1.36 | −0.01 | – | – | 0.04 |
| Butter and Fase (1981) [a]) | M2 | 1.19 | 1.45 | – | −0.25 | −0.28 | – |

*Notes:* With the exception of Butter and Fase (1981), the relationship used is of the type $M = AP^{\alpha_1}y^{\alpha_2} \times \exp(\alpha_3 r_k + \alpha_4 r_l + \alpha_5 \dot{p} + \alpha_6 cs)$, in which $P$ is the price level, $y$ real income, $r_k$ and $r_l$ short-term and long-term interest rate, respectively, $\dot{p}$ the rate of inflation and $cs$ a measure for currency substitution. This latter variable is not used in every study. In the study by Kremers and Lane, the restriction is imposed that the income and price elasticities equal 1. Testing shows that this hypothesis does not need to be rejected. In the study by Monticelli and Strauss-Kahn, the estimated relationships contain a significant trend variable.

[a]) calculated as averages of country estimates.

US. Kremers and Lane also present own estimation results of an error-correction model. Their sample period is 1978:IV–1987:IV and they consider the seven EU member states, Belgium, Denmark, Germany, France, Ireland, Italy and The Netherlands. The estimates for the elasticities and semi-elasticities are also given in Table 4.7. Striking, though not reflected in the table, is the fact that they find a substantial influence of the error-correction mechanism: 95% of the adjustment to the equilibrium situation is realized after only one quarter. Monticelli and Strauss-Kahn (1992) also use an error-correction model for the demand for money in the EU as a whole – excluding Portugal, Greece and Luxembourg – and present estimates obtained in both a direct and indirect way – indicated in Table 4.7 by I and II, respectively – for the estimation period 1979:I–1989:IV. They use the same final year as we did but only consider M3. Our study differs from the three studies mentioned here in that they also examine the effects of international currency substitution. Kremers and Lane use the level of the ECU–dollar exchange rate as explanatory variable, Monticelli and Strauss-Kahn opt for the change in exchange rates, which – from a theoretical viewpoint – is more logical, whereas Bekx and Tullio assume uncovered interest parity and use the interest rate differential between the US and the EMS.

Finally, Table 4.7 comprises the price, income and interest rate elasticities which can be calculated on the basis of the demand for money relationships for the individual EU countries as estimated by Butter and Fase (1981). By contrast to all other estimates with respect to interest rates and inflation rates in Table 4.7, these are elasticities. The elasticities follow from the semi-elasticities by multiplying by about 10.

As far as price elasticities are concerned, the estimates obtained by Bekx and Tullio seem hardly plausible. The most remarkable is that our outcomes for M1, M2 and M3 are slightly below 1, a value imposed by Kremers and Lane and Monticelli and Strauss-Kahn. In our study, as in that by Kremers and Lane, the income elasticity is restricted to be 1. In this respect, too, the results of Bekx and Tullio, Monticelli and Strauss-Kahn and Butter and Fase differ strongly. As far as interest rate and inflation rate elasticities are concerned, our study and that by Butter and Fase show remarkable similarities. When compared with the studies by Kremers and Lane and Monticelli and Strauss-Kahn, a striking difference is that in present study both the short- and long-term interest rates and the rate of inflation are assumed to play a role in the long-run. According to Kremers and Lane, the long-term interest rate only has influence in the short-run, whereas Monticelli and Strauss-Kahn consider the inflation rate to be of importance only for the description of the adjustment processes emerging in the short-run. Consequently, both studies assume the long-run elasticities for these variables to be 0, which is not plausible.

Although it does not concern the EU and focuses on the velocity of circulation instead of on the demand for money, it may be useful to examine the results of a study conducted by Bomhoff (1991) for the G 7 countries. His study implies a long-term interest rate elasticity for M1 and M2, calculated by us as an average, in the four European G 7 countries (Germany, France, Italy and the United Kingdom) of −0.17 and −0.10, respectively, results which for M1 agree with our outcome. The interest rate elasticity calculated for M2 in our study is slightly higher. It is remarkable that Bomhoff too finds a small interest rate elasticity for France. It should be noted, however, that, in many respects, Bomhoff's approach differs completely from that used in the studies on the demand for money mentioned here. The most important difference is that Bomhoff focuses on the predictability of the velocity of circulation, introducing a stochastic trend as explanatory variable. Admittedly, this improves the predictive performance but it lacks an economic interpretation. Moreover, Bomhoff wrongly identifies predictive performance with stability and predictability of monetary policy.[5]

As mentioned earlier, the estimates found for the EU in the present study and in that made by Butter and Fase represent a weighted average, using the money shares in the various member states, summarized in Table 4.8, as the weights. This method largely bypasses the complex problem of aggregation for which no unequivocal solution exists and a well-considered practical solution will have to suffice. For the aggregation of the countries' data on the money stock and income to EU level, three conversion methods can be used, in principle. The first method uses the actual exchange rates. Following the analysis of the aggregate demand for money for the group of ten by Gray, Ward, and Zis (1976), this method is used in the study conducted by Monticelli and Strauss-Kahn, which opts for the exchange rate *vis-à-vis* the ECU. This conversion method is applied here too, using the rates against the dollar. The second method, applied by Bekx and Tullio, uses the average 1979 exchange rate *vis-à-vis* the Deutsche Mark as a basis instead of the actual exchange rates. A third alternative, applied by Kremers and Lane, uses purchasing power parities. We have also calculated the EU elasticities using the last

[5] Bomhoff (1991, p. 631) stresses the general character of his model and its similarities with the error-correction model. The latter is, however, only correct insofar as the coefficient of the error-correction term is smaller than 1. As for the general character of Bomhoff's model, it can be stated that more general descriptions are conceivable, for example, descriptions regarding the broader category of time series models.

*Table 4.8: Country shares in EU monetary aggregates (percentages)*

| Country | Monetary aggregate | | |
|---|---|---|---|
| | M1 | M2 | M3 |
| Belgium | 3.56 | 4.36 | 4.50 |
| Denmark | 2.51 | 2.53 | 1.91 |
| France | 24.58 | 21.98 | 21.52 |
| Germany | 19.30 | 18.41 | 20.18 |
| Greece | 0.89 | 1.36 | 1.55 |
| Ireland | 0.36 | 0.63 | 0.74 |
| Italy | 23.93 | 21.62 | 19.33 |
| The Netherlands | 5.04 | 4.59 | 5.01 |
| Portugal | 1.08 | 1.58 | 1.27 |
| Spain | 6.78 | 7.14 | 7.73 |
| United Kingdom | 11.97 | 15.80 | 16.26 |

*Notes:* Average share in the EU total over the period 1977:I–1989:II. For this period, data on M1, M2 and M3 are available for all countries.

two conversion methods with base year 1988. The resulting values are similar to those reported in Table 4.7 and are therefore not mentioned here again. If the nominal exchange rates are stable over time, the first method is identical to the second method. If all EMS countries have the same rate of inflation, the second and third method are each other's equivalent while in the case PPP holds permanently, the first and third method yield identical results. Interest rates and inflation rates are calculated at an aggregate level as weighted averages, using weights from the ECU. Various authors are examining the effects of the alternative method of aggregation on the estimation results, but confine themselves generally to presenting the best results and the corresponding method of aggregation.

## 4.6 Conclusions and Final Remarks

A first distinguishing and unique characteristic of our study is that it pays attention to the demand for money in the individual EU countries instead of providing an aggregate demand for money equation for the whole EU. This approach does justice to possible differences in money demand behaviour in the various countries and avoids the – inevitably arbitrary – aggregation with its loss of information and the almost intractable problem of currency substitution. The price to be paid is a marked increase in estimation workload and the risk that the empirical evidence will become less clear. A second characteristic of our study is that it distinguishes between the short-run dynamics of the demand for money and the long-run equilibrium relationship, implied by the economic theory of the demand for money. Also, an extensive specification analysis, as in earlier studies made by us on the demand for money in The Netherlands, has been carried out. This is a third, methodological characteristic of this study.

For each EU member state, the demand for M1, M2 and M3 was analysed, resulting in a total of 33 demand for money equations. Quarterly data were used, compiled on the basis of – the most uniform possible – definitions for M1, M2 and M3 for the sample period 1970–1989. This relatively long time series is required due to the time series methodology used, which is, however, sufficiently flexible to allow for shifts in economic structure and behaviour in time.

Our empirical analysis shows that, in most cases, the price elasticities are slightly below 1. This means that the assumption of linear homogeneity of the demand for money in the prices, which is often made, is for the EU member states not fully supported by the estimation results. A second remarkable result is that in the southern member states, interest rate and inflation rate sensitivity is lower than in the northern member states. This might be due to the fact that there are less portfolio investment opportunities in the southern European countries as compared with the northern member states; as a result, liquid assets are held partly because of a lack of sufficient alternatives for portfolio investment. Third, our empirical analysis shows that in The Netherlands, the interest rate and inflation rate sensitivity is higher than in Germany, particularly with respect to M2 and M3. For M1, the inflation rate sensitivity is also higher in The Netherlands, but the interest rate semi-elasticities are similar. Fourth, the stability of the demand for money seems to increase for broader definitions of monetary aggregates but also show to some extent a remarkable pattern suggesting less stability for the smaller countries. However, the results for the United Kingdom seem to contradict this regularity with the size of the country. In any case, stability is remarkably higher in Germany than in The Netherlands. Fifth, the results for the individual countries provide interesting keys for the interpretation of the monetary developments in the various countries. The increase in the liquidity ratio in Denmark, for instance, is partly the result of a relatively high price elasticity, whereas our empirical analysis shows that, in The Netherlands and in the United Kingdom, an important role can be ascribed to the notable interest rate and inflation rate sensitivity, or in other words to investment considerations. A sixth, final remark, is that it proves to be possible to obtain very plausible price elasticities and semi-elasticities for interest rates and inflation rates for the EU as a whole, by weighting the estimation results for the individual member states.

A basic assumption for this study is that it is possible to estimate the demand for money. Despite the fact that this assumption is generally accepted in empirically oriented monetary econometrics, it is not completely undisputed. Cooley and LeRoy (1981) – and, following them Bomhoff (1991) – argued that the estimated interest rate elasticities of the demand for money reflect the researcher's *a priori* opinions rather than sample information. Moreover, they are of the opinion that demand for money studies pay insufficient attention to the issue of simultaneity.[6] Their plea, which is interesting from a methodological viewpoint, is, however, hardly convincing as they do not provide the practical researcher with an alternative and ignore the fact that earlier literature on the subject of money demand did focus on this issue, as illustrated by the work of Teigen (1964, 1970). At the time, Teigen concluded that the simultaneity bias is limited and that imposing *a priori* restrictions is an essential part of the formulation of theories. Moreover, unacceptable results from an empirical methodological viewpoint were exceptions. Interesting as it may be, Bomhoff's alternative, focusing not on the demand for money but on the velocity of circulation is hardly convincing either, since the two approaches are, in a way, identical.

Returning to the demand for money in the EU, our analysis shows that there are considerable differences between the various member states with respect to the nature of the demand for money and its stability which partly relate to the size of the country involved. Consequently, the degree to which the supply of money is exogenous in terms of demand for money determinants – strictly speaking a condition for the estimation of the demand for money as such – probably depends on the size of the economy. This underlines the importance of per country analyses prior to the estimation of the aggregated demand for money. The preceding discussion also shows that the stability of the demand for money is only one aspect of the issue to what extent there is room for an independent monetary policy regarding the control of the money stock.

---

[6] Simultaneity can formally be tested for. However, the commonly used statistics to test the hypothesis of orthogonality between the explanatory variables and the disturbance term have poor small sample properties (see *e.g.* Kiviet (1985)). Following common practice we refrained therefore from testing the hypothesis of exogeneity.

# 5. In Search for Stability: An Empirical Appraisal of the Demand for Money in the G7 and EU Countries

The demand for money has been at the centre of monetary econometrics. The demand for money research focuses on the factors determining money-holding behaviour of the private sector of the economy. Knowledge of this reaction pattern is of great importance for assessing the effectiveness of monetary policy or the impact of monetary or other shocks. However, views on this matter differ widely. On the one hand, there is a general approach, focusing on the monetary climate, which regards monetary ease or tightness as the main driving force without specifying the nature of the underlying transmission process. On the other hand, a more specific approach is discernible, which regards all changes in money-holding behaviour, or, in other words the reallocation within the range of components of wealth, as the most important channel for spending effects.

The demand for money is a well-explored field of monetary econometrics. Against that background and in view of the traditionally ample availability of data to examine the various theoretical views empirically, this is not surprising. Moreover, research on the demand for money conducted in the recent past has been an important source of inspiration for innovations in both monetary theory and econometric technique. This has resulted in an abundant flow of interesting empirical research on the demand for money covering many countries and regions. This survey aims at presenting an inventory and assessing these innovative activities from the viewpoint of monetary policy. It focuses on four aspects in particular. The first is the evolution of the theory on the demand for money, of which a brief survey is presented. The second is a

Reprinted from *De Economist*, **142**(4) (1994), M.M.G. Fase, 'In search for stability: An empirical appraisal of the demand for money in the G 7 and EC countries', 421–454, ©1994 with kind permission from Kluwer Academic Publishers.

summary of empirical studies carried out since 1970. Because virtually all recent surveys of money demand research – see *e.g.* Judd and Scadding (1982a), Goldfeld and Sichel (1990) or Boughton (1992) – focus primarily on the US, the present survey, following Fase and Kuné (1975, pp. 344–345) for the 1960s and before, broadens the perspective by including the G 7 and EU countries in particular. The third aspect concerns the most important theoretical and methodological lessons to be learned from the empirical survey presented here. This, as it were, reflects the practical interpretation of the recent theoretical and empirical evolution of research into the demand for money. The fourth and last aspect focuses on the policy conclusions to be drawn from this survey, based on the view that empirical econometrics in the field of money demand also derives its significance from its task in support of policy. The above four viewpoints determine the structure of this chapter. For the sake of brevity and clarity, the empirical findings which underlie this review have been listed partially in an appendix to this chapter. A comprehensive survey can be found in Fase (1993).

## 5.1 The Evolution of the Theory on the Demand for Money

An interesting question is why the demand for money – in contrast with most other monetary phenomena – has been the focus of so much econometric attention. An answer to this question may be sought in the circumstance that, in addition to the ample availability of data required for estimation, the theory on the demand for money is reasonably well-developed and that knowledge of the stability of the demand for money is relevant for monetary policy. The availability of a well-developed theory is supported by the historiography of views on the demand for money. They all originate from reflections by the French political economist Bodin, the Florentine merchant Davanzati and the Spanish writer Navarrus. The history of the neoclassical theory on the demand for money starts with the quantity theory of money by Fisher at the turn of the century. This theory, which is usually summarized as $MV = PT$, opposes the flow of money $MV$ to the flow of goods and services $PT$. This implies that the volume of current transactions determines the demand for money. In Fisher's theory, interest rates are irrelevant. This can presumably be ascribed to the fact that the classical quantity theory abstracted from financial transactions. This exclusion of wealth is a major difference with the closely related Cambridge variant of this classical quantity theory, which is often summarized as $M =$

$kPT$. This theory, known as the cash balance theory of, among others, Marshall, Pigou and Robertson, also paid explicit attention to money as a store of value. It was assumed implicitly that with regard to the cash ratio $k$, which is typical of this cash balance theory, a certain degree of dependence of interest rates could, in principle, not be ruled out. Furthermore, Fisher's presumption that velocity $V$ was only determined by technical factors was abandoned to some extent. The next important step in the development of the theory on the demand for money was Keynes' analysis of cash-holding behaviour with his famous three motives for holding money. This resulted in income, the bond rate, and wealth as explanatory variables. For practical reasons the latter is usually ignored in empirical research. The absence of the short-term interest rate as an explanatory variable was a purely practical matter as this rate was more or less constant in England in Keynes' days.

It should be noted that an unsatisfactory element of Keynes' distinction by liquidity motives is the fact that a means of payment can simultaneously serve all three motives. In this view, Friedman's reformulation of Fisher's quantity theory is a major step forward. He regarded the demand for money as a special case of the demand for goods and services. Consequently, Friedman's explanation does not differ substantially from those used in a general demand function for goods and services resulting from the general equilibrium framework. In this approach, the demand for money is as a matter of fact just one equation from a broad system of demand equations. Consequently, Friedman's theory was closely connected, in principle, to the portfolio approach of *e.g.* Tobin, developed in the vein of the general equilibrium approach mentioned above. By contrast to Friedman, Tobin's approach explicitly took restrictions into account resulting from the fact that total wealth must be allocated to some financial or real asset. In this view, money is the most liquid financial asset in the whole range of assets.

While the above-mentioned views can mostly be characterized as macroeconomic, a number of more microeconomically oriented theories with regard to the demand for money were formulated. An interesting approach is by MacCallum and Goodfriend (1988), who derived the demand for money within an intertemporal utility-maximization framework. The other theories were developed by Baumol and Tobin and focus notably on the demand for money by the business sector. Uncertainty was subsequently incorporated in these theories by *e.g.* Whalen or Miller and Orr, and these models found their way into finance theory. The special aspect of these approaches based on microeconomics is that they result in testable theoretical specifications. Unlike the research reported in the present chapter this interesting microeconomic line of empirical research is mainly based on cross-section data, but is beyond the scope of our survey which focuses on the macroeconomics of money demand.

In the research tradition of the demand for money the Keynesian liquidity preference theory and Friedman's general demand theory seem to offer the main building blocks. However, the two approaches differ strongly. Therefore, it is interesting to take a brief look at the fundamental differences between the two approaches. Keynes simplifies the world to two financial assets: money and bonds – serving as the aggregate for other financial assets – consequently using one interest rate as the determinant for this dichotomy. The focus of Friedman's theory is that money is considered one of many alternative assets within the spectrum of wealth. A whole set of interest rates and other prices is therefore used to explain the demand for money. Another major characteristic is that Keynes assumes only one substitute for money, whereas Friedman even considers real goods as substitutes. Consequently, by contrast to Keynes, interest rates play a less dominant role in Friedman's theory. A third difference is the prominent role played by wealth: in Friedman's theory this also includes human capital. Friedman actually underlaid his views empirically by using permanent income as an explanatory variable. In Keynes' theory, income plays the much more modest role as measure of the need for transactions.

As mentioned above, empirical research of the demand for money is one of the oldest research fields of econometrics in general and monetary econometrics in particular. The first studies were already published before World War II. It is therefore not surprising that the research on the demand for money shows an interesting life cycle from an econometric viewpoint. The survey articles mentioned above, and notably those by Boughton or Goldfeld and Sichel bear witness to this. In this historical evolution, four issues require special attention.

The first is the use of the so-termed partial adjustment hypothesis. When quarterly or monthly figures became available – the first studies on the demand for money used annual figures – the application of this mechanism gained importance. Its essence is that a distinction is made between the optimal demand for money and the actual demand. The latter might deviate from optimal demand, *i.e.* the demand assumed in theory, as a result of inertia in behaviour, lack of information and shortcomings in the actual efforts to achieve the optimal outcome. The key of the mechanism is the assumption that the actual size of the cash balance $m_t$ does not adjust instantaneously, but with a lag to the optimal cash balance $m^*$. To be more specific, the assumption is:

$$m_t - m_{t-1} = \lambda(f_t(y, r, \dots) - m_{t-1}) \quad \text{or:} \quad \Delta m_t = \lambda(m_t^* - m_{t-1})$$

with $0 \leq \lambda < 1$ the adjustment parameter and $m_t^* = f_t(y, r, \dots)$. By means of substitution the unobservable $m_t^*$ disappears, resulting in a demand for money in which $m$ also occurs with a lag. This formulation, in which the nominal or the real cash balance was used as the dependent variable, has served as the most important paradigm of empirical research of the demand for money for a long time. Nevertheless, this approach has some shortcomings. These shortcomings are notably of a technical-econometric nature with consequences for empirical results. These technical problems concern the restrictions implied by the above formulation, the unreliability and bias of the estimation results due to misspecification and the restrictive partial adjustment mechanism. This was also attended by the fundamental impossibility to estimate the demand for money formulated in the traditional manner in some cases, for instance when adaptive expectations and the partial adjustment mechanism were applied simultaneously. The relevant estimation problems have led to a less restrictive formulation of the lag structure in the demand for money, imposed by *e.g.* the Koyck-lag or the Almon-lag, which were popular notably in the early 1970s, and later the often used ARIMA-modelling. Consequently, explicit attention was paid to, among other things, seasonal sensitivity (see *e.g.* Butter and Fase (1981)). The result was, however, that the elegant theoretical motivation of the lag structure inspired by Koyck was lost. Feige (1967) presented a theoretical basis for this alternative approach to the lag structure by assuming the optimization of a loss function. Incidentally, the introduction of expectational variables according to the adaptive scheme also undermined this approach. In a number of studies, the rational expectations hypothesis was tested as an alternative to the adaptive expectations hypothesis. This forward-looking approach explicitly models the rational expectations of economic agents. A characteristic of this approach is that the parameter estimations obtained are independent of changes in the regime, thus accommodating the so-called Lucas critique.

The so-termed buffer-stock hypothesis was another, perhaps slightly artificial alternative. In the buffer-stock model – see *e.g.* Carr and Darby (1981) – unexpected shocks in the money supply are temporarily offset. In this view an accumulation of money takes place because economic agents temporarily deviate from their short-run optimal demand for money. According to this hypothesis, cash balances act as a buffer for discrepancies between the spontaneous demand for and supply of money on the road towards the equilibrium situation.

The second step in the evolution of the econometrics of the demand for money is the introduction of the error-correction mechanism and the related cointegration analysis. According to Granger's theorem (Engle and Granger 1987), the variables $x_t$ and $y_t$, are cointegrated if and only if an error-correction specification exists. Of course the generality of this lemma does not preclude cointegration analysis *per se*, although in small samples the analysis of static relationships frequently yields unreliable results (see *e.g.* Banerjee, Dolado, Hendry, and Smith (1986), Kremers, Ericsson, and Dolado (1992)). In Hendry's error-correction approach – see *e.g.* Hendry (1979) – an explicit distinction is made between an equilibrium situation applying in the long-run and the short-run dynamics. In spirit, this approach is related to the buffer-stock approach, albeit that the technical details differ fundamentally. In the short-run, deviations from the equilibrium path are explicitly allowed and modelled in the error-correction term. The so-called cointegration analysis statistically verifies the existence of the assumed equilibrium path. To illustrate this, assume that the long-run money demand relationship is as follows:

$$\ln m_t = \alpha_1 \ln y_t + \alpha_2 r_t$$

with $y$ income and $r$ the long-term interest rate. (For reasons of simplicity, we have abstracted here from the short-term interest rate and inflation as determinants of the demand for money.) A prerequisite for the existence of error-correction specification is the presence of cointegration. The error-correction formulation is a dynamic equation describing the change in the real money supply as a function of the changes of the explanatory variables plus the deviation from the equilibrium path with a one-period lag. This is illustrated by the following example:

$$\Delta \ln m_t = \beta_1 \Delta \ln y_t + \beta_2 \Delta r_t + \beta_3 (\ln m - \alpha_1 \ln y - \alpha_2 r)_{t-1}.$$

The last term in this equation is called the error-correction term in the cointegration literature.[1] Consequently, short-run deviations from the equilibrium equation, for instance cyclical influences on money-holding which are commonly used in Dutch studies on the demand for money – *cf.* Fase and Kuné (1974a), Fase and Winder (1990, 1993) – can easily be modelled within such a general specification.

Another important econometric innovation is the specification analysis which is related to the error-correction approach and cointegration

1 If desired, this equation may be rewritten as follows:

$$\Delta \ln m_t = \beta_1 \Delta y_t + \beta_2 \Delta r_t + \beta_3 (\ln m - \alpha_1 \ln y)_{t-1} + \gamma r_{t-1},$$

where $\gamma = -\beta_3 \alpha_2$. As is the case in a large number of studies, the term $(\ln m - \alpha_1 \ln y)_{t-1}$ – or $(\ln m - \ln y)_{t-1}$ if income elasticity is equal to 1 – may be assumed to be the error-correction term. Any divergence can be ascribed to differences in terminology. The interpretation in the text of the error-correction term as a deviation from the equilibrium path as used in our formula is somewhat broader than the interpretation given here, due to the fact that no restrictions are imposed on the parameters, while the interest rate is also included in the error-correction term.

analysis described above. For our purpose, however, this is an interesting side issue rather than a main issue. Nevertheless, this statistical and technical novelty has had an important impact on empirical research into the demand for money, rendering it possible to conduct more thorough analyses of the stability of the demand for money than before.

A third econometric innovation has been the research into the functional form. This field of attention, which was popular in the 1970s in particular, aimed at testing the type of demand for money specification: linear, loglinear and semi-loglinear. Basic to this approach was the so-termed Box–Cox transformation which was tested on the demand for money in the US by Zarembka (1968) and in The Netherlands by Butter and Kuné (1976). This type of research, often supporting the hypothesis of a loglinear demand for money specification, has presently disappeared completely from the stage, being superseded by the econometrically much more refined specification and cointegration tests mentioned above.

The old discussion whether money demand and supply should be estimated simultaneously underwent a similar fate. This is the fourth point of attention I would like to mention. Sometimes it is argued within this tradition that, in general, single equation estimations of the demand for money are insufficiently justified from an econometric viewpoint – for instance by Cooley and LeRoy (1981) and recently by Bomhoff (1991) – but these arguments have never really been found convincing as becomes evident from the practice of demand for money econometrics. This is, incidentally, in line with the modest attention paid within theoretical and applied econometrics to simultaneous estimation methods as well as with the fact that large-scale application of these methods has nowadays virtually fallen into disuse in econometric practice.

## 5.2 Empirical Survey of Demand for Money Studies in the G7 and EU

As mentioned before, the main objective of this chapter is to present a survey of empirical research over the past 20 years into the demand for money for the member states of the EU and the non-EU countries of the G 7. The countries of the G 7 were included not only to enlarge the sample, but also because most surveys focus rather one-sidedly on the US. In view of the strong tradition in the US of monetary regulation, this may explain the close attention paid to financial innovations. In Europe this phenomenon was clearly less evident. There is a danger, however, that focusing all attention on the US in this respect might have a distorting effect, as illustrated by the survey given in Judd and

Scadding (1982b).

The empirical demand for money studies surveyed in this chapter have been summarized into a number of tables of which only one example is shown in the appendix of this chapter.[2] This appendix also contains a table with a countrywise enumeration of the consulted research work. Given the large number of money demand studies examined, it is impossible to present an exhaustive survey here. However, a rather large number, *viz.* almost 400, has been considered for the present overview.

The 10 tables with estimation results of the demand for money in Fase (1993) cover a wide range of countries or areas – *viz.* The Netherlands, the US, Japan, Germany, France, the UK, Canada, Belgium, Denmark, Greece, Ireland, Italy, Spain, Portugal, as well as the EU as a whole – for the sake of brevity we only present the table for the multicountry studies here in Table 5.A.1.

This table successively indicates for each country considered the model and functional form used, the estimation period, the monetary aggregate used, and the long-run elasticities of real income, the price, short- and long-term interest rates, the inflation rate and any other additional variables included. Finally, the table reports the standard error of the regressions as a proximate measure of stability. It should be noted that it was not always possible to represent long-run elasticities in a numerical form. This is the case for instance with a semi-logarithmic demand for money specification. Usually, only the semi-elasticities in parametric form are shown then. The product of the semi-elasticity and this variable – *e.g.* interest or inflation rate – is equal to the elasticity.

In line with the modern quantity theory, in many studies the price level is not used as an explanatory variable; instead, the real money supply is used. If the implied restriction on the long-run price elasticity has been tested, a value of 1.0 appears in Table 5.A.1. The studies in which price homogeneity is not tested, but imposed *a priori*, have been indicated by $a^*$. Incidentally, examination of the real demand for money meets the Friedmanian interpretation of the demand for money which is confronted with the nominal supply of money to explain the general price level.

Table 5.A.1 presents an overview of the multicountry studies available. These concern studies on the demand for money, performed according to some fixed model specification for a number of countries with more or less uniform data, clearly revealing the actual differences between the countries. Large differences across countries are discernible. It is furthermore noteworthy that usually a relatively simple model has been

---

[2] For an extensive presentation the reader may wish to consult the full report by Fase (1993), available on request.

used – usually a static regression model – restricted mostly to income and one interest rate as the explanatory variables. As was to be expected, the error-correction model has only been applied in the most recent research papers. With regard to country groups, it must be noted that they usually concern the EU or the G 7.

The overview in Fase (1993) of the most important Dutch studies with regard to the demand for money over the past 20 years, conducted on the basis of quarterly data shows some interesting characteristics. In most studies, a broad monetary aggregate has been used; in a few cases the narrow monetary aggregate M 1 has been used or disaggregation by holdership has been applied. The large divergence in long-term interest rate elasticities is noteworthy. In studies of the demand for money by researchers of De Nederlandsche Bank, the use of a cyclical indicator as an explanatory variable must be noted. The gradual shift over time from the partial adjustment specification towards error-correction modelling is also interesting. This shift reflects the fact that research in The Netherlands has followed international research tendencies in this respect, without abandoning interest in the cyclical effects on the demand for money, which has always been typical of Dutch studies.

Studies on the aggregated 'European' demand for money characteristically regard Europe as one single country, the demand for money being estimated analogous to the studies on the demand for money in the individual countries. The results in Fase (1993) show that various aggregation techniques were considered and that the estimates obtained show remarkable differences depending on the aggregation method applied. Another striking characteristic is that a number of studies pay attention to the possible effects of currency substitution on the demand for money. In country studies this is often regarded as a source of instability of the demand for money. However, the relevant empirical findings usually do not support this point of view convincingly.

Classifying the 10 tables in Fase's (1993) appendix by country according to model type, functional form and monetary aggregate used, offers the basis for the schematic summary in our Table 5.1. This shows that for the 15 countries or country-sets considered here a total of 396 studies on the demand for money were collected. The majority of these country studies relate to the US, while France, the UK and Germany also account for a large number. With 34, The Netherlands and Japan score equally well in terms of numbers. For most other EU countries, about 10 studies are available.

As far as the *model formulation* is concerned, it is remarkable that the error-correction model is used most often, followed at a large distance by the partial adjustment model. In addition, and in line with the quantity

*Table 5.1: Schematic overview of estimations of the demand for money*

| Country | Number of | Model type | | | | | | | | | | Form | | | Monetary aggregate | | | |
|---|---|---|---|---|---|---|---|---|---|---|---|---|---|---|---|---|---|---|
| | equations | NPA | RPA | PA | BS | AE | FL | DL | EU | CO | SR | L | LL | SLL | M 1 | M 2 | M 3 | other |
| The Netherlands | 34 | 7 | 3 | 0 | 1 | 7 | 0 | 2 | 21 | 0 | 0 | 1 | 14 | 19 | 12 | 21 | 1 | 0 |
| United States | 75 | 9 | 25 | 1 | 5 | 2 | 0 | 9 | 21 | 5 | 0 | 0 | 42 | 33 | 46 | 23 | 0 | 6 |
| Japan | 34 | 0 | 19 | 0 | 5 | 3 | 0 | 0 | 10 | 0 | 0 | 0 | 11 | 23 | 17 | 17 | 0 | 0 |
| Germany | 49 | 3 | 22 | 2 | 5 | 4 | 0 | 2 | 13 | 0 | 2 | 0 | 3 | 46 | 27 | 3 | 18 | 1 |
| France | 50 | 3 | 19 | 2 | 5 | 1 | 0 | 3 | 14 | 0 | 4 | 0 | 12 | 38 | 23 | 17 | 10 | 0 |
| United Kingdom | 44 | 5 | 7 | 2 | 7 | 1 | 4 | 10 | 21 | 0 | 2 | 0 | 2 | 53 | 26 | 7 | 18 | 4 |
| Canada | 17 | 4 | 6 | 0 | 1 | 0 | 0 | 6 | 0 | 0 | 0 | 0 | 0 | 17 | 9 | 6 | 0 | 2 |
| Italy | 10 | 1 | 2 | 2 | 0 | 1 | 0 | 1 | 3 | 1 | 0 | 0 | 0 | 10 | 4 | 4 | 2 | 0 |
| Belgium | 15 | 7 | 2 | 0 | 0 | 0 | 0 | 1 | 5 | 0 | 0 | 0 | 8 | 7 | 7 | 5 | 2 | 1 |
| Denmark | 10 | 1 | 1 | 0 | 0 | 0 | 0 | 1 | 7 | 0 | 0 | 0 | 1 | 9 | 3 | 5 | 1 | 1 |
| Greece | 11 | 5 | 3 | 0 | 0 | 2 | 0 | 0 | 3 | 0 | 0 | 0 | 2 | 9 | 6 | 3 | 1 | 1 |
| Ireland | 8 | 1 | 2 | 0 | 1 | 1 | 0 | 1 | 3 | 0 | 0 | 1 | 1 | 6 | 4 | 2 | 2 | 0 |
| Spain | 6 | 0 | 0 | 2 | 0 | 0 | 0 | 0 | 4 | 0 | 0 | 0 | 0 | 6 | 2 | 1 | 1 | 2 |
| Portugal | 11 | 1 | 1 | 0 | 0 | 0 | 0 | 0 | 9 | 0 | 0 | 0 | 1 | 10 | 5 | 3 | 1 | 2 |
| Europe | 11 | 0 | 0 | 0 | 0 | 0 | 0 | 1 | 8 | 0 | 2 | 0 | 0 | 11 | 5 | 3 | 3 | 0 |
| | 396 | 47 | 112 | 11 | 30 | 22 | 4 | 37 | 142 | 6 | 10 | 2 | 97 | 297 | 196 | 120 | 60 | 20 |

*Notes:* Model type: AE = 'adaptive expectations', BS = 'buffer stock', CO = 'cointegration model', DL = 'distribution lag', EC = 'error-correction', FL = 'forward-looking model', NPA = 'nominal partial adjustment', RPA = 'real partial adjustment', PA = 'partial adjustment', SR = 'static regression'. Functional form: L = linear, LL = loglinear, SLL = semi-loglinear.

theory of money, application to the demand for money adjusted for price changes is the most frequent. Strictly speaking, application to the nominal demand for money is only correct insofar as testing of the assumption of price homogeneity comes first. In a number of cases – indicated in the scheme as PA – it has proven to be impossible to trace whether the estimation concerned the real or the nominal demand for money.

It is evident that, within the group of partial adjustment specifications the model type of real demand for money, which is best defendable on theoretical grounds, is the most commonly used, accounting for 112 applications. The buffer-stock model, which in fact comprises a hybrid of demand and supply elements and which is closely connected with the partial adjustment model in the sense that it also assumes temporary disequilibria, is used notably in money demand studies of the major G 7 countries, the UK in particular. Dynamic specification by assuming adaptive expectations is used less frequently than would be expected, given the criticism of this method. This also applies *mutatis mutandis* to the use of the rational expectations approach, which according to this scheme has only been tested in the UK. The more general dynamic specification without explicit economic-theoretical justification, including the Almon technique which was popular during the early 1970s, has also been applied frequently in demand for money studies for the UK. The error-correction model is most frequently used for six countries, with The Netherlands, the US and the UK jointly topping the list. The cointegration model, being a relatively new approach, has as yet only been applied in the US. The static specification is hardly applied any more. In view of the primitive character of this approach this is not surprising. Like the cointegration and the rational expectations models, this model is only used infrequently.

Where *functional form* is concerned, the lion's share of all studies opt for the semi-logarithmic specification. The major advantage of this specification is that the interest rate elasticity depends in part on the interest rate level, which seems plausible. This is presumably the main justification for this choice, which is not explained in most studies.

With regard to the *monetary aggregate* used, it must be noted that the number of studies decreases as a broader monetary aggregate is chosen: just 190 studies relate to M1, 120 to M2 and almost 60 to M3. It must be noted, however, that over time the attention has shifted from the narrow M1 to the broader monetary aggregates M2 and M3. This is undoubtedly related to the fading of boundaries, in practice, between the various short-term financial assets. The fact that studies on M1 are the most common in terms of numbers reflects that this shift in focus is still going on in the empirical demand for money research. This has become manifest most clearly in the major European countries and in Europe as a whole, but not yet in the US or Japan.

In addition to the angle considered above, in which the functional form of the demand for money is the central issue, a more substance-oriented approach can also be opted for, a case in point being the choice of the monetary aggregate used as already noted above. Moreover, an assessment of the estimation results or elasticities obtained and the aggregation level applied may offer an angle to gain some systematic insight into the numerous money demand studies shown here.

In view of the importance of the question whether real or nominal demand for money must be the focus of attention, the survey indicates that the majority of the reported studies simply use the requirement of price homogeneity as a starting point. This is done without paying too much attention to the question whether this assumption, which is testable, requires further examination. The fact that this always applies to studies for the US leads us to presume that, at least in the US, this is a lasting tradition. The fact that in some other studies – relating mainly to the UK and The Netherlands and in some of the reported multicountry studies – the assumption of price homogeneity is hardly supported, leads to the conclusion that the empirical basis of this hypothesis is weak and that money demand studies in this tradition must be regarded with some suspicion.

Where long-run income elasticity is concerned, the empirical results differ widely. At first sight, no systematic pattern shows up. However, on further examination of the frequency distribution of the income elasticities shown in Figure 5.1, a certain tendency is discernible towards an income elasticity of 1 with more downward than upward outliers. This is in conformity with the theory of the transactions demand. Particularly striking is that especially in the UK, for both the narrow and broad monetary aggregates, very high income elasticities of 1.5 or more are found. For the US – although this is not directly evident from the diagram – the opposite is true for M1.

With respect to interest rate elasticities, it becomes evident that irrespective of the monetary aggregate used, the elasticity for short-term interest rates is nearly always below that for long-term interest rates. This pattern manifests itself more sharply when, instead of M1, a broad monetary aggregate is used. However, large divergences are present within the estimates obtained, both by country and among the various countries. The same applies to the inflation rate elasticity. It is striking, however, that this is lower for M1 than for the broad monetary aggregate. The estimate found is usually closely in line with the short-

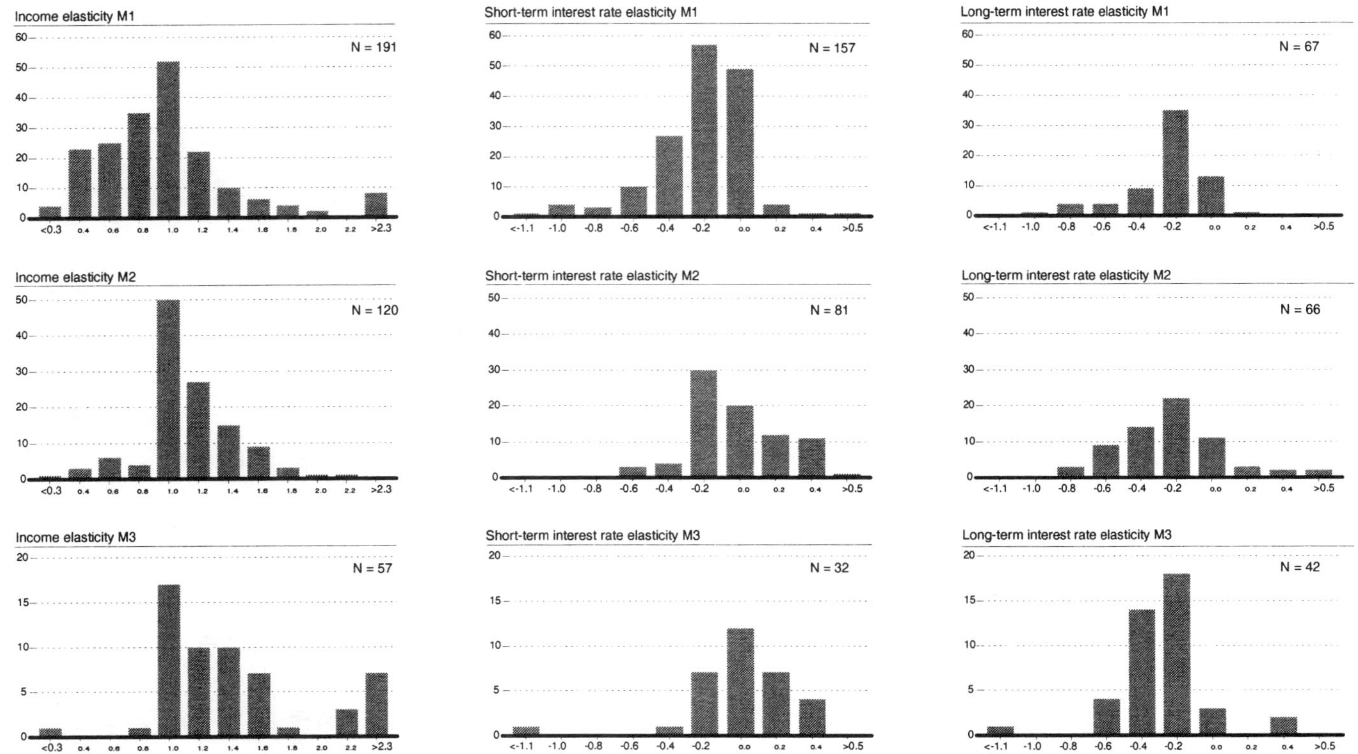


*Figure 5.1: Frequency distributions of money demand characteristics*

term interest rate elasticity. This seems a plausible result.

Inspection of the residual standard errors of the money demand equations – which is an alternative measure of stability – shows a similarly large variety in findings. In order to abstract from differences in model formulation and functional form, it serves to consider the multicountry studies, since they use a common model specification and methodology for a number of countries. The results in Table 5.A.1 indicate that among the large EU countries, Germany has the most stable money demand compared with *e.g.* the UK and France. Noteworthy is that the residual standard errors in money demand equations for the UK are often twice as large as the standard errors in Germany. The standard errors of French money demand equations are generally larger than for Germany, but smaller than those for the UK. Considering the various monetary aggregates individually reveals that in Germany the demand for broad money is generally more stable than the demand for narrow money. This regularity is also present in other countries and also found in earlier studies. For instance Fase and Winder (1993) find that for all EU countries the residual standard error in the M3 equations is smaller than in the M1 and M2 equations.

## 5.3 An Interpretation

An important question is what lessons may be drawn from the studies gathered here. It has become evident from this survey that the number of empirical money demand studies conducted is large. This is true for studies of both the countries of the EU and the G7 and for many studies within the countries considered. However, the survey shows that, even when more or less similar specifications are used, the variability between estimated elasticities is considerable. This is very well shown in Figure 5.1 with frequency distributions of money demand elasticities according to the monetary aggregate used. The resulting picture means that the present survey hardly shows any convergence of empirical findings, with clear outliers for certain coefficient values. This leads to the conclusion that the theoretical simplicity of the demand for money fades away in an empirical approach and raises doubts on the stability of estimates.

In Table 5.1 and Figure 5.1 the estimation results over almost two decades have been at the centre of our considerations. However, over the years statistical models generating the estimation results show a slow evolution which may be summarized – using the terminology of Hendry and Starr (1993) – as general-to-simple models. The authors reviewed here did not follow this approach and this perhaps may bias the picture presented here. To illustrate this, recall that perhaps the most important econometric innovation has been Hendry's model encompassing technique, which was particularly developed to detect misspecification. This shows that a number – but not all – estimated demand for money equations show specification errors and thus produce misleading results. Though this is an important issue, we do not believe that it will bias either our findings of Table 5.1 or Figure 5.1 seriously.

A second remarkable conclusion which might be drawn from this empirical survey – which certainly applies by country – is that the continuous divergence in estimation results does not in the least indicate the existence of a systematic empirical relationship. The question immediately arises whether the extensive focus on this aspect of money demand is justified or whether it should be regarded as a wandering from the initial objective of empirical research on the demand for money: a statistical estimation or verification of a behavioural equation resulting from a well-developed theory. The survey further suggests that this was attended by progressing econometric refinement without leading to a substantial enhancement of actual economic insight. Be that as it may, the survey presented here renders it clear that empirical results differ widely. In the quest for demand for money stability this arouses at least some doubts with regard to the findings in respect of this key focus of research into the demand for money.

A third conclusion is that – according to the size of the residual standard errors of the money demand equations – money demand in Germany is relatively stable compared to other EU countries. Obviously, a highly integrated world reduces the scope for an independent monetary policy in small countries strongly. The possibilities for pursuing a policy of monetary targeting are also limited for larger EU countries, due to their relatively unstable money demand. Controlling money supply in the individual countries may be important, however, to avoid putting a spoke in the Bundesbank's wheel. The reviewed studies also indicate that the demand for broad money is generally more stable than the demand for narrow money. This finding is supportive for monetary practice in Germany, which focuses on the broad money concept, and is well in line with the view, advocated by Friedman for instance, that money is a particular component of wealth.

The fourth remarkable aspect resulting from this survey is the steady progress in refinement of the empirical analysis. This refinement refers to both the aggregation level and the methodology used and can presumably be ascribed to dissatisfaction with the estimation results obtained initially. This may also be the reason why additional explanatory variables were included in numerous studies. An exception may be the inclusion of the cyclical variable, which is justified by the first formulation of the neoclassical quantity theory of money with a velocity sensitive to the level of economic activity.[3] However, as becomes evident from this survey, only a limited number of studies dares to tackle this well-known phenomenon in an empirical manner. An interesting question is why most studies hesitate to pay attention to this aspect, the more so as the introduction of the error-correction mechanism renders it possible to make a sharp empirical distinction between cyclical fluctuations and long-run relationships. Incidentally, it must be noted that the econometric refinement indicated here requires ever-longer time series, reducing the possibilities for the classical stability analysis.

Fifth, on the basis of an analysis of the frequency distributions and the various income elasticities by country, it follows that notably in the US, the income elasticity of M1 deviates markedly from that in other countries; most elasticities in the US centre around the low level of 0.7 (lower elasticities have been found only for France, for which, incidentally, fewer studies were available). This implies that in the US, and to a lesser degree in France, marked economies of scale occur with regard to M1-holdings. This contrasts sharply with the situation in *e.g.* Germany, the UK, The Netherlands or the EU as a whole. A possible interpretation might be that in the US, more than anywhere else, M1 serves mainly transaction motives.

Sixth, our survey shows that for The Netherlands, the US and the UK a disaggregated money demand analysis by sector has been conducted in a number of cases. This analysis reveals marked differences in underlying behaviour. Most striking, however, is that in the US and in the UK, interest in this disaggregated money demand has presently disappeared almost completely, despite the ample availability of data. In The Netherlands, on the other hand, this focus on sectoral disaggregation is of recent date, which can be ascribed particularly to the availability of the relevant data.

Another issue – the seventh point of our attention – is the virtual absence of wealth as an explanatory variable in the single money demand equations. This is all the more surprising as modern monetary theory considers the demand for money to be an element of a portfolio allocation process. This absence of wealth as an explanatory variable can be ascribed undoubtedly in part to the lack of time series data on wealth. The few studies which do take the concept of wealth into consideration,

---

[3] This concerns a refinement which is typical of The Netherlands. See Verrijn Stuart (1953), Kessler (1958), Stevers (1963), Dierick (1967), Fase and Kuné (1974a).

albeit indirectly – see *e.g.* Fase and Winder (1990, pp. 297–299), and Sterken (1992) – imply that this extension might help to explain the decreasing transactions velocity of money since the 1980s. This justifies an intensification of this line of research.

As far as the aggregation level is concerned – the eighth point of attention in this survey – it is noteworthy that, on the one hand, refinement by ownership is tested whereas, on the other hand, globalization by countries is apparent. One may wonder whether this is not a slightly contradictory development. Certainly, the main inspiration is the sustained search for a stable demand for money equation. A definite answer to this question cannot as yet be given. This does not, however, diminish the contradiction found here. For the time being, it appears that multicountry studies reveal more evidence for the stability of the demand for money than studies aggregated across countries. This finding may be due to the fact that in the former group a measure for stability may easily be formulated permitting immediate mutual comparison.

An interesting question, the ninth point of attention, is whether the elasticities to be calculated from the various demand for money studies in the EU member states present a view which corresponds with the estimations for EMU which are already available. For this purpose, Table 5.2 combines a number of elasticities for the demand for M3 in the EU. These elasticities are calculated on the basis of the empirical country studies collected here and are compared to earlier research by others or ourselves.

It is noteworthy that the average income elasticity calculated by us is virtually the same as that found by Monticelli and Strauss-Kahn and nearly 40% higher than that of Fase and Winder, who after testing assume the income elasticity to be one. This may be too restrictive. On

*Table 5.2: Average long-term elasticities for the demand for* M3 *in the EU*

| | Income | Price | Short-term interest rate | Long-term interest rate | Inflation |
|---|---|---|---|---|---|
| Calculated average | 1.38 | 0.96 | 0.02 | −0.28 | −0.12 |
| Fase and Winder (1993) | 1.00 | 0.97 | 0.05* | −0.12* | −0.12* |
| Monticelli and Strauss-Kahn (1992) | 1.33 | - | −0.04 | – | – |

*Notes:* * Short- and long-term interest rates are assumed at 5% and 6% respectively and the inflation rate is assumed at 6% per annum.

the other hand, Monticelli and Strauss-Kahn's money demand equation is so much more restricted that further comparisons are impossible. The other elasticities are more or less in line with each other. This is also the general picture when another country group – for instance Germany and the Benelux – or when M 1 or M 2 are taken into consideration. It appears that the divergences from the aggregate country studies disappear when average elasticities are used in weighting with, for instance, GDP.

An important issue and the last point of attention in this survey concerns the type of money demand which is most desirable within the context of EMU: by country or aggregate demand for EMU. Advocates of the aggregated approach – Beckx and Tullio, Kremers and Lane, Monticelli and Strauss-Khan and Lane and Poloz – stress the fact that in this approach the question of currency substitution can be treated systematically, causing the stability of the demand for money to increase. For the time being, however, this characteristic has not become convincingly evident from the studies available. Moreover, it is not clear whether this assumed gain in stability compensates for the aggregation bias, that is to say the sensitivity of the estimation results for the method of aggregation.

## 5.4 Conclusion

There are several ways to study stability of an equation in general and the demand for money equation in particular. For some time testing the constancy of the estimated coefficients over time has been fashionable and for that purpose a whole bunch of statistical tests have been developed. Examining residual errors has been popular for some time too and *e.g.* Fase and Winder (1993) employed this approach to examine the relative stability of money demand in Germany and The Netherlands (or the Benelux countries). However, a very natural way to proceed on this issue is perhaps just to study estimation results drawn from various research fields, *i.e.* frequency distributions of comparable estimates. We believe this to be a useful and effective method, as this chapter illustrates.

The most important conclusion is that our survey presents little explicit indication for the stability of the demand for money. It has become evident that a large diversity of estimation results exists, even when studies are restricted to one country or a group of countries. Among European countries, however, Germany has a relatively stable money demand. The survey also indicates that the demand for broad money is frequently more stable than the demand for narrow money.

The question arises whether this finding implies that there is little ground, for the time being, to presume that a stable demand for money exists. Perhaps this important question deserves additional attention here. The next question immediately arising is whether this is crucial and whether searching for a stable demand for money is as useful as tradition would have us believe. Money control policy primarily focuses on the supply side and is aimed at achieving the desired monetary developments. These elements together are decisive for the predictability and controllability of the money stock as it results from supply and demand. Stability of the demand for money may admittedly facilitate an assessment of the path to be followed, but no more than that. The above survey shows that the range of estimates collected at least raises doubts with regard to the robustness of the parameters of the money demand. However, stability of the demand for money is only one element of the conditions for a successful money supply policy. The degree of controllability of the supply of money and its independence of the factors determining the demand for money are of major importance too. It is not inconceivable that the various other elements combined may lead to a controllable and predictable development of the money stock.

## Appendix 5.A

*Table 5.A.1: Multicountry studies*[4]

| Study | Model[a] | Functional form[b] | Country[c] | Estimation period | Monetary aggregate |
|---|---|---|---|---|---|
| Canarella and Roseman (1978) | RFA | ll | B | 1957–1972 | M1 |
| | | | Den | 1957–1972 | M1 |
| | | | G | 1957–1972 | M1 |
| | | | F | 1957–1972 | M1 |
| | | | Ire | 1957–1972 | M1 |
| | | | N | 1957–1972 | M1 |
| | | | P | 1957–1972 | M1 |
| Carr and Darby (1981) | BS | sll | US | 1957:I–1976:IV | M1 |
| | | | J | 1957:I–1976:IV | M1 |
| | | | G | 1957:I–1976:IV | M1 |
| | | | F | 1957:I–1976:IV | M1 |
| | | | UK | 1957:I–1976:IV | M1 |
| | | | C | 1957:I–1976:IV | M1 |
| | | | I | 1957:I–1976:IV | M1 |
| | | | N | 1957:I–1976:IV | M1 |
| Boughton (1981) | RPA | sll | J | 1960:I–1977:IV | M1 |
| | | | G | 1960:I–1977:IV | M1 |
| | | | F | 1960:I–1977:IV | M1 |
| | | | UK | 1960:I–1977:IV | M1 |
| | | | C | 1960:I–1977:IV | M1 |
| | | | US | 1960:I–1977:IV | M2 |
| | | | J | 1960:I–1977:IV | M2 |
| | | | G | 1960:I–1977:IV | M3 |
| | | | F | 1960:I–1977:IV | M2 |
| | | | C | 1960:I–1977:IV | M2 |
| Butter and Fase (1981) | DL | sll | B | 1961:IV–1976:IV | M2 |
| | | | Den | 1971:I–1976:IV | M2 |
| | | | G | 1960:I–1976:IV | M2 |
| | | | F | 1960:IV–1976:IV | M2 |
| | | | Ire | 1963:I–1973:IV | M2 |
| | | | I | 1962:II–1976:IV | M2 |
| | | | N | 1960:I–1976:IV | M2 |
| | | | UK | 1964:IV–1970:IV | M2 |

[4] For the detailed table the reader may wish to consult the appendix in Fase (1993).

| Long-term elasticities | | | | | Additional variables | SE of regression ($\times 10^{-2}$) |
|---|---|---|---|---|---|---|
| Income (real) | Price | Short-term interest rate[i] | Long-term interest rate[i] | Inflation[i] | | |
| 1.39 | * | – | −0.68 | – | – | – |
| 1.12 | * | – | −0.10 | – | – | – |
| 0.86 | * | – | −0.16 | – | – | – |
| 1.23 | * | – | −0.86 | – | – | – |
| 1.46 | * | – | −0.85 | – | – | – |
| 1.06 | * | – | −0.32 | – | – | – |
| 1.01 | * | – | −0.51 | – | – | – |
| 1.87[d] | * | $-0.30r_k$ | – | – | – | 0.40 |
| 1.15[d] | * | $-0.16r_k$ | – | – | – | 1.30 |
| 0.87[d] | * | $-0.00r_k$ | – | – | – | 0.74 |
| 2.32[d] | * | $-0.36r_k$ | – | – | – | 0.98 |
| −1.27[d] | * | $-0.70r_k$ | – | – | – | 1.21 |
| 0.72[d] | * | $-0.04r_k$ | – | – | – | 1.35 |
| 1.73[d] | * | $0.01r_k$ | – | – | – | 1.10 |
| 0.91[d] | * | $0.01r_k$ | – | – | – | 1.47 |
| 1.07 | * | – | −0.38 | $-0.004\dot{p}$ | – | 1.44 |
| 1.07 | * | −0.05 | −0.07 | $-0.001\dot{p}$ | Euro-dollar rate | 0.72 |
| 0.92 | * | −0.37 | – | $-0.004\dot{p}$ | – | 1.25 |
| 1.32 | * | −0.51 | – | $-0.003\dot{p}$ | – | 1.38 |
| 0.79 | * | −0.19 | – | $-0.001\dot{p}$ | – | 1.26 |
| 1.20 | * | −0.11 | – | $-0.003\dot{p}$ | – | 0.42 |
| 1.00 | * | – | −0.46 | $-0.006\dot{p}$ | – | 0.56 |
| 1.51 | * | – | −0.40 | $-0.010\dot{p}$ | – | 0.81 |
| 1.26 | * | −0.51 | −0.55 | $-0.011\dot{p}$ | – | 0.85 |
| 1.57 | * | −0.09 | – | $-0.003\dot{p}$ | Euro-dollar rate | 0.97 |
| 1.09 | * | −0.31 | – | – | | 0.22 |
| 1.58 | * | −0.16 | – | $-0.009\dot{p}$ | | 0.36 |
| 1.21 | * | −0.20 | – | – | | 0.34 |
| 1.61 | * | −0.26 | – | $-0.001\dot{p}$ | cyclical variable | 0.25 |
| 1.41 | * | – | – | $-0.014\dot{p}$ | | 0.70 |
| 1.78 | * | −0.12 | – | – | | 0.43 |
| 1.19 | * | −0.30 | – | $-0.015\dot{p}$ | | 0.18 |
| 1.89 | * | −0.18 | – | $-0.005\dot{p}$ | | 0.60 |

*Table 5.A.1: Multicountry studies (continued)*

| Study | Model[a] | Functional form[b] | Country[c] | Estimation period | Monetary aggregate |
|---|---|---|---|---|---|
| Atkinson *et al.*, (1984) | RFA + AE RPA | sll | US | 1973–1983:I | M2 |
| | | | J | 1973–1983:I | M1 |
| | | | G | 1973–1983:I | M3 |
| | | | F | 1973–1983:I | M2 |
| | | | UK | 1972–1983:I | M1 |
| | | | C | 1970–1983:I | M1A |
| | | | I | 1973–1983:I | M1 |
| Fair (1987) | NPA | sll | US | 1954:I–1986:II | M1 |
| | | | US | 1954:I–1986:II | M1[h] |
| | RPA | | J | 1966:I–1985:IV | M1[b] |
| | NPA | | G | 1969:I–1985:IV | M1[b] |
| | | | F | 1964:I–1985:IV | M1[b] |
| | | | UK | 1958:I–1986:I | M1[b] |
| | | | C | 1962:I–1985:IV | M1[b] |
| | | | I | 1971:I–1985:III | M1[b] |
| | | | Den | 1969:I–1984:IV | M1[b] |
| | | | N | 1961:I–1984:IV | M1[b] |
| | RPA | | B | 1961:I–1984:IV | M1[b] |
| | NPA | | Ire | 1961:I–1984:IV | M1[b] |
| | | | P | 1961:I–1983:IV | M1[b] |
| | | | Gr | 1961:I–1984:IV | M1[b] |
| Boughton and Tavlas (1990) | RPA | sll | US | 1973:I–1985:IV | M1 |
| | | | J | 1973:I–1985:IV | M1 |
| | | | D | 1973:I–1985:IV | M1 |
| | | | F | 1973:I–1985:IV | M1 |
| | | | UK | 1974:III–1985:IV | M1 |
| | | | US | 1973:I–1985:IV | M2 |
| | | | J | 1973:I–1985:IV | M2+CDs |
| | | | G | 1973:I–1985:IV | M3 |
| | | | F | 1973:I–1985:IV | M2 |
| | | | UK | 1974:III–1985:IV | M3 |
| | BS | sll | US | 1973:I–1985:IV | M1 |
| | | | J | 1973:I–1984:IV | M1 |
| | | | G | 1973:I–1985:IV | M1 |
| | | | F | 1973:I–1985:IV | M1 |
| | | | UK | 1974:III–1985:IV | M1 |

| Long-term elasticities | | | | | Additional variables | SE of regression ($\times 10^{-2}$) |
|---|---|---|---|---|---|---|
| Income (real) | Price | Short-term interest rate[i] | Long-term interest rate[i] | Inflation[i] | | |
| 0.95 | * | −0.07 | – | −0.11[e] | – | 0.70 |
| 0.37 | * | −0.13 | – | −0.06[e] | – | 1.40 |
| 1.62 | * | −0.11 | – | – | – | 0.90 |
| 0.99 | * | −0.11 | – | – | – | 1.00 |
| 0.87 | * | −0.48 | – | – | – | 2.20 |
| 0.56 | * | −0.26 | – | – | – | 1.70 |
| 1.13 | * | −0.42 | – | – | – | 1.70 |
| 0.80 | * | $-0.050r_k$ | – | – | population as deflator for M and $Y$ | 1.40 |
| 1.05 | * | $-0.138r_k$ | – | – | | 2.37 |
| 0.76 | * | $-0.063r_k$ | – | – | | 2.28 |
| 1.19 | * | $-0.018r_k$ | – | – | | 1.28 |
| 0.36 | * | $-0.007r_k$ | – | – | | 2.15 |
| 1.70 | * | $-0.061r_k$ | – | – | | 2.23 |
| 0.98 | * | $-0.073r_k$ | – | – | | 2.82 |
| 1.88 | * | $-0.052r_k$ | – | – | | 1.88 |
| 1.67 | * | $-0.019r_k$ | – | – | | 3.70 |
| 0.71 | * | $-0.015r_k$ | – | – | | 1.83 |
| 0.41 | * | $-0.036r_k$ | – | – | | 1.93 |
| 1.48 | * | $-0.090r_k$ | – | – | | 3.10 |
| 0.95 | * | $-0.027r_k$ | – | – | | 3.22 |
| 1.25 | * | $-0.010r_k$ | – | – | | 3.89 |
| 10.00 | * | $-0.020r_k$ | – | – | – | 0.83 |
| 0.62 | * | $-0.001r_k$ | – | – | – | 1.23 |
| 1.23 | * | $-0.002r_k$ | – | – | – | 1.02 |
| 0.42 | * | – | $-0.001r_l$ | – | – | 1.09 |
| 2.75 | * | $-0.009r_k$ | – | – | – | 1.85 |
| 1.50 | * | $-0.003r_k$ | – | – | – | 0.87 |
| 1.45 | * | $-0.001r_k$ | – | – | – | 0.93 |
| 1.15 | * | $0.002r_k$ | $-0.004r_l$ | – | – | 1.25 |
| 1.30 | * | $-0.000r_k$ | – | – | – | 0.66 |
| 3.71 | * | $-0.001r_k$ | – | – | – | 1.73 |
| 2.75 | * | $-0.005r_k$ | – | – | – | 0.74 |
| 0.68 | * | $-0.001r_k$ | – | – | – | 1.20 |
| 1.36 | * | $-0.002r_k$ | – | – | – | 0.84 |
| 0.41 | * | – | $-0.001r_l$ | – | – | 1.04 |
| 2.44 | * | $-0.006r_k$ | – | – | – | 1.81 |

*Table 5.A.1: Multicountry studies (continued)*

| Study | Model[a] | Functional form[b] | Country[c] | Estimation period | Monetary aggregate |
|---|---|---|---|---|---|
| | | | US | 1973:I–1985:IV | M2 |
| | | | J | 1973:I–1985:IV | M2+CDs |
| | | | G | 1973:I–1985:IV | M3 |
| | | | F | 1980:I–1985:IV | M2 |
| | | | UK | 1974:III–1985:IV | M3 |
| | EC | sll | US | 1973:I–1985:IV | M2 |
| | | | J | 1973:IV –1985:IV | M1 |
| | | | J | 1973:II –1985:IV | M2 |
| | | | G | 1973:III–1985:IV | M3 |
| | | | F | 1974:I–1985:IV | M1 |
| | | | UK | 1974:IV –1985:IV | M1 |
| | | | UK | 1973:I–1985:IV | M3 |
| Domowitz and Hakkio (1990) | EC | sll | US | 1961:III–1972:IV | M1 |
| | | | G | 1961:III–1972:IV | M1 |
| | | | F | 1961:III–1972:IV | M1 |
| | | | UK | 1961:III–1972:IV | M1 |
| | | | US | 1977:I–1985:I | M1 |
| | | | G | 1977:I–1985:I | M1 |
| | | | F | 1977:I–1985:I | M1 |
| | | | UK | 1977:I–1985:I | M1 |
| Boughton (1991) | EC | sll | US | 1964:I–1988:IV | M1 |
| | | | J | 1964:I–1988:IV | M1 |
| | | | G | 1964:I–1988:IV | M1 |
| | | | F | 1964:I–1988:IV | M1 |
| | | | UK | 1964:I–1988:IV | M1 |
| | | | US | 1964:I–1988:IV | M2 |
| | | | J | 1964:I–1988:IV | M2 |
| | | | G | 1964:I–1988:IV | M3 |
| | | | F | 1964:I–1988:IV | M2 |
| | | | UK | 1964:I–1988:IV | M3 |
| Boughton and Tavlas (1991) | RPA | sll | US | 1965:I–1988:IV | M1 |
| | | | J | 1965:I–1988:IV | M1 |
| | | | G | 1965:I–1988:IV | M1 |
| | | | F | 1965:I–1988:IV | M1 |
| | | | UK | 1965:I–1988:IV | M1 |

| Long-term elasticities | | | | | Additional variables | SE of regression ($\times 10^{-2}$) |
|---|---|---|---|---|---|---|
| Income (real) | Price | Short-term interest rate[i] | Long-term interest rate[i] | Inflation[i] | | |
| 1.43 | * | $-0.001r_k$ | – | – | – | 0.54 |
| 1.57 | * | $-0.001r_k$ | – | – | – | 0.85 |
| 1.11 | * | $-0.001r_k$ | $-0.003r_l$ | – | – | 1.17 |
| 1.34 | * | $-0.000r_k$ | – | – | – | 0.67 |
| 5.20 | * | $0.020r_k$ | – | – | – | 1.66 |
| 0.65 | 1.10 | $-0.007r_k$ | $-0.000r_l$ | – | – | 0.40 |
| 1.00 | 0.50 | $0.023r_k$ | $-0.049r_l$ | – | – | 1.01 |
| 1.31 | 1.00 | $0.029r_k$ | $-0.036r_l$ | – | – | 0.58 |
| – | 1.53 | $0.035r_k$ | $-0.055r_l$ | – | – | 0.70 |
| 0.43 | 1.00 | $0.007r_k$ | $-0.014r_l$ | – | – | 0.56 |
| – | 0.87 | $0.035r_k$ | $-0.041r_l$ | – | – | 1.02 |
| 2.53 | 0.66 | $0.025r_k$ | $-0.048r_l$ | – | – | 0.87 |
| 0.76 | * | $-0.030r_k$ | – | $-0.011\dot{p}$ | | - |
| 1.23 | * | $-0.015r_k$ | – | $-0.003\dot{p}$ | | - |
| 0.86 | * | $-0.008r_k$ | – | $-0.006\dot{p}$ | anticipated | - |
| 0.57 | * | $-0.046r_k$ | – | $-0.002\dot{p}$ | exchange | - |
| 0.20 | * | $-0.023r_k$ | – | $-0.003\dot{p}$ | rate | - |
| −2.15 | * | $-0.030r_k$ | – | $-0.004\dot{p}$ | change[f] | - |
| 0.19 | * | $-0.010r_k$ | – | $-0.001\dot{p}$ | | - |
| 1.66 | * | $-0.031r_k$ | – | $-0.004\dot{p}$ | | - |
| 1.34 | 0.65 | $0.015r_k$ | $-0.030r_l$ | – | – | 0.66 |
| 0.83 | 0.83 | – | $-0.026r_l$ | – | – | 1.42 |
| 1.20 | 1.00 | $0.025r_k$ | $-0.015r_l$ | – | – | 1.19 |
| 0.43 | 1.00 | $-0.012r_k$ | $0.010r_l$ | – | – | 2.34 |
| 3.33 | 1.00 | $-0.103r_k$ | – | – | – | 1.43 |
| 1.00 | 1.00 | $-0.008r_k$ | – | – | – | 0.51 |
| 1.60 | 0.39 | $0.018r_k$ | $-0.056r_l$ | – | – | 0.42 |
| 2.24 | 0.42 | $0.022r_k$ | $-0.032r_l$ | – | – | 0.73 |
| 1.97 | 0.69 | $-0.013r_k$ | – | – | – | 1.34 |
| 3.28 | 0.70 | – | $-0.034r_l$ | – | – | 1.63 |
| 0.77 | 1.00 | $-0.040r_k$ | – | – | – | 0.81 |
| 0.60 | 1.00 | $-0.070r_k$ | – | – | – | 1.72 |
| 1.17 | 1.00 | $-0.030r_k$ | – | – | – | 1.35 |
| 0.46 | 1.00 | $-0.011r_k$ | – | – | – | 2.86 |
| 3.42 | 1.00 | $-0.134r_k$ | – | – | – | 1.78 |

*Table 5.A.1: Multicountry studies (continued)*

| Study | Model[a] | Functional form[b] | Country[c] | Estimation period | Monetary aggregate |
|---|---|---|---|---|---|
| | | | US | 1965:I–1988:IV | M2 |
| | | | J | 1965:I–1988:IV | M2 |
| | | | G | 1965:I–1988:IV | M3 |
| | | | F | 1965:I–1988:IV | M2 |
| | | | UK | 1965:I–1988:IV | M3 |
| | BS | sll | US | 1965:I–1985:IV | M1 |
| | | | J | 1965:I–1985:IV | M1 |
| | | | G | 1965:I–1985:IV | M1 |
| | | | F | 1965:I–1985:IV | M1 |
| | | | UK | 1965:I–1985:IV | M1 |
| | | | US | 1965:I–1985:IV | M2 |
| | | | J | 1965:I–1985:IV | M2 |
| | | | G | 1965:I–1985:IV | M3 |
| | | | F | 1965:I–1985:IV | M2 |
| | | | UK | 1965:I–1985:IV | M3 |
| | EC | sll | US | 1964:I–1985:IV | M1 |
| | | | J | 1973:I–1985:IV | M1 |
| | | | G | 1964:I–1985:IV | M1 |
| | | | F | 1964:I–1985:IV | M1 |
| | | | UK | 1964:I–1985:IV | M1 |
| | | | US | 1964:I–1985:IV | M2 |
| | | | J | 1964:I–1985:IV | M2 |
| | | | G | 1964:I–1985:IV | M3 |
| | | | F | 1964:I–1985:IV | M2 |
| | | | UK | 1964:I–1985:IV | M3 |
| Fase and Winder (1993) | EC | sll | B | 1971:III–1989:IV | M1 |
| | | | Den | 1971:II–1989:IV | M1 |
| | | | G | 1971:I–1989:IV | M1 |
| | | | F | 1971:II–1989:IV | M1 |
| | | | Gr | 1971:II–1989:IV | M1 |
| | | | Ire | 1971:III–1989:IV | M1 |
| | | | I | 1971:I–1989:IV | M1 |
| | | | N | 1971:I–1989:IV | M1 |
| | | | P | 1971:I–1989:IV | M1 |
| | | | S | 1971:II–1989:IV | M1 |
| | | | UK | 1971:II–1989:IV | M1 |
| | | | B | 1971:II–1989:IV | M2 |

| Long-term elasticities | | | | | Additional variables | SE of regression ($\times 10^{-2}$) |
|---|---|---|---|---|---|---|
| Income (real) | Price | Short-term interest rate[i] | Long-term interest rate[i] | Inflation[i] | | |
| 1.03 | 1.00 | $-0.032r_k$ | $0.024r_l$ | — | — | 0.69 |
| 1.12 | 1.00 | — | $-0.062r_l$ | — | — | 1.06 |
| 1.35 | 1.00 | $-0.025r_k$ | — | — | — | 1.15 |
| 1.28 | 1.00 | — | $-0.029r_l$ | — | — | 1.73 |
| 4.25 | 1.00 | — | $-0.152r_l$ | — | — | 2.38 |
| 0.72 | 1.00 | $-0.036r_k$ | — | — | — | 0.74 |
| 0.51 | 1.00 | $-0.078r_k$ | — | — | — | 1.59 |
| 1.17 | 1.00 | $-0.033r_k$ | — | — | — | 1.29 |
| 0.49 | 1.00 | $-0.015r_k$ | — | — | — | 2.66 |
| 3.08 | 1.00 | $-0.123r_k$ | — | — | — | 1.77 |
| 0.95 | 1.00 | $-0.036r_k$ | $0.028r_l$ | — | — | 0.66 |
| 1.09 | 1.00 | — | $-0.058r_l$ | — | — | 0.93 |
| 1.33 | 1.00 | $-0.021r_k$ | — | — | — | 1.12 |
| 1.27 | 1.00 | — | $-0.027r_l$ | — | — | 1.66 |
| 3.35 | 1.00 | — | $-0.114r_l$ | — | — | 2.36 |
| 1.46 | 0.54 | — | — | — | — | 0.56 |
| 0.89 | 0.42 | — | $-0.028r_l$ | — | — | 0.97 |
| 1.00 | 1.00 | — | $-0.071r_l$ | — | — | 1.11 |
| 0.47 | 1.00 | $-0.008r_k$ | — | — | — | 2.48 |
| 3.85 | 1.00 | $-0.166r_k$ | — | — | — | 1.32 |
| 1.00 | 1.00 | $-0.007r_k$ | — | — | — | 0.50 |
| 1.65 | 0.35 | $-0.024r_k$ | $-0.061r_l$ | — | — | 0.44 |
| 2.51 | 0.25 | $-0.016r_k$ | $-0.033r_l$ | — | — | 0.78 |
| 2.20 | 0.56 | — | — | — | — | 1.29 |
| 3.79 | 0.55 | — | — | — | — | 1.72 |
| 1.00 | 0.59 | −0.11 | −0.12 | −0.07 | | 1.20 |
| 1.00 | 1.24 | −0.21 | −0.26 | −0.14 | | 2.00 |
| 1.00 | 1.00 | −0.18 | −0.21 | −0.06 | | 1.10 |
| 1.00 | 0.82 | −0.04 | −0.04 | −0.03 | | 1.00 |
| 1.00 | 1.00 | −0.28 | — | −0.32 | | 2.80 |
| 1.00 | 0.73 | −0.13 | −0.15 | −0.10 | cyclical | 1.90 |
| 1.00 | 0.87 | −0.15 | — | −0.11 | variable[g] | 1.60 |
| 1.00 | 0.84 | −0.20 | −0.23 | −0.14 | | 2.00 |
| 1.00 | 0.85 | −0.16 | −0.17 | −0.17 | | 2.60 |
| 1.00 | 0.83 | −0.13 | −0.13 | −0.12 | | 1.20 |
| 1.00 | 1.00 | −0.27 | −0.30 | −0.25 | | 2.60 |
| 1.00 | 1.00 | 0.38 | −0.39 | −0.23 | | 1.40 |

*Table 5.A.1: Multicountry studies (continued)*

| Study | Model[a] | Functional form[b] | Country[c] | Estimation period | Monetary aggregate |
|---|---|---|---|---|---|
| | | | Den | 1975:IV–1989:IV | M2 |
| | | | G | 1971:II–1989:IV | M2 |
| | | | F | 1971:II–1989:IV | M2 |
| | | | Gr | 1971:I–1989:IV | M2 |
| | | | Ire | 1971:III–1988:IV | M2 |
| | | | I | 1971:III–1989:IV | M2 |
| | | | N | 1971:II–1989:IV | M2 |
| | | | P | 1977:IV–1988:IV | M2 |
| | | | S | 1971:II–1989:IV | M2 |
| | | | UK | 1971:II–1989:II | M2 |
| | | | B | 1971:II–1989:IV | M3 |
| | | | Den | 1975:III–1989:IV | M3 |
| | | | G | 1971:II–1989:IV | M3 |
| | | | F | 1971:I–1989:IV | M3 |
| | | | Gr | 1971:I–1989:IV | M3 |
| | | | Ire | 1971:III–1988:IV | M3 |
| | | | I | 1971:II–1989:IV | M3 |
| | | | N | 1971:I–1989:IV | M3 |
| | | | P | 1971:II–1988:IV | M3 |
| | | | S | 1971:III–1989:IV | M3 |
| | | | UK | 1971:II –1989:II | M3 |
| Angeloni, Cottarelli, and Levy (1991) | PA | sll | G | 1982:I–1990:IV | M1 |
| | | | F | 1982:I–1990:IV | M1 |
| | | | UK | 1982:I–1990:IV | M0 |
| | | | I | 1982:I–1990:IV | M1 |
| | | | S | 1982:I–1990:IV | M1 |
| | | | G | 1982:I–1990:IV | M3 |
| | | | F | 1982:I–1990:IV | M3 |
| | | | UK | 1982:I–1990:IV | M4 |
| | | | I | 1982:I–1990:IV | M2 |
| | | | S | 1982:I–1990:IV | ALP |

*Notes:*
[a] AE = 'adaptive expectations', BS = 'buffer stock', DL = 'distributed lag', EC = 'error-correction', NPA = 'nominal partial adjustment', RPA = 'real partial adjustment', PA = 'partial adjustment'.
[b] ll = loglinear, sll = semi-loglinear.
[c] B = Belgium, C = Canada, Den = Denmark, F = France, G = (West)Germany, Gr = Greece, Ire = Ireland, I = Italy, J = Japan, N = The Netherlands, P = Portugal, S = Spain, UK = United Kingdom, US = United States.

| Long-term elasticities | | | | | Additional variables | SE of regression ($\times 10^{-2}$) |
|---|---|---|---|---|---|---|
| Income (real) | Price | Short-term interest rate[i] | Long-term interest rate[i] | Inflation[i] | | |
| 1.00 | 1.18 | 0.11 | −0.40 | −0.21 | cyclical variable[g] | 1.50 |
| 1.00 | 1.00 | 0.16 | −0.31 | −0.17 | | 1.30 |
| 1.00 | 0.89 | – | −0.18 | −0.13 | | 1.20 |
| 1.00 | 1.00 | 0.44 | – | −0.51 | | 2.10 |
| 1.00 | 0.88 | 0.14 | −0.16 | −0.13 | | 2.30 |
| 1.00 | 1.00 | – | −0.16 | −0.16 | | 1.20 |
| 1.00 | 0.89 | 0.38 | −0.45 | −0.27 | | 2.50 |
| 1.00 | 0.94 | 0.16 | −0.16 | −0.19 | | 1.50 |
| 1.00 | 0.75 | 0.10 | −0.10 | −0.09 | | 1.30 |
| 1.00 | 1.00 | 0.42 | −0.47 | −0.39 | | 2.80 |
| 1.00 | 1.00 | 0.32 | −0.33 | −0.20 | | 0.90 |
| 1.00 | 1.25 | 0.05 | −0.34 | −0.18 | | 1.30 |
| 1.00 | 1.00 | 0.09 | −0.31 | −0.14 | | 0.90 |
| 1.00 | 0.92 | – | −0.13 | −0.10 | | 0.80 |
| 1.00 | 1.21 | 0.34 | – | −0.39 | | 1.00 |
| 1.00 | 1.00 | 0.14 | −0.17 | −0.14 | | 1.70 |
| 1.00 | 1.00 | – | −0.13 | −0.12 | | 0.90 |
| 1.00 | 0.94 | 0.33 | −0.46 | −0.28 | | 1.60 |
| 1.00 | 0.95 | 0.18 | −0.19 | −0.22 | | 1.20 |
| 1.00 | 0.79 | 0.29 | −0.10 | −0.09 | | 1.00 |
| 1.00 | 1.00 | 0.36 | −0.41 | −0.34 | | 2.00 |
| 1.38[h] | – | $-0.017r_k$ | – | – | – | 1.35 |
| 0.73[h] | – | – | $-0.012r_l$ | – | – | 1.27 |
| 0.62[h] | – | $-0.012r_k$ | – | – | – | 0.49 |
| 0.90[h] | – | $-0.007r_k$ | – | – | own interest rate | 0.86 |
| 0.48[h] | – | – | $-0.005r_l$ | – | linear and quadratic trend | 1.62 |
| 1.14[h] | – | $0.041r_k$ | $-0.041r_l$ | – | – | 0.68 |
| 1.24[h] | – | $0.008r_k$ | – | – | – | 0.67 |
| 0.11[h] | – | $0.017r_k$ | $-0.017r_l$ | – | wealth | 0.51 |
| 0.92[h] | – | $-0.013r_k$ | $-0.006r_l$ | – | – | 0.95 |
| 1.06[h] | – | $0.007r_k$ | $-0.007r_l$ | – | – | 0.75 |

[d] Permanent income.
[e] With regard to anticipated inflation.
[f] Calculated as the difference between the interest rate in the US and the domestic interest rate.
[g] Only in the short-term relationship.
[h] Nominal income.
[i] $r_k$ is the short-, $r_l$ the long-term interest rate; $\dot{p}$ is the inflation rate.
* Homogeneity imposed.

*Table 5.A.2: Countrywise enumeration of demand for money research by authors**

| | |
|---|---|
| 1 | The Netherlands: Fase and Kuné (1974a), Butter and Kuné (1976), Blommestein and Palm (1982), Knoop and Hooijmans (1985), Taylor (1986), Huijser (1987), Kuipers and Boertje (1988), Cesar, Haan, and Jacobs (1990), Fase and Winder (1990), Traa (1991), Sterken (1992). |
| 2 | United States: Goldfeld (1973), Goldfeld (1976), Lieberman (1977), Hafer and Hein (1979), Arango and Nadiri (1981), Judd and Scadding (1982a), Rose (1985), Mankiw and Summers (1986), Judd and Trehan (1987), Baba, Hendry, and Starr (1987), Goldfeld and Sichel (1987), Ebrill (1988), Wenniger (1988), Mehra (1989), Miller (1989), Baade and Nazmi (1989), Miller (1991), Hafer and Jansen (1991), Hoffman and Rasche (1991). |
| 3 | Japan: Suzuki (1984), Dooley and Spinelli (1985), Hamada and Hayashi (1985), Baade and Nazmi (1989), Corker (1990), Rasche (1990), Yoshida and Rasche (1990). |
| 4 | Germany: Hamburger (1977), Akhtar and Putnam (1980), Langfeldt and Lehment (1980), Arango and Nadiri (1981), Buscher and Schröder (1983), Neumann (1983), Buscher (1984, 1985), Heri (1985), Taylor (1986), Trehan (1988), Baade and Nazmi (1989), Herz and Röger (1990). |
| 5 | France: Grandmont (1973), Fröchen and Roubine (1979), Dooley and Spinelli (1985), Fröchen and Voisin (1986), Taylor (1986), Bennett (1987), Bethenod (1988), Bordes and Strauss-Kahn (1989). |
| 6 | United Kingdom: Price (1972), Hacche (1974), Hamburger (1977), Hendry and Mizon (1978), Arango and Nadiri (1981), Artis and Lewis (1984), Hendry (1985), Patterson (1987), Cuthbertson and Taylor (1987a, 1987b), Cuthbertson (1988), Muscatelli (1989), Hall, Henry, and Wilcox (1989), Cuthbertson and Taylor (1990), Hendry and Ericsson (1991a,1991b). |
| 7 | Canada: White (1976), Bordo and Choudhri (1982), Ghosh (1989), Caramazza (1989). |
| 8 | Belgium: Quintijn (1986, 1988), Jeanfils (1992). |
| 9 | Denmark: Juselius (1987), Juselius (1991), Juselius (1992), Johansen and Juselius (1990). |
| 10 | Greece: Brissimis and Leventakis (1981), Himarios (1986), Himarios (1987). |
| 11 | Ireland: Browne (1986). |
| 12 | Italy: Dooley and Spinelli (1985), Muscatelli and Papi (1990). |
| 13 | Portugal: Marques and Lopes (1992). |
| 14 | Spain: Dolado and Escriva (1992). |
| 15 | Europe: Butter and Fase (1981), Bekx and Tullio (1989), Kremers and Lane (1990), Monticelli and Strauss-Kahn (1992), Fase and Winder (1993), Artis, Bladen-Hovell, and Zhang (1993). |

*Notes:* * For the detailed table the reader may consult the appendix in Fase (1993).

# 6. Wealth and the Demand for Money: Empirical Evidence for The Netherlands and Belgium

## 6.1 Introduction

Research on the demand for money is one of the oldest research areas of econometrics. The reason for this is the reasonably well-developed theory of the demand for money, the ample availability of data required for estimation and the fact that knowledge of the stability of the demand for money is relevant for a monetary policy aimed at controlling money growth. This perhaps explains the emphasis on the stability issue rather than on the role of wealth in money demand research efforts (see also Fase (1994)). However, in this historical perspective the role of wealth is unarticulated and almost ignored in empirical research on money demand. This has raised the question of whether income or wealth, or perhaps both, should be included in empirical demand for money functions.

The availability of a well-developed theory is supported by the historiography of views on the demand for money. The history of the neoclassical theory of the demand for money starts with the quantity theory of money advanced by Irving Fisher at the turn of the century, although writers of the Classical School like Locke and Hume already established the basic idea (see e.g. Blaug *et al.* (1995)). This theory, usually summarized by the equation of exchange, opposes the flow of money and the flow of goods and services. This implies that the volume of current transactions determines the demand for money. In Fisher's theory, interest rates and wealth are irrelevant. This can presumably be ascribed to the fact that the classical quantity theory abstracts from financial transactions. The explicit exclusion of wealth is the major difference between this theory and the closely related Cambridge variant

Reprinted from *De Economist*, **144**(4) (1996), M.M.G. Fase and C.C.A. Winder, 'Wealth and the demand for money: Empirical evidence for The Netherlands and Belgium', 568–589, ©1996 with kind permission from Kluwer Academic Publishers.

of Fisher's quantity theory, known as the cash balance theory with the cash ratio as a crucial parameter. This parameter, which also pays explicit attention to money as a store of value and thus wealth, was implicitly assumed to depend on interest rates. The next important step in the development of the theory on the demand for money was Keynes' liquidity preference theory setting out his famous three motives for holding money. This resulted in income, the bond rate, and wealth as explanatory variables, the inclusion of wealth mainly due to the speculative motive. For several reasons wealth is usually ignored as an explanatory variable in empirical research. One reason is the purely practical matter that either wealth was assumed to be more or less constant in the short-run or proportional to income. Another and perhaps more important reason was the fact that appropriate time series data on wealth were not available.

It should be noted that a means of payment can simultaneously serve all three motives. Therefore, Friedman's reformulation of Fisher's quantity theory is a major step forward. He regarded the demand for money as a special case of the demand for goods and services. Consequently, Friedman's approach does not differ from a general equilibrium approach to the demand for goods and services. In this approach, the demand for money is in fact just one equation from a complete system of demand equations. Consequently, Friedman's theory was closely connected, in principle, to the portfolio approach of e.g. Tobin which naturally included wealth. Therefore, Friedman's and Tobin's approach explicitly take wealth into account to explain money-holding behaviour. In this view, money is the most liquid financial asset of the whole range of assets.

The purpose of this chapter is to examine empirically money demand with wealth as one of the explanatory variables. A first and very preliminary attempt to examine this for The Netherlands is offered in Fase and Winder (1990); the present chapter aims to investigate this matter further. As data availability is still a problem we confine our empirical analysis to Belgium and The Netherlands.

## 6.2 Theoretical Framework and Empirical Results

The theoretical framework adopted to examine the impact of wealth on money demand is similar to that in Fase and Winder (1990, 1993, 1994). The starting point is a traditional demand for money relationship according to which desired money balances not only depend on familiar determinants such as real income, interest rates and inflation, but also on real wealth. The postulated long-run demand for money relationship is

$$M \propto P^{\alpha_1} y^{\alpha_2} w^{\alpha_3} \exp\left(\alpha_4 r_k + \alpha_5 r_l + \alpha_6 \dot{p}\right) \qquad (6.1)$$

with M the desired nominal money stock in a steady state situation, $P$ the price level, $y$ real income, $w$ real wealth, $\dot{p}$ the inflation rate while $r_k$ and $r_l$ represent the short- and long-term interest rates, respectively. The price elasticity equals $\alpha_1$, while $\alpha_2$ and $\alpha_3$ represent the income and wealth elasticities; $\alpha_4$, $\alpha_5$ and $\alpha_6$ measure the relative change of money demand as a result of a one percentage point increase of the short-term interest rate, long-term interest rate and the inflation rate, respectively. These parameters are therefore the semi-elasticities with respect to the short- and long-term interest rates and inflation. The much-made assumption of price homogeneity – e.g. $\alpha_1 = 1$ – is not imposed as an *a priori* restriction, but considered as a testable hypothesis in our empirical analysis. If this restriction is valid the steady state in (6.1) relates real money balances to the explanatory variables, with $y$ reflecting the impact of the transactions' volume and wealth the scale variable reflecting portfolio investment considerations. An alternative interpretation of this determinant is that it is a proxy for the influence of the demand for financial transactions. These transactions are not accounted for appropriately by the income variable (see e.g. Knoop and Hooijmans (1985)). The interest rates and inflation rate describe, following Friedman (1971), the substitution processes between financial and physical assets. The short-term interest rate is the representative yield on near-money. For the narrow money concept M1 $\alpha_4$ should therefore be negative, while for broader aggregates like M2 and M3 a positive sign is plausible. Including both the short- and long-term interest rate is also intended to take into account the influence of the yield curve on the demand for money.

Equation (6.1) is our maintained hypothesis and describes the steady state demand for money relationship. When deviations from this long-run equilibrium occur, adjustment processes provoke a tendency towards restoring the equilibrium. These short-run adjustment processes are modelled by means of lagged values of the variables in (6.1), leading to a dynamic equation in which the short- and long-run properties of the demand for money are described jointly. Following earlier studies carried out at the bank, a cyclical indicator has been included to describe the short-run adjustment processes (see e.g. Fase and Kuné (1974a) and Butter and Fase (1981)). The resulting dynamic equation is reformulated as an error-correction specification, which provides an easy way to discriminate between the long-run steady state and the short-run adjustment processes. Appendix 6.A contains a discussion and derivation of the money demand function which has served as the general formulation used in the estimation and specification analysis.

The demand for money and the specific impact of wealth have been analysed for both The Netherlands and Belgium. In order to obtain an comprehensive picture of the monetary developments we did not restrict the analysis to one monetary aggregate, but considered a broad spectrum i.e. three money concepts: M1, M2 and M3. Data on real income refer to GNP figures. The wealth concept used is net financial wealth, and derived from the balance sheets for The Netherlands and Belgium used in Boeschoten, Bondt, and Bikker (1995). Net financial wealth is defined as the differential between total assets – the sum of M3, government bonds, other capital market investments and gross foreign assets – and total liabilities – credit plus gross foreign liabilities – of the non-monetary private sector. A more general wealth concept, which includes both financial wealth and non-financial components like capital stock, houses and perhaps durable consumption goods, has not been considered, because these data are not readily available. One may argue that for money demand behaviour portfolio investment considerations are dominant. Focusing on financial wealth is therefore fully justified. However, even if a broader wealth concept would be more appropriate, the reported results remain valid if it is assumed that financial wealth is a reliable proxy or instrumental variable for total wealth. The price of GNP is used to deflate nominal financial wealth and to construct the inflation rate variable. For The Netherlands the short-term interest rate is the three-month money market loans to local authorities and for Belgium the interest rate on three-month deposits on the Euro market. Data for the long-term interest rate are the yields on long-term government bonds. In the analysis we considered seasonally unadjusted quarterly data. Since for Belgium no quarterly data on GNP and its price are available, quarterly data are constructed from the annual figures by means of industrial production and consumer prices, respectively. The sample period considered for The Netherlands is 1970:I–1994:IV. As data on financial wealth for Belgium are only available from 1979:IV onwards, the sample period for Belgium is 1979:IV–1994:IV.

Rather than reporting all estimation results – relegating details to the appendices – we will focus on the long-run properties implied by the estimated demand for money relationships. The estimation results for M1, M2 and M3 of The Netherlands and Belgium are reported in Appendix 6.B. The results of the statistical evaluation of the estimated demand for money relationships are given in Appendix 6.C, showing that from a statistical point of view the specifications are appropriate.

In evaluating the empirical results we will not discuss the estimated specifications in detail. In order to gain insight into the properties of the demand for money, a discussion of the steady state is obviously most revealing. To this end the estimates of the parameters of the steady state demand for money relationships for the distinguished monetary aggregates are summarized in Table 6.1.

Table 6.1 shows that wealth has a significant impact on the demand for money. The sole exception is M1 for Belgium, for which no influence is found at all. The demand for M1 in Belgium is also distinct from the other monetary aggregates considered in that it has a price elasticity lower than 1. For all the other money concepts price homogeneity applies. For those aggregates having a wealth elasticity unequal to 0, the restriction has been imposed that the income and wealth elasticities sum to 1. This restriction constitutes a testable hypothesis and the results in Appendix 6.C show that the hypothesis that this restriction is valid cannot be rejected. The finding that the income and wealth elasticities sum to 1 corresponds with the results obtained by Sterken (1992) for The Netherlands. This result has also been reported for other countries. Examples are the Deutsche Bundesbank (1995) for Germany, Hall, Henry, and Wilcox (1989) for the UK, Hunt and Volker (1981) for Australia, and Corker (1990) for Japan. Table 6.1 shows furthermore that both for The Netherlands and Belgium the demand for M1 has a higher income elasticity than M2 and M3, reflecting that M1-balances are mainly held for the purpose of carrying out transactions. For The Netherlands the income elasticity of the demand for M2 and M3 is about 0.6 – and thus a wealth elasticity of about 0.4 – whereas for Belgium both the income and wealth elasticities are equal to about 0.5. A striking feature is also that for both The Netherlands and Belgium the wealth elasticity of M2 is slightly higher than that of M3. The wealth elasticity of M2 in The Netherlands is similar to the value of 0.36 found in Fase and Winder (1990).

With respect to the semi-elasticities of the short- and long-term interest rate and the inflation rate, Table 6.1 shows that all the estimates obtained have the theoretically plausible signs and are, with the exception of M2 for both The Netherlands and Belgium, significantly different from 0. For all monetary aggregates restrictions with respect to the semi-elasticities have been imposed. For M1 in The Netherlands for instance, the semi-elasticities of the long-term interest and inflation rate are assumed to be equal. Testing these restrictions shows that in all cases the hypotheses concerning the semi-elasticities cannot be rejected (see Appendix 6.C). For Belgium the semi-elasticities obtained for M2 are 0.04 and substantially higher than those for M1 and M3, whereas for The

*Table 6.1: Estimates of parameters of long-run money demand relationships*

| Country | Monetary aggregate | $\alpha_1$ | $\alpha_2$ | $\alpha_3$ | $\alpha_4$ | $\alpha_5$ | $\alpha_6$ |
|---|---|---|---|---|---|---|---|
| The Netherlands | M 1 | 1 | 0.807<br>(20.92) | 0.193<br>(5.03) | −0.021<br>(2.55) | −0.012<br>(2.47) | −0.012<br>(2.47) |
| | M 2 | 1 | 0.593<br>(8.64) | 0.407<br>(5.96) | 0.010<br>(1.59) | −0.010<br>(1.59) | −0.010<br>(1.59) |
| | M 3 | 1 | 0.635<br>(18.56) | 0.365<br>(10.77) | 0.025<br>(5.16) | −0.015<br>(4.27) | −0.015<br>(4.27) |
| Belgium | M 1 | 0.726<br>(11.03) | 0.699<br>(7.08) | 0 | −0.003<br>(2.66) | −0.003<br>(2.66) | −0.003<br>(2.66) |
| | M 2 | 1 | 0.503<br>(2.09) | 0.497<br>(2.07) | 0.040<br>(1.46) | −0.040<br>(1.46) | −0.040<br>(1.46) |
| | M 3 | 1 | 0.523<br>(3.71) | 0.477<br>(3.38) | 0.026<br>(2.62) | −0.026<br>(2.62) | −0.026<br>(2.62) |

*Note:* *t*-values are given in parentheses.

Netherlands the mutual differences between the monetary aggregates considered are relatively small. Table 6.1 shows also that the demand for the broad money concepts M 2 and M 3 in Belgium is more sensitive to changes in the interest rates and the inflation rate than their counterparts of The Netherlands, although the semi-elasticity of M 3 with respect to the short-term interest rate has a similar magnitude. M 1-balances in The Netherlands on the other hand have higher interest rates and inflation rate semi-elasticities than those in Belgium.

An alternative way to evaluate the estimation results is to consider the properties of near-money. The elasticities found for M 1, M 2 and M 3 imply elasticities of the demand for M 2−M 1, M 3−M 1 and M 3−M 2 and these elasticities must of course be economically plausible.[1] This offers a possibility to assess the mutual consistency of the results obtained for M 1, M 2 and M 3. Therefore, the elasticities of the various near-money concepts are presented in Table 6.2 together with the elasticities for M 1,

[1] It can easily be verified that $d \ln M2 = \omega d \ln M1 + (1-\omega) d \ln(M2 - M1)$ with $\omega = M1/M2$. Similar relationships hold for the other assets. In the calculation of the elasticities for the various near-money concepts, the sample means of $\omega$ were used. These elasticities should be considered as approximations, since constancy of the elasticities of M 1, M 2 and M 3 implies that the elasticities of near-monies are not constant.

M2 and M3. The price, income and wealth elasticities for M1, M2 and M3 follow from Table 6.1, whereas the elasticities with respect to the short- and long-term interest rate and the inflation rate have been calculated by multiplying the semi-elasticities given in Table 6.1 by the sample means of the respective variables.

Table 6.2 shows that the elasticities of the various near-money concepts have an economically plausible sign and a reasonable magnitude, implying that the results for M1, M2 and M3 are mutually consistent. The price elasticities of the various near-monies in The Netherlands equal 1. For Belgium, however, a price elasticity larger than 1 is found for M2−M1 and M3−M1, reflecting a price elasticity smaller than 1 for M1 and price homogeneity for M2 and M3. Both for The Netherlands and Belgium the income elasticities of the various near-money concepts are smaller than for M1. The demand for short-term savings deposits, e.g. M3−M2, has a higher income elasticity than M2−M1. The demand for short-term time deposits and foreign currency deposits, e.g. M2−M1, is on the other hand characterized by a higher wealth elasticity. A relatively high wealth elasticity of M2−M1 for The Netherlands was also found by Sterken (1992). The sum of the income and wealth elasticities equals 1 for the various near-money concepts in The Netherlands and for M3−M2 in Belgium. This result reflects the similar properties of M1, M2 and M3 in The Netherlands and M2 and M3 in Belgium.

The general picture following from Table 6.2 for the interest rates and inflation elasticities of M1, M2 and M3 is similar to that found for the semi-elasticities discussed before. This is not surprising given the procedure to calculate these elasticities. Table 6.2 shows also that the demand for M2 − M1 in Belgium is characterized by relatively high interest rates and inflation rate elasticities, whereas for The Netherlands these elasticities are more in line with those for the other near-money concepts. A notable feature of Table 6.2 is finally that for both The Netherlands and Belgium the demand for M2 − M1 is particularly sensitive to changes in the short-term interest rate.

## 6.3 A Further Assessment of the Role of Wealth

The discussion of the empirical results in Section 6.2 revealed a substantial impact of real wealth on the demand for money. Only for M1 in Belgium could no influence of wealth be found. This section goes further and investigates the role of wealth. Particularly, the issue will be addressed whether the development of wealth over time offers an explanation for the monetary expansion experienced in The Netherlands

*Table 6.2: Long-run elasticities*

| Country | Monetary aggregate | Price | Income | Wealth | Short-term interest rate | Long-term interest rate | Inflation |
|---|---|---|---|---|---|---|---|
| The Netherlands | M1 | 1 | 0.807 | 0.193 | −0.146 | −0.095 | −0.051 |
| | M2 | 1 | 0.593 | 0.407 | 0.067 | −0.077 | −0.042 |
| | M3 | 1 | 0.635 | 0.365 | 0.179 | −0.118 | −0.064 |
| | M2 − M1 | 1 | 0.242 | 0.758 | 0.419 | −0.049 | −0.027 |
| | M3 − M1 | 1 | 0.536 | 0.464 | 0.365 | −0.132 | −0.071 |
| | M3 − M2 | 1 | 0.693 | 0.307 | 0.337 | −0.176 | −0.094 |
| Belgium | M1 | 0.726 | 0.699 | 0 | −0.029 | −0.030 | −0.016 |
| | M2 | 1 | 0.503 | 0.497 | 0.362 | −0.371 | −0.205 |
| | M3 | 1 | 0.523 | 0.477 | 0.235 | −0.241 | −0.133 |
| | M2 − M1 | 1.248 | 0.326 | 0.946 | 0.716 | −0.680 | −0.376 |
| | M3 − M1 | 1.106 | 0.456 | 0.661 | 0.337 | −0.322 | −0.178 |
| | M3 − M2 | 1 | 0.554 | 0.446 | 0.046 | −0.047 | −0.026 |

and Belgium over the last decade or so. To throw some light on this issue the development of the wealth-income ratio and the liquidity ratio, e.g. the money stock as a percentage of output in nominal terms, for the various money concepts considered are depicted in the charts of Figure 6.1. Since data on net financial wealth for Belgium are only available from 1979:IV onwards, the wealth-income ratio for Belgium covers a shorter time span than the other ratios which are given for the period 1971–1994.

Figure 6.1 shows that in both The Netherlands and Belgium the wealth-income ratio has increased strongly in the first half of the 1980s. From 1987 onwards this ratio has increased only modestly in The Netherlands and has on balance been at a constant level in Belgium. In contrast, the wealth-income ratio was relatively constant in The Netherlands during the 1970s and has actually shown a slight decrease. Obviously, wealth has evolved far from proportional to income, thus causing serious doubts about the much-made assumption that income serves as an appropriate proxy for wealth. A salient feature of the charts in Figure 6.1 is the large diversity in the liquidity ratios. Not only the differences between The Netherlands and Belgium are substantial, but the differences between the monetary aggregates within one country are also large. This goes notably for Belgium: the M1-ratio has decreased steadily over the sample period, the M2-ratio was almost constant until 1989, rising strongly since then, and the growth of the M3-ratio accelerated in 1986. As compared with Belgium, the development of the various liquidity ratios in The

Netherlands has been similar. M1, M2 and M3 have all grown stronger than income. The M1- and M2-ratio, however, have risen especially in the 1980s, whereas the M3-ratio shows a steady increase from the early 1970s onwards.

A feature of Figure 6.1 that catches the eye is the similar development of the various liquidity ratios and the wealth-income ratio in The Netherlands. This holds notably for the M1- and M2-ratio and to a somewhat lesser extent for the M3-ratio. This stylized fact supports the hypothesis that the relatively strong growth of wealth explains the rise of the liquidity ratios in The Netherlands (see also Fase and Winder (1990)). For Belgium, however, the developments of the various liquidity ratios are not in line with that of the wealth-income ratio. Obviously, the growth of wealth offers no explanation for the falling M1-ratio. It is therefore not surprising that the impact of wealth on the demand for M1 was absent in the empirical analysis for Belgium. The falling M1-ratio seems to be related to the specific values of the income and price elasticities which are both smaller than 1. In contrast, the M2- and M3-ratios have increased, but Figure 6.1 shows that this increase clearly lagged behind the growth of the wealth-income ratio. This does not mean, however, that wealth is no determinant of the demand for M2 and M3. The empirical results discussed in Section 6.2 showed a substantial impact of wealth on the demand for M2 and M3 in Belgium. The charts in Figure 6.1 do suggest, however, that interest rates and inflation are very important to explain the development of the liquidity ratios over time.

In the spirit of Fisher's quantity theory, liquidity ratios – or their inverse, the velocities of money – are frequently used as a simple indicator to assess monetary developments. It is well known that these ratios are fairly rough measures because substitution processes resulting from changes of interest rates and inflation may cause large fluctuations of the money stock. Perhaps more importantly, however, wealth also exerts a major influence on the demand for money. In a study of Divisia aggregates for the EU, Fase and Winder (1994) for instance argue that the sharp increase of the liquidity ratios for the broad money concepts in the 1980s should be attributed to increases in the volume of liquid assets held for investment purposes. Therefore, they advocate the use of Divisia aggregates as a more appropriate measure of the amount of money held for transactions purposes. An alternative procedure to take into account the growing importance of portfolio investment considerations is to include wealth among the determinants of the demand for money.

The long-run demand for money relationship (6.1) implies

$$\mathrm{M} \propto P^{\alpha_1-\alpha_2-\alpha_3} Y^{\alpha_2} W^{\alpha_3} f\left(r_k, r_l, \dot{p}\right)$$

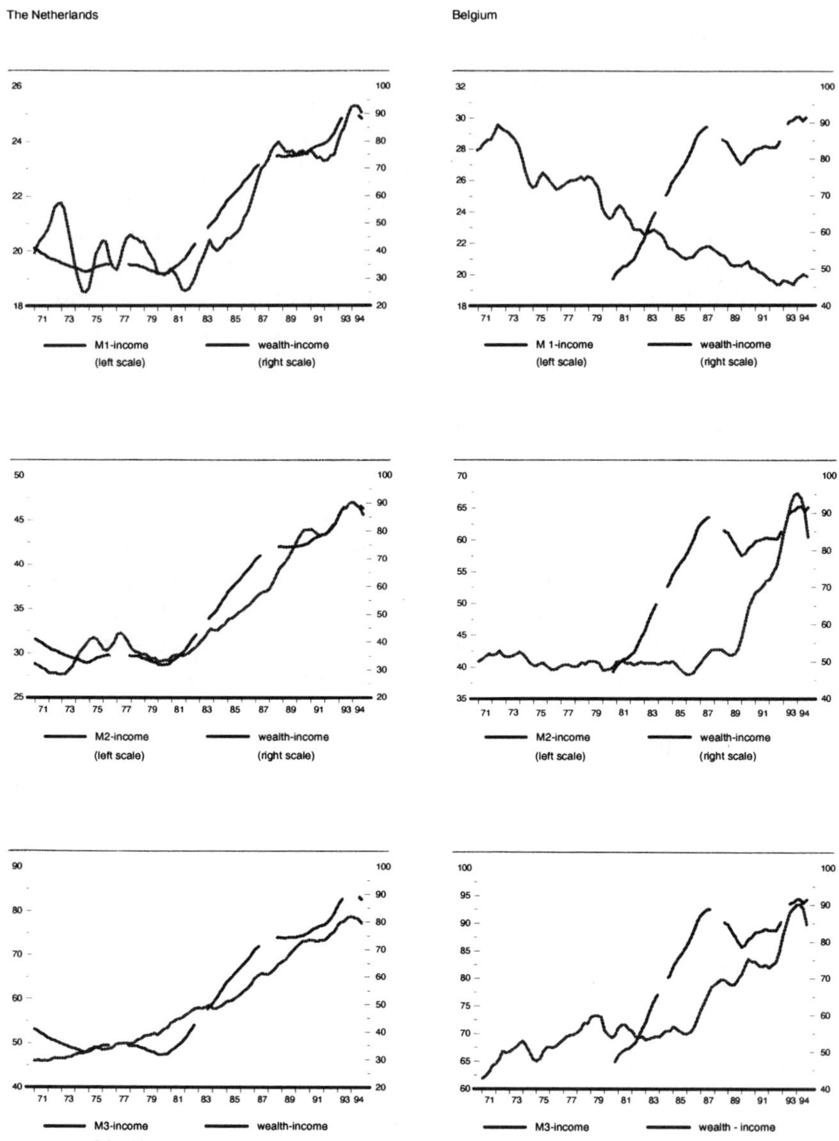


*Figure 6.1: Liquidity ratios and wealth-income ratios*

with $Y$ and $W$ nominal income and nominal wealth, respectively, and $f(r_k, r_l, \dot{p}) = \exp(\alpha_4 r_k + \alpha_5 r_l + \alpha_6 \dot{p})$. Thus,

$$\frac{\mathrm{M}}{Y} \propto P^{\alpha_1-\alpha_2-\alpha_3} Y^{\alpha_2-1} W^{\alpha_3} f(r_k, r_l, \dot{p})$$

showing that the liquidity ratio, and hence the velocity of money, depends also on wealth. If the price elasticity equals 1 and the income and wealth elasticities sum to 1, we have

$$\frac{\mathrm{M}}{Y} \propto \left(\frac{W}{Y}\right)^{1-\alpha_2} f(r_k, r_l, \dot{p}).$$

The relationship between the liquidity ratio and the wealth-income ratio has been considered in Figure 6.1. With the above restrictions concerning the price, income and wealth elasticities, we also have

$$\frac{\mathrm{M}}{Y^{\alpha_2} W^{1-\alpha_2}} \propto f(r_k, r_l, \dot{p}).$$

Since the interest and inflation rates do not display trend-like behaviour, it may be expected that the same property holds for $\mathrm{M}/(Y^{\alpha_2} W^{1-\alpha_2})$. It may therefore be interesting to consider this ratio for the monetary aggregates. It goes without saying that we use this ratio only as a descriptive statistic without much economic content. In Figure 6.2 this statistic is depicted together with the liquidity ratio for each of the money concepts considered. Since the wealth elasticity of M1 in Belgium is 0, the ratio $\mathrm{M}/Y^{\alpha_2}$ has been given for this aggregate. The sample period considered is 1971–1994 for The Netherlands, and due to the fact that data on wealth are only available for a shorter time span, 1981–1994 for Belgium. If the income and wealth elasticities sum to 1, the modified ratio is independent from the unit in which the money stock, income and wealth are expressed. This situation applies to all monetary concepts considered, except M1 in Belgium for which the income elasticity equals 0.70 and the wealth elasticity is 0. If the elasticities do not sum to 1, the level of the modified ratio depends on the unit in which the variables are expressed. Thus, it makes a difference whether M1, income and wealth are expressed in millions or billions of Belgium francs. It can easily be shown, however, that the development over time is not influenced by the choice of unit. It is only the level that is affected. Therefore, the chart for the M1-ratio and the corresponding modified ratio for Belgium is depicted with a double scale. In all other cases one scale suffices.

Figure 6.2 shows that the modified ratios for The Netherlands are relatively constant over the period 1971–1994. The modified M1-ratio fluctuates between narrow margins around the level of 25. The fluctuations of the modified M2-ratio are somewhat larger but its values remain within the interval (40, 50). The M3-ratio shows an upward tendency during the 1970s, but is relatively constant from 1980 onwards. A salient feature of all these modified ratios is that no upward tendency is present during the 1980s. This result indicates that in The Netherlands no excessive monetary expansion has occurred, a conclusion that is in line with the modest development of the inflation rates during the 1980s. This does not mean, however, that the real and financial sectors have evolved in line. As witnessed by the increase of the liquidity ratios – and the relative constantness of the macroeconomic capital coefficient implying that the capital stock has grown more or less in line with output – the expansion of the real sector has lagged behind that of the financial sector. In the spirit of portfolio models of money demand behaviour, the broadening and deepening of the financial sector since the 1980s should have had an impact on money demand. The charts for The Netherlands therefore suggest that the increase of the liquidity ratios can be attributed primarily to portfolio investment considerations, a conclusion that is in line with the research findings of Fase and Winder (1994). The relatively stable monetary development according to the modified ratios may therefore be taken as a justification of the reserved policy reactions of the monetary authorities to the growth of the liquidity ratios.

As compared with The Netherlands, the modified ratios for Belgium are rather volatile. In contrast to the downward tendency of the M1-ratio, the modified M1-ratio has increased over time. The modified M2- and M3-ratios decreased during the first half of the 1980s. This reflects the relatively strong increase of wealth, while M2 and M3 grew more or less in line with income. During the second half of the 1980s, the movements of the modified M2- and M3-ratios were parallel to those of the M2- and M3-ratios. As before, this suggests that interest rates and inflation are important in explaining the development of the liquidity ratios for M2 and M3 in Belgium.

A final aspect in the evaluation of the role of wealth concerns the short-run adjustment processes if an increase of wealth occurs. In Section 6.2 we discussed the impact in the long-run, but it is also important to consider the short-run effects. For all the monetary aggregates considered, except M1 in Belgium for which no wealth dependency was found, the initial effect of an increase of wealth on the demand for money is smaller than the impact in the long-run. Only for M2 in The Netherlands is the initial effect larger than the long-run effect. A similar finding for this monetary aggregate was reported in Fase and Winder (1990).

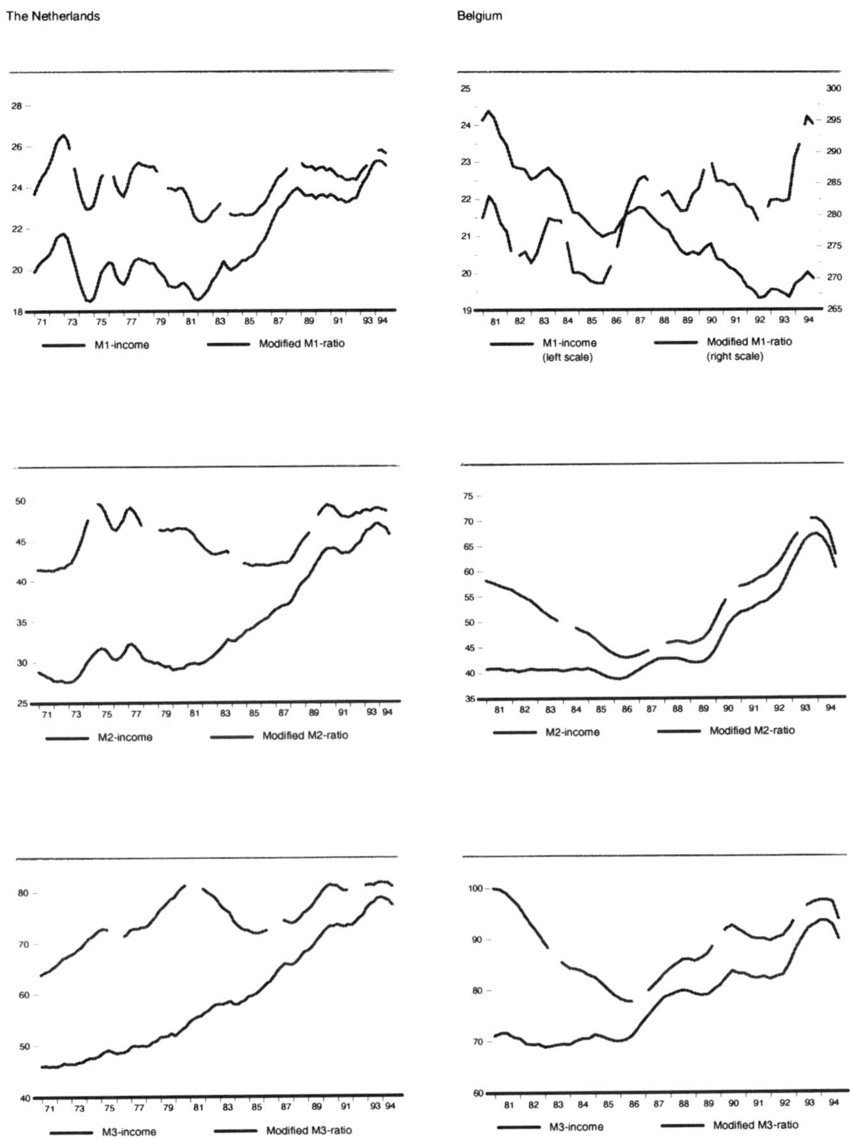


*Figure 6.2: Liquidity ratios and modified ratios*

## 6.4 Concluding Remarks

The main novelty of the research reported in this chapter is the inclusion of wealth as an explanatory variable for the demand for money. Following the theory this hypothesis has been verified empirically for both Belgium and The Netherlands because for these countries data on wealth have become available.

The most important finding is that with the exception of one case we found substantial wealth elasticities. The only exception is the demand for M1 in Belgium which does not show wealth dependency. Another finding is that very often income and wealth elasticities add up to 1. An important implication of wealth dependency of the demand for money is that the velocity of money will also depend on wealth. For The Netherlands, incorporating wealth effects on the demand for money seems to mitigate the volatility of the monetary picture. For Belgium this is not the case, indicating that interest and inflation rates are important factors in understanding monetary developments.

## APPENDIX 6.A ECONOMETRIC METHODOLOGY

This appendix discusses the equation that has served as the basis for the specification and estimation analysis. As argued in the main text, a dynamic formulation of the steady state relationship

$$\mathrm{M} \propto P^{\alpha_1} y^{\alpha_2} w^{\alpha_3} \exp\left(\alpha_4 r_k + \alpha_5 r_l + \alpha_6 \dot{p}\right) \tag{6.A.1}$$

has been chosen, including the cyclical indicator as explanatory variable, as the model describing the long-run properties and short-run adjustment processes in case deviations from the steady state occur:

$$\begin{aligned}\alpha(L)\ln \mathrm{M} = {} & \beta_1(L)\ln P + \beta_2(L)\ln y + \beta_3(L)\ln w + \beta_4(L)r_k + \beta_5(L)r_l \\ & + \beta_6(L)\dot{p} + \beta_7(L)conj \end{aligned} \tag{6.A.2}$$

with $L$ the lag operator and $\alpha(L)$ and $\beta(L)$ lag polynomials. Fase and Winder (1993) discuss extensively the identification problem concerning the parameters of the lag polynomials $\beta_1(L)$ and $\beta_6(L)$. In line with their analysis a number of *a priori* restrictions have been imposed, leading to

$$\begin{aligned}\alpha(L)\ln\frac{\mathrm{M}}{P} = {} & (\beta_{10}-1)\ln P + \beta_2(L)\ln y + \beta_3(L)\ln w + \beta_4(L)r_k \\ & + \beta_5(L)r_l + \beta_6(L)\dot{p} + \beta_7(L)conj \end{aligned} \tag{6.A.3}$$

with $\beta_{10}$ the constant of the lag polynomial of $\beta_1(L)$. Reformulating (6.A.3) yields the estimation equation considered in the empirical analysis:

$$\begin{aligned}\bar{\alpha}(L)\Delta\ln\frac{\mathrm{M}}{P} = {} & (\beta_{10}-1)\ln P - \alpha\left(\ln(\mathrm{M}/P)_{-1} - \ln y_{-1}\right) \\ & + \beta_3\left(\ln w_{-1} - \ln y_{-1}\right) + (\beta_2+\beta_3-\alpha)\ln y_{-1} + \beta_4 r_k \\ & + \beta_5 r_l + \beta_6\dot{p} + \bar{\beta}_2(L)\Delta\ln y + \bar{\beta}_3(L)\Delta\ln w \\ & + \bar{\beta}_4(L)\Delta r_k + \bar{\beta}_5(L)\Delta r_l + \bar{\beta}_6(L)\Delta\dot{p} \\ & + \beta_7(L)conj \end{aligned} \tag{6.A.4}$$

with $\beta_i$, $i = 2,\ldots,6$ equal to the sum of the coefficients of the lag polynomial $\beta_i(L)$. From equation (6.A.4) the long-run (semi-)elasticities can easily be determined. The semi-elasticities with respect to the short- and long-term interest rates and the inflation rate are equal to $\beta_4/\alpha$, $\beta_5/\alpha$ and $\beta_6/\alpha$, respectively. The price elasticity equals $(\beta_{10} - 1 + \alpha)/\alpha$, whereas the income and wealth elasticities are equal to $\beta_2/\alpha$ and $\beta_3/\alpha$. With equation (6.A.4) it is relatively simple to test restrictions with respect to the long-run price, income and wealth elasticities. The hypothesis that the price elasticity equals 1 can be tested by assessing the significance of the estimate of the coefficient of $\ln P$. The hypothesis that the wealth elasticity equals 0 corresponds with the restriction that the coefficient of $(\ln w_{-1} - \ln y_{-1})$ is 0. The hypothesis that the income and wealth elasticities sum to 1 corresponds with the restriction that the coefficient of $\ln y_{-1}$ is equal to 0. Obviously, these restrictions can easily be tested by means of the $t$-statistics of the estimates of these parameters.

## Appendix 6.B Estimation Results

This appendix presents the estimated demand for money equations for The Netherlands and Belgium. Since the data used are not seasonally adjusted, seasonal dummies $s_1$, $s_2$ and $s_3$ are included in the estimation equation. The notation of the other variables is the same as in the main text. The $t$-values of the estimates, reported between brackets in the following equations, are adjusted for the possible presence of heteroscedasticity. $\bar{R}^2$ denotes the multiple correlation coefficient adjusted for degrees of freedom and $SE$ is the standard error of the residuals.

*The Netherlands:*

$$\begin{aligned}
\Delta \ln \frac{\mathrm{M1}}{P} = & - \underset{(3.13)}{0.1554} (\ln(\mathrm{M1}/P)_{-1} - \ln y_{-1}) + \underset{(2.23)}{0.0300} (\ln w - \ln y_{-1}) \\
& - \underset{(2.93)}{0.3629} \Delta \ln(\mathrm{M1}/P)_{-1} + \underset{(3.16)}{0.2847} \Delta \ln y - \underset{(2.67)}{0.2761} \Delta \ln w_{-1} \\
& - \underset{(3.22)}{0.0032} r_k - \underset{(2.11)}{0.0044} \Delta r_{k-1} - \underset{(5.98)}{0.0018} r_l - \underset{(2.32)}{0.0112} \Delta r_l \\
& - \underset{(5.98)}{0.0018} \dot{p} - \underset{(6.38)}{0.0020} \Delta \dot{p}_{-1} - \underset{(3.37)}{0.0010} \Delta \dot{p}_{-2} \\
& - \underset{(2.78)}{0.0139} \Delta conj_{-1} - \underset{(1.14)}{0.0238} + \underset{(2.80)}{0.0326} s_1 + \underset{(10.71)}{0.0898} s_2 \\
& + \underset{(0.88)}{0.0155} s_3
\end{aligned}$$

Estimation period 1971:I–1994:IV $\bar{R}^2 = 0.94$ $SE = 0.018$

$$\begin{aligned}
\Delta \ln \frac{\mathrm{M2}}{P} = & - \underset{(2.70)}{0.0796} (\ln(\mathrm{M2}/P)_{-1} - \ln y_{-1}) + \underset{(2.35)}{0.0324} (\ln w - \ln y_{-1}) \\
& + \underset{(2.75)}{0.2335} \Delta \ln(\mathrm{M2}/P)_{-1} + \underset{(3.89)}{0.3705} \Delta \ln y + \underset{(5.49)}{0.4573} \Delta \ln w \\
& - \underset{(3.65)}{0.2715} \Delta \ln w_{-1} - \underset{(2.03)}{0.1080} \Delta \ln w_{-2} + \underset{(2.23)}{0.0008} r_k \\
& + \underset{(3.29)}{0.0037} \Delta r_{k-2} - \underset{(2.23)}{0.0008} r_l - \underset{(3.29)}{0.0037} \Delta r_{l-1} - \underset{(2.23)}{0.0008} \dot{p} \\
& - \underset{(0.53)}{0.0012}\, conj_{-2} + \underset{(0.15)}{0.0011} + \underset{(1.81)}{0.0226} s_1 + \underset{(0.71)}{0.0057} s_2 \\
& + \underset{(1.12)}{0.0127} s_3
\end{aligned}$$

Estimation period 1971:III–1994:IV $\bar{R}^2 = 0.86$ $SE = 0.018$

$$\begin{aligned}
\Delta \ln \frac{\mathrm{M3}}{P} = & - \underset{(4.36)}{0.1004} (\ln(\mathrm{M3}/P)_{-1} - \ln y_{-1}) \\
& + \underset{(3.66)}{0.0367} (\ln w_{-1} - \ln y_{-1}) + \underset{(2.11)}{0.1125} \Delta \ln y + \underset{(7.41)}{0.2967} \Delta \ln w \\
& - \underset{(4.00)}{0.1784} \Delta \ln w_{-1} - \underset{(4.17)}{0.1172} \Delta \ln w_{-2} + \underset{(3.26)}{0.0026} r_{k-1} \\
& + \underset{(6.86)}{0.0045} \Delta r_k - \underset{(7.93)}{0.0015} r_l - \underset{(6.86)}{0.0045} \Delta r_{l-1} - \underset{(7.93)}{0.0015} \dot{p} \\
& - \underset{(2.84)}{0.0007} \dot{p}_{-1\frac{1}{2}} - \underset{(1.16)}{0.0016}\, conj_{-2} + \underset{(5.43)}{0.0590} + \underset{(2.39)}{0.0157} s_1 \\
& + \underset{(3.73)}{0.0207} s_2 + \underset{(1.15)}{0.0073} s_3
\end{aligned}$$

Estimation period 1971:II–1994:IV $\bar{R}^2 = 0.95$ $SE = 0.009$

*Belgium:*

$$\Delta \ln \frac{\text{M1}}{P} = \underset{(4.13)}{-\ 0.6050}\,(\ln(\text{M1}/P)_{-1} - \ln y_{-1}) \ \underset{(2.45)}{+\ 0.3627}\,\Delta \ln(\text{M1}/P)_{-4}$$
$$\underset{(2.24)}{-\ 0.1824}\ln y_{-1} \ \underset{(3.67)}{-\ 0.1660}\ln P \ \underset{(2.25)}{-\ 0.4048}\,\Delta \ln y_{-1\frac{1}{2}}$$
$$\underset{(3.17)}{-\ 0.0019}r_{k-1} \ \underset{(2.29)}{-\ 0.0082}\,\Delta r_k \ \underset{(3.17)}{-\ 0.0019}r_{l-1} \ \underset{(2.11)}{-\ 0.0193}\,\Delta r_l$$
$$\underset{(3.17)}{-\ 0.0019}\dot{p}_{-1} \ \underset{(3.10)}{-\ 0.0047}\,\Delta \dot{p} \ \underset{(2.67)}{-\ 0.0255}\,\Delta conj_{-2}$$
$$\underset{(2.23)}{+\ 1.2578} \ \underset{(1.20)}{-\ 0.0176}s_1 \ \underset{(1.52)}{+\ 0.0434}s_2 \ \underset{(1.41)}{-\ 0.0262}s_3$$

Estimation period 1980:I–1994:IV $\bar{R}^2 = 0.91$ $SE = 0.018$

$$\Delta \ln \frac{\text{M2}}{P} = \underset{(2.28)}{-\ 0.0682}\,(\ln(\text{M2}/P)_{-1} - \ln y) \ \underset{(2.41)}{+\ 0.0339}\,(\ln w_{-1} - \ln y)$$
$$\underset{(1.93)}{+\ 0.2442}\,\Delta \ln(\text{M2}/P)_{-1} \ \underset{(2.34)}{+\ 0.3778}\,\Delta \ln(\text{M2}/P)_{-4}$$
$$\underset{(1.63)}{+\ 0.0027}r_k \ \underset{(1.91)}{+\ 0.0109}\,\Delta r_{k-\frac{1}{2}} \ \underset{(1.63)}{-\ 0.0027}r_l \ \underset{(1.63)}{-\ 0.0027}\dot{p}$$
$$\underset{(2.84)}{+\ 0.0133}\,\Delta \dot{p}_{-3} \ \underset{(1.09)}{-\ 0.0134}\,\Delta conj_{-2\frac{1}{2}} \ \underset{(0.56)}{+\ 0.0116} \ \underset{(1.54)}{+\ 0.0268}s_1$$
$$\underset{(0.41)}{+\ 0.0052}s_2 \ \underset{(0.18)}{-\ 0.0021}s_3$$

Estimation period 1980:I–1994:IV $\bar{R}^2 = 0.56$ $SE = 0.026$

$$\Delta \ln \frac{\text{M3}}{P} = \underset{(3.32)}{-\ 0.0794}\,(\ln(\text{M3}/P)_{-1} - \ln y) \ \underset{(4.26)}{+\ 0.0378}\,(\ln w - \ln y)$$
$$\underset{(2.05)}{+\ 0.3395}\,\Delta \ln(\text{M3}/P)_{-2} \ \underset{(3.88)}{+\ 0.0020}r_k \ \underset{(2.54)}{+\ 0.0036}\,\Delta r_k$$
$$\underset{(3.88)}{-\ 0.0020}r_l \ \underset{(2.54)}{-\ 0.0036}\,\Delta r_{l-2} \ \underset{(3.88)}{-\ 0.0020}\dot{p} \ \underset{(1.88)}{-\ 0.0123}\,\Delta conj$$
$$\underset{(2.87)}{+\ 0.0592} \ \underset{(1.79)}{+\ 0.0131}s_1 \ \underset{(0.87)}{+\ 0.0052}s_2 \ \underset{(1.48)}{-\ 0.0117}s_3$$

Estimation period 1980:I–1994:IV $\bar{R}^2 = 0.53$ $SE = 0.014$

# Appendix 6.C Results of Specification Analysis

This appendix discusses the results of the statistical evaluation of the demand for money equations presented in the former appendix. A first issue concerns the restrictions imposed on the parameters of the estimated equations. With respect to these restrictions two categories can be distinguished. The first one concerns restrictions on the parameters of the long-run demand for money relationship. Examples are for instance the restriction that the price elasticity equals one or the restriction that the sum of the income and wealth elasticity is equal to one. Frequently a restriction has been imposed on the semi-elasticities with respect to the interest rates and the inflation rate. All these restrictions constitute testable hypotheses, which can be tested by means of $t$- and $F$-tests. The values of the $t$- and $F$-statistics for the respective hypotheses are reported in Table 6.C.1 and indicate that all the restrictions imposed are justified from a statistical point of view.

The second class of restrictions concerns the parameters describing the short-run adjustment processes. An example is the formulation of the error-correction term which reads as $(\ln(\mathrm{M}/P)_{-1} - \ln y)$ in the equations for M2 and M3 for Belgium. This formulation results if one imposes a restriction on the coefficients of the familiar error-correction term $(\ln(\mathrm{M}/P)_{-1} - \ln y_{-1})$ and the explanatory variables $\Delta \ln y$ and $(\ln w_{-1} - \ln y_{-1})$. An economic interpretation of this restriction is that the partial effect on money demand as a result of current income growth and a change in the wealth-income ratio equals the equilibrium restoring effect following from a value $\ln(\mathrm{M}/P)_{-1}$ of deviating from its equilibrium. These restrictions on the parameters describing the short-run dynamics have been tested as well. The results are not reported in this appendix, but again all the restrictions imposed are valid from a statistical point of view.

A second aspect of the statistical evaluation concerns the properties of the residuals. For all demand for money equations, the hypothesis that the residuals are white noise has been tested. To this end, the Ljung–Box test statistic has been calculated, using the first $p$ autocorrelations of the residuals $p = 1$, 4, 8, 12. Under the null hypothesis of white noise error processes, these statistics are $\chi^2(p)$ distributed. The results are reported in Tabel 6.C.2 and show that no significant residual autocorrelation is present.

The long-run relationships, implied by the dynamic demand for money equations, have been analysed by means of cointegration tests. One way to examine cointegration is to apply Johansen-type tests. Since these tests require the specification of a VAR-model rather than a single-

*Table 6.C.1: Results of the specification analysis, long-run relationship*

| Country | Monetary aggregate | Elasticities $\alpha_1 = 1$ | $\alpha_2 + \alpha_3 = 1$ | $\alpha_3 = 0$ | Semi-elasticities Restriction imposed | Test statistic |
|---|---|---|---|---|---|---|
| The Netherlands | M1 | 1.46 | 0.35 | 2.23* | $\alpha_5 = \alpha_6$ | 0.95 |
| | M2 | 1.65 | 0.70 | 3.35* | $-\alpha_4 = \alpha_5 = \alpha_6$ | $F(2, 78) = 2.77$ |
| | M3 | 0.68 | 0.66 | 3.66* | $\alpha_5 = \alpha_6$ | 0.47 |
| Belgium | M1[a] | 3.67* | 2.24* | 0.00 | $\alpha_4 = \alpha_5 = \alpha_6$ | $F(2, 44) = 0.09$ |
| | M2 | 0.97 | 0.41* | 2.41* | $-\alpha_4 = \alpha_5 = \alpha_6$ | $F(2, 46) = 2.36$ |
| | M3 | 0.42 | 0.32 | 4.26* | $-\alpha_4 = \alpha_5 = \alpha_6$ | $F(2, 48) = 1.85$ |

*Notes:*
Long-run money demand M $\propto P^{\alpha_1} y^{\alpha_2} w^{\alpha_3} \exp(\alpha_4 r_k + \alpha_5 r_l + \alpha_6 \dot{p})$. Unless specified otherwise, the values of the $t$-test statistics are given.
* Significant at a significance level of 0.05.
[a] $\alpha_2 + \alpha_3 = 1$ corresponds to the restriction that the income elasticity equals 1.

equation approach, the Johansen procedure has not been carried out. Instead, we have investigated whether the deviations of the long-run relationship follow a stationary process. Since the data used are not seasonally adjusted, the procedure put forward by Hylleberg, Engle, Granger, and Yoo (1990) has been applied. The equation

$$\Delta_4 x_t = \pi_1 y_{1t-1} + \pi_2 y_{2t-1} + \pi_3 y_{3t-2} + \pi_4 y_{3t-1} + \varepsilon_t, \qquad (6.C.1)$$

with $x_t$ the deviations from the long-run relationship, $y_{1t} = (1 + L + L^2 + L^3)x_t$, $y_{2t} = -(1 - L)(1 + L^2)x_t$, $y_{3t} = -(1 - L)(1 + L)x_t$, and $\varepsilon_t$ the disturbance term, has been estimated. Lags of $\Delta_4 x_t$ have been included as explanatory variables to eliminate possible autocorrelation of the residuals. The restriction $\pi_1 = 0$ corresponds with a unit root equal to 1. The restriction $\pi_2 = 0$ implies that a unit root $L = -1$ is present and if $\pi_3$ and $\pi_4$ both equal 0, the unit roots $L = \pm i$ are present. As these unit roots are each other's complex conjugates both $\pi_3$ and $\pi_4$ must be equal to 0. These restrictions can be tested by means of the $t$-values of $\pi_i$, $i = 1, \ldots, 4$ and the $F$-test for the hypothesis $\pi_3 = \pi_4 = 0$. Since the conventional statistical theory does not apply for these unit root tests, the critical values derived by Hylleberg, Engle, Granger, and Yoo (1990) have been used.

For the cointegration test, equation (6.C.1) has been estimated with seasonal dummies, a constant term and the first four lags of $\Delta_4 x_t$ included as additional explanatory variables. Subsequently, the most insignificant lag of $\Delta_4 x_t$ has been removed from the equation. Repeating this procedure ultimately yields an equation with only significant lags of $\Delta_4 x_t$ as explanatory variables. The results of the $t$- and $F$-tests for this ultimate equation are shown in Table 6.C.3. For both The Netherlands and Belgium the hypothesis that the unit root $L = 1$ is present cannot

*Table 6.C.2: Results of LB-tests on residual autocorrelation*

| Country | Monetary aggregate | Order $p$ 1 | 4 | 8 | 12 |
|---|---|---|---|---|---|
| The Netherlands | M1 | 0.23 | 1.89 | 3.61 | 13.45 |
| | M2 | 1.49 | 3.09 | 4.28 | 5.76 |
| | M3 | 1.65 | 5.19 | 9.26 | 10.41 |
| Belgium | M1 | 0.20 | 5.19 | 10.23 | 11.52 |
| | M2 | 0.09 | 2.34 | 12.19 | 16.17 |
| | M3 | 0.11 | 0.78 | 8.64 | 16.76 |

be rejected. Seasonal unit roots, however, are not present. The results in Table 6.C.3 indicate that cointegration must be rejected. Banerjee, Dolado, Hendry, and Smith (1986) argue, however, that the small sample properties of the above tests are rather poor. An alternative test for cointegration put forward by Kremers, Ericsson, and Dolado (1992) is based on the $t$-statistic of the estimate of the coefficient of the error-correction term. Under particular assumptions this statistic is normally distributed. If these assumptions are violated, the Dickey–Fuller critical values can be used. Using this procedure to test for cointegration, the empirical results reported in Appendix 6.B yield supportive evidence for the cointegration hypothesis.

*Table 6.C.3: Results of cointegration analysis*

| Country | Monetary aggregate | $t(\pi_1)$ | $t(\pi_2)$ | $t(\pi_3)$ | $t(\pi_4)$ | $F(\pi_3, \pi_4)$ |
|---|---|---|---|---|---|---|
| The Netherlands | M1 | −1.60 | −6.23* | −5.34* | −4.28* | 31.35* |
| | M2 | −1.47 | −6.22* | −4.29* | −4.78* | 26.94* |
| | M3 | −1.78 | −5.79* | −2.31 | −3.56* | 10.14* |
| Belgium | M1 | −2.17 | −3.08* | −3.55* | −1.42 | 7.78* |
| | M2 | −1.73 | −3.10* | −4.77* | −4.44* | 46.53* |
| | M3 | −1.98 | −3.01* | −3.88* | −3.79* | 28.22* |

*Note:* * Significant at a level of significance of 0.05.

# 7. Money Demand Within EMU: An Analysis With the Divisia Measure

## 7.1 INTRODUCTION

A noteworthy monetary phenomenon in many countries is the diminishing emphasis on the money supply as a key monetary target. This development cannot be viewed in isolation from the fact that, notably in small countries, the controllability of the money supply has decreased as a result of the greater volatility of international capital movements and the shift towards the exchange rate as the policy target. In addition, and perhaps also in connection with this development, many countries have experienced considerable money growth since the 1980s. This monetary expansion has been especially evident for the broad monetary aggregates M2 and M3, although in various countries M1 has also expanded at a higher rate than national income.

A restrictive monetary policy induced by increases in short-term interest rates often results in a flat or even inverted yield curve, as long-term rates, determined as they are in the world capital market, increase to a lesser extent or do not rise at all. Consequently, liquid assets become a more attractive investment opportunity. This leads to shifts from capital market investments towards monetary assets, thus automatically increasing the traditionally defined money stock. In itself, this is not a new phenomenon, as illustrated by the shift of funds from savings accounts to time deposits in The Netherlands during the 1970s (*cf.* Fase (1978b, 1979)). However, it does illustrate once again that proper assessment of the movements in the traditional monetary indicators calls for careful interpretation and detailed analysis. One major aspect that merits attention in this context is the fact that money growth resulting

---

Reprinted with kind permission from *De Nederlandsche Bank, Quarterly Bulletin*, 1994/3 (September 1994), M.M.G. Fase and C.C.A. Winder, 'Money demand within EMU: An analysis with the Divisia measure', 25–55, ©1994 by De Nederlandsche Bank NV.

from an increase in monetary assets for investment purposes lowers the velocity of circulation. This means that the probability of these monetary assets being used for transactions purposes is small. The view that this mechanism accounted for a substantial distortion of money growth during the 1980s explains to a large extent the reserved policy reactions of the national monetary authorities.

In the light of these monetary experiences from the past decade, there is a need for a monetary aggregate whose growth rate is adjusted to eliminate the growth ensuing from investment considerations. Such an aggregate would constitute a less biased measure of the quantity of money held for transactions purposes than the usual aggregates. For its construction, various alternatives have been proposed, such as the Divisia measures of money or the currency-equivalent aggregate. These alternatives avoid a drawback inherent in the usual monetary aggregates such as M1, M2 or M3, which represent simple sum aggregates of their components and thus implicitly assume perfectly equal degrees of liquidity and, hence, perfect substitutability. In principle, the Divisia measures of money meet the need to adjust for the evident differences in degrees of liquidity in a fairly objective manner.

There is a second reason for paying attention to the construction of such monetary aggregates as the Divisia measure of money. This reason has to do with the desirability of defining a European monetary aggregate which constitutes an unbiased reflection of the monetary assets available for transactions purposes within Economic and Monetary Union (EMU). Moreover, such an aggregate could serve as a basis for analysis of the overall demand for money within the EU.

The central aim of such research is to gain an insight into the properties of the demand for money within EMU. In addition to insight into the income and interest rate sensitivities of the demand for money, the conduct of monetary policy also requires an insight into the stability of the demand for money within EMU, the more so as it is not simple to ascertain this with sufficient accuracy (*cf.* Fase (1994)). In various studies, such as Kremers and Lane (1990), Monticelli and Strauss-Kahn (1992), and Fase and Winder (1993), various monetary aggregates have been examined. These studies, however, only consider the traditional unweighted aggregates. Thus far, Divisia aggregates for EMU as a whole have not been examined. The present study seeks to fill this gap by constructing Divisia aggregates for EMU and analysing their properties.

This chapter has been organized as follows. Section 7.2 briefly discusses and evaluates the theoretical foundations of Divisia aggregates. Section 7.3 deals with the construction of the Divisia aggregates for EMU. For the construction of aggregates at the EMU level, several methods of aggregation are available; hence, this section first addresses the aggregation problem itself. Subsequently, using a number of descriptive statistics, a preliminary analysis is conducted of the properties of the various aggregates calculated, after which a choice is made. Section 7.4 presents the results of our econometric analysis of the demand for money within EMU on the basis of Divisia aggregates, the economic properties being established by means of error-correction models. Section 7.5 examines the Divisia aggregates more closely, also in the light of the results obtained in earlier demand for money studies. Section 7.6 summarizes the main conclusions. Additional empirical results and explanatory notes are presented in two appendices.

## 7.2 THEORY OF DIVISIA AGGREGATES

This section briefly discusses the concept of Divisia aggregates.[1] Most of the conventional monetary aggregates are constructed by summing the constituent liquid assets; this implicitly assumes that these components have identical properties and are thus perfect substitutes. In practice, however, this heroic assumption can only be maintained as an approximation and may be misleading. For instance, currency and demand deposits are held primarily for transactions purposes, whereas in the case of near-money investment considerations will also play a major role. Hence, it is not surprising that there is a need of aggregates in which the various components are weighted by their degree of liquidity, thus providing a measure of the volume of liquid assets held for transactions purposes. The view that the traditional monetary aggregates are not perfect is not new. Friedman and Schwartz (1970), for instance, noted this problem in 1970 in the statistical supplement to their famous 1963 study of the monetary history of the US and proposed the use of a weighting procedure.

Divisia aggregates take explicit account of, and seek to adjust for, the differences in degrees of liquidity of the various liquid assets. The underlying notion is that holding an asset for transactions purposes involves a price, which may be viewed as the price of the moneyness

[1] The notion of a monetary index was first formulated in a series of articles by F. Divisia, published in *Revue d'Economie Politique* in 1925 and 1926 (*cf.* Divisia (1925, 1926)).

For an extensive discussion, illustrating the relationship between economic theory on index numbers and monetary aggregation, see Barnett, Fisher, and Serletis (1992). Fase and Schuit (1992), and Fisher, Hudson, and Pradhan (1993). The last-mentioned authors also give an application for the UK, as Fase (1985b) does for The Netherlands and Lecarpentier (1993) for France.

or liquidity provided by the asset concerned. This price concerns the costs of using the asset, i.e. its user cost. In this view, different user costs of assets reflect differences in the extent to which these assets serve transactions purposes. For the determination of the user cost, it is obvious to consider the rates of return of the various assets, since the fact that the various liquid assets are not perfect substitutes is reflected in differences in these return rates. The user cost is determined by comparing the rate of return of a liquid asset with that of a benchmark financial asset which is completely non-liquid and where, consequently, the transactions motive plays no role whatever. Thus, the cost of holding an asset consists of the return foregone as a result of the decision not to hold it in the alternative form of the non-liquid benchmark asset. The return foregone is the price which the economic agent is prepared to pay for the degree of liquidity provided by an asset.

This reasoning may be illustrated as follows. Suppose that the interest paid in period $t$ on a monetary asset $i$ is $r_{it}$ and that on a completely non-liquid asset offering no transactions services, is $R_t$. The user cost of holding a unit of asset $i$, say $p_{it}$ is equal to[2]

$$p_{it} = R_t - r_{it}. \tag{7.1}$$

If $A_{it}$ is the volume of asset $i$ in the portfolio, the amount of the corresponding user cost is therefore equal to $A_{it}p_{it}$. The total user cost of the portfolio is then equal to $\sum_i A_{it}p_{it}$. The share in total user cost accounted for by asset $i$, $s_{it}$, is the expenditure share of asset $i$, where $s_{it} = A_{it}p_{it}/\sum_j A_{jt}p_{jt}$. Monetary Divisia aggregates are expressed as index numbers. The growth of the Divisia index is defined as the weighted sum of the growth rates of the individual liquid assets. The weights are equal to the two-period moving averages of the corresponding expenditure shares. If the value of the Divisia aggregate in period $t$ is defined as $D_t$, then

$$\Delta \ln D_t = \sum_i n_{it} \Delta \ln A_{it}, \tag{7.2}$$

where $n_{it} = (s_{it} + s_{it-1})/2$, so that by definition $\sum_i n_{it} = 1$ while $\Delta \ln D$ and $\Delta \ln A_{it}$ indicate the relative growth rates of the aggregate concerned.

From a theoretical viewpoint, Divisia aggregates are to be preferred to the conventional unweighted monetary aggregates. However, their

[2] The formula used here is a simplification of the theoretical user cost, derived by Barnett (1978). The simplification concerns the conversion into present value of interest yield and does not affect the level of and the movements in the Divisia aggregates.

practical use involves a number of problems. The principal problem concerns the choice of the completely non-liquid benchmark asset serving to determine the degree of liquidity of the monetary assets. This benchmark asset should not provide any transactions services. Moreover, it should not be possible to convert it easily into a liquid form. This implies that financial assets which are actively traded in a secondary market are not, in principle, eligible for use as the benchmark asset. In addition – this is of major practical significance – the return on the benchmark asset must be higher than that on the liquid assets; otherwise, according to equation (7.1), the user cost, constituting the price for a monetary asset's liquidity, would be negative. In practice, it will be difficult or even impossible to select a financial asset meeting all of these requirements. Hence, any benchmark asset chosen will only partially meet the requirements mentioned.

Another drawback – the last to be discussed here – concerns the measurement of an asset's degree of liquidity. In the calculation of Divisia aggregates, it is implicitly assumed that the interest received and the corresponding user cost adequately define the asset's degree of liquidity, with differences in user cost reflecting differences in liquidity. However, the question is to what extent observed interest rates provide unbiased information in this respect. In a general equilibrium framework with full competition within the financial services sector, the equilibrium values resulting for the interest rates will exactly mirror the properties of the liquid assets. In the event of market imperfections, price setting behaviour, etc., it cannot be ruled out, however, that the user cost determined on the basis of actual interest rates may present a biased picture of the degree of liquidity of the asset concerned.

The above discussion shows that, despite the theoretical advantages of Divisia aggregates over unweighted monetary aggregates, the practical application of Divisia aggregates entails a number of imperfections. To what extent these should be assigned practical significance is above all an empirical matter, where the informational content for the purpose of the conduct of monetary policy is a crucial issue (*cf.* also Issing, Tödter, Herrmann, and Reimers (1993)). Moreover, monetary policy will generally not focus on a single indicator or aggregate. Usually, a range of indicators is used and, in this respect, weighted and unweighted aggregates may both serve a useful purpose.

## 7.3 The Divisia Aggregates for EMU

An analysis of monetary variables aggregated across EMU countries involves specific aggregation problems. Hence, we will first discuss the data and the various aggregation methods considered in this study. In order to get an impression of the sensitivity of the results to the specific aggregation method chosen, data constructed in a number of ways were subjected to a preliminary examination. This section concludes with a discussion of the results of this general comparison.

### 7.3.1 Data and Aggregation Methods

The data used in this study have been taken in part from the data set used in Fase and Winder (1993) to estimate the demand for money in the individual EMU countries. The sample period is 1970:I–1992:IV. With a few exceptions, seasonally unadjusted quarterly figures for the unweighted monetary aggregates M1, M2 and M3, gross domestic product in current and 1985 prices, money market interest rates and capital market interest rates are available for the entire sample period. For Greece, no reliable data for long-term interest rates could be obtained, so that it was decided to exclude this country from the analysis. The EMU variables discussed below consequently concern all EMU countries, except Greece and Luxembourg, for which no separate monetary statistics are available.

For the construction of EMU-wide data, several options are open. In order to measure the monetary aggregates and nominal national products of the various countries in a common currency, exchange rates and purchasing power parities were used as the conversion factor. Both conversion methods permit the use of either actual – that is, current – values or the values in a base period, resulting in a total of four different options. In the present study, these four options have all been examined, the monetary aggregates and nominal national products of the individual EMU countries being expressed in Deutsche Marks with 1985 being taken as the base period. The figures for the countries' national products in 1985 prices have been converted into 1985 Deutsche Mark prices using the 1985 exchange rates and purchasing power parities against the Deutsche Mark. The resulting series of the monetary aggregates for EMU as a whole and EMU's supranational product in current and constant prices have been obtained by summing the corresponding transformed variables for the individual EMU countries.[3] The price index at the

[3] As residents' cross-border holdings do not form part of the national monetary aggregates, the money supply calculated for EMU understates the actual money

EMU level has been determined as the ratio of EMU product in current to that in constant prices.

The short- and long-term interest rates for EMU have been calculated as weighted averages of the corresponding interest rates in the individual countries, using both a constant and a time-varying weighting scheme. In the constant weighting scheme, the weights chosen are the current shares of the EMU currencies in the ECU.[4] The time-varying weighting scheme consists of the shares of the national products of the individual countries in aggregated EMU product. Since four different conversion factors were used in calculating aggregated EMU product, this leads to four weighting schemes on the basis of the income shares of the individual countries, so that a total of five weighting schemes results for short- and long-term interest rates.

Divisia indices for EMU-wide M2 and M3 have been determined in two ways: directly and indirectly. In the *direct* manner of calculation, data were first constructed for the monetary aggregates and short- and long-term interest rates at the EMU level, and subsequently the corresponding Divisia indices were calculated. Four different definitions of monetary aggregates (depending on the conversion factors) and five different interest rates (depending on the weighting scheme chosen) were considered. In the calculation of the Divisia indices, two definitions of the EMU interest rate were considered for each of the four monetary aggregates: that based on ECU weights and that based on an income weighting scheme, that particular scheme being selected which follows from the calculation of EMU product using the same conversion factor as for the monetary aggregate. Consequently, if the monetary aggregate was determined on the basis of current exchange rates, the income weighting scheme based on current exchange rates was also used. In the *indirect* manner of calculation, Divisia indices were first calculated for the individual countries, the Divisia indices at the EMU level subsequently being determined as the weighted averages of the individual Divisia indices. The same five weighting schemes – based on ECU and the four different income shares – as used in the construction of the EMU interest rates were applied.

Divisia indices for M2 and M3 were calculated using the definition in Section 7.2 by weighting the growth rates of the components M1 and M2 – M1 and M3 – M1, respectively, by the two-period moving averages

supply (*cf.* Angeloni, Cottarelli, and Levy (1991)). However, for the sample period no appropriate data on cross-border holdings are available.

4 The relevant shares (after adjustment for leaving out Luxembourg and Greece) are: Belgium 8.3%, Denmark 2.6%, Germany 32.8%, France 20.0%, Ireland 1.1%, Italy 8.2%, The Netherlands 10.3%, Portugal 0.7%, Spain 4.5% and the United Kingdom 11.5%.

of the expenditure shares. The user cost involved depends on the benchmark interest rate for the non-liquid asset and the rates of return on the various liquid assets themselves. Following, for instance, Belongia and Chrystal (1991), the benchmark interest rate was taken to be the long-term rate, plus a constant mark-up equal to the maximum differential between short- and long-term rates during the sample period 1970:I–1992:IV.[5] This procedure guarantees that the user cost is positive. As regards the return on the liquid assets themselves, it has been assumed that for M1 it is equal to 0 and for $M2 - M1$ and $M3 - M1$ equal to the short-term interest rate. The latter assumption is in line with Fase and Winder (1993), who take the short-term interest rate to be representative of the return on near-money. The Divisia indices thus constructed are based on a relatively rough breakdown of the broadly defined monetary aggregates. However, a further refinement distinguishing between more categories of liquid assets with their corresponding rates of return leads to data requirements which cannot be met in an analysis at the EMU level.

### 7.3.2 Preliminary Analysis

The various possibilities of calculating variables at the EMU level lead to a large number of alternative series of the Divisia aggregates. The above discussion gives rise to 13 different time series for the Divisia M2 aggregates: eight following from the direct manner of calculation and five from the indirect manner. On the basis of theoretical arguments, it is not possible to make a definite choice. Therefore, the selection of the most appropriate construction method is more or less an empirical matter. However, should the alternative calculation methods lead to sharply differing results, the question would arise whether an analysis at the EMU level is at all meaningful. For this reason, the Divisia series calculated were first subjected to a preliminary analysis. The unweighted monetary aggregates and income have also been included in this analysis. With the aid of such statistics as the mean, the standard deviation and the coefficient of variation, the properties of the series have been assessed. In addition, the correlation with M1 and nominal EMU product has been determined. As the Divisia aggregates weight the various components by their degree of liquidity, which is greatest for M1, it is to be expected that the Divisia aggregates for M2 and M3 would be correlated more closely with M1 than with M2 and M3 themselves. In addition, the

[5] The mark-up factors for the EMU interest rates based on income weights (current and 1985 exchange rates, current and 1985 purchasing power parities) and ECU weights are 1.85, 1.67, 1.63, 1.64 and 2.10 percentage points, respectively.

correlation with nominal income was considered.

For the sake of brevity and clarity, the discussion is confined to the results for those Divisia aggregates which were also subjected to a more detailed econometric analysis, to be discussed in Section 7.4. These Divisia aggregates consist of the series determined by the direct method of calculation, the 1985 exchange rates being used as the aggregation method and the EMU interest rates being determined using the income weighting scheme following from the calculation of EMU product using 1985 exchange rates as the conversion factor. The results of the preliminary statistical analysis are summarized in Table 7.1; the results for the series resulting from the other aggregation methods are contained in Appendix 7.A.[6]

The results presented in Table 7.1 have a number of characteristics which – unless stated otherwise – prove to be representative, irrespective of the specific aggregation method used. First, the growth of the unweighted monetary aggregates proves to be higher as the concept of money used is broader. For all monetary aggregates, the average growth rate exceeds that of income. This is reflected in an increase in the liquidity ratios (the money supply expressed as a percentage of income), which has been apparent for a number of years for the broad monetary aggregates in particular. Second, the average growth rate of the Divisia aggregates is smaller than that of the corresponding unweighted aggregates and is more closely in line with the average growth rate for M1. Third, the standard deviations of the Divisia aggregates exceed those of the corresponding unweighted aggregates. This result is not, however, insensitive to the aggregation method chosen, as is illustrated by the analysis in Appendix 7.A. Fourth, the growth of the Divisia aggregates proves to be correlated more closely with that of M1 than with the growth of the unweighted aggregates. This is not unexpected, since the Divisia indices aim to adjust for differences in degrees of liquidity between the various components, and M1 best matches the notion of pure transactions balances. The fifth and last characteristic concerns the correlation with income growth. In this respect, no unequivocal pattern is evident. The correlation of Divisia M2 with income growth is greater than that for M2 with income, the reverse being the case for Divisia M3. Moreover, this result proves to be fairly sensitive to the aggregation method used.

The results shown in Table 7.1 suggest that the movements in the Divisia aggregates are comparable with those in M1, a property ascer-

[6] This appendix also contains the outcomes for the aggregates considered for the individual EMU countries. This countrywise inventory provides the possibility to examine whether the stylized facts of the series at EMU level correspond to those at the level of the individual EMU countries.

*Table 7.1: Descriptive statistics for the growth of monetary aggregates and income for EMU*

| Variable | Mean growth rate (%) | Standard deviation | Coefficient of variation | Correlation with M 1 | Correlation with income |
|---|---|---|---|---|---|
| M 1 | 9.63 | 2.76 | 0.28 | 1.00 | 0.56 |
| M 2 | 11.47 | 2.34 | 0.20 | 0.40 | 0.54 |
| DiM 2 | 9.96 | 2.44 | 0.24 | 0.96 | 0.60 |
| M 3 | 11.69 | 2.14 | 0.18 | 0.71 | 0.76 |
| DiM 3 | 10.24 | 2.54 | 0.25 | 0.97 | 0.63 |
| Income | 9.58 | 2.32 | 0.24 | 0.56 | 1.00 |

*Notes:* The Divisia indices have been determined by the direct method. All variables have been calculated using 1985 exchange rates as the conversion factor.

tained earlier by Fase (1985b) for The Netherlands. This impression is confirmed by Figures 7.1 and 7.2. Figure 7.1 presents the annual growth rates of the unweighted aggregates M 1 and M 2 and of Divisia M 2. Figure 7.2 shows the movements in the growth of M 1, M 3 and Divisia M 3. From the figures it becomes clear that M 1 and the Divisia aggregates exhibit similar patterns. During three sub-periods, the growth of the unweighted aggregates differs sharply from that of the corresponding Divisia aggregates: 1972:IV–1974:IV, 1979:III–1982:II and 1989:I–1992:II. Especially during the last period, the divergences between the movements in M 2 and those in Divisia M 2 are prominent. The three sub-periods show turbulent interest rate movements, with sharp increases in short-term rates leading to a flat or even an inverted yield curve. The resulting shift from capital market investments to near-money led to a high growth rate of the broad monetary aggregates relative to M 1. As part of this increase was the result of portfolio considerations, the observed growth rate presents a biased picture of the growth of money held for transactions purposes. The adjustment for differences in degrees of liquidity implicit in the Divisia aggregates causes the movements in the Divisia aggregates to correspond fairly closely to those in M 1. This suggests that the Divisia aggregates considered here constitute a more appropriate measure of the volume of money for transactions purposes than the traditional monetary aggregates.

A comparison of the movements in the monetary aggregates considered here with EMU income provides further information about the monetary developments which have occurred during the sample period. To this end, the liquidity ratio was calculated for each of the monetary

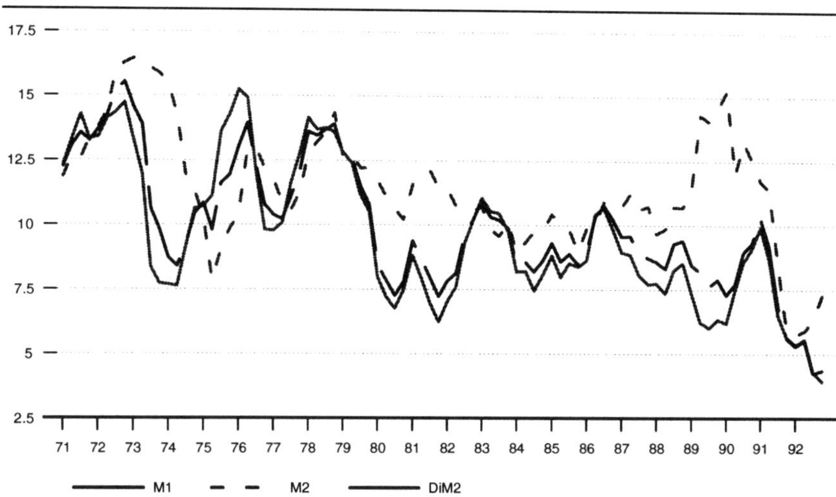


*Figure 7.1: Growth of* M1, M2 *and Divisia* M2 *for EMU Percentages*

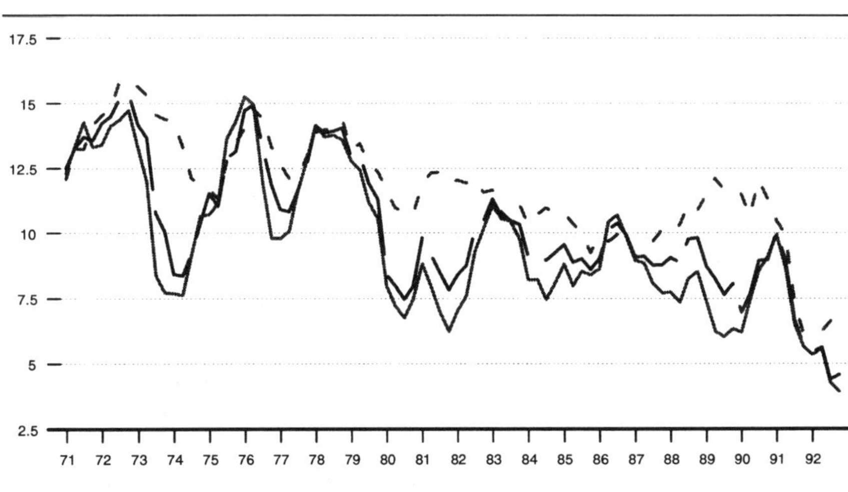


*Figure 7.2: Growth of* M1, M3 *and Divisia* M3 *for EMU Percentages*

aggregates. As the Divisia aggregates represent index numbers, with the 1970 level set at 100, the unweighted aggregates M1, M2 and M3 as well as EMU income have been scaled with their values in 1970. Hence, for all monetary aggregates, the money supply as a percentage of EMU income in 1970 was set at 100. Figure 7.3 shows the movements in the liquidity ratios of M1, M2 and Divisia M2, while Figure 7.4 presents the movements in the ratios for M1, M3 and Divisia M3. The differences between the ratios shown in Figure 7.3 and Figure 7.4 reflect the divergent movements in the various monetary aggregates. Whereas Figures 7.1 and 7.2 show the differences in terms of annual growth rates, Figures 7.3 and 7.4 present the growth differentials accumulated over time.

Figures 7.3 and 7.4 make clear that both M2 and M3 have increased much more sharply than EMU income. During the 1980s in particular, the M2 ratio showed a sharp increase, with a pronounced growth acceleration in the second half of the 1980s. The increase in the M3 ratio has been relatively much more smooth, but is already present from the early 1970s onwards. The movements in the M1 ratio, on the other hand, are comparatively stable. Figures 7.3 and 7.4 reveal that the movements in the liquidity ratios for the Divisia aggregates are similar to those in the M1 ratio. For the 1970s, the Divisia M2 ratio moves in close harmony with the M1 ratio. From 1980 onwards, however, a discrepancy becomes evident, with Divisia M2 growing at a faster rate than M1. The Divisia M3 ratio diverges from the M1 ratio from as early as the beginning of the 1970s. The movements in the liquidity ratios for the Divisia aggregates indicate that, during the 1980s, the volume of money held for transactions purposes increased somewhat more rapidly than EMU income. However, according to the Divisia ratios, this monetary expansion was limited, suggesting that the very considerable increases in the ratios for the corresponding unweighted monetary aggregates should primarily be attributed to increases in the volume of liquid assets held for investment purposes.

The use of alternative aggregation methods yields a picture which corresponds fairly closely to that outlined in this section. This warrants the conclusion that the specific choice of aggregation method, though influencing the results in terms of their details, generally does not affect the overall pattern. Moreover, it appears that the stylized facts found for EMU as a whole correspond closely to those for the individual EMU countries (see Appendix 7.A).

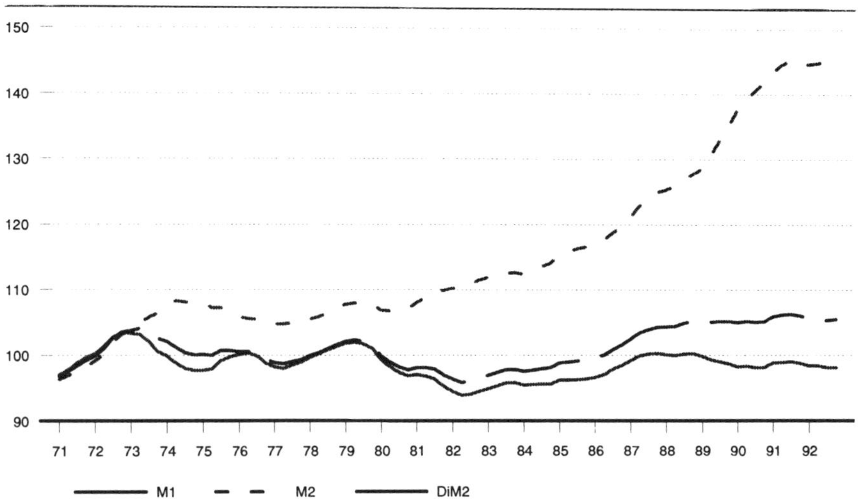


*Figure 7.3: Liquidity ratios for* M1, M2 *and Divisia* M2 *for EMU* 1970 = 100

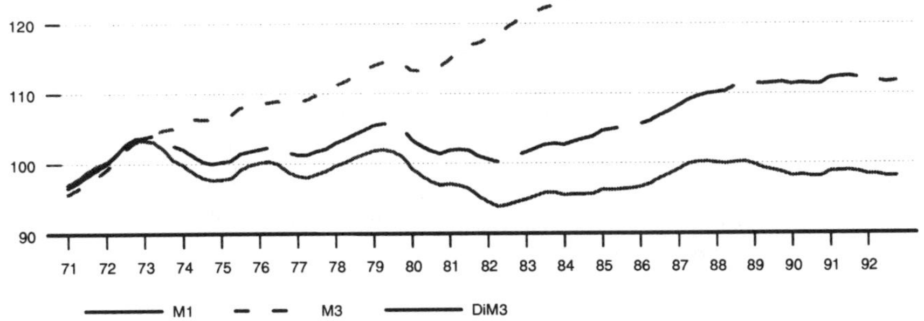


*Figure 7.4: Liquidity ratios for* M1, M3 *and Divisia* M3 *for EMU* 1970 = 100

## 7.4 Divisia Aggregates and the Demand for Money Within EMU

The Divisia aggregates discussed in Section 7.3 were used to estimate the demand for money. Therefore, this Section first discusses the model used. This model is the same as that in Fase and Winder (1990, 1993). The estimation results are reviewed in Subsection 7.4.2.

### 7.4.1 Statistical Model

For the estimation of the demand for money based on Divisia aggregates, an error-correction model has been chosen. An essential characteristic of this model is the distinction between a long-run equilibrium relationship and the short-run adjustment processes which, if deviations from the equilibrium path occur, establish a return to the long-run equilibrium relationship. The postulated long-run relationship reads as follows:

$$\mathrm{M} = AP^{\alpha_1}y^{\alpha_2}\exp(\alpha_3 oc + \alpha_4\dot{p}), \tag{7.3}$$

where M is the demand of the Divisia money desired in the equilibrium situation, $P$ the price index and $y$ real income. The relevant interest rate variable is $oc$ (opportunity costs), representing the cost of holding liquid assets and $\dot{p}$ represents inflation, defined as the percentage change in the price index on an annual basis. The long-run price and income elasticities are equal to $\alpha_1$ and $\alpha_2$, respectively; $\alpha_3$ and $\alpha_4$ are the semi-elasticities with respect to the interest rate variable and the inflation rate; $A$ is a constant term. Following Fase and Winder (1993), it has not been assumed *a priori* that the price elasticity is equal to 1. The more general specification used here permits this frequently made assumption to be tested statistically.

If deviations occur from the long-run equilibrium path, equilibrating mechanisms are triggered. These short-run adjustment processes have been modelled by considering a dynamic variant of equation (7.3). In addition, and in line with our earlier demand for money research, a cyclical indicator, $conj$, has been included in the estimation equation as an explanatory variable to describe the short-run dynamics (*cf.*, for instance, Fase and Kuné (1974a), Butter and Fase (1981)). The equation which served as the basis for the specification and estimation analysis is:

$$\begin{aligned}\alpha(L)\Delta\ln(\mathrm{M}/P) = {} & \beta_1\ln P - \alpha(\ln(\mathrm{M}/P)_{-1} - \ln y_{-1}) \\ & + (\beta_2 - \alpha)\ln y_{-1} + \beta_3 oc + \beta_4\dot{p} + \beta_2(L)\Delta\ln y \\ & + \beta_3(L)\Delta oc + \beta_4(L)\Delta\dot{p} + \beta_5(L)conj, \end{aligned} \tag{7.4}$$

where $L$ represents the lag operator and $\alpha(L)$ and $\beta_i(L)$, $i = 2,3,4,5$ lag polynomials. Owing to the fact that the data considered are not seasonally adjusted, a constant and three seasonal dummies $s_i$ have been included in the estimation equation. Estimates of the long-run (semi-)elasticities can be determined with equation (7.4). The semi-elasticities with respect to the interest rate variable and the inflation rate are equal to $\beta_3/\alpha$ and $\beta_4/\alpha$, respectively. The income elasticity is $\beta_2/\alpha$ and the price elasticity is equal to $(\beta_1 + \alpha)/\alpha$. The hypothesis that the income elasticity is equal to 1 corresponds to the constraint that the coefficient of $\ln y_{-1}$ is equal to 0. This hypothesis can thus be tested easily. The same holds for the hypothesis that the price elasticity is equal to 1, since this hypothesis corresponds to the constraint that the coefficient of $\ln P$ in equation (7.4) is equal to 0.

### 7.4.2 Estimation Results

The estimated equations for the demand for money for Divisia M2 and Divisia M3 for EMU as a whole are:

$$\begin{aligned}
\Delta \ln(\mathrm{DiM}2/P) = &- \underset{(2.41)}{0.1087}(\ln(\mathrm{DiM}2/P)_{-1} - \ln y_{-1}) \\
&+ \underset{(5.41)}{0.4457}\Delta \ln(\mathrm{DiM}2/P)_{-4} + \underset{(2.03)}{0.1813}\Delta \ln y \\
&+ \underset{(2.11)}{0.3525}\Delta \ln y_{-1\frac{1}{2}} - \underset{(2.35)}{0.0071}\ln P \\
&- \underset{(3.28)}{0.0015}oc_{1-\frac{1}{2}} - \underset{(2.06)}{0.0036}\Delta R - \underset{(4.24)}{0.0041}\Delta r_{k-1} \\
&- \underset{(3.28)}{0.0015}\dot{p} - \underset{(3.95)}{0.0053}\Delta \dot{p} - \underset{(2.91)}{0.0066}\Delta conj \\
&- \underset{(2.17)}{0.1100} - \underset{(0.90)}{0.0116}s_1 \\
&- \underset{(0.74)}{0.0074}s_2 + \underset{(0.32)}{0.0037}s_3
\end{aligned} \tag{7.5}$$

Estimation period 1972:I–1992:IV $\bar{R}^2 = 0.78$ $SE = 0.007$

$$\begin{aligned}
\Delta \ln(\mathrm{DiM}3/P) = &- \underset{(2.43)}{0.0981}(\ln(\mathrm{DiM}3/P)_{-1} - \ln y) \\
&+ \underset{(6.44)}{0.5689}\Delta \ln(\mathrm{DiM}3/P)_{-4} + \underset{(2.43)}{0.4170}\Delta \ln y_{-1\frac{1}{2}}
\end{aligned}$$

$$
\begin{aligned}
&- \underset{(2.20)}{0.0010 oc_{2_{-1}}} - \underset{(2.33)}{0.0044 \Delta R} - \underset{(4.14)}{0.0042 \Delta r_{k-1}} \\
&- \underset{(2.20)}{0.0010 \dot{p}} - \underset{(4.34)}{0.0054 \Delta \dot{p}} - \underset{(3.91)}{0.0085 \Delta conj} \\
&- \underset{(2.19)}{0.0956} - \underset{(2.62)}{0.0171 s_1} - \underset{(2.18)}{0.0146 s_2} \\
&- \underset{(0.54)}{0.0022 s_3} \qquad (7.6)
\end{aligned}
$$

Estimation period 1972:I–1992:IV $\bar{R}^2 = 0.74 \quad SE = 0.007$,

where the Divisia aggregates for M2 and M3 have been denoted as DiM2 and DiM3, respectively. For the other variables, the notation explained in the preceding subsection has been used. The interest rate variables $oc_1$ and $oc_2$ represent the cost of holding M2 and M3 and have been defined as the weighted average of the user costs of the various components:

$$
\begin{aligned}
oc_1 &= R(\text{M}1/\text{M}2) - (R - r_k)(\text{M}1 - \text{M}2)/\text{M}2 \\
&= R - r_k(\text{M}2 - \text{M}1)/\text{M}2 \qquad (7.7)
\end{aligned}
$$

and

$$
\begin{aligned}
oc_2 &= R(\text{M}1/\text{M}3) - (R - r_k)(\text{M}1 - \text{M}3)/\text{M}3 \\
&= R - r_k(\text{M}3 - \text{M}1)/\text{M}3. \qquad (7.8)
\end{aligned}
$$

In equations (7.5) and (7.6), $t$-values, adjusted for potential heteroscedasticity, are given in parentheses. $SE$ and $\bar{R}^2$ are the standard error of the residuals and the coefficient of determination adjusted for degrees of freedom, respectively. Measured by the $\bar{R}^2$, the goodness of fit for DiM2 is slightly better than that for DiM3. In both equations, the standard error of the residuals is of the same order of magnitude. The $t$-values found indicate that all estimates, except for a number of seasonal parameters, differ significantly from 0.

The estimated models have a similar dynamic structure. A striking difference is that the price level has a significant influence on DiM2, whereas it does not feature as a separate explanatory variable in the equation for DiM3. This indicates that the price elasticity for DiM2 is not equal to 1, whereas price homogeneity holds for DiM3. For both aggregates, the long-run income elasticity is equal to 1. Testing the hypothesis that these constraints are valid leads to the conclusion that imposing these constraints is justified (see also Appendix 7.B).

In both equations, the error-correction term has a significant influence on the movements in the Divisia aggregates. In the specification for DiM 3, the error-correction mechanism does not have its traditional form $\ln(\text{DiM}\,3/P)_{-1} - \ln y_{-1}$, but is $\ln(\text{DiM}\,3/P)_{-1} - \ln y$.[7] This means that the equilibrating influence of a differential between actual $\ln(\text{DiM}\,3/P)_{-1}$ and its equilibrium value and that of the partial effect of income growth are equally large. In the DiM 2 equation, the explanatory variables $\ln(\text{DiM}\,2/P)_{-1} - \ln y_{-1}$ and $\Delta \ln y$ have been included separately, so that these effects are not equal.

In addition to the above constraints, the equations for DiM 2 and DiM 3 include the constraint that the long-run semi-elasticities with respect to the interest rate variable and the inflation rate are equal. For DiM 2, the interest rate has a more direct effect than for DiM 3, as $oc_2$ has been included with a lag of one quarter. Changes in $oc_1$ and $oc_2$ proved to exert no significant influence, contrary to the first differences of the underlying benchmark interest rate $R$ and the short-term interest rate $r_k$. Consequently, $\Delta R$ and $\Delta r_k$ (with a lag of one quarter) have been included in both equations as explanatory variables. It is also noteworthy that, for both DiM 2 and DiM 3, the cyclical indicator has a significant influence. This result, which is in line with earlier findings of Fase and Winder (1993), illustrates once again the importance of including a cyclical indicator as an explanatory variable in demand for money equations.

## 7.5 ASSESSMENT

Our evaluation of the estimation results obtained focuses on two aspects in particular. First, a more detailed analysis is presented of the sensitivity of the results to the aggregation method chosen. Second, a comparison is made between the results of the present study and those of other empirical studies on the demand for money within EMU as a whole.

### 7.5.1 Sensitivity to the Aggregation Method Chosen

Whether or not the empirical results presented in the preceding section are highly sensitive to the aggregation method used can be examined in a simple manner by additional estimation of equations (7.5) and (7.6) for

---

7 This formulation follows if the equation with the explanatory variables $\ln(\text{DiM}\,3/P)_{-1} - \ln y_{-1}$ and $\Delta \ln y$ is subjected to the constraint that the corresponding coefficients are each other's opposite.

the Divisia aggregates determined using the other construction methods. These supplementary calculations show that the use of EMU interest rates based on ECU weights instead of income weights leads to similar results. The parameter estimates are of the same order of magnitude as in (7.5) and (7.6) and again differ significantly from 0. This exercise also shows that the use of 1985 purchasing power parities instead of 1985 exchange rates as the conversion factor does not give rise to major differences. However, the use of current exchange rates and purchasing power parities instead of 1985 values does have a considerable effect on the estimation results: the size of the parameter estimates changes markedly and becomes implausible. Moreover, from an econometric viewpoint – that is, considering their statistical properties – the estimation results are frequently not acceptable.

The long-run properties of the reasonable estimates for the demand for money according to the Divisia aggregates are summarized in Table 7.2. The elasticities shown in Table 7.2 for the Divisia aggregates determined using the 1985 exchange rates and the EMU interest rates based on income weights follow directly from the estimated demand for money equations (7.5) and (7.6). For both Divisia aggregates, the long-run income elasticity is equal to 1. For Divisia M3, the price elasticity is also equal to 1, so that in the long-run price homogeneity is found. For Divisia M2, on the other hand, the estimated price elasticity is slightly less than 1. The semi-elasticities in respect of interest and inflation rates are equal, having a value of −0.014 for Divisia M2 and −0.010 for Divisia M3. Hence, a one percentage point increase in the interest rate ultimately leads to a decrease in Divisia M2 by 1.4% and of Divisia M3 by 1.0%. Multiplying these semi-elasticities by the sample averages for interest and inflation rates provides an estimate of the corresponding elasticities. The resulting values for the interest rate and the inflation rate elasticity of Divisia M2 are −0.101 and −0.094, respectively. For Divisia M3, the interest rate and inflation rate elasticities are equal to −0.057 and −0.071, respectively.

As is evident from Table 7.2, the alternative Divisia aggregates reviewed here have similar long-run properties. The estimates of price elasticity show a remarkably robust pattern. This is also true of the estimates of the interest rate and the inflation rate sensitivity of the demand for the Divisia aggregates, although the differences between the resulting semi-elasticities are somewhat greater than those between the price elasticities. In all cases the demand for Divisia M2 is more sensitive to changes in interest and inflation rates than that for Divisia M3. The results also show that the Divisia aggregates constructed with EMU interest rates based on ECU weights have semi-elasticities for the

*Table 7.2: Long-run properties of Divisia aggregates constructed by various aggregation methods*

| Aggregation method | Monetary aggregate | Elasticities | | Semi-elasticities | |
|---|---|---|---|---|---|
| | | Price | Income | Interest rate | Inflation rate |
| 1985 exchange rates | DiM 2 | 0.935 | 1 | −0.014 | −0.014 |
| | DiM 3 | 1 | 1 | −0.010 | −0.010 |
| | DiM 2 − ECU | 0.932 | 1 | −0.018 | −0.018 |
| | DiM 3 − ECU | 1 | 1 | −0.014 | −0.014 |
| 1985 purchasing power parities | DiM 2 | 0.934 | 1 | −0.013 | −0.013 |
| | DiM 3 | 1 | 1 | −0.009 | −0.009 |
| | DiM 2 − ECU | 0.932 | 1 | −0.017 | −0.017 |
| | DiM 3 − ECU | 1 | 1 | −0.013 | −0.013 |

*Notes:* Divisia aggregates calculated using interest rates based on ECU weights are indicated by the addition ECU. The other Divisia aggregates have been calculated on the basis of income weights, income in the member countries being expressed in a common currency using the conversion method stated in the first column.

interest and the inflation rate which are systematically higher than in the case of interest rates based on income weights. All in all, however, the differences are relatively small.

In summary, it may be concluded that the decision to construct the variables aggregated across the EMU countries, using either current conversion factors or conversion factors in a base period, has a definite influence on the empirical results. The results discussed here also indicate that the use of exchange rates or of purchasing power parities and the use of ECU or income weights in constructing the EMU interest rates affect the results to a much lesser extent.

### 7.5.2 Comparison With Previous Research

A comparison with the findings obtained in previous demand for money research for EMU provides an effective way of assessing the results reported here. As the present study is the first to analyse Divisia aggregates for EMU as a whole, the comparison focuses on studies considering the traditional unweighted monetary aggregates: those of Bekx and Tullio (1989), Kremers and Lane (1990), and Monticelli and Strauss-

Kahn (1992).[8] The discussion centres on three aspects. First, some general characteristics are reviewed, followed by a discussion of the long-run properties of the demand for money within EMU. Third, two characteristics of the dynamic demand for money equations are compared.

An assessment of the studies reviewed here demands first of all an insight into their mutual differences, since these differences will have an impact on the results obtained. The first difference concerns the group of countries considered. Bekx and Tullio, like Kremers and Lane, consider the original participants in the exchange rate mechanism – except Luxembourg – at the time of the establishment of the EMS. Monticelli and Strauss-Kahn add Spain and the United Kingdom to this group of seven. The second difference relates to the aggregation method chosen. For the construction of aggregated data for EMU as a whole, Bekx and Tullio use exchange rates in a base period. The two other studies consider various aggregation methods. On the basis of a preliminary analysis, Kremers and Lane ultimately opt for purchasing power parities in a base period, whereas Monticelli and Strauss-Kahn prefer current exchange rates as the conversion factor. The third difference concerns the length of the sample period. For all three studies, the start of the estimation period roughly coincides with the establishment of the EMS. Bekx and Tullio analyse data up to and including 1986:IV. The estimation period of Kremers and Lane ends with 1987:IV, while Monticelli and Strauss-Kahn consider data for the period up to and including 1990:II. This survey of general characteristics shows that the present study differs in a number of respects. The principal differences concern the sample period and the group of countries examined: our sample period is considerably longer and our study gives a more comprehensive view of the demand for money within EMU as it covers practically all EMU countries.

For the purposes of an evaluation of the economic properties of the demand for money within EMU, Table 7.3 presents the long-run elasticities as found in the three studies. The table also indicates the monetary aggregates considered in each of them. The results found by Bekx and Tullio and those of Kremers and Lane relate to M1, whereas Monticelli and Strauss-Kahn consider the broad monetary aggregate M3. Monticelli and Strauss-Kahn use two different techniques to estimate the demand for money. In the first – marked I in the table – the long-run demand for money relationship has been estimated directly by means of cointegration regression. In the second – marked II in the table – the long-run properties have been estimated simultaneously

[8] The evaluation is confined to studies which provide direct estimates of the aggregated demand for money within EMU. Riet (1993) presents a discussion which includes a comparison with the properties of the demand for money within EMU obtained by weighting the country results in Fase and Winder (1993).

with the short-term dynamics. To facilitate comparison, the results for the monetary Divisia aggregates from the present study are also shown. The semi-elasticities with respect to short- and long-term interest rates have been calculated with equations (7.7) and (7.8). As – apart from a constant mark-up factor – the benchmark interest rate is equal to the long-term interest rate, the long-term interest rate semi-elasticity can be determined directly. The short-term interest rate semi-elasticity, however, can only be approximated. Using the sample means of $(M2 - M1)/M2$ and $(M3 - M1)/M3$, the semi-elasticities with respect to the short-term interest rate have been calculated.

Table 7.3 also shows that Bekx and Tullio found an implausibly low value of 0.42 for the price elasticity. In the other two studies, the price elasticity was set equal to 1. The resulting pattern with respect to the income elasticity is diverse. Bekx and Tullio obtain a value of 0.91. After testing, Kremers and Lane find a value of 1 and the results of Monticelli and Strauss-Kahn are considerably larger than 1.

Our results for the Divisia aggregates correspond most closely to those of Kremers and Lane. For both Divisia aggregates, the income elasticity is equal to 1, while the price elasticity of Divisia M3 is also equal to 1. For the price elasticity of Divisia M2, however, the resulting estimate is slightly below 1.

In the studies reviewed here, the long-run relationship includes only one interest rate: the long-term rate in Bekx and Tullio and the short-term rate in the other two studies. The negative short-term interest rate semi-elasticity found by Monticelli and Strauss-Kahn is surprising. They regard the short-term interest rate as representative of the return on financial assets which do not form part of M3. However, as the short-term interest rate represents a return on liquid assets and, hence, is more in the nature of return on near-money, a positive value would have been more plausible. In view of the measures of money used, the signs of the interest rate semi-elasticities in the other studies are plausible. Moreover, the estimation results of Kremers and Lane show that changes in the long-term interest rate do have an effect on the demand for money. Thus, the effect of the long-term interest rate is restricted to the short-term and the long-run semi-elasticity has thus been assumed to be equal to 0. This result is not convincing. In the study by Monticelli and Strauss-Kahn, changes in the inflation rate only have short-term effects, so that a long-run inflation rate semi-elasticity of 0 is found. In the case of the Divisia aggregates, the long-term and short-term interest rates and the inflation rate all have long-run effects. The values found for the semi-elasticities correspond fairly well to those found in the other studies, although the Divisia aggregates would appear

*Table 7.3: Long-run properties of the demand for money within EMU*

| Study | Monetary aggregate | Elasticities | | Semi-elasticities | | |
|---|---|---|---|---|---|---|
| | | Price | Income | Short-term interest rate | Long-term interest rate | Inflation rate |
| Bekx and Tullio | M 1 | 0.42 | 0.91 | – | −0.010 | – |
| Kremers and Lane | M 1 | 1 | 1 | −0.007 | 0 | −0.004 |
| Monticelli and Strauss-Kahn | M 3(I) | 1 | 1.33 | −0.007 | – | 0 |
| | M 3(II) | 1 | 1.36 | −0.009 | – | 0 |
| Present study | DiM 2 | 0.93 | 1 | 0.006 | −0.014 | −0.014 |
| | DiM 3 | 1 | 1 | 0.007 | −0.010 | −0.010 |

to be somewhat more sensitive to changes in the inflation rate than the unweighted monetary aggregates.

In addition to the variables shown in Table 7.3, the three studies considered here also review the effect of currency substitution. As this effect has been modelled in highly different ways, its influence is not shown in Table 7.3. Bekx and Tullio have chosen the interest rate differential between the US and Europe as the measure of currency substitution. Kremers and Lane have included the level of the ECU–dollar rate in the estimation equation, while Monticelli and Strauss-Kahn have opted for the change in this exchange rate in order to represent the effect of currency substitution. The last choice is to be preferred from an economic viewpoint since exchange rate changes provide a better measure of the return on assets than the exchange rate level. Finally, it is noteworthy that Monticelli and Strauss-Kahn have added as an extra explanatory variable a trend variable which is operational from the mid-1980s onwards. They regard this trend variable as a proxy for wealth which they assume to have been a major determinant of the demand for money, considering the continuing liberalization of financial markets. Inclusion of this trend variable causes the income elasticity to decrease from the implausible value of 1.7 to 1.3; however, without further empirical underpinning, this is still not really convincing.

To conclude this assessment, we take a look at the short-run properties of the demand for money. The dynamic equations of Kremers and Lane and of Monticelli and Strauss-Kahn, like our estimated equations for the Divisia aggregates, form part of the class of error-correction models. Bekx and Tullio do not consider a dynamic specification, so that their study will not be discussed further in this respect. The first issue regarding the dynamic properties of the demand for money concerns the speed of adjustment in the event of deviations from the equilibrium path. Kremers and Lane find that about 95% of the total adjustment has already been effected after one quarter. This very rapid adjustment is noteworthy, but may present a biased picture, as re-estimation by Barr (1992) – with slightly modified data but for the same sample period – leads to a sharp decrease in the extent of adjustment after one quarter, to 50%. Monticelli and Strauss-Kahn find that 30 to 40% of the total adjustment has been effected after one quarter. For the Divisia aggregates, a much slower adjustment is found, of about 10% after one quarter. This estimate corresponds to the speed of adjustment frequently found in demand for money analyses at the national level (*cf.* Fase and Winder (1993)). A second issue, the last to be reviewed here, relates to the standard errors of the residuals, which constitute a measure of the stability of the demand for money. Kremers and Lane find a value of 0.008, while Monticelli and Strauss-Kahn come to an estimate of 0.005. These results are in line with the findings for the Divisia aggregates – 0.007 for both DiM2 and DiM3 – and are significantly below the values found for the individual countries (*cf.* Fase and Winder (1993)), suggesting that, at the EMU level, the demand for money is more stable than at the country level.

## 7.6 Conclusions

Under the Maastricht Treaty, a common monetary policy must be pursued within EMU in 1999 at the latest. Because of the far-reaching nature of this commitment, the monetary authorities are already faced with the question how to give concrete shape to this common policy. Although the principle of price stability has been endorsed as the ultimate objective by all member countries, the intermediate monetary objective to be chosen is not yet clear. However, in view of the monetary practice in Germany, the money supply is a logical and serious candidate. For such a policy to be successful, a number of conditions must be satisfied, among which stability of the demand for money and controllability of the supply of money are the most important. Hence, it is not surprising that in recent years the demand for money within EMU has been a major research topic. The present study aims to contribute to this discussion by analysing monetary Divisia aggregates for EMU. In this respect, it differs from other studies, which have thus far focused solely on the traditional unweighted monetary aggregates at the EMU level. In Divisia aggregates, the various components of the money supply are weighted by their degree of liquidity, so that the money stock is expressed as a weighted sum total of the constituent liquid assets. The weighting process seeks to eliminate liquidity held for investment purposes from the unweighted monetary aggregates, so that, in principle, the Divisia aggregates constitute a better measure of the quantity of money held for transactions purposes.

In this study, monetary Divisia aggregates for M2 and M3 have been constructed at the EMU level and their properties have been examined. Two aspects were given special attention. The first concerns the sensitivity of the results to the specific construction method chosen to aggregate data across the EMU countries. The second concerns a comparison of the properties of the Divisia aggregates with those of the unweighted monetary aggregates at the EMU level.

The principal results of our analysis may be summarized as follows. First, the Divisia aggregates for M2 and M3 show similar movements during the period 1970–1992, corresponding fairly well to those in M1 but differing sharply from those in the unweighted aggregates M2 and M3. Especially in periods characterized by interest rate turbulence, with sharp increases in short-term rates leading to a flat or even inverted yield curve, the Divisia aggregates and the corresponding unweighted monetary aggregates show widely diverging patterns. This result provides empirical support for the hypothesis that, during the 1980s, the unweighted aggregates regularly presented a biased picture of underlying monetary developments as the money growth recorded was largely due to increases in money held for investment purposes.

Second, our study shows that, according to the Divisia aggregates, money growth relative to income growth within EMU has been modest during the 1980s and in any case much smaller than suggested by the unweighted broad monetary aggregates. This outcome may be taken to constitute a justification – and perhaps an explanation – of the reserved policy reactions of the monetary authorities to the growth of the broad monetary aggregates during the 1980s.

Third, our calculations show that the aggregation method chosen affects the ultimate results, although its influence is often limited. The sensitivity analysis conducted provides a number of major insights. It becomes evident, for instance, that the use of exchange rates or of purchasing power parities as the factor to convert the national aggregates into a common currency does not have a significant effect on the results. However, the use of current values or of values in a base period does have a definite influence on the results. Furthermore, our analysis shows that the use of ECU or of income weights in the construction of EMU interest rates has little effect.

The fourth and last conclusion is that the econometric analysis performed for the demand for money based on Divisia aggregates yields plausible results, which are in line with those of earlier demand for money studies for EMU. The income elasticity of the Divisia aggregates comes out at a value equal to 1. For Divisia M3, the price elasticity is likewise equal to 1. For Divisia M2, the value is slightly less than one, so that the hypothesis of price homogeneity for Divisia M2 must be rejected. The interest and inflation rate sensitivities of the Divisia aggregates correspond fairly well to the values found in other studies of the demand for money within EMU. Finally, the analysis shows that the standard error of the residuals, which provides a measure of the stability of the demand for money, is distinctly smaller than the values usually found for the individual countries. This suggests that, at the EMU level, the demand for money is more stable than at the national level and that the condition of stability of the demand for money, necessary for a common monetary policy, would appear to be fulfilled.

# Appendix 7.A Descriptive Statistics for EMU Variables for Various Aggregation Methods

This appendix offers further information about the extent to which the series at the EMU level considered in this study are sensitive to the specific method of aggregation used. To this end, for all series obtained by the aggregation procedures discussed in the main text, a number of statistics are provided. In all cases, the annual growth rates are considered. The results of this preliminary analysis are shown in Tables 7.A.1 to 7.A.3. Subsequently, we examine whether the stylized facts thus established for the series at the EMU level match the properties of the corresponding series for the individual EMU countries. The results of this countrywise analysis are shown in Tables 7.A.4 and 7.A.5.

Table 7.A.1 presents the means, the standard deviations and the coefficients of variation for the Divisia aggregates calculated by the direct method and for the traditional, unweighted monetary aggregates as well as nominal income and the corresponding price. Table 7.A.2 shows the results for the Divisia aggregates calculated by the indirect method. For the unweighted monetary aggregates and the Divisia aggregates calculated by the direct method, Table 7.A.3 shows the correlations with M1 and nominal income (again annual growth rates have been considered). The results in Tables 7.A.1 to 7.A.3 yield roughly the same pattern as the analysis discussed in Section 7.3, so that we need not dwell on the figures at great length. We focus on a few salient points here.

Table 7.A.1 indicates that the average growth rates of the monetary aggregates (both unweighted and Divisia) calculated with the aid of current exchange rates and purchasing power parities are definitely lower than for the corresponding aggregates calculated with the aid of 1985 exchange rates and purchasing power parities. This is a consequence of the choice made to express the country variables in Deutsche Marks. The depreciation of all EMU currencies against the Deutsche Mark during the sample period decreases the growth rates of the variables based on current conversion factors. This effect is eliminated if a conversion factor in a particular base period is used. The same depreciation effect is apparent for inflation. In terms of Deutsche Marks, inflation within EMU is lower if current conversion factors are used. The weighted appreciation of the Deutsche Mark can be calculated and comes out at an average of 3.25% in the case of current exchange rates and of 3.89% in the case of current purchasing power parities. If these figures are added to the average inflation rates on the basis of current conversion factors, as shown in Table 7.A.1, the resulting values are of the same order of magnitude as those based on 1985 conversion factors. The second observation concerns the standard deviation of the growth rates of the monetary aggregates, listed in Table 7.A.1. This is greater when based on current exchange rates than on current purchasing power parities; the latter, in turn, exceed those on the basis of 1985 conversion factors (1985 exchange rates and purchasing power parities yield comparable results). The greater standard deviation in the case of current exchange rates reflects the volatile exchange rate movements.

Considering the above depreciation effect, the results in Table 7.A.2 are best compared with the Divisia indices calculated by the direct manner on the basis of 1985 conversion factors. The results correspond fairly well, although slight differences are apparent. Comparison shows that the average growth rates of the Divisia aggregates weighted by ECU weights are slightly lower and that these aggregates have smaller standard deviations than the Divisia indices calculated by the direct method. For the Divisia aggregates weighted by income shares, the resulting average growth rates are slightly higher than the values for the Divisia aggregates calculated by the direct method, with similar standard deviations.

Table 7.A.3 shows that, irrespective of the specific aggregation method used, the growth rates of the Divisia aggregates for both M2 and M3 exhibit a higher correlation with M1 growth than the unweighted aggregates. The difference is relatively large in the case of 1985 conversion factors. The other results correspond to the findings presented in the main text.

The results of the countrywise inventory are summarized in Tables 7.A.4 and 7.A.5. Table 7.A.4 shows the statistics as Table 7.A.1, except that the figures now relate to the individual EMU countries. Table 7.A.5 is analogous to Table 7.A.3. The properties of the relevant series for the individual countries are well in line with those for the EMU-wide variables. Usually, for at least eight out of the 10 countries considered, the stylized facts prove to correspond to those for EMU as a whole. As a result of this robust pattern, the EMU variables constructed gain in plausibility.

In addition to the results presented in Table 7.A.4, it might be noted that the outcomes correspond to the results found by Fase (1985b) for The Netherlands. The results reported there indicate, as do the figures in Table 7.A.4, that the average growth rate of the unweighted monetary aggregates is higher as the concept of money considered is broader and that the Divisia aggregates for M2 and M3 show lower average growth rates and have smaller standard deviations than the corresponding unweighted aggregates.

*Table 7.A.1: Descriptive statistics for the growth of monetary aggregates, income and price for EMU (direct method of calculation)*

| Aggregation method | Variable | Mean | Standard deviation | Coefficient of variation |
|---|---|---|---|---|
| Current exchange rates | M1 | 6.15 | 4.36 | 0.71 |
| | M2 | 7.75 | 4.34 | 0.56 |
| | DiM2 | 5.47 | 4.27 | 0.66 |
| | DiM2–ECU | 6.55 | 4.30 | 0.66 |
| | M3 | 8.23 | 4.15 | 0.50 |
| | DiM3 | 6.84 | 4.24 | 0.62 |
| | DiM3–ECU | 6.94 | 4.26 | 0.61 |
| | income | 6.64 | 3.69 | 0.56 |
| | price | 4.08 | 4.05 | 0.99 |
| 1985 exchange rates | M1 | 9.63 | 2.76 | 0.28 |
| | M2 | 11.47 | 2.34 | 0.20 |
| | DiM2 | 9.96 | 2.44 | 0.24 |
| | DiM2–ECU | 10.09 | 2.35 | 0.23 |
| | M3 | 11.69 | 2.14 | 0.18 |
| | DiM3 | 10.24 | 2.54 | 0.25 |
| | DiM3–ECU | 10.39 | 2.44 | 0.23 |
| | income | 9.58 | 2.32 | 0.24 |
| | price | 7.01 | 2.34 | 0.33 |
| Current purchasing power parities | M1 | 5.97 | 3.62 | 0.61 |
| | M2 | 7.59 | 2.57 | 0.47 |
| | DiM2 | 6.27 | 3.56 | 0.57 |
| | DiM2–ECU | 6.39 | 3.57 | 0.56 |
| | M3 | 8.12 | 2.93 | 0.36 |
| | DiM3 | 6.61 | 3.43 | 0.52 |
| | DiM3–ECU | 6.78 | 3.39 | 0.50 |
| | income | 6.55 | 2.30 | 0.35 |
| | price | 3.97 | 1.60 | 0.40 |
| 1985 purchasing power parities | M1 | 9.87 | 2.70 | 0.27 |
| | M2 | 11.65 | 2.31 | 0.20 |
| | DiM2 | 10.19 | 2.43 | 0.24 |
| | DiM2–ECU | 10.32 | 2.34 | 0.23 |
| | M3 | 11.93 | 2.14 | 0.18 |
| | DiM3 | 10.47 | 2.51 | 0.24 |
| | DiM3–ECU | 10.63 | 2.41 | 0.23 |
| | income | 9.80 | 2.32 | 0.24 |
| | price | 7.22 | 2.35 | 0.33 |

*Note:* See Table 7.2.

*Table 7.A.2: Descriptive statistics for the growth of EMU Divisia indices (indirect method of calculation)*

| Weighting method | Variable | Mean | Standard deviation | Coefficient of variation |
|---|---|---|---|---|
| Income – current exchange rates | DiM2 | 10.79 | 2.35 | 0.22 |
| | DiM3 | 11.41 | 2.41 | 0.21 |
| Income – 1985 exchange rates | DiM2 | 10.64 | 2.58 | 0.24 |
| | DiM3 | 11.25 | 2.60 | 0.23 |
| Income – current purchasing power parities | DiM2 | 10.96 | 2.52 | 0.23 |
| | DiM3 | 11.59 | 2.51 | 0.22 |
| Income – 1985 purchasing power parities | DiM2 | 10.94 | 2.56 | 0.23 |
| | DiM3 | 11.57 | 2.56 | 0.22 |
| ECU weights | DiM2 | 9.82 | 2.13 | 0.22 |
| | DiM3 | 10.31 | 2.28 | 0.22 |

*Table 7.A.3: Correlation between growth of monetary aggregates and growth of* M1 *and income for* ECU

| Aggregation method | Variable | Correlation with M1 | Correlation with income |
|---|---|---|---|
| Current exchange rates | M1 | 1.00 | 0.75 |
| | M2 | 0.85 | 0.80 |
| | DiM2 | 0.99 | 0.77 |
| | DiM2 – ECU | 0.98 | 0.77 |
| | M3 | 0.89 | 0.89 |
| | DiM3 | 0.99 | 0.80 |
| | DiM3 – ECU | 0.98 | 0.81 |
| | income | 0.75 | 1.00 |
| 1985 exchange rates | M1 | 1.00 | 0.56 |
| | M2 | 0.40 | 0.54 |
| | DiM2 | 0.96 | 0.60 |
| | DiM2 – ECU | 0.94 | 0.58 |
| | M3 | 0.71 | 0.76 |
| | DiM3 | 0.97 | 0.63 |
| | DiM3 – ECU | 0.94 | 0.62 |
| | income | 0.56 | 1.00 |
| Current purchasing power parities | M1 | 1.00 | 0.65 |
| | M2 | 0.80 | 0.67 |
| | DiM2 | 0.99 | 0.67 |
| | DiM2 – ECU | 0.98 | 0.67 |
| | M3 | 0.86 | 0.75 |
| | DiM3 | 0.99 | 0.68 |
| | DiM3 – ECU | 0.98 | 0.68 |
| | income | 0.65 | 1.00 |
| 1985 purchasing power parities | M1 | 1.00 | 0.56 |
| | M2 | 0.45 | 0.56 |
| | DiM2 | 0.97 | 0.60 |
| | DiM2 – ECU | 0.95 | 0.58 |
| | M3 | 0.71 | 0.76 |
| | DiM3 | 0.97 | 0.63 |
| | DiM3 – ECU | 0.96 | 0.63 |
| | income | 0.56 | 1.00 |

*Table 7.A.4: Descriptive statistics for growth of monetary aggregates, national income and price for EMU countries*

| Country | Variable | Mean | Standard deviation | Coefficient of variation |
|---|---|---|---|---|
| Belgium | M1 | 6.16 | 3.93 | 0.64 |
| | M2 | 9.28 | 4.11 | 0.44 |
| | DiM2 | 7.40 | 3.44 | 0.46 |
| | M3 | 9.13 | 3.68 | 0.40 |
| | DiM3 | 7.90 | 3.77 | 0.48 |
| | income | 7.79 | 4.11 | 0.53 |
| | price | 5.36 | 2.68 | 0.50 |
| Denmark | M1 | 10.72 | 6.29 | 0.59 |
| | M2 | 10.20 | 5.26 | 0.52 |
| | DiM2 | 10.49 | 5.63 | 0.54 |
| | M3 | 10.65 | 5.02 | 0.47 |
| | DiM3 | 10.65 | 5.44 | 0.51 |
| | income | 8.83 | 4.03 | 0.46 |
| | price | 6.93 | 3.21 | 0.46 |
| France | M1 | 8.22 | 4.20 | 0.51 |
| | M2 | 10.97 | 2.40 | 0.22 |
| | DiM2 | 9.16 | 3.28 | 0.36 |
| | M3 | 11.14 | 4.52 | 0.32 |
| | DiM3 | 9.51 | 3.84 | 0.40 |
| | income | 9.91 | 3.58 | 0.36 |
| | price | 7.26 | 3.38 | 0.47 |
| Germany | M1 | 8.11 | 4.79 | 0.59 |
| | M2 | 8.83 | 5.25 | 0.59 |
| | DiM2 | 7.90 | 4.37 | 0.55 |
| | M3 | 8.11 | 3.31 | 0.41 |
| | DiM3 | 7.76 | 3.71 | 0.48 |
| | income | 6.85 | 3.06 | 0.45 |
| | price | 4.00 | 1.68 | 0.42 |

*Table 7.A.4: (continued)*

| Country | Variable | Mean | Standard deviation | Coefficient of variation |
|---|---|---|---|---|
| Ireland | M1 | 9.58 | 6.34 | 0.66 |
| | M2 | 12.61 | 4.94 | 0.39 |
| | DiM2 | 10.93 | 4.94 | 0.45 |
| | M3 | 13.08 | 5.53 | 0.42 |
| | DiM3 | 11.62 | 5.33 | 0.46 |
| | income | 12.61 | 5.89 | 0.47 |
| | price | 9.07 | 6.23 | 0.69 |
| Italy | M1 | 13.42 | 5.46 | 0.41 |
| | M2 | 13.46 | 4.85 | 0.36 |
| | DiM2 | 13.23 | 4.87 | 0.37 |
| | M3 | 15.34 | 3.99 | 0.26 |
| | DiM3 | 14.16 | 4.32 | 0.31 |
| | income | 14.01 | 5.90 | 0.42 |
| | price | 11.39 | 5.01 | 0.44 |
| The Netherlands | M1 | 7.63 | 5.32 | 0.70 |
| | M2 | 8.81 | 5.07 | 0.58 |
| | DiM2 | 7.65 | 3.42 | 0.45 |
| | M3 | 9.07 | 3.27 | 0.36 |
| | DiM3 | 7.98 | 3.16 | 0.40 |
| | income | 6.85 | 4.01 | 0.59 |
| | price | 4.57 | 3.37 | 0.74 |
| Portugal | M1 | 15.66 | 6.53 | 0.42 |
| | M2 | 18.56 | 4.62 | 0.25 |
| | DiM2 | 17.28 | 4.84 | 0.28 |
| | M3 | 19.32 | 6.06 | 0.31 |
| | DiM3 | 17.67 | 5.33 | 0.30 |
| | income | 18.83 | 5.19 | 0.28 |
| | price | 15.32 | 5.39 | 0.35 |
| Spain | M1 | 14.09 | 5.32 | 0.38 |
| | M2 | 13.31 | 4.71 | 0.35 |
| | DiM2 | 13.75 | 5.01 | 0.36 |
| | M3 | 15.07 | 3.97 | 0.26 |
| | DiM3 | 14.63 | 4.13 | 0.28 |
| | income | 14.20 | 4.62 | 0.33 |
| | price | 11.03 | 4.41 | 0.40 |

*Table 7.A.4: (continued)*

| Country | Variable | Mean | Standard deviation | Coefficient of variation |
|---|---|---|---|---|
| United Kingdom | M1 | 7.83 | 6.43 | 0.82 |
| | M2 | 14.25 | 6.86 | 0.48 |
| | DiM2 | 10.72 | 5.45 | 0.51 |
| | M3 | 13.97 | 4.21 | 0.30 |
| | DiM3 | 11.38 | 4.63 | 0.41 |
| | income | 11.12 | 4.74 | 0.43 |
| | price | 9.18 | 5.26 | 0.57 |

*Table 7.A.5: Correlation between growth of monetary aggregates and growth of* M1 *and national income for EMU countries*

| Country | Variable | Correlation with M1 | Correlation with income |
|---|---|---|---|
| Belgium | M1 | 1.00 | 0.30 |
| | M2 | 0.26 | 0.18 |
| | DiM2 | 0.80 | 0.22 |
| | M3 | 0.77 | 0.47 |
| | DiM3 | 0.90 | 0.34 |
| Denmark | M1 | 1.00 | 0.27 |
| | M2 | 0.81 | 0.48 |
| | DiM2 | 0.96 | 0.39 |
| | M3 | 0.81 | 0.50 |
| | DiM3 | 0.96 | 0.41 |
| France | M1 | 1.00 | 0.77 |
| | M2 | 0.63 | 0.32 |
| | DiM2 | 0.97 | 0.69 |
| | M3 | 0.87 | 0.78 |
| | DiM3 | 0.97 | 0.78 |
| Germany | M1 | 1.00 | 0.53 |
| | M2 | 0.32 | 0.75 |
| | DiM2 | 0.77 | 0.76 |
| | M3 | 0.73 | 0.78 |
| | DiM3 | 0.92 | 0.70 |

*Table 7.A.5: (continued)*

| Country | Variable | Correlation with M1 | Correlation with income |
|---|---|---|---|
| Ireland | M1 | 1.00 | 0.46 |
| | M2 | 0.56 | 0.35 |
| | DiM2 | 0.87 | 0.47 |
| | M3 | 0.62 | 0.64 |
| | DiM3 | 0.84 | 0.64 |
| Italy | M1 | 1.00 | 0.53 |
| | M2 | 0.79 | 0.64 |
| | DiM2 | 0.96 | 0.62 |
| | M3 | 0.69 | 0.74 |
| | DiM3 | 0.94 | 0.66 |
| The Netherlands | M1 | 1.00 | 0.32 |
| | M2 | −0.07 | 0.52 |
| | DiM2 | 0.67 | 0.51 |
| | M3 | 0.19 | 0.79 |
| | DiM3 | 0.78 | 0.65 |
| Portugal | M1 | 1.00 | 0.21 |
| | M2 | 0.40 | 0.25 |
| | DiM2 | 0.83 | 0.19 |
| | M3 | 0.23 | 0.37 |
| | DiM3 | 0.69 | 0.26 |
| Spain | M1 | 1.00 | 0.46 |
| | M2 | 0.94 | 0.57 |
| | DiM2 | 0.99 | 0.50 |
| | M3 | 0.59 | 0.66 |
| | DiM3 | 0.89 | 0.62 |
| United Kingdom | M1 | 1.00 | 0.55 |
| | M2 | 0.01 | 0.01 |
| | DiM2 | 0.70 | 0.32 |
| | M3 | 0.25 | 0.18 |
| | DiM3 | 0.81 | 0.41 |

# Appendix 7.B Results of Specification Analysis

The demand for money equations for the Divisia aggregates discussed in Section 7.4 have been subjected to an econometric specification analysis. The results are discussed in this appendix. First, the constraints imposed upon the parameters are reviewed. Subsequently, the residuals of the estimated equations have been tested for autocorrelation. The appendix concludes with a cointegration analysis of the long-run relationships.

The estimated demand for money equations (7.5) and (7.6) include a number of constraints imposed on the parameters. These constraints constitute testable hypotheses, whose validity has been examined with the aid of $t$- and $F$-tests. In the equation for Divisia M2, the long-run income elasticity is equal to one. A $t$-test for this constraint yields an insignificant value of 1.79. Upon the coefficients $oc_1$, $oc_{1_{-1}}$ and $\dot{p}$, constraints were imposed which imply that the long-run semi-elasticities are equal. The $F$-test for the two constraints is not significant: $F(2,68) = 0.58$. An additional constraint has been imposed in that the coefficients of $\Delta \ln y_{-1}$ and $\Delta \ln y_{-2}$ are equal, for which the $t$-test yields a value of 0.20. In the equation for Divisia M3, it has been assumed that the long-run income and price elasticities are equal to one. The $t$-tests for these constraints (0.46 and 0.78, respectively) indicate that these constraints need not be rejected. The long-run semi-elasticities of $oc_2$ and $\dot{p}$ are equal ($t$-test 0.69). The error-correction term $\ln(\text{DiM}3/P)_{-1} - \ln y$ follows if the equation with explanatory variables $\ln(\text{DiM}3/P)_{-1} - \ln y_{-1}$ and $\Delta \ln y$ is subjected to the constraint that the corresponding coefficients are each other's opposite. The $t$-test for this constraint yields a value of 0.74. Moreover, a constraint has been imposed in that the coefficients of $\Delta \ln y_{-1}$ and $\Delta \ln y_{-2}$ are equal. The $t$-test for this constraint yields a value of 0.54. In summary, it may be concluded that, for each constraint imposed, the hypothesis that the constraint is valid need not be rejected.

Subsequently, we have tested whether the residuals of the demand for money equations show autocorrelation. To this end, the Ljung–Box test statistic, based on the first $p$ autocorrelations of the residuals – $p = 1$, 4, 8 and 12 – has been calculated. Under the null hypothesis of white noise disturbances, the test statistics have been $\chi^2(p)$ distributed. The results are ashown in Table 7.B.1 and indicate that no significant autocorrelation is present.

The long-run relationships implied by the estimated dynamic demand for money equations have been examined further by means of cointegration tests to verify whether the deviations from the equilibrium path follow a stationary process. As the data used are seasonally unadjusted, the procedure of Hylleberg, Engle, Granger, and Yoo (1990) has been

*Table 7.B.1: Results of LB-test for residual autocorrelation*

| $p$ | DiM 2 | DiM 3 |
|---|---|---|
| 1 | 0.00 | 0.00 |
| 4 | 1.65 | 3.25 |
| 8 | 6.53 | 10.28 |
| 12 | 9.93 | 13.26 |

used. The estimated equation is:

$$\Delta_4 x_t = \pi_1 y_{1t-1} + \pi_2 y_{2t-1} + \pi_3 y_{3t-2} + \pi_4 y_{3t-1} + \varepsilon_t, \qquad (7.B.1)$$

where $x_t$ represents the deviations from the equilibrium path, $y_{1t} = (1 + L + L^2 + L^3)x_t$, $y_{2t} = -(1 - L)(1 + L^2)x_t$, $y_{3t} = -(1 - L)(1 + L)x_t$, and $\varepsilon_t$ a disturbance term. Lags of $\Delta_4 x_t$ have been added to eliminate any autocorrelation in the residuals. The constraint $\pi_1 = 0$ corresponds to a unit root $L = 1$. The constraint $\pi_2 = 0$ implies that a unit root equal to $L = -1$ is present. If $\pi_3$ and $\pi_4$ are both equal to 0, the complex roots $L = \pm i$ are present. These various constraints can be tested with the $t$-ratios of $\pi_i$, $i = 1, \ldots, 4$ and the $F$-test for the constraint $\pi_3 = \pi_4 = 0$. However, the test statistics do not have the standard distributions. Hylleberg, Engle, Granger, and Yoo (1990) present the critical values for the test statistics obtained with simulation experiments.

The cointegration test has been carried out by estimating equation (7.B.1) with seasonal dummies, a constant term and the first four lags of $\Delta_4 x_t$ being included as additional explanatory variables. Subsequently, in several rounds, the most insignificant of the lags of $\Delta_4 x_t$ has been

*Table 7.B.2: Results of cointegration tests*

| Monetary aggregate | $t(\pi_1)$ | $t(\pi_2)$ | $t(\pi_3)$ | $t(\pi_4)$ | $F(\pi_3, \pi_4)$ |
|---|---|---|---|---|---|
| DiM 2 | −2.191 | −3.512[1] | −5.989[1] | −1.126 | 19.263[1] |
| DiM 3 | −1.733 | −3.168[2] | −5.083[1] | −1.164 | 13.933[1] |

*Notes:*

[1] Significant at a level of significance of 0.01.

[2] Significant at a level of significance of 0.05.

eliminated successively from the estimation equation. The results of the above $t$- and $F$-tests for the ultimate equation are listed in Table 7.B.2, showing that, for both Divisia M2 and Divisia M3, the deviations from the equilibrium path are not stationary. However, according to the results in Table 7.B.2, seasonal unit roots are absent.

# 8. Divisia Aggregates and the Demand for Money in Core EMU

Knowledge of money-holding behaviour in the private sector – *i.e.* households and businesses – is of great importance for assessing the impact of monetary and other shocks on the economy and the effectiveness of monetary policy. This, together with the fact that the theory of the demand for money is fairly well developed with the required data readily available, explains why the demand for money has been so well explored econometrically. The underlying thought in all this work has been the belief that money demand should be stable (see Fase (1993, 1994)). The present chapter is in this research tradition but with a slight shift of emphasis away from econometric techniques towards the substantial issues of considering various money concepts and geographical areas. Our main concern is the stability of money demand across various geographical areas within EMU for various simple sum *versus* index number theory-based aggregates. Of these the Divisia measure is a prominent example. As to geographical areas we accept the view that Germany is the anchor country for EMU and should therefore have a relatively stable money demand *vis-à-vis* other member countries such as the Netherlands.

This chapter examines the narrow problem of money demand stability across a particular set of EMU countries in view of the broader political issue of a multi-speed Europe. The economics behind this debate is the fact that there are weak and strong countries in terms of the economic convergence measures defined in the Maastricht Treaty of 1992. Of course, this political debate on the creation of core EMU would by definition exclude other member countries.

Reprinted with kind permission from *DNB-Staff Reports* no. 5 (1996), M.M.G. Fase and C.C.A. Winder, 'Divisia aggregates and the demand for money in core EMU',

## 8.1 Aggregation and the Divisia Index

### 8.1.1 Aggregation Method

A difficult problem in constructing monetary and income aggregates across countries is the conversion of national units into a common unit. A similar problem arises in constructing common price and interest rate variables. Because no unique conversion method exists, arbitrary decisions need to be made. This, perhaps, affects the monetary picture and the resulting policy diagnosis, the sensitivity of which is shown, in part, by comparisons of results from some of the conversion techniques most prevalent in other research. Before addressing this important issue we first discuss the aggregation issue in general.

For the construction of (sub)EMU-wide data, several options are open. In order to place the monetary aggregates and nominal national product of the various countries on the same footing, current and 1985 exchange rates and purchasing power parities were successively used as the conversion factor, resulting in a total of four options. Moreover, we experimented with the current US dollar for conversion to illustrate the importance of the conversion method for the results.

In the study of Fase and Winder (1994) on Divisia aggregates for EMU, four options were tested, the monetary aggregates and nominal national products of the individual EMU countries being expressed in Deutsche Marks with 1985 as the base period. The data for the member states' national products in 1985 prices were converted into 1985 Deutsche Mark prices using the 1985 exchange rates and purchasing power parities against the Deutsche Mark. The resulting series of (sub)EMU-wide monetary aggregates and (sub)EMU's supranational product in current and constant prices were obtained by summing the corresponding uniformized variables for the individual member states. The price index at the (sub)EMU level was determined as the quotient of (sub)EMU product in current and constant prices.

The (sub)EMU short- and long-term interest rates were calculated as weighted averages of the corresponding interest rates in the individual countries, using both a constant and a time-varying weighting scheme. In the constant weighting scheme, the weights chosen are the current shares of the EMU currencies in the ECU. The time-varying weighting scheme consists of the shares of the national products of the individual countries in aggregated EMU product. Since four different conversion factors were used in calculating aggregated EMU product, this leads to four weighting schemes on the basis of the income shares of the individual member states, so that a total of five weighting schemes results for short-

and long-term interest rates.

### 8.1.2 Divisia Aggregates

For monetary aggregation we use the Divisia index as it focuses on money for transactions purposes, adjusted for money-holding for portfolio or speculative purposes. The notion of a monetary index was first brought to the fore in a series of articles by F. Divisia, published in the French 'Revue d'Economie Politique' in the 1920s (see Divisia (1925, 1926)), and rediscovered by Barnett (1978, 1980) almost half a century later. As is known, Divisia aggregates take explicit account of, and seek to adjust for, the differences in degrees of liquidity of the various liquid assets.

Divisia indices for (sub)EMU-wide money stock were determined in two ways: directly and indirectly. In the direct manner of calculation, data were first constructed for the monetary aggregates and short- and long-term interest rates at the EMU level, after which the corresponding Divisia indices were calculated. This results in four different definitions of monetary aggregates (depending on the conversion factor chosen) while five different interest rates (depending on the weighting scheme chosen) were used. In the calculation of the Divisia indices, two definitions of the EMU interest rate were considered for each of the four monetary aggregates: that based on ECU weights and that based on an income weighting scheme, that particular scheme being selected which follows from the calculation of EMU product using the same conversion factor as for the monetary aggregate. Consequently, if the monetary aggregate was determined on the basis of current exchange rates, the income weighting scheme based on current exchange rates was likewise used. In the indirect manner of calculation, Divisia indices were first calculated for the individual countries, the Divisia indices at the (sub)EMU level subsequently being determined as the weighted averages of the individual Divisia indices. The same five weighting schemes – ECU and the four different income shares – were used in the construction of the EMU interest rates. The various possible combinations results in 13 different series for both Divisia M2 and M3 are shown in Table 8.1. This chapter focuses in particular on the subset resulting from the direct manner of calculation and (sub)EMU interest rates based on ECU shares. Divisia indices for M2 and M3 were calculated in conformity with the definition discussed above by weighting the growth rates of the components M1 and M2–M1 and M3–M1, respectively, with the two-period moving averages of the expenditure shares. The user cost required to this end is dependent on the benchmark interest rate carried by the illiquid asset and the return rates on the various monetary assets.

*Table 8.1: Various methods of constructing Divisia measures for (sub)EMU*

| Method of calculation | Aggregation method: monetary aggregates | Weighting scheme interest rates | | | | |
|---|---|---|---|---|---|---|
| | | ECU shares | income shares | | | |
| | | | exchange rates | | PPP | |
| | | | current | base period | current | base period |
| Direct | exchange rates | | | | | |
| | – current | × | × | · | · | · |
| | – base period | × | · | × | · | · |
| | PPP | | | | | |
| | – current | × | · | · | × | · |
| | – base period | × | · | · | · | × |
| Indirect | | × | × | × | × | × |

*Notes:* × means considered in present chapter, · means not considered.

Following, for instance, Belongia and Chrystal (1991), the benchmark interest rate was taken to be the long-term rate, raised by a constant equal to the maximum differential between short- and long-term rates during the sample period 1970:I–1992:IV. This procedure warrants positive user cost. As Barnett, Fisher, and Serletis (1992) point out, however, another and perhaps preferred method, consistent with the consumer's optimization problem, is to choose the maximum available holding period yield in each period as the benchmark rate. As regards the return on the liquid assets themselves, it has been assumed that for M 1 it is equal to 0 and for M 2–M 1 and M 3–M 1 to the short-term interest rate. The Divisia indices thus constructed are based on a relatively rough breakdown of the broadly defined monetary aggregate. However, further refinement to distinguish between more categories of liquid assets with their rates of return would give rise to serious data problems in an analysis at the (sub)EMU level.

### 8.1.3 Preliminary Analysis of Divisia Aggregates for Core EMU

To gain some feeling for the meaning of Divisia aggregates as a monetary measure, Table 8.2 sets out summary statistics for possible core EMU countries Germany plus the Benelux. The table shows a close correspondence between the M1 growth rate and the two Divisia aggregates M2 and M3 while the correlation of the latter with M1 of 0.80 to almost 0.95 is quite impressive. This seems to support the view that the relevant monetary expansion, i.e. the growth rate of transaction money, is close to the growth rate of M1, which is in line with the growth of real income $y$. This picture hardly changes with the conversion technique used; the same holds for the core countries Germany, the Benelux plus France (see Appendix 8.B). At the same time, the simple sum variants of M2 and M3 demonstrate much lower correlation with M1 than the equivalent Divisia indices.

## 8.2 Money Demand and Simple Sum Aggregates

### 8.2.1 General Theoretical Framework

A traditional demand for money relationship typically expresses that the desired demand for money is determined by real income, the rate of inflation, and short- and long-term interest rates. Assuming a price elasticity possibly unequal to one, the following macroeconomic demand for money equation is postulated:

$$\mathrm{M} = AP^{\alpha_1} y^{\alpha_2} \exp(\alpha_3 r_s + \alpha_4 r_l + \alpha_5 \dot{p}) \tag{8.1}$$

with M the desired money stock in a steady state situation, $P$ the price index – so that $\mathrm{M}/P$ is the real money stock – $y$ real income, $\dot{p}$ the rate of inflation, $r_s$ the short-term interest rate and $r_l$ the long-term interest rate. The price and income elasticities are equal to $\alpha_1$ and $\alpha_2$, respectively; $\alpha_3$, $\alpha_4$ and $\alpha_5$ measure the relative change in the demand for money due to a one percentage point change in short- and long-term interest rates and inflation, respectively. These coefficients are therefore semi-elasticities. Following, for example, Butter and Fase (1981) and a recent study by Boughton (1991), the usual assumption of a price elasticity of 1 – i.e. price homogeneity of order 1 – is not made *a priori*, but considered as a testable hypothesis.

Equation (8.1) describes the relationship between the optimum nominal amount of liquid assets held, on the one hand, and the expected

*Table 8.2: Summary statistics for core EMU countries Germany plus Benelux (all variables in growth rates)*

| Conversion technique | Variable | Mean | Standard deviation | Correlation with | |
|---|---|---|---|---|---|
| | | | | M1 | $y$ |
| Current DM exchange rates | M1 | 7.45 | 4.48 | 1.00 | 0.38 |
| | M2 | 8.54 | 4.04 | 0.26 | 0.62 |
| | M3 | 8.05 | 2.79 | 0.70 | 0.54 |
| | DiM2 | 7.43 | 3.69 | 0.85 | 0.60 |
| | DiM3 | 7.46 | 3.46 | 0.94 | 0.50 |
| | Real income | 2.73 | 2.63 | 0.38 | 1.00 |
| | Price | 3.95 | 1.85 | 0.20 | −0.20 |
| 1985 DM exchange rates | M1 | 7.82 | 4.24 | 1.00 | 0.39 |
| | M2 | 8.89 | 4.07 | 0.20 | 0.61 |
| | M3 | 8.38 | 2.71 | 0.66 | 0.54 |
| | DiM2 | 7.80 | 3.48 | 0.82 | 0.64 |
| | DiM3 | 7.80 | 3.23 | 0.93 | 0.52 |
| | Real income | 2.73 | 2.63 | 0.39 | 1.00 |
| | Price | 4.20 | 1.78 | 0.11 | −0.21 |
| Current DM–PPP | M1 | 7.48 | 4.17 | 1.00 | 0.42 |
| | M2 | 8.59 | 4.13 | 0.22 | 0.61 |
| | M3 | 8.12 | 2.63 | 0.65 | 0.59 |
| | DiM2 | 7.47 | 3.53 | 0.82 | 0.65 |
| | DiM3 | 7.50 | 3.20 | 0.93 | 0.56 |
| | Real income | 2.73 | 2.63 | 0.42 | 1.00 |
| | Price | 3.99 | 1.63 | 0.04 | −0.20 |
| 1985 DM–PPP | M1 | 7.81 | 4.22 | 1.00 | 0.39 |
| | M2 | 8.89 | 4.05 | 0.20 | 0.61 |
| | M3 | 8.39 | 2.70 | 0.66 | 0.54 |
| | DiM2 | 7.79 | 3.46 | 0.82 | 0.63 |
| | DiM3 | 7.80 | 3.22 | 0.93 | 0.52 |
| | Real income | 2.73 | 2.63 | 0.39 | 1.00 |
| | Price | 4.21 | 1.78 | 0.12 | −0.21 |

equilibrium value of the explanatory variables, on the other. As such, equation (8.1) is a description of the long-run equilibrium relationship based on an aggregated macroeconomic approach. An advantage of this approach is its fundamental distinction between the steady state and the short-run, which makes such an expression especially suitable for practical purposes like forecasting. In this case, where it is desirable to model deviations from the equilibrium relationship, a dynamic formulation of (8.1) must be found for the estimation process and the long-run properties of the demand for money are determined jointly with the short-run adjustment processes. An error-correction specification was chosen for this purpose, together with the introduction of lags. In accordance with our earlier studies (see Fase and Kuné (1974a, 1974b) and Fase (1979) and Butter and Fase (1981) and Fase and Winder (1990, 1993)), a cyclical indicator, *conj* – defined as some measure of unused capacity – was used to describe the short-run dynamics of the demand for money. This variable represents the tendency of money hoarding in times of recession and of dishoarding during an economic boom. An alternative, and perhaps deeper economic interpretation, is to regard this variable as a proxy for the costs of real assets, for which liquid financial assets provide a substitute. In this view hoarding and dishoarding reflect substitution processes.

With respect to the long-run relationship (8.1), income represents the influence of the transaction volume or wealth, while the rate of inflation and the two interest rates determine the composition of the monetary aggregate, for which the holding of, for example, less liquid financial assets such as bonds offers an alternative. Including both short- and long-term interest rates is also intended to take into account the influence of the yield curve on the demand for money.

The above leads to the following general dynamic specification of the demand for money:

$$\alpha(L)\ln \mathrm{M} = \beta_1(L)\ln P + \beta_2(L)\ln y + \beta_3(L)r_s + \beta_4(L)r_l + \beta_5(L)\dot{p} + \beta_6(L)conj \tag{8.2}$$

with $\alpha(L) = 1 - \alpha_1 L - \ldots - \alpha_p L^p$ and $\beta_i(L) = \beta_{i0} + \beta_{i1}L + \ldots + \beta_{ip_i}L^{pi}$, with $i = 1, \ldots, 6$. Of course, the indices $p$ and $pi$ rather than $i$ indicate the number of lags. The parameters of $\beta_1(L)$ and $\beta_5(L)$ are not all identified as a result of perfect multicollinearity between the $\ln P$ and $\dot{p}$. This identification problem can be solved by imposing *a priori* restrictions on the polynomials concerned.

One possible method is to consider real money balances as the dependent variable. This means – in terms of equation (8.2) – that the restrictions $\beta_{10} = 1$ and $\beta_{1i} = -\alpha_i$, for $i = 1, \ldots, p$ are imposed. These

$p+1$ restrictions imply that the long-run price elasticity is equal to 1. As only $p$ restrictions are needed, the imposed restrictions are sufficient, but not necessary, to obviate the identification problem. In the present study we deliberately impose the restrictions $\beta_{1i} = -\alpha_i$, for $i = 1, \ldots, p$. Because these restrictions serve to avoid the identification problem, they cannot be tested.

In view of this, equation (8.3) can be rewritten as:

$$\alpha(L)\ln(\mathrm{M}/P) = (\beta_{10}-1)\ln P + \beta_2(L)\ln y + \beta_3(L)r_s + \beta_4(L)r_l + \beta_5(L)\dot{p} + \beta_6(L)conj \tag{8.3}$$

so that it is no longer assumed *a priori* that the price elasticity equals 1.

For further analysis we consider the following reformulation of (8.3):

$$\begin{aligned}\bar{\alpha}(L)\Delta\ln(\mathrm{M}/P) = {} & (\beta_{10}-1)\ln P - \alpha(\ln(\mathrm{M}/P)_{-1} - \ln y_{-1}) \\ & + (\beta_2 - \alpha)\ln y_{-1} + \beta_3 r_s + \beta_4 r_l + \beta_5\dot{p} \\ & + \bar{\beta}_2(L)\Delta\ln y + \bar{\beta}_3(L)\Delta r_s + \bar{\beta}_4(L)\Delta r_l \\ & + \bar{\beta}_5(L)\Delta\dot{p} + \beta_6(L)conj \end{aligned} \tag{8.4}$$

with $\alpha = 1 - \alpha_1 - \ldots - \alpha_p, \beta_i = \beta_{i0} + \cdots + \beta_{ipi}, i = 2, \ldots, 6$, while $\bar{\alpha}(L)$ and $\bar{\beta}_i(L), i = 2, \ldots, 5$, are lag polynomials of order $p-1$ and $pi-1$. The parameters of $\bar{\alpha}(L)$ and $\bar{\beta}_i(L)$ are linear combinations of those of $\alpha(L)$ and $\beta_i(L)$. For example, $\bar{\alpha}_i = -\sum_{j=i+1}^{p}\alpha_j, i = 1, \ldots, p-1$, with $\bar{\alpha}_i$ the parameters of polynomial $\bar{\alpha}(L)$.

Equation (8.4) serves as the general formulation for the estimation and specification analysis. Estimating equation (8.4) instead of (8.3) has several advantages. The most important is that it provides the possibility to obtain the long-run (semi-)elasticities in a relatively simple way, as they equal the ratio of two estimates. The long-run semi-elasticities are $\beta_3/\alpha$ for the short-term interest rate, $\beta_4/\alpha$ for the long-term rate, $\beta_5/\alpha$ for the rate of inflation, and the elasticity is $\beta_2/\alpha$ for real income. Obviously, the hypothesis that the income elasticity equals 1 corresponds with the restriction that the coefficient of $\ln y_{-1}$ equals 0. The price elasticity is equal to $(\beta_{10} - 1 + \alpha)/\alpha$. Thus, the hypothesis whether the price elasticity is equal to 1 can be tested by assessing the significance of the estimate of the coefficient of $\ln P$. This, together with the identifying restrictions $\beta_{1i} = -\alpha_i$ for $i = 1, \ldots, p$, implies that the polynomial $\beta_1(L) - \alpha(L)$ has a unit root. Therefore, this is an alternative interpretation of the hypothesis that $\alpha_{10} - 1 = 0$. The economic interpretation is that the price elasticity equals 1. The second advantage of equation (8.4) over (8.3) is that equation (8.4) circumvents the multicollinearity problem by expressing the explanatory variables in first differences.

It is also worth noting that formulation (8.4), which belongs to the class of error-correction models, is in line with the first studies into the demand for money. This linkage is made by noting that the error-correction term represents the inverse velocity of circulation, the dependent variable in Latané's (1954) study of the demand for money. Christ (1993) offers a thorough review of this relationship between early and modern studies.[1]

### 8.2.2 Estimation Results for Simple Sum Aggregates

To begin with, equation (8.4) was estimated for the simple sum monetary aggregates M1, M2 and M3 for Germany, Belgium, the Netherlands and France as well as for the potential core countries Germany and the Benelux – say GB – and for GB plus France. A full report of the estimation results is given in Appendix 8.A. By way of illustration we report here the estimation result for M3 for the core group Germany plus the Benelux. Using the current DM exchange rates as conversion methods, $s_i$ as seasonal dummies, $\text{dum}_{90:\text{III}}$ a binary variable to account for the German unification in October 1990, and the sample period of 1971:II–1992:IV, the estimated equation is:

$$\begin{aligned}
\Delta \ln(\mathrm{M3}/P) = &- \underset{(4.39)}{0.1056}(\ln(\mathrm{M3}/P)_{-1} - \ln y) + \underset{(2.51)}{0.0381} \ln y_{-1} \\
&+ \underset{(1.31)}{0.0010} r_s - \underset{(2.18)}{0.0024} \Delta r_{s_{-1}} - \underset{(3.42)}{0.0046} r_{l_{-\frac{1}{2}}} - \underset{(7.14)}{0.0018} \dot{p} \\
&- \underset{(2.18)}{0.0003} \Delta \dot{p}_{-2} - \underset{(2.03)}{0.0019} conj_{-4} - \underset{(1.39)}{0.1149} + \underset{(0.11)}{0.0005} s_1 \\
&- \underset{(1.06)}{0.0037} s_2 - \underset{(5.07)}{0.0197} s_3 + \underset{(36.80)}{0.0928} \text{dum}_{90:\text{III}}
\end{aligned}$$

$\bar{R}^2 = 0.88 \qquad SE = 0.006$

Without firm guidance from theory, the choice of the conversion method is an important decision for the examination of monetary behaviour

[1] Our formulation (8.4) differs from that used in the more technically oriented cointegration literature put forward by Engle and Granger (1987). In this cointegration approach, the error-correction term is defined as the deviations from the equilibrium relationship (8.1), and hence is given a somewhat different interpretation. Collecting the level terms in (8.4) yields the formulation commonly used in the cointegration literature and shows that real income, the price level as well as interest rates and inflation are important in the long-run.

across countries. This is the more so as several alternatives are reasonable. To illustrate the potential effects of these choices, equation (8.4) was re-estimated using data converted by current DM purchasing power parity. The resulting estimated equation for Germany plus the Benelux is:

$$\begin{aligned}\Delta \ln(\mathrm{M3}/P) = &- \underset{(4.39)}{0.1001}(\ln(\mathrm{M3}/P)_{-1} - \ln y) + \underset{(2.35)}{0.0350} \ln y_{-1} \\ &+ \underset{(2.52)}{0.0012} r_s - \underset{(5.56)}{0.0045} r_{l_{-3\frac{1}{2}}} - \underset{(5.15)}{0.0144} \Delta r_{l_{-1\frac{1}{2}}} - \underset{(13.03)}{0.0024} \dot{p} \\ &- \underset{(3.37)}{0.0026} conj_{-3} - \underset{(1.19)}{0.0956} - \underset{(3.28)}{0.0093} s_1 \\ &- \underset{(3.17)}{0.0088} s_2 - \underset{(6.89)}{0.0165} s_3 + \underset{(33.29)}{0.0924} \mathrm{dum}_{90:\mathrm{III}}\end{aligned}$$

$\bar{R}^2 = 0.90 \quad SE = 0.006$

The above two examples show remarkable differences in empirical specification and estimation results, but not in the error-correction term and goodness of fit. In any case the two equations illustrate that the method of conversion may affect the results. To investigate this matter further we also estimated the equation for data converted by using the US$ exchange rate rather than DM exchange rate. This yields:

$$\begin{aligned}\Delta \ln(\mathrm{M3}/P) = &- \underset{(2.14))}{0.0842}(\ln(\mathrm{M3}/P)_{-1} - \ln y) + \underset{(1.19)}{0.0316} \ln y_{-1} \\ &+ \underset{(1.56)}{0.0019} r_s - \underset{(2.22)}{0.0035} \Delta r_{s_{-1}} - \underset{(3.65)}{0.0072} r_{l_{-\frac{1}{2}}} - \underset{(1.12)}{0.0001} \dot{p} \\ &- \underset{(2.36)}{0.0001} \Delta \dot{p}_{-2} - \underset{(2.44)}{0.0031} conj_{-4} - \underset{(0.51)}{0.0581} + \underset{(7.75)}{0.0232} s_1 \\ &+ \underset{(3.46)}{0.0137} s_2 - \underset{(3.33)}{0.0108} s_3 + \underset{(24.81)}{0.1002} \mathrm{dum}_{90:\mathrm{III}}\end{aligned}$$

$\bar{R}^2 = 0.76 \quad SE = 0.009$

Obviously, these results differ from those obtained with the other equations. Consequently the long-run or equilibrium elasticities also differ as Table 8.3 illustrates, doubling the size of the long-run interest rate elasticity, which seems implausible.

One explanation of this difference is that movements in the price variable are influenced by the specific exchange rate used. When expressing the national aggregates in another currency, the change in the transformed price is the result of changes in both domestic prices and

*Table 8.3: Equilibrium elasticities for* M3

| | Short-term interest rate | Long-term interest rate | Inflation |
|---|---|---|---|
| – Current DM exchange rates | | | |
| Germany and Benelux | 0.07 | −0.35 | −0.07 |
| Idem, plus France | 0.04 | −0.24 | −0.02 |
| – Current DM PPP | | | |
| Germany and Benelux | 0.09 | −0.37 | −0.10 |
| Idem, plus France | 0.13 | −0.33 | −0.06 |
| – Current US$ exchange rates | | | |
| Germany and Benelux | 0.16 | −0.70 | −0.01 |

exchange rates. To illustrate this, Figure 8.1 presents the inflation rates in Belgium, Germany and the Netherlands with the DM conversion method and the US$ conversion method. When using the dollar as the conversion factor, the first half of the 1980s shows strong deflation, whereas in 1985–1986 excessive inflation is in evidence. Naturally, this reflects the change in the value of the US dollar.

## 8.3 Money Demand With Divisia Measures in Core EMU

This section discusses estimated money demand equations using Divisia monetary measures for the hard core of EMU, focusing in particular on stability issues of Divisia measures *vis-à-vis* simple sum aggregates discussed in Section 8.1. Moreover, the statistical properties of the estimated equation are briefly examined.

### 8.3.1 Estimation Results for Divisia Measures

As before, the estimated equations are based on the general theoretical framework set out in Section 8.2.1 and particularly on equation (8.4). As before for simple sum aggregates, this equation was estimated for Divisia M2 and M3 for Germany, the Netherlands, Belgium and France as well as for the potential core countries Germany and the Benelux – say GB – and for GB plus France. A full report of the estimation results

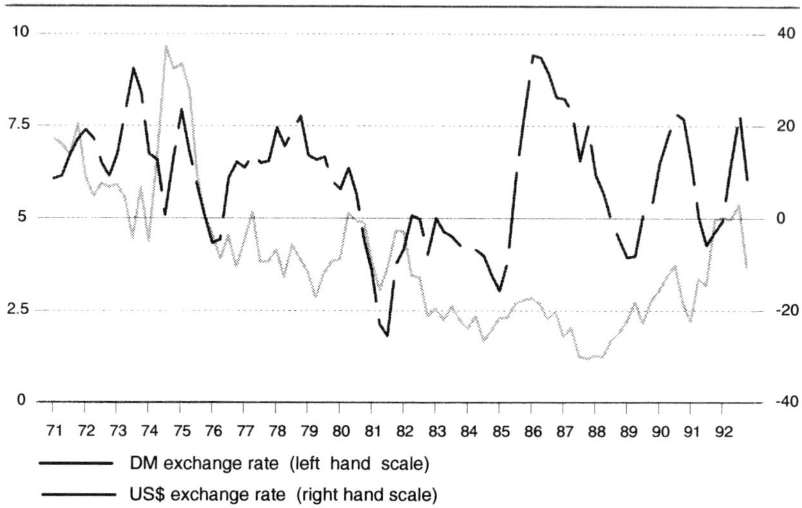


*Figure 8.1: Inflation in Germany plus Benelux using* DM *and US$ exchange rates*

is given in Appendix 8.A. By way of illustration we report below the estimated equation for Divisia M3 in the core group Germany–Benelux. Using the 1985 DM exchange rates as conversion technique, $oc2$ the user costs of M3, $s_i$ as seasonal dummies; $\mathrm{dum}_{90:\mathrm{III}}$ is a binary variable to account for the German unification in October 1990 and sample period 1971:II–1992:IV. The estimated equation is:

$$\begin{aligned}\Delta \ln(\mathrm{DiM3}/P) = & -\underset{(2.01)}{0.0736}(\ln(\mathrm{DiM3}/P)_{-3} - \ln y) \\ & + \underset{(3.78)}{0.3659}\Delta \ln(\mathrm{DiM3}/P)_{-4} - \underset{(2.32)}{0.0022}oc2_{-2\frac{1}{2}} \\ & - \underset{(1.69)}{0.0055}\Delta R - \underset{(2.32)}{0.0022}\dot{p} - \underset{(3.00)}{0.0042}conj_{-1} - \underset{(0.98)}{0.0184} \\ & + \underset{(0.97)}{0.0044}s_1 + \underset{(2.95)}{0.0113}s_2 - \underset{(3.18)}{0.0148}s_3 \\ & + \underset{(29.86)}{0.0900}\mathrm{dum}_{90:\mathrm{III}}\end{aligned}$$

$\bar{R}^2 = 0.70$ $SE = 0.011$ $t$-values in parentheses

The estimation results for Divisia measures of money also depend on the conversion technique chosen. Therefore we also present the corresponding estimates, using 1985 DM purchasing power parity as conversion method. The estimated equation is:

$$\begin{aligned}
\Delta \ln(\mathrm{DiM3}/P) = & -\underset{(2.02)}{0.0738}(\ln(\mathrm{DiM3}/P)_{-3} - \ln y) \\
& + \underset{(3.80)}{0.3694}\Delta \ln(\mathrm{DiM3}/P)_{-4} - \underset{(2.32)}{0.0021} oc2_{-2\frac{1}{2}} \\
& - \underset{(1.68)}{0.0054}\Delta R - \underset{(2.32)}{0.0021}\dot{p} - \underset{(3.02)}{0.0043} conj_{-1} - \underset{(1.01)}{0.0192} \\
& + \underset{(0.98)}{0.0044}s_1 + \underset{(2.96)}{0.0113}s_2 - \underset{(3.18)}{0.0149}s_3 \\
& + \underset{(29.42)}{0.0890}\mathrm{dum}_{90:\mathrm{III}}
\end{aligned}$$

$\bar{R}^2 = 0.71 \quad SE = 0.011$

Comparing the two equations shows that in this case the technique of conversion affects the specification and estimates only slightly. The results differ substantially, however, if the US$ or current value of DM are used (see Appendix 8.A). The size of the standard error of residuals, which is a measure of stability – our main focus – is only slightly affected by the conversion method but larger than for simple sum money demand. Therefore we may conclude that money demand stability for the Divisia measure and simple sum aggregate differ considerably.

Finally, Table 8.4 sets out the (semi-)elasticities over countries/region and monetary aggregates, showing that very often the results are rather plausible. They are also in agreement with the implications of the simple sum estimates.

### 8.3.2 A Closer Look at the Results

Relative stability is our main concern in this chapter. The statistic for stability used here is the residual standard error for the monetary aggregate over two core EMU countries set out in Table 8.5. This table also includes the standard errors for the equations for Belgium, France, Germany and the Netherlands.

The results in Table 8.5 indicate first that, regardless of the monetary measure used, stability measured by standard errors of residuals is greater for Germany and France than for the low countries. Second, stability does not increase by using Divisia measures although the pattern according to the size of the countries still holds. Third, Table 8.5 suggests a slight increase in stability for the core EMU. However, stability is much greater for EMU as a whole.

Table 8.5 shows the remarkable result that aggregation across countries reduces the standard error of residuals in the demand for money. As far as this standard error is the measure for stability, it increases stability for the particular countries considered. This result suggests that aggregation across countries should be examined further. Table 8.5 also shows that M3 is more stable than the narrowly defined aggregates, a result that constitutes a justification for considering M3 as the central monetary policy variable.

### 8.3.3 Statistical Properties

The demand for money equations discussed in this chapter have been subjected to an econometric specification analysis. The results are summarized in Appendix 8.C on which the following discussion draws. First, the constraints imposed upon the parameters are tested. Subsequently, the residuals of the estimated equations have been tested for autocorrelation. Finally, a cointegration analysis of the long-run relationships is set out.

The estimated demand for money equation (8.4) includes a number of constraints imposed on the parameters and long-run elasticities. These constraints constitute testable hypotheses, whose validity has been examined with $t$- and $F$-tests. The test for these constraints, set out in Table 8.C.2, indicate that these constraints need not be rejected.

Subsequently, we have tested whether the residuals of the demand for money equations show autocorrelation. To this end, the Ljung–Box test statistic, based on the first $p$ autocorrelations of the residuals – $p = 2, 4, 8$ and 12 – has been calculated. Under the null hypothesis of white noise disturbances, the test statistics are distributed $\chi^2(p)$. The results are shown in Table 8.C.1 and indicate that no significant autocorrelation is present.

The long-run relationships implied by the estimated dynamic demand for money have been examined further by means of cointegration tests to verify whether the deviations from the equilibrium path follow a stationary process. As the data used are seasonally adjusted, the procedure of Hylleberg, Engle, Granger, and Yoo (1990) has been used. The estimated equation is:

$$\Delta_4 x_t = \pi_1 y_{1t-1} + \pi_2 y_{2t-1} + \pi_3 y_{3t-2} + \pi_4 y_{3t-1} + \varepsilon_t \tag{8.5}$$

where $x_t$ represents the deviations from the equilibrium path, $y_{1t} = 1 + L + L^2 + L^3)x_t, y_{2t} = -(1 - L)(1 + L^2)x_t, y_{3t} = -(1 - L)(1 + L)x_t$

*Table 8.4: Long-run properties of money demand*

| Country(ies) | Monetary aggregate | Elasticities | | Semi-elasticities | | |
|---|---|---|---|---|---|---|
| | | Price | Income | Short-term int. rate | Long-term int. rate | Inflation |
| Germany | DiM 2 | 1 | 1 | 0.012 | −0.029 | −0.029 |
| | DiM 3 | 1 | 1 | 0.021 | −0.032 | −0.032 |
| The Netherlands | DiM 2 | 1 | 1 | 0.011 | −0.029 | −0.029 |
| | DiM 3 | 1 | 1 | 0.022 | −0.034 | −0.034 |
| Belgium | DiM 2 | 0.746 | 1 | 0.025 | −0.058 | −0.011 |
| | DiM 3 | 0.745 | 1 | 0.039 | −0.059 | −0.026 |
| France | DiM 2 | 0.830 | 1 | 0.004 | −0.010 | −0.010 |
| | DiM 3 | 0.849 | 1 | 0.004 | −0.007 | −0.007 |
| Germany plus | M 1 | 1 | 1.391 | −0.010 | −0.010 | −0.010 |
| Benelux | M 2 | 1 | 1.229 | 0.041 | −0.041 | −0.041 |
| – 1985 DM | M 3 | 1 | 1 | 0.021 | −0.043 | −0.043 |
| exchange rates | DiM 2 | 1 | 1 | 0.014 | −0.035 | −0.035 |
| | DiM 3 | 1 | 1 | 0.019 | −0.029 | −0.029 |
| – Current DM exchange rates | M 3 | 1 | 1.361 | 0.010 | −0.043 | −0.017 |
| Germany plus | M 1 | 1 | 1.384 | −0.010 | −0.010 | −0.010 |
| Benelux | M 2 | 1 | 1.225 | 0.041 | −0.041 | −0.041 |
| – 1985 DM PPP | M 3 | 1 | 1 | 0.021 | −0.043 | −0.043 |
| | DiM 2 | 1 | 1 | 0.014 | −0.035 | −0.035 |
| | DiM 3 | 1 | 1 | 0.019 | −0.029 | −0.029 |
| – Current DM PPP | M 3 | 1 | 1.349 | 0.012 | −0.045 | −0.024 |
| Germany, France | M 1 | 1 | 1 | −0.007 | −0.007 | −0.008 |
| plus Benelux | M 2 | 1 | 1 | 0.054 | −0.054 | −0.054 |
| – 1985 DM | M 3 | 1 | 1 | 0.035 | −0.035 | −0.035 |
| exchange rates | DiM 2 | 1 | 1 | 0.015 | −0.035 | −0.015 |
| | DiM 3 | 1 | 1 | 0.015 | −0.024 | −0.024 |
| – Current DM exchange rates | M 3 | 1.254 | 1 | 0.004 | −0.027 | −0.004 |
| Germany, France | M 1 | 1 | 1 | −0.007 | −0.007 | −0.007 |
| plus Benelux | M 2 | 1 | 1 | 0.054 | −0.054 | −0.054 |
| – 1985 DM PPP | M 3 | 1 | 1 | 0.035 | −0.035 | −0.035 |
| | DiM 2 | 1 | 1 | 0.015 | −0.036 | −0.015 |
| | DiM 3 | 1 | 1 | 0.015 | −0.024 | −0.024 |
| – Current DM PPP | M 3 | 1 | 1.289 | 0.015 | −0.037 | −0.015 |

*Table 8.5: Standard error of residuals* ($\times 10^3$)

| | M1 | M2 | M3 | DiM2 | DiM3 |
|---|---|---|---|---|---|
| Germany plus Benelux | 14 | 12 | 8 | 12 | 11 |
| Germany, France plus Benelux | 8 | 11 | 8 | 9 | 9 |
| EMU[a] | 6 | 6 | 5 | 7 | 7 |
| Germany[b] | 11 | 13 | 9 | 14 | 12 |
| France[b] | 10 | 12 | 8 | 11 | 9 |
| Belgium[b] | 12 | 14 | 9 | 15 | 15 |
| The Netherlands[b] | 20 | 25 | 16 | 19 | 19 |

*Notes:*
The results for (sub)EMU follow by using 1985 DM exchange rates as conversion factor.
[a] The results for M1, M2 and M3 are calculated as a weighted average of the country results in Fase and Winder (1993). The results for DiM2 and DiM3 are found in Fase and Winder (1994).
[b] The results for M1, M2 and M3 are obtained from Fase and Winder (1993).

and $\varepsilon_t$ a disturbance term. Lags of $\Delta_4 x_t$ have been added to eliminate any autocorrelation in the residuals. The constraint $\pi_1 = 0$ corresponds to a unit root $L = 1$. The constraint $\pi_2 = 0$ implies that a unit root equal to $L = -1$ is present. If $\pi_3$ and $\pi_4$ are both equal to 0, the complex roots $L = \pm i$ are present. These various constraints can be tested with the $t$-ratios of $\pi_i, i = 1, \ldots, 4$ and the $F$-test for the constraint $\pi_3 = \pi_4 = 0$. However, the test statistics do not have the standard distributions. Hylleberg, Engle, Granger, and Yoo (1990) present the critical values for the test statistics obtained with simulation experiments.

The cointegration test was carried out by estimating equation (8.5) with seasonal dummies, a constant term and the first four lags of $\Delta_4 x_t$ being included as additional explanatory variables. Subsequently, in several rounds, the most insignificant of the lags of $\Delta_4 x_t$ was eliminated successively from the equation. The results of the above $t$- and $F$- tests for the ultimate equation are listed in Table 8.C.3 showing that cointegration can be accepted for the core EMU including France. On the other hand, cointegration has to be rejected for the monetary aggregates for Germany plus Benelux, with the exception of M2. According to the results in Table 8.C.3, seasonal unit roots are absent.

## 8.4 Conclusion

The main objective of this chapter is to examine the properties of the demand for money measured as a simple sum and Divisia aggregate for various groups of EMU countries. The groups studied are the potential hard core EMU countries, in particular the country-set Germany, Belgium and the Netherlands and this country-set extended with France.

Our analysis results in five clear cut conclusions. First, we found evidence for the hypothesis of price homogeneity. Second, the method of converting individual country data to a common basis does affect the estimation results in some instances. Third, the estimation results differ slightly according to the monetary aggregate used, but are consistent between potential core EMU countries and EMU as a whole. Fourth, money demand in the core countries has a similar stability as in Germany, a finding which holds for both simple sum and Divisia aggregates. The empirical results also indicate that for EMU as a whole, demand for Divisia monetary aggregates displays greater stability than for core EMU. Finally, the monetary picture resulting for Divisia aggregates differs substantially from that given by the traditional monetary aggregates but converges to simple sum M1 monetary growth. Perhaps this means that one may wish to consider M1 again as a useful monetary aggregate.

# APPENDIX 8.A ESTIMATION RESULTS

*Germany*

$$\Delta \ln(\text{DiM}\,2/P) = \underset{(1.80)}{-\,0.0629}(\ln(\text{DiM}\,2/P)_{-3} - \ln y) + \underset{(2.59)}{0.2565}\Delta \ln(\text{DiM}\,2/P)_{-4}$$
$$\underset{(2.14)}{-\,0.0018}oc1_{-2} \underset{(2.47)}{-\,0.0085}\Delta R_{-1\frac{1}{2}} \underset{(2.14)}{-\,0.0018}\dot{p} \underset{(0.50)}{-\,0.0008}conj$$
$$\underset{(0.66)}{+\,0.0131} \underset{(2.55)}{-\,0.0174}s_1 \underset{(0.48)}{-\,0.0024}s_2$$
$$\underset{(2.82)}{-\,0.0157}s_3 + \underset{(29.69)}{0.1324}\text{dum}_{90:\text{III}}$$

Sample period: 1971:II–1992:IV $\bar{R}^2 = 0.64$ $SE = 0.014$

$$\Delta \ln(\text{DiM}\,3/P) = \underset{(2.16)}{-\,0.0681}(\ln(\text{DiM}\,3/P)_{-3} - \ln y) + \underset{(2.20)}{0.2424}\Delta \ln(\text{DiM}\,3/P)_{-4}$$
$$\underset{(2.24)}{-\,0.0022}oc2_{-3} \underset{(2.72)}{-\,0.0081}\Delta R_{-1} \underset{(2.24)}{-\,0.0022}\dot{p} \underset{(1.50)}{-\,0.0022}conj_{-\frac{1}{2}}$$
$$\underset{(0.57)}{+\,0.0066} \underset{(0.44)}{+\,0.0021}s_1 \underset{(0.20)}{+\,0.0007}s_2$$
$$\underset{(2.47)}{-\,0.0103}s_3 + \underset{(35.91)}{0.1235}\text{dum}_{90:\text{III}}$$

Sample period: 1971:II–1992:IV $\bar{R}^2 = 0.58$ $SE = 0.012$

*The Netherlands*

$$\Delta \ln(\text{DiM}\,2/P) = \underset{(1.71)}{-\,0.0464}(\ln(\text{DiM}\,2/P)_{-1} - \ln y_{-1}) + \underset{(4.02)}{0.3833}\Delta \ln y$$
$$\underset{(3.67)}{+\,0.3334}\Delta \ln y_{-2} \underset{(7.74)}{+\,0.6607}\Delta \ln(\text{DiM}\,2/P)_{-4} \underset{(2.44)}{-\,0.0013}oc1_{-1}$$
$$\underset{(2.89)}{-\,0.0132}\Delta R \underset{(2.44)}{-\,0.0013}\dot{p} \underset{(3.57)}{-\,0.0090}\Delta \dot{p}_{-\frac{1}{2}}$$
$$\underset{(4.95)}{+\,0.0117}\Delta \dot{p}_{-1\frac{1}{2}} \underset{(1.28)}{-\,0.0022}conj_{-1} \underset{(0.89)}{+\,0.0348}$$
$$\underset{(4.38)}{+\,0.0729}s_1 \underset{(2.66)}{+\,0.0285}s_2 \underset{(3.22)}{+\,0.0560}s_3$$

Sample period: 1971:II–1992:IV $\bar{R}^2 = 0.89$ $SE = 0.019$

$$\Delta \ln(\text{DiM}\,3/P) = \underset{(1.80)}{-\,0.0512}(\ln(\text{DiM}\,3/P)_{-1} - \ln y_{-1}) + \underset{(4.44)}{0.3615}\Delta \ln y$$

$$
\begin{aligned}
&+ \underset{(2.68)}{0.2450}\Delta \ln y_{-2} + \underset{(7.95)}{0.6070}\Delta \ln(\mathrm{DiM}\,3/P)_{-4} - \underset{(2.99)}{0.0017}oc2_{-1} \\
&+ \underset{(3.46)}{0.0090}\Delta oc2 - \underset{(2.99)}{0.0017}\dot{p} - \underset{(1.84)}{0.0031}conj_{-2} \\
&+ \underset{(1.40)}{0.0605} + \underset{(3.05)}{0.0514}s_1 + \underset{(1.73)}{0.0143}s_2 + \underset{(2.42)}{0.0394}s_3
\end{aligned}
$$

Sample period: 1971:II–1992:IV $\quad \bar{R}^2 = 0.86 \quad SE = 0.019$

*Belgium*

$$
\begin{aligned}
\Delta \ln(\mathrm{DiM}\,2/P) = &- \underset{(2.59)}{0.1211}(\ln(\mathrm{DiM}\,2/P)_{-1} - \ln y_{-1}) + \underset{(3.37)}{0.2838}\Delta \ln(\mathrm{DiM}\,2/P)_{-4} \\
&- \underset{(1.08)}{0.1328}\Delta \ln y_{-1\frac{1}{2}} - \underset{(2.29)}{0.0308}\Delta \ln P - \underset{(3.89)}{0.0070}oc1_{-4} \\
&- \underset{(1.66)}{0.0013}\dot{p} - \underset{(3.15)}{0.0073}\Delta\dot{p} - \underset{(1.19)}{0.0022}conj_{-3} \\
&- \underset{(1.74)}{0.0769} - \underset{(0.26)}{0.0029}s_1 + \underset{(2.24)}{0.0375}s_2 + \underset{(3.82)}{0.0329}s_3
\end{aligned}
$$

Sample period: 1971:II–1992:IV $\quad \bar{R}^2 = 0.83 \quad SE = 0.015$

$$
\begin{aligned}
\Delta \ln(\mathrm{DiM}\,3/P) = &- \underset{(0.69)}{0.0440}(\ln(\mathrm{DiM}\,3/P)_{-1} - \ln y_{-1}) + \underset{(3.20)}{0.3180}\Delta \ln(\mathrm{DiM}\,3/P)_{-4} \\
&- \underset{(1.09)}{0.0112}\Delta \ln P - \underset{(1.87)}{0.0026}oc2_{-4} - \underset{(1.13)}{0.0011}\dot{p} \\
&- \underset{(2.97)}{0.0078}\Delta\dot{p} - \underset{(1.40)}{0.0032}conj_{-3} - \underset{(0.30)}{0.0203} \\
&- \underset{(1.31)}{0.0062}s_1 + \underset{(4.20)}{0.0206}s_2 - \underset{(1.85)}{0.0238}s_3
\end{aligned}
$$

Sample period: 1971:II–1992:IV $\quad \bar{R}^2 = 0.79 \quad SE = 0.015$

*France*

$$
\begin{aligned}
\Delta \ln(\mathrm{DiM}\,2/P) = &- \underset{(2.71)}{0.1823}(\ln(\mathrm{DiM}\,2/P)_{-1} - \ln y) - \underset{(3.02)}{0.0310}\ln P \\
&- \underset{(3.32)}{0.0018}oc1_{-1} - \underset{(3.32)}{0.0018}\dot{p}_{-1} - \underset{(3.22)}{0.0042}conj_{-3} \\
&- \underset{(2.11)}{0.1091} - \underset{(9.41)}{0.0365}s_1 - \underset{(1.53)}{0.0066}s_2 + \underset{(1.44)}{0.0193}s_3
\end{aligned}
$$

Sample period: 1971:II–1992:IV $\quad \bar{R}^2 = 0.67 \quad SE = 0.011$

$$
\Delta \ln(\mathrm{DiM}\,3/P) = \underset{(1.66)}{0.0930}(\ln(\mathrm{DiM}\,3/P)_{-1} - \ln y) - \underset{(2.97)}{0.0140}\ln P
$$

$$\begin{aligned}&+\underset{(3.85)}{0.3417}\Delta\ln(\mathrm{DiM3}/P)_{-4}-\underset{(2.30)}{0.0007}oc2-\underset{(2.30)}{0.0007}\dot{p}\\&-\underset{(7.30)}{0.0079}\Delta\dot{p}-\underset{(4.13)}{0.0039}conj_{-3}-\underset{(1.26)}{0.0506}\\&-\underset{(4.55)}{0.0187}s_1-\underset{(1.67)}{0.0057}s_2+\underset{(0.66)}{0.0072}s_3\end{aligned}$$

Sample period: 1971:II–1992:IV $\bar{R}^2 = 0.71$ $SE = 0.009$

*Germany plus Benelux*
(1985 DM exchange rates)

$$\begin{aligned}\Delta\ln(\mathrm{M1}/P)=&-\underset{(2.09)}{0.1134}(\ln(\mathrm{M1}/P)_{-2}-\ln y)+\underset{(4.44)}{0.3682}\Delta\ln y_{-4}\\&+\underset{(2.21)}{0.0443}\ln y_{-1}-\underset{(2.74)}{0.0011}r_{s-2}-\underset{(2.74)}{0.0011}r_{l-2}\\&-\underset{(2.74)}{0.0011}\dot{p}-\underset{(5.74)}{0.0094}conj_{-2}-\underset{(2.13)}{0.2991}\\&+\underset{(0.63)}{0.0075}s_1+\underset{(6.91)}{0.0323}s_2-\underset{(4.25)}{0.0244}s_3\\&+\underset{(18.91)}{0.0874}\mathrm{dum}_{90:\mathrm{III}}\end{aligned}$$

Sample period: 1971:II–1992:IV $\bar{R}^2 = 0.82$ $SE = 0.014$

$$\begin{aligned}\Delta\ln(\mathrm{M2}/P)=&-\underset{(3.02)}{0.0837}(\ln(\mathrm{M2}/P)_{-3}-\ln y_{-1})+\underset{(3.99)}{0.3527}\Delta\ln(\mathrm{M2}/P)_{-4}\\&+\underset{(2.70)}{0.2936}\Delta\ln y+\underset{(3.02)}{0.0192}\ln y_{-1}+\underset{(3.78)}{0.0034}r_s\\&-\underset{(3.78)}{0.0034}r_l+\underset{(2.07)}{0.0069}\Delta r_{l-2}-\underset{(3.78)}{0.0034}\dot{p}\\&+\underset{(2.01)}{0.0047}\Delta\dot{p}_{-2}-\underset{(2.85)}{0.0048}conj_{-3\frac{1}{2}}-\underset{(2.91)}{0.0978}\\&+\underset{(2.52)}{0.0315}s_1+\underset{(2.50)}{0.0114}s_2+\underset{(0.33)}{0.0023}s_3\\&+\underset{(10.98)}{0.0985}\mathrm{dum}_{90:\mathrm{III}}\end{aligned}$$

Sample period: 1971:II–1992:IV $\bar{R}^2 = 0.68$ $SE = 0.012$

$$\begin{aligned}\Delta\ln(\mathrm{M3}/P)=&-\underset{(2.96)}{0.0600}(\ln(\mathrm{M3}/P)_{-3}-\ln y)+\underset{(2.60)}{0.3168}\Delta\ln(\mathrm{M3}/P)_{-4}\\&+\underset{(1.90)}{0.0013}r_s-\underset{(2.20)}{0.0028}\Delta r_{s-1}-\underset{(2.97)}{0.0026}r_{l-1}\end{aligned}$$

$$\underset{(2.12)}{-\,0.0064\Delta r_{l_{-2\frac{1}{2}}}} \underset{(2.97)}{-\,0.0026\dot{p}_{-1}} \underset{(2.48)}{-\,0.0073\Delta\dot{p}_{-\frac{1}{2}}}$$

$$\underset{(3.14)}{+\,0.0090\Delta\dot{p}_{-1\frac{1}{2}}} \underset{(2.50)}{-\,0.0029conj_{-3\frac{1}{2}}} \underset{(3.19)}{+\,0.0668}$$

$$\underset{(4.52)}{+\,0.0184s_1} \underset{(2.12)}{+\,0.0052s_2} \underset{(2.94)}{-\,0.0095s_3}$$

$$\underset{(30.49)}{+\ 0.1015\text{dum}_{90:\text{III}}}$$

Sample period: 1971:IV–1992:IV $\bar{R}^2 = 0.82$ $SE = 0.008$

$$\Delta\ln(\text{DiM}2/P) = \underset{(1.34)}{-\,0.0529(\ln(\text{DiM}2/P)_{-3} - \ln y)} \underset{(3.78)}{+\,0.3352\Delta\ln(\text{DiM}2/P)_{-4}}$$

$$\underset{(2.89)}{-\,0.0018oc1_{-2}} \underset{(2.28)}{-\,0.0081\Delta R_{-\frac{1}{2}}} \underset{(2.89)}{-\,0.0018\dot{p}} \underset{(2.06)}{-\,0.0030conj_{-2}}$$

$$\underset{(0.09)}{-\,0.0026} \underset{(1.34)}{-\,0.0080s_1} \underset{(2.73)}{+\,0.0121s_2}$$

$$\underset{(3.48)}{-\,0.0202s_3} \underset{(29.51)}{+\ 0.0931\text{dum}_{90:\text{III}}}$$

Sample period: 1971:II–1992:IV $\bar{R}^2 = 0.75$ $SE = 0.012$

$$\Delta\ln(\text{DiM}3/P) = \underset{(2.01)}{-\,0.0736(\ln(\text{DiM}3/P)_{-3} - \ln y)} \underset{(3.78)}{+\,0.3659\Delta\ln(\text{DiM}3/P)_{-4}}$$

$$\underset{(2.32)}{-\,0.0022oc2_{-2\frac{1}{2}}} \underset{(1.69)}{-\,0.0055\Delta R} \underset{(2.32)}{-\,0.0022\dot{p}} \underset{(3.00)}{-\,0.0042conj_{-1}}$$

$$\underset{(0.98)}{-\,0.0184} \underset{(0.97)}{+\,0.0044s_1} \underset{(2.95)}{+\,0.0113s_2}$$

$$\underset{(3.18)}{-\,0.0148s_3} \underset{(29.86)}{+\ 0.0900\text{dum}_{90:\text{III}}}$$

Sample period: 1971:II–1992:IV $\bar{R}^2 = 0.70$ $SE = 0.011$

*Germany plus Benelux*
(1985 DM purchasing power parities)

$$\Delta\ln(\text{M}1/P) = \underset{(2.04)}{-\,0.1111(\ln(\text{M}1/P)_{-2} - \ln y)} \underset{(4.42)}{+\,0.3644\Delta\ln y_{-4}}$$

$$\underset{(2.16)}{+\,0.0426\ln y_{-1}} \underset{(2.72)}{-\,0.0011r_{s_{-2}}} \underset{(2.72)}{-\,0.0011r_{l_{-2}}}$$

$$\underset{(2.72)}{-\,0.0011\dot{p}} \underset{(5.73)}{-\,0.0093conj_{-2}} \underset{(2.08)}{-\,0.2877}$$

$$\underset{(0.60)}{+\,0.0072s_1} \underset{(7.02)}{-\,0.0328s_2} \underset{(4.21)}{-\,0.0245s_3}$$

$$+ \underset{(18.93)}{0.0867}\text{dum}_{90:\text{III}}$$

Sample period: 1971:II–1992:IV $\bar{R}^2 = 0.82$ $SE = 0.014$

$$\begin{aligned}
\Delta\ln(\text{M}2/P) = &-\underset{(3.00)}{0.0826}(\ln(\text{M}2/P)_{-3} - \ln y_{-1}) + \underset{(4.03)}{0.3579}\Delta\ln(\text{M}2/P)_{-4} \\
&+ \underset{(2.68)}{0.2917}\Delta\ln y + \underset{(3.00)}{0.0186}\ln y_{-1} + \underset{(3.80)}{0.0034}r_s \\
&- \underset{(3.80)}{0.0034}r_l + \underset{(2.08)}{0.0069}\Delta r_{l-2} - \underset{(3.80)}{0.0034}\dot{p} \\
&+ \underset{(1.99)}{0.0047}\Delta\dot{p}_{-2} - \underset{(2.87)}{0.0048}conj_{-3\frac{1}{2}} - \underset{(2.90)}{0.0943} \\
&+ \underset{(2.52)}{0.0317}s_1 + \underset{(2.53)}{0.0117}s_2 + \underset{(0.38)}{0.0027}s_3 \\
&+ \underset{(10.91)}{0.0973}\text{dum}_{90:\text{III}}
\end{aligned}$$

Sample period: 1971:IV–1992:IV $\bar{R}^2 = 0.68$ $SE = 0.012$

$$\begin{aligned}
\Delta\ln(\text{M}3/P) = &-\underset{(2.96)}{0.0597}(\ln(\text{M}3/P)_{-3} - \ln y) + \underset{(2.63)}{0.3224}\Delta\ln(\text{M}3/P)_{-4} \\
&+ \underset{(1.91)}{0.0013}r_s - \underset{(2.18)}{0.0028}\Delta r_{s-1} - \underset{(2.98)}{0.0026}r_{l-1} \\
&- \underset{(2.14)}{0.0065}\Delta r_{l-2\frac{1}{2}} - \underset{(2.98)}{0.0026}\dot{p}_{-1} - \underset{(2.51)}{0.0073}\Delta\dot{p}_{-\frac{1}{2}} \\
&+ \underset{(3.16)}{0.0091}\Delta\dot{p}_{-1\frac{1}{2}} - \underset{(2.54)}{0.0029}conj_{-3\frac{1}{2}} + \underset{(3.19)}{0.0668} \\
&+ \underset{(4.49)}{0.0182}s_1 + \underset{(2.11)}{0.0052}s_2 - \underset{(2.93)}{0.0095}s_3 \\
&+ \underset{(29.99)}{0.1003}\text{dum}_{90:\text{III}}
\end{aligned}$$

Sample period: 1971:II–1992:IV $\bar{R}^2 = 0.82$ $SE = 0.008$

$$\begin{aligned}
\Delta\ln(\text{DiM}2/P) = &-\underset{(1.33)}{0.0526}(\ln(\text{DiM}2/P)_{-3} - \ln y) + \underset{(3.80)}{0.3384}\Delta\ln(\text{DiM}2/P)_{-4} \\
&- \underset{(2.89)}{0.0018}oc1_{-2} - \underset{(2.27)}{0.0081}\Delta R_{-\frac{1}{2}} - \underset{(2.89)}{0.0018}\dot{p} - \underset{(2.08)}{0.0030}conj_{-2} \\
&- \underset{(0.11)}{0.0032} - \underset{(1.29)}{0.0078}s_1 + \underset{(2.78)}{0.0122}s_2
\end{aligned}$$

$$\begin{aligned}&- \underset{(3.47)}{0.0202}s_3 + \underset{(29.15)}{0.0921}\text{dum}_{90:\text{III}}\end{aligned}$$

Sample period: 1971:II–1992:IV $\bar{R}^2 = 0.76$ $SE = 0.012$

$$\begin{aligned}\Delta \ln(\text{DiM}3/P) = &- \underset{(2.02)}{0.0738}(\ln(\text{DiM}3/P)_{-3} - \ln y) + \underset{(3.80)}{0.3694}\Delta \ln(\text{DiM}3/P)_{-4}\\ &- \underset{(2.32)}{0.0021}oc2_{-2\frac{1}{2}} - \underset{(1.68)}{0.0054}\Delta R - \underset{(2.32)}{0.0021}\dot{p} - \underset{(3.02)}{0.0043}conj_{-1}\\ &- \underset{(1.01)}{0.0192} + \underset{(0.98)}{0.0044}s_1 + \underset{(2.96)}{0.0113}s_2\\ &- \underset{(3.18)}{0.0149}s_3 + \underset{(29.42)}{0.0890}\text{dum}_{90:\text{III}}\end{aligned}$$

Sample period: 1971:II–1992:IV $\bar{R}^2 = 0.71$ $SE = 0.011$

*Germany plus Benelux*
(current DM exchange rates)

$$\begin{aligned}\Delta \ln(\text{M}3/P) = &- \underset{(4.39)}{0.1056}(\ln(\text{M}3/P)_{-1} - \ln y) + \underset{(2.51)}{0.0381}\ln y_{-1}\\ &+ \underset{(1.31)}{0.0010}r_s - \underset{(2.18)}{0.0024}\Delta r_{s-1} - \underset{(3.42)}{0.0046}r_{l-\frac{1}{2}}\\ &- \underset{(7.14)}{0.0018}\dot{p} - \underset{(2.18)}{0.0003}\Delta\dot{p}_{-2} - \underset{(2.03)}{0.0019}conj_{-4}\\ &- \underset{(1.39)}{0.1149} + \underset{(0.11)}{0.0005}s_1 - \underset{(1.06)}{0.0037}s_2 - \underset{(5.07)}{0.0197}s_3\\ &+ \underset{(36.80)}{0.0928}\text{dum}_{90:\text{III}}\end{aligned}$$

Sample period: 1971:II–1992:IV $\bar{R}^2 = 0.88$ $SE = 0.006$

*Germany plus Benelux*
(current DM purchasing power parities)

$$\begin{aligned}\Delta \ln(\text{M}3/P) = &- \underset{(4.39)}{0.1001}(\ln(\text{M}3/P)_{-1} - \ln y) + \underset{(2.35)}{0.0350}\ln y_{-1}\\ &+ \underset{(2.52)}{0.0012}r_s - \underset{(5.56)}{0.0045}r_{l-3\frac{1}{2}} - \underset{(5.15)}{0.0144}\Delta r_{l-1\frac{1}{2}}\\ &- \underset{(13.03)}{0.0024}\dot{p} - \underset{(3.37)}{0.0026}conj_{-3} - \underset{(1.19)}{0.0956}\\ &- \underset{(3.28)}{0.0093}s_1 - \underset{(3.17)}{0.0088}s_2 - \underset{(6.89)}{0.0165}s_3\\ &+ \underset{(33.29)}{0.0924}\text{dum}_{90:\text{III}}\end{aligned}$$

Sample period: 1971:I–1992:IV $\bar{R}^2 = 0.90$ $SE = 0.006$

*Germany, Benelux plus France*
(1985 DM exchange rates)

$$\begin{aligned}
\Delta \ln(\mathrm{M}1/P) = &- \underset{(4.33)}{0.2544}(\ln(\mathrm{M}1/P)_{-1} - \ln y) + \underset{(4.81)}{0.3282}\Delta \ln(\mathrm{M}1/P)_{-4} \\
&- \underset{(4.93)}{0.0017}r_s - \underset{(2.65)}{0.0038}\Delta r_{s-1} - \underset{(4.93)}{0.0017}r_l \\
&+ \underset{(2.24)}{0.0061}\Delta r_{l-2} - \underset{(2.47)}{0.0020}\dot{p} - \underset{(3.03)}{0.0098}\Delta \dot{p}_{-\frac{1}{2}} \\
&+ \underset{(2.28)}{0.0059}\Delta \dot{p}_{-1\frac{1}{2}} - \underset{(2.41)}{0.0035}conj_{-1\frac{1}{2}} - \underset{(0.65)}{0.0071} \\
&- \underset{(1.99)}{0.0100}s_1 + \underset{(2.18)}{0.0078}s_2 - \underset{(0.00)}{0.0000}s_3 \\
&+ \underset{(6.81)}{0.0358}\mathrm{dum}_{90:\mathrm{III}}
\end{aligned}$$

Sample period: 1971:IV–1992:IV $\bar{R}^2 = 0.89$ $SE = 0.008$

$$\begin{aligned}
\Delta \ln(\mathrm{M}2/P) = &- \underset{(1.97)}{0.0453}(\ln(\mathrm{M}2/P)_{-1} - \ln y) + \underset{(4.78)}{0.5318}\Delta \ln(\mathrm{M}2/P)_{-4} \\
&+ \underset{(2.27)}{0.3809}\Delta \ln y_{-1\frac{1}{2}} + \underset{(2.24)}{0.0024}r_s - \underset{(2.24)}{0.0024}r_l \\
&- \underset{(2.24)}{0.0024}\dot{p} - \underset{(3.50)}{0.0084}\Delta \dot{p} - \underset{(1.57)}{0.0023}conj_{-2} \\
&+ \underset{(3.50)}{0.0497} - \underset{(2.96)}{0.0274}s_1 - \underset{(2.40)}{0.0243}s_2 \\
&- \underset{(2.94)}{0.0190}s_3 + \underset{(11.07)}{0.0564}\mathrm{dum}_{90:\mathrm{III}}
\end{aligned}$$

Sample period: 1971:II–1992:IV $\bar{R}^2 = 0.74$ $SE = 0.011$

$$\begin{aligned}
\Delta \ln(\mathrm{M}3/P) = &- \underset{(2.26)}{0.0481}(\ln(\mathrm{M}3/P)_{-1} - \ln y) + \underset{(4.19)}{0.5719}\Delta \ln(\mathrm{M}3/P)_{-4} \\
&+ \underset{(2.28)}{0.0017}r_s - \underset{(1.86)}{0.0027}\Delta r_{s-2\frac{1}{2}} - \underset{(2.28)}{0.0017}r_{l-1} \\
&- \underset{(2.12)}{0.0045}\Delta r_{l-1} - \underset{(2.28)}{0.0017}\dot{p} - \underset{(3.15)}{0.0093}\Delta \dot{p}_{-\frac{1}{2}} \\
&+ \underset{(2.18)}{0.0053}\Delta \dot{p}_{-1\frac{1}{2}} - \underset{(2.27)}{0.0028}conj_{-3} + \underset{(2.59)}{0.0549}
\end{aligned}$$

$$
\begin{aligned}
&+ 0.0026s_1 - 0.0027s_2 - 0.0096s_3 \\
&\quad (1.09) \qquad (1.08) \qquad (1.55) \\
&+ 0.0606\text{dum}_{90:\text{III}} \\
&\quad (11.85)
\end{aligned}
$$

Sample period: 1971:IV–1992:IV $\bar{R}^2 = 0.82$ $SE = 0.008$

$$
\begin{aligned}
\Delta\ln(\text{DiM}2) = &- 0.2017(\ln(\text{DiM}2)_{-1} - \ln y) + 0.4480\Delta\ln(\text{DiM}2/P)_{-4} \\
&\quad (4.83) \qquad\qquad\qquad\qquad (6.04) \\
&- 0.0071oc1 + 0.0075\Delta oc1_{-1} + 0.0128\Delta oc1_{-2\frac{1}{2}} \\
&\quad (3.32) \qquad (2.50) \qquad (2.74) \\
&- 0.0030\dot{p} - 0.0107\dot{p}_{-\frac{1}{2}} + 0.0069\dot{p}_{-1\frac{1}{2}} - 0.0037conj_{-2} \\
&\quad (2.75) \qquad (3.19) \qquad (2.66) \qquad (2.20) \\
&- 0.1076 - 0.0042s_1 + 0.0067s_2 \\
&\quad (3.60) \qquad (0.92) \qquad (1.94) \\
&+ 0.0011s_3 + 0.0430\text{dum}_{90:\text{III}} \\
&\quad (0.15) \qquad (8.81)
\end{aligned}
$$

Sample period: 1971:IV–1992:IV $\bar{R}^2 = 0.84$ $SE = 0.009$

$$
\begin{aligned}
\Delta\ln(\text{DiM}3) = &- 0.1218(\ln(\text{DiM}3)_{-1} - \ln y) + 0.5449\Delta\ln(\text{DiM}3/P)_{-4} \\
&\quad (2.86) \qquad\qquad\qquad\qquad (4.74) \\
&- 0.0029oc2_{-\frac{1}{2}} + 0.0085\Delta oc2_{-1} + 0.0109\Delta oc2_{-2\frac{1}{2}} \\
&\quad (3.19) \qquad (2.93) \qquad (3.32) \\
&- 0.0029\dot{p} - 0.0097\dot{p}_{\frac{1}{2}} - 0.0066\dot{p}_{1\frac{1}{2}} - 0.0024conj_{-3} \\
&\quad (3.19) \qquad (3.56) \qquad (2.57) \qquad (1.97) \\
&- 0.0688 - 0.0002s_1 + 0.0028s_2 \\
&\quad (2.29) \qquad (0.06) \qquad (0.86) \\
&- 0.0039s_3 + 0.0420\text{dum}_{90:\text{III}} \\
&\quad (0.55) \qquad (7.98)
\end{aligned}
$$

Sample period: 1971:II–1992:IV $\bar{R}^2 = 0.81$ $SE = 0.009$

*Germany, Benelux plus France*
(1985 DM purchasing power parities)

$$
\begin{aligned}
\Delta\ln(\text{M}1/P) = &- 0.2546(\ln(\text{M}1/P)_{-1} - \ln y) + 0.3267\Delta\ln(\text{M}1/P)_{-4} \\
&\quad (4.31) \qquad\qquad\qquad\qquad (4.82) \\
&- 0.0017r_s - 0.0038\Delta r_{s-1} - 0.0017r_l \\
&\quad (4.99) \qquad (2.65) \qquad (4.99) \\
&+ 0.0061\Delta r_{l-2} - 0.0019\dot{p} - 0.0099\Delta\dot{p}_{-\frac{1}{2}} \\
&\quad (2.26) \qquad (2.42) \qquad (3.06) \\
&+ 0.0059\Delta\dot{p}_{-1\frac{1}{2}} - 0.0035conj_{-1\frac{1}{2}} - 0.0070 \\
&\quad (2.29) \qquad (2.41) \qquad (0.64)
\end{aligned}
$$

$$
\begin{aligned}
&- \underset{(1.99)}{0.0100 s_1} + \underset{(2.24)}{0.0081 s_2} - \underset{(0.02)}{0.0002 s_3} \\
&+ \underset{(6.81)}{0.0357 \text{dum}_{90:\text{III}}}
\end{aligned}
$$

Sample period: 1971:II–1992:IV $\bar{R}^2 = 0.89$ $SE = 0.008$

$$
\begin{aligned}
\Delta \ln(\text{M}2/P) = {} & - \underset{(1.97)}{0.0451}(\ln(\text{M}2/P)_{-1} - \ln y) + \underset{(4.82)}{0.5340} \Delta \ln(\text{M}2/P)_{-4} \\
& + \underset{(2.28)}{0.3822 \Delta \ln y_{-1\frac{1}{2}}} + \underset{(2.25)}{0.0024 r_s} - \underset{(2.25)}{0.0024 r_l} \\
& - \underset{(2.25)}{0.0024 \dot{p}} - \underset{(3.52)}{0.0084 \Delta \dot{p}} - \underset{(1.56)}{0.0023 conj_{-2}} \\
& + \underset{(3.51)}{0.0497} - \underset{(2.94)}{0.0274 s_1} - \underset{(2.40)}{0.0242 s_2} \\
& - \underset{(2.93)}{0.0189 s_3} + \underset{(11.01)}{0.0560 \text{dum}_{90:\text{III}}}
\end{aligned}
$$

Sample period: 1971:II–1992:IV $\bar{R}^2 = 0.74$ $SE = 0.011$

$$
\begin{aligned}
\Delta \ln(\text{M}3/P) = {} & - \underset{(2.28)}{0.0483}(\ln(\text{M}3/P)_{-1} - \ln y) + \underset{(4.21)}{0.5739} \Delta \ln(\text{M}3/P)_{-4} \\
& + \underset{(2.31)}{0.0017 r_s} - \underset{(1.87)}{0.0027 \Delta r_{s_{-2\frac{1}{2}}}} - \underset{(2.31)}{0.0017 r_{l_{-1}}} \\
& - \underset{(2.15)}{0.0045 \Delta r_{l_{-1}}} - \underset{(2.31)}{0.0017 \dot{p}} - \underset{(3.17)}{0.0093 \Delta \dot{p}_{-\frac{1}{2}}} \\
& + \underset{(2.19)}{0.0053 \Delta \dot{p}_{-1\frac{1}{2}}} - \underset{(2.30)}{0.0028 conj_{-3}} + \underset{(2.61)}{0.0551} \\
& + \underset{(1.13)}{0.0027 s_1} - \underset{(1.04)}{0.0026 s_2} - \underset{(1.54)}{0.0095 s_3} \\
& + \underset{(11.80)}{0.0602 \text{dum}_{90:\text{III}}}
\end{aligned}
$$

Sample period: 1971:IV–1992:IV $\bar{R}^2 = 0.82$ $SE = 0.008$

$$
\begin{aligned}
\Delta \ln(\text{DiM}2) = {} & - \underset{(4.77)}{0.2003}(\ln(\text{DiM}2)_{-1} - \ln y) + \underset{(6.04)}{0.4502} \Delta \ln(\text{DiM}2/P)_{-4} \\
& - \underset{(3.33)}{0.0071 oc1} + \underset{(2.51)}{0.0075 \Delta oc1_{-1}} + \underset{(2.72)}{0.0127 \Delta oc1_{-2\frac{1}{2}}} \\
& - \underset{(2.69)}{0.0029 \dot{p}} - \underset{(3.21)}{0.0108 \dot{p}_{-\frac{1}{2}}} + \underset{(2.65)}{0.0068 \dot{p}_{-1\frac{1}{2}}} - \underset{(2.19)}{0.0037 conj_{-2}}
\end{aligned}
$$

$$\begin{array}{l} - \underset{(3.57)}{0.1077} - \underset{(0.90)}{0.0041 s_1} + \underset{(1.97)}{0.0068 s_2} \\ + \underset{(0.14)}{0.0010 s_3} + \underset{(8.79)}{0.0428 \text{dum}_{90:\text{III}}} \end{array}$$

Sample period: 1971:IV–1992:IV $\bar{R}^2 = 0.84$ $SE = 0.009$

$$\begin{aligned} \Delta \ln(\text{DiM}3) = & - \underset{(2.87)}{0.1228}(\ln(\text{DiM}3/P)_{-1} - \ln y) + \underset{(4.76)}{0.5454} \Delta \ln(\text{DiM}3/P)_{-4} \\ & - \underset{(3.19)}{0.0030 oc2_{-\frac{1}{2}}} + \underset{(2.94)}{0.0085 \Delta oc2_{-1}} + \underset{(3.30)}{0.0109 \Delta oc2_{-2\frac{1}{2}}} \\ & - \underset{(3.19)}{0.0030 \dot{p}} - \underset{(3.58)}{0.0097 \dot{p}_{-\frac{1}{2}}} - \underset{(2.59)}{0.0066 \dot{p}_{-1\frac{1}{2}}} - \underset{(1.99)}{0.0024 conj_{-3}} \\ & - \underset{(2.30)}{0.0702} - \underset{(0.04)}{0.0001 s_1} + \underset{(0.90)}{0.0029 s_2} \\ & - \underset{(0.54)}{0.0038 s_3} + \underset{(7.97)}{0.0417 \text{dum}_{90:\text{III}}} \end{aligned}$$

Sample period: 1971:IV–1992:IV $\bar{R}^2 = 0.82$ $SE = 0.009$

*Germany, Benelux plus France*
(current DM exchange rates)

$$\begin{aligned} \Delta \ln(\text{M}3/P) = & - \underset{(2.79)}{0.1490}(\ln(\text{M}3/P)_{-1} - \ln y) + \underset{(1.94)}{0.1376} \Delta \ln(\text{M}3/P)_{-4} \\ & + \underset{(2.18)}{0.0378 \ln P} + \underset{(2.24)}{0.0007 r_{s\,-3\frac{1}{2}}} - \underset{(4.22)}{0.0040 r_{l\,-2\frac{1}{2}}} \\ & - \underset{(2.24)}{0.0007 \dot{p}_{-3\frac{1}{2}}} - \underset{(2.10)}{0.0010 \Delta \dot{p}} - \underset{(3.06)}{0.0033 conj_{-3\frac{1}{2}}} \\ & + \underset{(3.46)}{0.1669} + \underset{(1.95)}{0.0079 s_1} + \underset{(0.94)}{0.0038 s_2} \\ & - \underset{(0.05)}{0.0003 s_3} + \underset{(22.95)}{0.0552 \text{dum}_{90:\text{III}}} \end{aligned}$$

Sample period: 1972:I–1992:IV $\bar{R}^2 = 0.68$ $SE = 0.007$

*Germany, Benelux plus France*
(current DM purchasing power parities)

$$\begin{aligned} \Delta \ln(\text{M}3/P) = & - \underset{(3.57)}{0.1843}(\ln(\text{M}3/P)_{-1} - \ln y) + \underset{(2.32)}{0.0530 \ln y_{-1}} \\ & + \underset{(3.83)}{0.0028 r_s} - \underset{(4.88)}{0.0045 \Delta r_{s\,-1}} - \underset{(6.31)}{0.0068 r_{l\,-\frac{1}{2}}} \\ & - \underset{(3.83)}{0.0028 \dot{p}} - \underset{(4.33)}{0.0034 conj_{-4}} \end{aligned}$$

$$\begin{array}{l} - \underset{(1.32)}{0.1545} + \underset{(1.93)}{0.0041 s_1} + \underset{(0.48)}{0.0011 s_2} \\ - \underset{(0.21)}{0.0010 s_3} + \underset{(20.25)}{0.0548 \text{dum}_{90:\text{III}}} \end{array}$$

Sample period: 1971:II–1992:IV $\bar{R}^2 = 0.72$ $SE = 0.006$

# Appendix 8.B

*Table 8.B.1: Summary statistics for core EMU Germany, France plus Benelux*

| Conversion technique | Variable | Mean | Standard deviation | Correlation with | |
|---|---|---|---|---|---|
| | | | | M1 | $y$ |
| Current DM exchange rates | M1 | 6.17 | 4.45 | 1.00 | 0.11 |
| | M2 | 7.95 | 3.89 | 0.73 | 0.34 |
| | M3 | 7.81 | 3.50 | 0.90 | 0.26 |
| | DiM2 | 6.71 | 4.00 | 0.96 | 0.23 |
| | DiM3 | 6.89 | 3.99 | 0.98 | 0.20 |
| | Real income | 2.70 | 1.96 | 0.11 | 1.00 |
| | Price | 3.83 | 2.80 | 0.69 | −0.24 |
| 1985 DM exchange rates | M1 | 7.98 | 3.10 | 1.00 | 0.17 |
| | M2 | 9.75 | 2.46 | 0.21 | 0.64 |
| | M3 | 9.38 | 2.43 | 0.77 | 0.41 |
| | DiM2 | 8.51 | 2.32 | 0.88 | 0.44 |
| | DiM3 | 8.57 | 2.66 | 0.95 | 0.31 |
| | Real income | 2.70 | 1.96 | 0.17 | 1.00 |
| | Price | 5.13 | 1.90 | 0.37 | −0.29 |
| Current DM PPP | M1 | 6.30 | 3.04 | 1.00 | 0.41 |
| | M2 | 8.12 | 3.22 | 0.52 | 0.63 |
| | M3 | 7.98 | 2.65 | 0.81 | 0.60 |
| | DiM2 | 6.87 | 2.83 | 0.90 | 0.59 |
| | DiM3 | 7.05 | 2.82 | 0.96 | 0.54 |
| | Real income | 2.69 | 1.96 | 0.41 | 1.00 |
| | Price | 3.96 | 1.59 | 0.26 | −0.06 |
| 1985 DM PPP | M1 | 7.97 | 3.10 | 1.00 | 0.16 |
| | M2 | 9.74 | 2.46 | 0.21 | 0.64 |
| | M3 | 9.38 | 2.43 | 0.77 | 0.41 |
| | DiM2 | 8.50 | 2.32 | 0.88 | 0.44 |
| | DiM3 | 8.57 | 2.66 | 0.95 | 0.31 |
| | Real income | 2.69 | 1.96 | 0.16 | 1.00 |
| | Price | 5.13 | 1.90 | 0.37 | −0.29 |

# APPENDIX 8.C

*Table 8.C.1: LB-tests on residual autocorrelation*

| Country(ies) | Monetary aggregate | Order $p$ | | | |
|---|---|---|---|---|---|
| | | 1 | 4 | 8 | 12 |
| Germany | DiM 2 | 0.96 | 1.51 | 10.28 | 13.79 |
| | DiM 3 | 0.06 | 1.85 | 5.11 | 6.55 |
| The Netherlands | DiM 2 | 1.67 | 7.56 | 12.58 | 15.11 |
| | DiM 3 | 0.75 | 5.56 | 10.93 | 13.17 |
| Belgium | DiM 2 | 1.66 | 2.04 | 4.92 | 13.89 |
| | DiM 3 | 0.90 | 1.84 | 3.70 | 11.84 |
| France | DiM 2 | 0.45 | 3.33 | 5.65 | 11.69 |
| | DiM 3 | 0.45 | 2.21 | 7.38 | 10.48 |
| Germany plus | M 1 | 0.44 | 1.11 | 2.70 | 5.55 |
| Benelux | M 2 | 0.11 | 0.80 | 2.40 | 5.68 |
| – 1985 DM exchange | M 3 | 1.66 | 2.20 | 6.08 | 10.94 |
| rates | DiM 2 | 1.30 | 3.76 | 14.17 | 16.45 |
| | DiM 3 | 0.62 | 7.77 | 10.91 | 11.94 |
| – Current DM exchange rates | M 3 | 2.43 | 4.75 | 12.90 | 15.37 |
| Germany plus | M 1 | 0.46 | 1.13 | 2.76 | 5.64 |
| Benelux | M 2 | 0.13 | 0.87 | 2.44 | 5.82 |
| – 1985 DM PPP | M 3 | 1.61 | 2.16 | 6.09 | 10.92 |
| | DiM 2 | 1.30 | 3.85 | 14.03 | 16.27 |
| | DiM 3 | 0.65 | 7.98 | 11.04 | 12.03 |
| – Current DM PPP | M 3 | 0.75 | 3.88 | 8.48 | 11.56 |
| Germany, France | M 1 | 0.07 | 3.79 | 4.73 | 7.78 |
| plus Benelux | M 2 | 1.18 | 3.34 | 4.25 | 6.43 |
| – 1985 DM exchange | M 3 | 0.14 | 0.63 | 2.90 | 5.87 |
| rates | DiM 2 | 0.02 | 4.37 | 5.04 | 12.73 |
| | DiM 3 | 0.05 | 4.49 | 6.31 | 10.83 |
| – Current DM exchange rates | M 3 | 1.32 | 3.91 | 9.13 | 16.16 |
| Germany, France | M 1 | 0.08 | 3.84 | 4.74 | 7.73 |
| plus Benelux | M 2 | 1.14 | 3.35 | 4.34 | 6.48 |
| – 1985 DM PPP | M 3 | 0.13 | 0.63 | 2.86 | 5.77 |
| | DiM 2 | 0.02 | 4.40 | 5.07 | 12.73 |
| | DiM 3 | 0.05 | 4.53 | 6.38 | 10.86 |
| – Current DM PPP | M 3 | 2.01 | 2.99 | 4.92 | 6.68 |

*Table 8.C.2: Results of specification analysis, long-run relationship*

| Country(ies) | Monetary aggregate | Elasticities | | Semi-elasticities | |
|---|---|---|---|---|---|
| | | price $\alpha_1 = 1$ | income $\alpha_2 = 1$ | restriction | test statistic[b] |
| Germany | DiM 2 | 0.28 | 1.68 | $\alpha_3 = \alpha_4$ | 0.68 |
| | DiM 3 | 0.74 | 1.21 | $\alpha_3 = \alpha_4$ | 0.80 |
| The Netherlands | DiM 2 | 1.10 | 0.75 | $\alpha_3 = \alpha_4$ | 1.58 |
| | DiM 3 | 0.16 | 0.11 | $\alpha_3 = \alpha_4$ | 0.15 |
| Belgium | DiM 2 | 2.29* | 0.99 | – | – |
| | DiM 3 | 1.09 | 0.36 | – | – |
| France | DiM 2 | 3.02* | 1.64 | $\alpha_3 = \alpha_4$ | 0.77 |
| | DiM 3 | 2.97* | 0.97 | $\alpha_3 = \alpha_4$ | 1.76 |
| Germany plus Benelux | M 1 | 0.90 | 2.21* | $\alpha_3 = \alpha_4 = \alpha_5$ | $F(2,75) = 0.85$ |
| | M 2 | 0.62 | 1.74[a] | $\alpha_3 = -\alpha_4 = \alpha_5$ | $F(2,71) = 1.78$ |
| – 1985 DM exchange rates | M 3 | 0.85 | 1.06 | $\alpha_3 = \alpha_5$ | 1.54 |
| | DiM 2 | 1.25 | 0.13 | $\alpha_3 = \alpha_4$ | 1.91 |
| | DiM 3 | 0.21 | 0.98 | $\alpha_3 = \alpha_4$ | 1.18 |
| – Current DM exchange rates | M 3 | 0.64 | 2.51 | – | – |
| Germany plus Benelux | M 1 | 0.93 | 2.16* | $\alpha_3 = \alpha_4 = \alpha_5$ | $F(2,75) = 0.87$ |
| | M 2 | 0.63 | 1.76[a] | $\alpha_3 = -\alpha_4 = \alpha_5$ | $F(2,71) = 1.78$ |
| – 1985 DM PPP | M 3 | 0.85 | 1.07 | $\alpha_3 = \alpha_5$ | 1.56 |
| | DiM 2 | 1.27 | 0.10 | $\alpha_3 = \alpha_4$ | 1.93 |
| | DiM 3 | 0.21 | 0.97 | $\alpha_3 = \alpha_4$ | 1.20 |
| – Current DM PPP | M 3 | 1.22 | 2.35* | – | – |
| Germany, France plus Benelux | M 1 | 0.97 | 1.13 | $\alpha_3 = \alpha_4$ | 0.06 |
| | M 2 | 0.43 | 0.62 | $\alpha_3 = -\alpha_4 = \alpha_5$ | $F(2,74) = 1.54$ |
| – 1985 DM exchange rates | M 3 | 1.23 | 0.03 | $\alpha_3 = -\alpha_4 = \alpha_5$ | $F(2,70) = 1.23$ |
| | DiM 2 | 0.18 | 0.14 | – | – |
| | DiM 3 | 0.96 | 0.44 | $\alpha_3 = \alpha_4$ | 0.72 |
| – Current DM exchange rates | M 3 | 2.18* | 0.51 | $\alpha_4 = -\alpha_5$ | 0.35 |
| Germany, France plus Benelux | M 1 | 0.90 | 1.09 | $\alpha_3 = \alpha_4$ | 0.03 |
| | M 2 | 0.42 | 0.60 | $\alpha_3 = -\alpha_4 = \alpha_5$ | $F(2,74) = 1.53$ |
| – 1985 DM PPP | M 3 | 1.21 | 0.03 | $\alpha_3 = -\alpha_4 = \alpha_5$ | $F(2,70) = 1.24$ |
| | DiM 2 | 0.23 | 0.09 | – | – |
| | DiM 3 | 0.92 | 0.43 | $\alpha_3 = \alpha_4$ | 0.71 |
| – Current DM PPP | M 3 | 0.31 | 2.32* | $\alpha_4 = -\alpha_5$ | 1.03 |

*Notes:*
Long-run relationship for M 1, M 2, M 3: $M = P^{\alpha_1} y^{\alpha_2} \exp(\alpha_3 r_l + \alpha_4 r_s + \alpha_5 \dot{p})$; for DiM 2, DiM 3: $M = p^{\alpha_1} y^{\alpha_2} \exp(\alpha_3 oc + \alpha_4 \dot{p})$.

* Significant at significance level of 0.05.

[a] $t$-test for restriction implying that the price elasticities of M 2 – M 1 and M 3 – M 1 are equal to 1.

[b] Unless stated otherwise, the values of the $t$-test statistic are given.

*Table 8.C.3: Results of cointegration analysis*

| Country(ies) | Monetary aggregate | $t(\pi_1)$ | $t(\pi_2)$ | $t(\pi_3)$ | $t(\pi_4)$ | $F(\pi_3, \pi_4)$ |
|---|---|---|---|---|---|---|
| Germany | DiM 2 | 1.20* | −4.51 | −6.12 | −4.53 | 44.66 |
| | DiM 3 | 2.81 | −4.56 | −6.25 | −4.64 | 47.87 |
| The Netherlands | DiM 2 | −1.86* | −6.04 | −4.24 | −3.90 | 20.93 |
| | DiM 3 | −2.51* | −6.03 | −4.78 | −3.89 | 24.77 |
| Belgium | DiM 2 | −2.83 | −4.14 | −5.28 | −5.01 | 40.75 |
| | DiM 3 | −4.08 | −4.50 | −4.84 | −5.72 | 43.89 |
| France | DiM 2 | −3.94 | −2.05* | −2.64* | −1.83* | 5.03* |
| | DiM 3 | −1.73* | −2.29* | −2.35* | −2.41 | 5.13* |
| Germany plus Benelux | M 1 | −1.57* | −4.14 | −5.75 | −2.29 | 21.33 |
| | M 2 | −2.86 | −4.85 | −5.70 | −6.01 | 60.71 |
| – 1985 DM exchange rates | M 3 | −2.31* | −4.39 | −6.47 | −4.86 | 54.06 |
| | DiM 2 | −1.78* | −4.06 | −5.80 | −5.39 | 51.50 |
| | DiM 3 | −2.50* | −4.15 | −5.60 | −5.63 | 52.41 |
| – Current DM exchange rates | M 3 | −2.45* | −2.56* | −4.59 | −1.29* | 12.02 |
| Germany plus Benelux | M 1 | −1.55* | −4.15 | −5.79 | −2.29 | 21.60 |
| | M 2 | −2.86 | −4.84 | −5.70 | −6.03 | 60.92 |
| – 1985 DM PPP | M 3 | −2.31* | −4.40 | −6.49 | −4.86 | 54.34 |
| | DiM 2 | −1.79* | −4.06 | −5.81 | −5.38 | 51.58 |
| | DiM 3 | −2.50* | −4.15 | −5.61 | −5.63 | 52.39 |
| – Current DM PPP | M 3 | −3.02 | −2.75 | −3.15 | −2.20 | 8.64 |
| Germany, France plus Benelux | M 1 | −2.91 | −3.98 | −3.40 | −2.50 | 9.36 |
| | M 2 | −3.89 | −5.27 | −4.63 | −6.23 | 47.36 |
| – 1985 DM exchange rates | M 3 | −2.19* | −5.73 | −1.54* | −4.25 | 10.51 |
| | DiM 2 | −3.56 | −4.85 | −5.95 | −5.45 | 54.39 |
| | DiM 3 | −3.53 | −4.35* | −5.69* | −5.67 | 54.25 |
| – Current DM exchange rates | M 3 | −3.37 | −5.53 | −6.85 | −4.41 | 54.02 |
| Germany, France plus Benelux | M 1 | −2.90 | −3.99 | −3.40 | −2.47 | 9.27 |
| | M 2 | −3.88 | −5.27 | −4.62 | −6.24 | 47.42 |
| – 1985 DM PPP | M 3 | −2.21* | −5.72 | −1.55* | −4.25 | 10.55 |
| | DiM 2 | −3.57 | −4.87 | −5.95 | −5.44 | 54.30 |
| | DiM 3 | −3.55 | −4.35 | −5.71* | −5.66 | 54.35 |
| – Current DM PPP | M 3 | −3.22 | −4.82 | −7.00 | −4.26 | 53.59 |

*Note:* * Not significant at significance level of 0.10, in $t(\pi_1)$-column indicates absence of cointegration.

PART TWO

# Monetary Disaggregation: Asset Demand, Bank Credit, Notes and Coins

*Whatever its proper role in monetary economics, the composition of the currency is a matter of great practical concern to central banks. By and large, central banks see their function in the currency realm as one of supplying the public demand.*

Manski and Goldin (1987, p. 99)

*De aanbodrelatie kan het best gezien worden als een prijsfixatierelatie voor kort krediet: door hun rentetarieven regelen de banken de omvang van hun kredietverlening.*

Tinbergen (1942, p. 135)

*L'affermarsi della moneta bancaria, la relazione stretta, anche se non rigida, che lega il credito e la massa monetaria all' andamento dell' attività economica e dei prezzi fanno rientrare a pieno titolo l' attività delle banche nell' ambito della politica monetaria.*

Fazio (1995)

# 9. The Demand for Financial Assets: Time Series Evidence for The Netherlands: 1963:II–1975:IV

## 9.1 Introduction

The choice of an appropriate definition of money is important for controlling the economy through monetary management, which requires the velocity of circulation to be a stable function of known determinants. In the early fifties, this led De Nederlandsche Bank to adopt a broadly defined money concept. In addition to currency and demand deposits this broad definition includes time deposits with banks, short-term claims on the government and local authorities, and foreign currency deposits with residents, insofar as these are held by others than money-creating institutions. Savings deposits are usually not included in The Netherlands definition of money. It is interesting to note that these liquid assets are easily convertible into money and that they have in common price certainty, i.e., the absence of possible gains or losses in terms of money. This does not mean, of course, that asset-holding does not respond to variations in the yields. The estimation of those elasticities has been the objective of a considerable number of studies employing both time series and cross-section data. Most of these studies, which were recently surveyed by Feige (1974) and Feige and Pearce (1977), focus on a single equation. Others prefer a systems approach and attempt to estimate a set of demand equations in order to find elasticities of substitution among various liquid assets.[1] In spite of the vast amount of research, Feige and Pearce remark in their 1977 survey that the substitutability question is likely to remain an important issue, pointing out a need for further time series investigations of a system of demand functions for liquid assets.

---

Reprinted from *European Economic Review*, **12**(4) (October 1979), M.M.G. Fase, 'The demand for financial assets: The time series evidence for The Netherlands: 1963:II–1975:IV', 381–394, ©1979 with kind permission from Elsevier Science-NL, Sara Burgherhartstraat 25, 1055 KV Amsterdam, The Netherlands.

[1] See Feige (1964), Feige and Swamy (1974), Gramlich and Kalchbrenner (1970).

The present study attempts to meet this demand by providing additional time series evidence for The Netherlands.[2]

The remainder of this chapter is laid out as follows. Section 9.2 presents some theoretical considerations underlying the empirical analysis. Section 9.3 discusses the statistical specification and the data. The estimation results and their interpretation are presented in Section 9.4. In Section 9.5 some conclusions are drawn.

## 9.2 The Demand for Liquid Assets

At least three approaches are possible for a theoretical basis of the demand for liquid assets. Of these the Baumol–Tobin inventory approach seems the least appropriate in the present case as it is restricted to transaction balances. The other two approaches, which are usually associated with Chicago and Yale, respectively, consider the whole spectrum of financial (and real) assets. The Chicago approach considers the demand for liquid assets as an application of the theory of consumer behaviour for durables whose non-pecuniary services enter the utility function (see e.g. Friedman (1959)). This flow of non-pecuniary services is assumed to vary proportionally to the real stock of liquid assets and the demand for the flow of services is therefore approximated by the demand for the real stock of liquid assets. The rates of return on these assets and real income become the appropriate arguments of the resulting demand functions.

The Yale approach views the demand for financial (liquid) assets as the selection of an optimal portfolio and emphasizes the logical constraints on the balance sheet explicitly (see Brainard and Tobin (1968), and Tobin (1969)). Like the Chicago approach, the portfolio approach is basically a microeconomic approach. It assumes that individual households choose their portfolio composition in order to maximize expected utility derived from the portfolio subject to a wealth constraint, given the expected rates of return and their variance–covariance matrix.[3] As a result, a set of demand equations is obtained with the demand for a particular asset dependent on the own and competing rates of return and the size of the portfolio considered.[4]

---

[2] As exemplified by Fase and Kuné (1974a) this evidence for The Netherlands is still scarce. For earlier and recent results of other countries see Barrett, Gray, and Parkin (1975), Christ (1963), Gramlich and Hullett (1972), Gramlich and Kalchbrenner (1970), Helliwell *et al.* (1971), Hendershott (1971), Kopcke (1977), Modigliani (1972), Saito (1977), and Sparks (1974).

[3] See e.g. Parkin (1970), Parkin, Gray, and Barrett (1970), Gramlich and Hullett (1972), and Barrett, Gray, and Parkin (1975).

[4] It can easily be shown that the mathematical form of asset demand equations

The above comments imply that both the portfolio theory and the Chicago approach help to postulate a set of demand equations, but do not offer really competing hypotheses. It is for this reason that we adopt an eclectic view in this chapter.

It may be argued that real rather than nominal rates of return are relevant, particularly because inflationary expectations may distort the allocation of liquid assets. To avoid the intricacies of generating four time series of real rates of return, we include price expectations as a separate independent variable. As a matter of fact this seems to be in line with the Chicago emphasis on durables as an alternative to financial assets. However, in comparison with the demand for consumer goods, the preference for financial assets may be more volatile, particularly over the trade cycle. In other words, we assume the income velocity of particular assets to vary with the cyclical state of the economy. We therefore include a cyclical variable in the demand equations to account for cyclical shifts.

Monetary economists differ on the precise justification of income in demand functions for liquid assets. Following Friedman, many theorists view income as a budget restraint variable. Others, adhering to the transactions approach, regard income as a proxy for outlays, requiring a certain flow of services generated by liquid asset-holdings. This view contrasts with the Yale approach, which regards income mainly as the rate of return on human and non-human capital. Empirically it is difficult to be dogmatic on this issue; but the Yale interpretation immediately raises the question of the precise role of our business cycle indicator as an explanatory variable.

Thus, taking a logarithmic linear form of the demand function, the typical equation for the $i$th asset would be

$$\begin{aligned} m_{it}^* = {} & \alpha_{i0} + \alpha_{i1} y_t + \alpha_{iP} r_{Pt} + \alpha_{iT} r_{Tt} + \alpha_{iO} r_{Ot} + \alpha_{iS} r_{St} + \alpha_{i2} \dot{p}_t \\ & + \alpha_{i3} c_t + \alpha_{i4} \dot{m}_t, \end{aligned} \tag{9.1}$$

with $m_{it}^*$ the desired or optimal stock in real terms of the $i$th liquid asset in quarter $t$ with $i = P$, $T$, $O$, $S$, indicating money, time deposits, near-moneys and savings deposits, respectively, $y_t$ current income in real terms, the $r_i$ the nominal rate of return on the $i$th asset, $\dot{p}_t$ a measure of inflationary expectations, $c_t$ a cyclical indicator and $\dot{m}_t$ a measure of total financial wealth. A justification for our selection of assets is given below.

Equation (9.1), like any other specification of the demand for liquid

varies considerably with the specific assumptions made on the utility function and the probability distribution on the rates of return. See Gray and Parkin (1973), and Blomgren-Hansen (1974).

assets, is based on a number of considerations. An important characteristic is our choice of the logarithmic linear form. This means that the $\alpha$'s in equation (9.1) are equilibrium elasticities. Of even more importance is the fact that this specification may be justified by the empirical study of Butter and Kuné (1976) on the functional form of the demand for money in The Netherlands. Using a Box–Cox power transformation they demonstrate that the logarithmic functional form is more appropriate than the linear form.

The use of liquid assets at constant prices assumes a price elasticity of one for the desired stock of liquid assets. This is a common assumption in the literature, which is for The Netherlands supported by empirical evidence from earlier investigations (see Fase and Kuné (1974a)).

Another characteristic is that the income variable refers to current income rather than to permanent income as is often the case in the literature. The literature nearly always employs cross-section data of individual households. The use of permanent rather than current income may be desirable even in an analysis employing time series data, if one believes the reaction to income changes to be more drawn-out than the response to changes in yields. Because little is known about the perception lag of income, we use the simple approach and include current income. Of course, this does not answer the question of which income measure is most appropriate (see Selden (1975)).

In our model no long-term rate of interest is included in the demand functions. The rationale for this is that we see the portfolio choice as a two-level decision. At the lower level a global distribution of wealth among liquid and other assets is accomplished with the long-term rate of interest as a key variable. At the second stage the broad category of liquid assets is allocated according to the rates of return on the various competing liquid assets. A representative rate of interest for the other assets is of particular importance in explaining the first stage. Our specification means that it is assumed that the separability theorem holds and that in the second stage the long-term rate of interest is irrelevant as a decision variable. This is in accordance with the literature, which nearly always limits itself to short-term interest rates as explanatory variables (see e.g. Feige (1964) or Parkin (1970)).

## 9.3 Statistical Specification and Data

Unlike, e.g. Parkin (1970) we want to incorporate adjustment lags into the demand functions to account for lagged responses to changes in the explanatory variables. As Brainard and Tobin have pointed out, the conventional stock adjustment model for each $m_i^*$ does not work out all that well. In order to keep the analysis simple we therefore postulate a common speed of adjustment $\beta_7$ and view the percentage change in total assets, $\dot{m}$, also as a variable to account for the temporary allocation to $m_{it}$ of an increase in total assets while the stock adjusts itself (see Helliwell *et al.* (1971)). When seasonal dummies and stochastic disturbances $u_i$ are included we obtain for the $i$th asset

$$\begin{aligned} m_{it} = {} & \beta_{i0}y_t + \beta_{i1}r_{Pt} + \beta_{i2}r_{Tt} + \beta_{i3}r_{Ot} + \beta_{i4}r_{St} + \beta_{i5}\dot{p}_t \\ & + \beta_{i6}c_t + \beta_7 m_{it-1} + \beta_{i8}\dot{m}_t + \beta_{i9}d_{1t} + \beta_{i10}d_{2t} \\ & + \beta_{i11}d_{3t} + \beta_{i12} + u_{it}. \end{aligned} \tag{9.2}$$

In view of our consumer theoretical approach, but also by analogy and plausibility, we simply postulate symmetry among interest rate responses across the system by constraining the short-run cross-elasticities.[5] Because of the common speed of adjustment, this symmetry also holds for the long-run elasticities. Incorporation of the symmetry condition into demand equations for liquid assets is not widely accepted among monetary econometricians. In fact, Brainard and Tobin do not even mention these restrictions in their pitfalls article. More common among econometric model builders is the Brainard–Tobin constraint that the coefficients of all variables except income or wealth must add up to 0 across equations. Since the set of liquid assets considered in this study constitutes only a subset of financial wealth, restrictions do not appear warranted. Moreover, the fact that our system is cast in a logarithmic-linear form makes it very difficult to impose these theoretical constraints in a straightforward way, thus exemplifying Brainard and Tobin's own words that 'the burden on empirical testing and estimation is very heavy'. Moreover, in applied work it is no good worrying about what cannot be helped. As a result we have deliberately decided not to impose the balance sheet constraint in carrying out the estimation.

Estimates were obtained by applying a modified version of the Aitken–Zellner operational generalized least-squares procedure under restrictions (see Zellner (1962)). Bearing the symmetry and equality restrictions in mind, we have estimated our system of four equations using quarterly data over the period 1963–1975.

Our choice of assets is dictated by monetary practice in The Netherlands, which defines money broadly as the sum total of currency outside banks and checking accounts with banks and giro institutions, time deposits and various near-moneys (notably Treasury bills, claims on local

[5] A theoretical justification for this is attempted by Bierwag and Grove (1968), Epps (1975) and Fischer (1972). An application is given in Gramlich and Kalchbrenner (1970) and Hendershott (1971).

authorities, foreign currency deposits and liquid savings) held by the public. In our disaggregation we follow this definition but have added savings deposits with money-creating institutions as we want to assess their moneyness. Because no reliable data on overdraft facilities are available we have ignored this item in spite of the fact that potentially they should be in the same class of liquid assets as money and time deposits.[6] The actual distribution over the four liquid assets considered here is given in Table 9.1.

The liquid assets $m_i$ are GNP price deflated quarterly averages. These assets are not available by ownership. This means that our analysis is necessarily based on the assumption that the pattern of reactions of households is the same as that of corporations. This is a heroic assumption as, for example, Price (1972) discovered in his analysis for the UK.

Income $y$ is measured in terms of the GNP of the relevant quarter at 1970 prices. In view of the openness of The Netherlands economy one may argue that GNP should be adjusted for international transactions by excluding exports and including imports. However, since the results are hardly affected by this measurement of GNP, we have ignored it.

The rates of interest used are quarterly averages. The rate of return on money ($r_P$) is a weighted average of the interest paid on ordinary credit deposits with banks, on credit balances of interest-bearing checking accounts with banks, and on credit balances at giro institutions. The choice of weights enables us to take into account the fact that the notes and coins included in $m_P$ do not bear any positive rate of return. The rate of return on time deposits, $r_T$, is approximated by the rate of interest on three-month loans to local authorities. The rate of return on other near-moneys, $r_O$, is a weighted average of the rates on three-month loans to local authorities, on ordinary deposits and on savings accounts with banks. The rate of return on savings deposits, $r_S$, is measured by the interest rate paid on ordinary savings deposits with commercial banks.

In view of an earlier study (see Fase and Nieuwkerk (1975)) $\dot{p}_t$ is measured as the actual rate of inflation lagged one quarter, derived from GNP prices.

We began by measuring the cyclical indicator $c$ as the quarterly average of the male labour reserve as a percentage of the total male labour force. However, later on in Section 9.4 we will consider several alternatives for this variable.

---

6 It is interesting to note that in the twenties Holtrop advocated the inclusion of overdraft facilities in the definition of money (see Holtrop (1928, p. 150)).

*Table 9.1: Distribution of liquid assets (end of 1975)*

| Asset $m_i$ | Millions of guilders | % |
|---|---|---|
| Currency and demand deposits ($m_P$) | 46 930 | 44 |
| Time deposits ($m_T$) | 18 764 | 17 |
| Other near-moneys ($m_O$) | 6 691 | 6 |
| Savings deposits at money-creating institutions ($m_S$) | 35 308 | 33 |
| | 107 693 | 100 |

## 9.4 Estimation Results

The estimation results for the system of demand equations (9.2) under the symmetry and equality constraints were, on the whole, not very satisfactory.

An interesting question is whether the estimation results would improve if more restrictions were added. In the conventional linear allocation model for a given volume of assets the coefficients of all the explanatory variables, except income, wealth and the lagged dependent variable, must add to 0 across equations. Since our model is linear in logarithms rather than in the variables itself – which means that the model is multiplicative in all variables, including the seasonal factors – the appropriate restrictions cannot be imposed on the estimated coefficients. Moreover, since the assets considered here do not necessarily add to total financial wealth, it is questionable whether the balance sheet constraint must be imposed. Therefore we have considered several alternatives, which we will discuss now.

One set of alternatives extends the present model by including all dependent variables lagged one quarter as additional explanatory variables (which is possible because the balance sheet constraint does not hold). The results, which for the sake of brevity are not reported here, do not improve substantially: out of 58 independently estimated coefficients 17, i.e. about 30%, are insignificant, while the implied elasticities do not seem very plausible. For instance, the calculated long-run income elasticities vary between 2.0 and 4.6. This may be due to the employed adjustment scheme in which all dependent variables are included as explanatory variables.

In the next alternative we have simplified equation (9.2) by omitting $\dot{p}$ – which was often insignificant – and $\dot{m}$ because we deliberately ignore the balance sheet constraint. Moreover, we include only the own dependent variable as a lagged variable, allowing the speed of adjustment to differ across equations. The estimation results for the simplified model (9.2) under the symmetry constraint are set out in Table 9.2 with $t$-values in parentheses. The residual variance SSE indicates the goodness of fit.

The regression coefficients of income invariably take the expected sign but are significant in one case only. At times insignificance also occurs in the interest rate coefficients. The real demand for currency and demand deposits shows a low and insignificant own interest rate elasticity, while the cross-elasticities appear to be significant with respect to $r_T$ and $r_S$. The negative sign of the coefficient of the rate of return on time deposits means that time deposits are a substitute for money. The positive cross-elasticities for the other rates of interest indicate weak complementarity between money, other near-moneys and savings deposits.

The own rate of interest of the demand for time deposits has the expected positive sign. The interest rate coefficients of other near-moneys and of savings deposits are insignificant. The signs do, however, indicate substitutability and complementarity, respectively.

The interest rate coefficient of the demand for other near-moneys is often insignificant. The signs would indicate that there is a weak complementarity relationship with money and a substitution relationship with the two other liquid assets.

The own interest elasticity of the real demand for savings deposits is insignificant, but does have the expected sign. The signs of the coefficients of $r_P$ and $r_T$ indicate complementarity, while we found a weak substitutability with other near-moneys.

The cyclical indicator is significant with respect to time and savings deposits. This is an interesting result which seems to support the view that in a recession hoarding is mainly discernible in these deposits.

The significance of the seasonal dummies varies considerably across equations, being totally absent in the savings equation. Although this is difficult to understand, it may be explained by the fact that the flow of savings consitutes only a minor part of the stock so that the seasonal pattern in the flows is hardly apparent in the stocks.

Apart from real money balances the actual real stock of liquid assets responds fairly slowly to changes in its determinants. Indeed, at most 20% of the adjustment is completed within the current quarter. This contrasts sharply with the behaviour of real money balances where 50% of the discrepancy between actual and desired stocks is absorbed within one quarter.

As mentioned above we have imposed the symmetry constraint upon

*Table 9.2: Restricted Aitken–Zellner estimates, 1963:II–1975:IV*

| Type of asset | $y_t$ | $r_P$ | $r_T$ | $r_O$ | $r_S$ | $c$ | $m_{i-1}$ | $d_1$ | $d_2$ | $d_3$ | Con-stant | SSE×$10^3$ (millions of guilders) |
|---|---|---|---|---|---|---|---|---|---|---|---|---|
| $m_P$ | 0.371 | 0.011* | −0.064 | 0.005* | 0.033 | −0.003* | 0.510 | 0.009 | 0.022 | 0.016 | −0.679 | 0.04 |
| | (6.75) | (1.57) | (4.92) | (0.23) | (3.67) | (0.50) | (10.00) | (3.00) | (11.00) | (8.00) | (5.96) | |
| $m_T$ | 0.085* | −0.064 | 0.171 | −0.024* | 0.019* | 0.063 | 0.829 | 0.026 | −0.001* | 0.015 | −0.276* | 0.80 |
| | (1.05) | | (4.28) | (0.36) | (0.66) | (2.52) | (25.91) | (2.60) | (0.10) | (1.67) | (0.73) | |
| $m_O$ | 0.104* | 0.005* | −0.024* | 0.147* | −0.108 | 0.002* | 0.797 | 0.012* | 0.018 | 0.030 | −0.216* | 0.40 |
| | (1.25) | | | (1.20) | (1.89) | (0.11) | (11.23) | (1.50) | (2.57) | (4.29) | (0.62) | |
| $m_S$ | 0.014* | 0.033 | 0.019* | −0.108 | 0.066* | 0.011 | 0.955 | −0.003* | −0.003* | 0.003* | 0.046* | 0.05 |
| | (0.20) | | | | (1.53) | (1.83) | (22.21) | (0.75) | (1.00) | (1.00) | (0.18) | |

*Note:* * Insignificant at the 5 % level.

the short-run elasticities across equations. Consequently this constraint applies only to the signs of the long-run interest elasticities, while their magnitude is entirely determined by the speed of adjustment. The latter introduces an inaccuracy of the long-run elasticities shown in Table 9.3.

Since we have imposed symmetry mainly by analogy, we have tested the symmetry hypothesis against the unrestricted model.[7] The resulting $F$-statistic of 1.9 is well below the 95% level of 2.4 with 6 and 160 degrees of freedom, thus rejecting the alternative hypothesis of asymmetric interest rate behaviour. In not rejecting the hypothesis on symmetrical impact interest rate elasticities on the basis of this statistic, we should be aware of the dangers of applying the test as pointed out by Klevmarken (1975).

In view of the large number of insignificant estimates no firm conclusions have yet been achieved. Nevertheless, the results displayed in Tables 9.2 and 9.3 can be summarized as follows:

- The income elasticities for each asset are positive and less than one.
- The own interest rate elasticities have the expected sign and are, with the exception of $m_P$, fairly large.
- Narrow money and time deposits show a significant but weak substitution relationship, while a complementarity relationship exists with respect to other near-moneys and savings deposits.
- Time deposits and savings deposits display a weak but insignificant complementarity, whereas time deposits and other near-moneys show a weak and insignificant substitutability.
- Other near-moneys and savings deposits display a weak but significant substitution relationship.
- The impact of the level of economic activity is most notably present in the time deposit equation but also in the savings equation. This may suggest that hoarding mainly occurs in these assets.

In the present study the choice of the cyclical indicator as explanatory variable is of particular importance. The inclusion of this variable bears on the traditional concern in monetary theory for the variability of the velocity of circulation over the trade cycle.[8] However, quantification of this idea introduces some ambiguity, as a wide variety of variables is available to describe this cyclical behaviour.

The use of the male labour reserve as an indicator may be criticized because of the fact that in recent years the structural component of

---

7 See Zellner (1962) for the appropriate test statistic.

8 See Kessler (1958) and Fase and Kuné (1974a).

*Table 9.3: Long-run income and interest elasticities*

| Type of asset | $y$ | $r_P$ | $r_T$ | $r_O$ | $r_S$ |
|---|---|---|---|---|---|
| $m_P$ | 0.757 | 0.022 | −0.131 | 0.010 | 0.067 |
| $m_T$ | 0.497 | −0.374 | 1.000 | −0.140 | 0.111 |
| $m_O$ | 0.512 | 0.025 | −0.118 | 0.724 | −0.532 |
| $m_S$ | 0.311 | 0.733 | 0.422 | −2.400 | 1.467 |

unemployment has increased. This criticism merely reflects the fact that our theoretical concept of the business cycle is not quite as sharp empirically as we would like. To meet this objection one may attempt to construct a synthetic cyclical indicator by carrying out a principal components analysis on a whole spectrum of economic series, presumably showing cyclical behaviour. As this attempt failed we subsequently considered five single alternative measures, viz.: percentage change in industrial fixed investment, $i_t$, percentage of the active population, $\nu_t$, amount of registered temporary short-time working, $mgu_t$, labour reserve plus welfare recipients according to the 'Incapacity for Work Benefit Act' as a percentage of the active population, $u'_t$, and capacity utilization indicator, $q_{l_t}$.

We will now discuss our findings, which for the sake of brevity are not reported here. The results for $i_t$ as a cyclical indicator, indicate that, with the exception of time deposits, the estimated cyclical coefficients do not differ significantly from 0. The time deposits show a positive correlation with the business cycle and seem to support our hypothesis that the demand increases during a recession. However, the question may be raised, in particular for the recent past, whether, for The Netherlands, investments provide a suitable cyclical indicator.

The indicator $\nu_t$ has the advantage of reflecting businesspeople's views on the actual economic situation and, therefore, seems most appropriate to measure the cyclical variation. The estimation results do not support our hypothesis on the cyclical influence. The results show an insignificant cyclical coefficient for the money equation, and a significant positive influence for the savings deposits' equation. These outcomes seem plausible, but the negative signs of the significant estimates for the two other equations are difficult to interpret. An explanation may be the fact that at the microeconomic level stocks are substitutes for money. In that case, however, the indicator $\nu_t$ fails to reflect the shifts in liquidity preference that we are attempting to quantify.

Application of the alternatives $mgu_t$, and $u'_t$ as cyclical indicators do not yield better estimates. In both cases the estimates appear to be insignificant across equations at the 5% level. In view of these results it is tempting to reject our hypothesis, but the question still remains whether the failure to substantiate our hypothesis empirically is not merely the result of the inadequacy of the data. In that case the underlying theory is not refuted.

Returning to our first approach with $c_t$, we have considered a variant of $c_t$, $q_{l_t}$, which may remedy the major criticism against $c_t$, because it attempts to take into account shifts in the level of structural unemployment more properly. The results, not reported here, show that in both the time deposit and in the savings deposit equation the estimated coefficients of $q_l$ are significant and take the expected sign. In the other two equations these estimates are insignificant. The remaining estimates appear to be fairly insensitive to replacement of $c_t$ by $q_l$. The major difference is the reversal of the sign of the coefficient of $y$ in the savings equation.

Concluding this section we note that in the course of the analysis we have considered several other specifications and, for some variables, different measurements. In addition to the cyclical indicators we experimented with gross national expenditure as the income variable, because that is the concept we used in earlier studies.[9] The results reported here, appeared to be quite consistent with our main findings and did not lead to different conclusions. Another approach attempted was to ignore the dynamics by leaving out the lagged dependent variable as an explanatory variable. Again we found most of the estimates to be in line with the above results.

## 9.5 CONCLUSION

The main conclusion to be drawn from our results is that estimates of the demand for liquid assets equations indicate surprisingly inelastic cross- and own interest-rate elasticities.

For time deposits and other near-moneys the own interest rate elasticities are in the range of 0.7 to 1.0 but for currency and demand deposits the elasticity is almost 0. The own elasticity for savings deposits with money-creating institutions seems to be implausibly high.

[9] The relationship between GNP and gross national expenditure at constant prices is as follows. GNP at constant prices = gross national expenditure at constant prices + balance on current account on transaction basis at constant prices − balance of income transfers at constant prices − term of trade gains.

The estimated cross-elasticities of savings and time deposits indicate complementarity. This is presumably due to the fact that there are two categories of holders for these deposits. It seems advisable therefore to apply the same method of monetary analysis to the savings deposits held with money-creating institutions as to the time deposits. It is noteworthy that time and savings deposits with money-creating institutions and other near-moneys show clear substitutability.

As to the cyclical indicator, it is particularly interesting to see how the cyclical influence varies across the asset equations. The sensitivity of time deposits to the trade cycle indicates that the velocity of these assets varies with the trade cycle. The fact that money and other near-moneys do not respond to cyclical movements might indicate that these assets primarily serve transaction purposes. The weaker responsiveness of savings deposits to the cyclical variable supports the idea that savings are a particular form of wealth.

Some of our estimates differ widely from the estimates given in Feige's (1974) survey of cross-section studies. Both Feige and Feige and Swamy (1974) suggest that the estimation results are somewhat sensitive to the statistical model used. They show that the elasticities obtained with the Aitken–Zellner model are often higher than those obtained with the random components model. However, it is reassuring to find that in our study a weighted average of the estimated income elasticities corresponds closely to the income elasticity of 0.85 estimated in our earlier work on the aggregated demand for money in The Netherlands.

# 10. The Demand for Commercial Bank Loans and the Lending Rate

## 10.1 Introduction

While economic literature contains much empirical research on the demand for money, there are surprisingly few studies on the demand for bank credit. Given the prominence of bank credit control in the conduct of monetary policy in the recent decade or so, plus the fact that, at least intuitively, bank credit is of great practical importance for economic activity, this neglect is remarkable, perhaps deserving the attention of historians of economic thought. Whereas there has been a strong focus on money the lack of attention to bank credit becomes even more intriguing in view of the fact that one of the first econometric analyses of bank credit was published in the early 1930s by Tinbergen (1934, 1937), a considerable time before Brown (1938, 1939) published his empirical work on the demand for money, which was a novelty at the time.

This emphasis on the demand for money is consistent with a common treatment of money, which views bank credit merely as the mirror image of money. However, it is quite easy, particularly for open economies, to illustrate by means of historical statistics on the sources of money growth that the view that the demand for money merely reflects the demand for bank credit is not necessarily true. For example, in the period 1970–1990 The Netherlands' domestic money supply of M2 increased by over 200 billion guilders or 500%. Of this increase two-thirds or 150 billion guilders was accounted for by money creation by banks and one-third by net inflows of funds from abroad, the contribution of the public sector being negligible. In The Netherlands, short-term bank credit is the main source of money creation, accounting for 50% of the total increase in

Reprinted from *European Economic Review*, **39**(1) (January 1995), M.M.G. Fase, 'The demand for commercial bank loans and the lending rate', 99–115, ©1995 with kind permission from Elsevier Science-NL, Sara Burgherhartstraat 25, 1055 KV Amsterdam, The Netherlands.

the money supply in the period 1970–1990. In addition, this mirror view on bank credit may be refuted by theoretical arguments as given in, for instance, Brunner (1971), Brunner and Meltzer (1966, 1968), as recalled recently in Laidler (1991). Monetarists, who are well aware of this approach, know that the issuing quotient, *i.e.* the amount of money issued per dollar of bank credit as well as the definition of money, are the key parameters. The issuing ratio is a constant only if changes in reserve requirements, the discount rate or market interest rates affect money and earning asset multipliers to the same extent. Monetarists, however, contend that this condition is rather restrictive and unlikely to occur in practice. An alternative to the money view is the credit view which emphasizes the importance of bank credit rather than money for economic activity. This credit view is less prominent in the literature although it goes back to Schumpeter (1912) and Hawtrey (1928) and has recently been put forward by *e.g.* Friedman (1981, 1983). As a matter of fact the credit view seems to gain prominence slowly. The present difficulties in a number of small European countries closely linked to the Deutsche Mark to control money supply has, perhaps, renewed interest in bank credit as an intermediate monetary target. A shift in emphasis from money to credit requires more accurate empirical knowledge of the determinants of the demand for bank credit.

The main purpose of this chapter is to estimate a two-equation structural model of the market for short-term bank credit in The Netherlands, taking into account the fact that the lending rate is observed as a zone rather than as a unique and directly measurable market price. Therefore, emphasis is also on statistical methodology rather than on monetary theory alone. Section 10.2 presents the general background to our model. In Section 10.3 we specify our loan demand and lending rate equation. The statistical implications of considering the lending rate as an unobservable independent and dependent variable are examined in Section 10.4. Section 10.5 discusses the estimation results obtained with quarterly observations for the sample period 1970:I–1990:IV. Section 10.6 examines in detail some of the statistical properties implicitly assumed in our analysis. Section 10.7 provides some concluding comments on the possible implications for monetary policy.

## 10.2 Theoretical Background

Reviewing the literature on the demand for bank loans two major hypotheses have come to the fore which, according to Mélitz (1975), may be labelled neo-Keynesian and neo-Fisherine. A third approach amerges from research on portfolio behaviour of banks.

The neo-Keynesian approach which, in one form or another, provides the basic premise of the work of e.g. Anderson (1964), Goldfeld (1966) and Jaffee (1971), considers the *firm* and thus the corporate balance sheet as the main framework for specifying business loan demand. In this view short-term commercial bank loans and long-term liabilities, including equity and long-term debt, serve to finance the asset side of the firms's balance sheet. Thus, each individual item of the asset side should to a certain proportion be financed by long-term liabilities and by short-term commercial bank loans. Because of the slow adjustment to equilibrium, short-term loans have the additional function of bridging the temporary gap between the desired and the actual financial structure of the firm.

A general implication of this reasoning is that the demand for bank loans is dependent on the assets composition of the balance sheet of the firm. The most relevant assets are inventory stock, real capital stock, and liquid assets (for which sales are frequently used as a proxy). Finally the relative cost of short-term bank loan and long-term liability financing plays a crucial role.

The Fisherine approach, which Mélitz and Pardue (1973) and Mélitz (1975) apply in their own work, assumes a process of utility maximization to generate the functional specification of the demand for bank credit. In contrast to the neo-Keynesian approach, the Fisherine approach considers the *household* rather than the firm as the basic unit of decision. Therefore this approach would not seem to be appropriate to explain corporate lending which constitutes the major part of the demand for bank credit, unless it is possible to translate, as Pardue and Mélitz do, the utility framework into the framework of production behaviour and corporate management.

The portfolio approach, followed by *e.g.* Parkin (1970), Parkin, Gray, and Barrett (1970), Hester and Pierce (1975) and Wood (1975), focuses on the behaviour of the *banking firm* rather the private sector as the decision unit. Starting from a utility function maximized under a set of balance sheet constraints, a set of estimable commercial bank asset supply functions is derived. In spite of its theoretical elegancy, the major difficulty with this approach is that it ignores the fact that individual banks do not operate in a fully competitive world with given prices while asset choice behaviour results from the interaction of banks and the whole private sector, *i.e.* households and firms.

This study focuses on short-term bank lending to the private sector, *i.e.* households and firms, recognizing the often neglected fact that little is known about the interest charged to the individual demander for bank credit. Studies of the bank credit market very often consider the sum total of loans to the private sector and government security portfolio of the banking system (see *e.g.* Brunner and Meltzer (1968), Zwick (1971), and Korteweg and Loo (1977)). This aggregation over sectors is perhaps inappropriate when one may expect different loan behaviour for the household, business, and public sectors. On the other hand, disaggregated time series for bank credit are usually not available. In the Dutch case the availability of data allows disaggregation and thus exploitation of the theories suggested by various authors mentioned above to specify estimable equations for the whole private sector.

## 10.3 A Model for the Commercial Loan Market

### 10.3.1 Demand for Short-term Bank Loans

The demand for short-term bank credit by the private sector of the economy, *i.e.* the household and the business sector, is the result of a variety of economic factors leading to the decision to borrow. On the one hand, the decision is made on the basis of expected cash flows. On the other, it is the outcome of deliberate economic calculations by those who have access to other sources of external finance than short-term bank credit alone.

We assume that the stock of outstanding bank credit, $CL$, is determined mainly by the demand side of the market. This means that banks follow the short-term loan demand of the private sector and that the lending rate, $r_B^*$, – the * indicates that this variable is unobservable – serves to adjust this demand to the banks' desired portfolio of short-term loans to the private sector. Therefore, we postulate the following equilibrium loan demand equation:

$$CL/P = \alpha SA^{\gamma_0} \exp(\gamma_1 r_B^* + \gamma_2 r_L) \tag{10.1}$$

with $CL/P$ being the equilibrium or optimal real stock of outstanding short-term debt of the private sector to commercial banks; $SA$ the volume of expected sales, $P$ the price level, $r_L$ the yield on long-term government bonds. It is assumed *a priori* that the optimal or long-run demand for bank credit is homogeneous of the first degree with respect to the price level.

The basic motivation of equation (10.1) is that expected sales determine the optimal balance sheet composition of the private sector, which in turn generates the desired or optimal amount of bank credit. Therefore we expect a positive sign for $\gamma_0$. Apart from cash, short-term bank credit may be viewed as the most flexible counterpart to cushion the inventory stock, although long-term debt and equity are alternatives. This means that bank credit may have to compete with these other financial sources. Accordingly we include $r_L$ as an explanatory variable. To circumvent collinearity it would be virtually impossible to include other relevant competing rates. Therefore $r_L$ should also be viewed as an index of the yield on alternative domestic or foreign earning assets. This assumption is supported empirically by *e.g.* a multivariate and a principal component analysis of interest rates and yields (see Fase (1973)). We anticipate a negative relationship between loans and its own rate, *i.e.* $\gamma_1 < 0$, and a positive relationship with the competing bond yield, *i.e.* $\gamma_2 > 0$.

It is likely that the adjustment of outstanding bank loans to the optimal stock does not take place immediately. Therefore we assume for the amount of outstanding loans in real terms a dynamic adjustment pattern with an error-correction formulation leading to equilibrium equation (10.1). This means that the variables in the long-run equilibrium loan demand equation are assumed to be cointegrated, which is a hypothesis to be tested later on in the chapter. Preliminary statistical analysis of the sort from general to specific suggests that the following equation should be considered in the empirical analysis:

$$\begin{aligned}\Delta_4 \ln(CL/P) = {} & \alpha_0 + \alpha_1(\ln(CL/P)_{-4} - \alpha_2 \ln SA_{-4}) + \alpha_3\Delta_4 \ln SA \\ & + \alpha_4 r_B^* + \alpha_5 r_L + \alpha_6 \Delta_4 \ln q_n + \alpha_7 \Delta_4 \ln(CL/P)_{-1} \\ & + \alpha_8 \Delta_4 \ln SA_{-4} + u_1 \qquad (10.2)\end{aligned}$$

with $\gamma_1 = -\alpha_4/\alpha_1$, $\gamma_2 = -\alpha_5/\alpha_1$ while $q_n$ equals the ratio of the volume of inventories $N_t$ to sales $SA_t$. Thus, $q_n = N/SA$ represents a buffer stock mechanism in the balance sheet composition of the private sector. In (10.2) the error-correction term equals $\ln(CL/P)_{-4} - \alpha_2 \ln SA_{-4}$, which differs from the conventional form because we do not impose *a priori* a long-run sales or income elasticity of one. The above specification means instantaneous adjustment of nominal loans to price shocks which, of course, is not necessarily true. However, as this is not the main focus of this chapter, we have, for the sake of simplicity, not tested this by *e.g.* considering $\Delta_4 \ln P_{-4}$ as an additional explanatory variable in the error-correcting term of equation (10.2). Equation (10.2) is our basic specification of the demand for loans' equation and is assumed to incorporate approximately the most important elements of the three theoretical approaches summarized in Section 10.2.

### 10.3.2 Determinants of the Loan Rate

Specification of the lending rate equation is necessary to complete our model of the market for short-term bank loans. According to economic theory, the behaviour of market participants is governed by the objective function in their mind, possible activities, and the economic and institutional environment. This is also true of the commerical banks' financial behaviour. Banks operate under oligopolistic market conditions. This means that banks do not move along the demand curve, but set a loan rate – or rather a loan rate zone – at which loans are provided to all customers meeting additional requirements, like collateral security, maturity, and repayment. Apart from credit rationing, we therefore consider the loan rate as the banks' major decision variable, generated by the rate-setting function for loans.

More specifically we assume, following Dutch banking practice, that the banks' loan rate $r_B^*$ is related to the discount rate $r_D$ and the yield obtainable on alternative earning assets $r_E$. In view of the fact that the openness of the Dutch economy is also reflected in the banking system's portfolio, the yield $r_E$ has to capture both foreign and domestic competing earning assets. It is measured as the Euro guilder rate. Inclusion of the discount rate $r_D$ in the lending rate equation is justified by the fact that it is the penalty rate at which the banking system has access to additional resources of reserves available either at the discount window of the central bank or in the call money market. This means that in case of money market shortage – and this is the common situation in The Netherlands – the central bank controls the money market rate and does not necessarily adjust its discount rate to the actual money market rate. Usually money market rates are tied to the bank's discount rate at which commercial banks can borrow. Occasionally however, when *e.g.* the guilder is too strong within the EMS, the bank will keep the discount rate low to prevent the guilder from appreciating and restrict access to its lending facilities. Money market rates will consequently rise spontaneously, reducing the commercial banks' spread, who will apply a flexible surcharge to avoid unprofitable lending. To account for this, two different money market regimes should be distinguished and accordingly two alternative loan rate equations should be considered. To model these different circumstances, a dummy variable, *dumrkk*, is introduced to describe the two money market regimes. Thus a general estimable loan rate specification is obtained taking into account additional explanatory variables switching, as a matter of fact, with the money market regime. These additional variables are, to begin with, the flexible surcharge $r_k - r_D$, $r_k$ being the money market rate. Commercial banks in The

Netherlands apply this surcharge as soon as the central bank's discount rate policy does not respond to domestic money market developments for exchange rate considerations. In these periods the discount rate $r_D$ is lower than the money market rate $r_k$. This situation defines the two regimes considered here and is covered by *dumrkk*, being equal to 1 for periods with $r_k > r_D$ and to 0 otherwise. In view of this and common practice in our macroeconomic modelling (see *e.g.* Fase, Kramer, and Boeschoten (1992)), we postulate the following loan rate-setting equation for short-term bank loans:

$$\begin{aligned} r_B^* = {} & r_D + \beta_0 + \beta_1 dumrkk(r_B - r_D)_{-1} + \beta_2 dumrkk(r_k - r_D) \\ & + \beta_3 dumrkk(D/BT) + \beta_4 dum73 + \beta_5 r_E + u_2. \end{aligned} \tag{10.3}$$

As before, * indicates that the variable is unobservable. The variable $D/BT$ is the proportion of short-term deposits of the domestic sector in the banking system's total liabilities. It is assumed that a limit is set, *ceteris paribus*, to the bank's lending potential so that banks will charge a higher rate on loans when this potential dries up. For additional discussion reference is made to Jaffee (1971), Monti (1972), Goodhart (1989), Hester and Pierce (1975), and Wood (1975). *dum*73 is a dummy equal to 1 in 1973:III and 1973:IV used to account for a money market perturbation at the time. Apart from the term $dumrkk(r_B - r_D)_{-1}$ our loan rate-setting equation ignores inertia. This seems to be justified by the banking practice, suggesting that rates adjust almost instantaneously within the observation period. Moreover, this assumption enables us to keep the analysis manageable in view of the statistical implications to be discussed in the following.

## 10.4 Structural and Regression Model

The model set out in the preceding section, containing a demand equation and a lending rate-setting equation, reads as

$$\begin{aligned} \Delta_4 \ln(CL/P) = {} & \alpha_0 + \alpha_1(\ln(CL/P)_{-4} - \alpha_2 \ln SA_{-4}) + \alpha_3 \Delta_4 \ln SA \\ & + \alpha_4 r_B^* + \alpha_5 r_L + \alpha_6 \Delta_4 \ln q_n + \alpha_7 \Delta_4 \ln(CL/P)_{-1} \\ & + \alpha_8 \Delta_4 \ln SA_{-4} + u_1, \end{aligned} \tag{10.4}$$

$$\begin{aligned} r_B^* = {} & r_D + \beta_0 + \beta_1 dumrkk(r_B - r_D)_{-1} \\ & + \beta_2 dumrkk(r_k - r_D) + \beta_3 dumrkk(D/BT) \\ & + \beta_4 dum73 + \beta_5 r_E + u_2, \end{aligned} \tag{10.5}$$

where $u_1$ and $u_2$ are stochastic error terms. However, as noted before, $r_B^*$ is unobservable. An unobservable variable is a variable that is measured with error, which may be due to several causes. It arises, in our case, because observed loan rates take a range of values whereas its theoretical counterpart is commonly understood to be a well-defined value. Our exercise may be viewed as an application of errors-in-variables in a simultaneity framework, for which Goldberger (1972, 1974), Zellner (1970), and Aigner and Goldberger (1977) developed efficient estimation procedures. Consistent with these theoretical studies we assume that the lending rate $r_B$ lies in a zone which can be expressed as

$$r_B = r_B^* + u_3. \tag{10.6}$$

Equations (10.4)–(10.6) can be viewed as a structural model with two causal relations, where $CL/P$ and $r_B$ are observable dependent variables, $r_B^*$ is an unobservable variable, and the $\alpha$ and $\beta$ are the structural parameters. Further, it is assumed that the structural disturbances $u_1$, $u_2$ and $u_3$ have 0 means, are serially uncorrelated and mutually independent, *i.e.* the contemporaneous variance–covariance matrix is assumed to be diagonal.

The reduced form of this model is obtained by solving (10.4)–(10.6) for $\ln(CL/P)$ and $r_B$ in terms of the predetermined variables. This yields

$$\begin{aligned}\Delta_4 \ln(CL/P) = {} & \alpha_0 + \alpha_4\beta_0 + \alpha_1(\ln(CL/P)_{-4} - \alpha_2 \ln SA_{-4}) \\ & +\alpha_3\Delta_4 \ln SA + \alpha_4 r_D + \alpha_4\beta_1 dumrkk(r_B - r_D)_{-1} \\ & +\alpha_4\beta_2 dumrkk(r_k - r_D) + \alpha_4\beta_3 dumrkk(D/BT) \\ & +\alpha_4\beta_4 dum73 + \alpha_4\beta_5 r_E + \alpha_5 r_L + \alpha_6\Delta_4 \ln q_n \\ & +\alpha_7\Delta_4 \ln(CL/P)_{-1} + \alpha_8\Delta_4 lnSA_{-4} + u_1 \\ & +\alpha_4 u_2 \qquad (10.7a) \\ r_B = {} & r_D + \beta_0 + \beta_1 dumrkk(r_B - r_D)_{-1} \\ & +\beta_2 dumrkk(r_k - r_D) + \beta_3 dumrkk(D/BT) \\ & +\beta_4 dum73 + \beta_5 r_E + u_2 + u_3. \qquad (10.7b)\end{aligned}$$

It is convenient to reparameterize the reduced form (10.7a) and (10.7b) as follows:

$$\begin{aligned}\Delta_4 \ln(CL/P) = {} & \pi_{01} + \pi_{11}(\ln(CL/P)_{-4} + \pi_{21} \ln SA_{-4}) \\ & + \pi_{31}\Delta_4 \ln SA + \pi_{41} r_D + \pi_{51} dumrkk(r_B - r_D)_{-1} \\ & + \pi_{61} dumrkk(r_k - r_D) + \pi_{71} dumrkk(D/BT) \\ & + \pi_{81} dum73 + \pi_{91} r_E + \pi_{101} r_L + \pi_{111}\Delta_4 \ln q_n \\ & + \pi_{121}\Delta_4 \ln(CL/P)_{-1} + \pi_{131}\Delta_4 lnSA_{-4} + \epsilon_1 \qquad (10.8a)\end{aligned}$$

$$
\begin{aligned}
r_B = r_D &+ \pi_{02} + \pi_{12} dumrkk(r_B - r_D)_{-1} \\
&+ \pi_{22} dumrkk(r_k - r_D) + \pi_{32} dumrkk(D/BT) \\
&+ \pi_{42} dum73 + \pi_{52} r_E + \epsilon_2, \qquad (10.8b)
\end{aligned}
$$

where the $\pi$'s summarize the corresponding parameters of (10.7a) and (10.7b) while the reduced-form disturbances are denoted by: $\epsilon_1 = u_1 + \alpha_4 u_2$ and $\epsilon_2 = u_2 + u_3$. The $\epsilon$'s have the disturbance $u_2$ in common and therefore, they may be not independent of each other. This pair of equations, like the reduced-form of a conventional simultaneous set of equations, constitutes a multivariate linear regression model. The 20 regression coefficients $\pi$ can be expressed in terms of exactly 15 structural parameters $\alpha$ and $\beta$. This means that five constraints are imposed on the regression coefficients, namely:

$$
\pi_{41} = \frac{\pi_{51}}{\pi_{12}} = \frac{\pi_{61}}{\pi_{22}} = \frac{\pi_{71}}{\pi_{32}} = \frac{\pi_{81}}{\pi_{42}} = \frac{\pi_{91}}{\pi_{52}}, \qquad (10.9)
$$

which are in fact nonlinear constraints, with $\pi_{41} = \alpha_4$.

Equations (10.8a) and (10.8b) can be estimated by applying a version of Zellner's (1962) operationally generalized least-squares procedure, viewing the system (10.8a) and (10.8b) as a stacked regression equation:

$$
\vec{y} = X\vec{\pi} + \vec{\epsilon}
$$

subject to the nonlinear constraint (10.9) where $\vec{\epsilon} = (\epsilon_1, \epsilon_2)'$.

We assume the contemporaneous variance–covariance matrix to take the form

$$
E(\epsilon\epsilon') = \begin{pmatrix} E\epsilon_1\epsilon_1 & E\epsilon_1\epsilon_2 \\ E\epsilon_2\epsilon_1 & E\epsilon_2\epsilon_2 \end{pmatrix} = \begin{pmatrix} \omega_{11} & \omega_{12} \\ \omega_{21} & \omega_{22} \end{pmatrix} \otimes I_T = \Omega \otimes I_T,
$$

which, however, is unknown in our case.

In the empirical analysis of the next section we follow the Asymptotic Least-Squares two-stage estimation procedure, suggested by Gouriéroux, Montfort, and Trognon (1985). In the first stage the two-equation system is estimated without the cross-equation restrictions. In the second stage estimates of the parameters of interest – which are asymptotically equivalent to the maximum-likelihood estimates – are obtained by employing the unrestricted estimates of the first stage and the relationships between the unrestricted parameters and the parameters of interest. For details reference is made to Gouriéroux, Montfort, and Trognon (1985) and Kodde, Palm, and Pfann (1990).

## 10.5 Data and Estimation Results

The system (10.8a) and (10.8b) is estimated with quarterly observations over a sample period containing the 84 quarters 1970:I to 1990:IV. To preserve the variability in the data as much as possible we employed seasonally unadjusted figures. Therefore we applied the $\Delta_4$-filter for a number of variables.

Analogous to common usage in the analysis of the demand for liquid assets we have defined the demand for bank loans in terms of stocks. $CL/P$ is the real stock of outstanding short-term loans granted to the private sector by banks. Confining ourselves to the private sector of the economy means that we want to distinguish between short-term loans, short-term credit to the government and the foreign sector. This and the fact that large-scale granting of long-term loans to the private sector has not been common practice in the Dutch banking industry is the main reason we focus on short-term banking loans.

Although sales by industries are available, we have approximated the volume of sales by enterprises and the income of the household sector, by the gross value added, derived from the quarterly accounts of national resources and expenditures. The main motivation for this is that we believe this to be the most appropriate measure for the whole private sector studied here, which, moreover, can be more easily deflated than sales alone.

As to the price level $P_t$ we took the price deflator of sales by enterprises. The quantity $D/BT$ measures the share of short-term deposit liabilities in total liabilities of the banking system. The interest rates $r_E$, $r_k$ and $r_L$ refer to net yields on three-month Euro-guilder deposits, the money market rate and yields on recent long-term government bonds. The variable $r_D$ measures the discount rate set by De Nederlandsche Bank. As pointed out before, this is the rate at which the banks have recourse to the bank to acquire additional liquidity. This explains why the loan rate, $r_B$, *i.e.* the interest rate charged by banks for short-term advances, is closely related to the discount rate. Usually $r_B$ equals $r_D$ plus an additional interest charge of 1.25 to 2.5 percentage points, which is prompted by Dutch central banking tradition. However, as The Netherlands' discount rate policy since 1979 also aims at stabilizing the exchange rate rather than just at following the money market, discrepancies between money market rates *vis-à-vis* the Deutsche Mark and the official discount rate repeatedly induced the banks to impose an additional surcharge in periods when the call rate $r_k$ exceeds the discount rate.

Constrained ordinary least-squares estimation of (10.8a) and (10.8b) yielded the results shown in the first line of Table 10.1, with $t$-values in parentheses. The ordinary least-squares residuals were deployed to obtain the sample variances and covariances of the residuals. Thus the contemporaneous sample estimate $\hat{\Omega}$ becomes:

$$10^{-2} \times \begin{pmatrix} 0.104 & 0.034 \\ 0.034 & 4.118 \end{pmatrix}.$$

In order to achieve greater efficiency we have applied Zellner's operational generalized least-squares procedure to estimate the system. This has yielded the result shown in the second line of Table 10.1. It should be noted that these generalized least-squares estimates do not differ substantially from the ordinary least-squares estimates. The coefficients in the two equations take the *a priori* expected sign and are significant, with three exceptions, *viz.* $\alpha_6$, $\alpha_8$ and $\beta_5$. Because of the highly insignificant estimate of $\beta_5$ the restriction $\beta_5 = 0$ is imposed, which means that the foreign sector is excluded from the interest rate equation. The estimation results – given in the third and fourth line of Table 10.1 – show that this restriction leads to only slightly different estimates of the remaining parameters. The exception is $\alpha_5$, which becomes insignificant and now has the wrong sign. Since the estimate of $\alpha_5$ in the unrestricted model was significant, we do not impose the restriction $\alpha_5 = 0$, but $\alpha_4 = -\alpha_5$. This constraint is the same as taking the interest differential $r_L - r_B^*$ as explanatory variable in the demand equation. Estimates for this specification are given in the last two lines of Table 10.1, and show that all the estimates have an economically plausible sign and are significantly different from 0.

It is evident that this modification has improved the estimation results. As to the loan rate equation, the results indicate that the prime rate, represented by the central bank's discount rate $r_D$, is a significant determinant of the unobservable loan rate $r_B^*$ and is therefore an important variable to explain demand, in principle. Our results also indicate that $\beta_2$ is significantly smaller than unity. This result implies that discount rate changes are not immediately fully passed on to the loan rates in case a surcharge is applied by the banking system. This seems to be a very plausible result, considering Dutch practice. The estimate of the coefficient of $r_E$ is insignificant: it contrasts with the fact that the discount rate in the open Dutch economy is set in view of the development of foreign interest rates, which, as shown in Fase (1976), used to be closely related to $r_E$.

With respect to the demand for credit equation, the parameters of the steady state relationship are the most important. The long-run elasticities obtained for the various equations are summarized in Table 10.2.

*Table 10.1: Estimation results*[a]

| Estimation method | Restriction | Parameter $\alpha_0$ | $\alpha_1$ | $\alpha_2$ | $\alpha_3$ | $\alpha_4$ | $\alpha_5$ | $\alpha_6$ | $\alpha_7$ | $\alpha_8$ | $\beta_0$ | $\beta_1$ | $\beta_2$ | $\beta_3$ | $\beta_4$ | $\beta_5$ |
|---|---|---|---|---|---|---|---|---|---|---|---|---|---|---|---|---|
| OLS | – | −2.190 | −0.123 | 2.447 | 0.322 | −0.014 | 0.010 | 0.200 | 0.791 | −0.193 | 2.403 | 0.457 | 0.529 | −1.901 | −1.041 | 0.004 |
| | | (2.96) | (2.85) | (8.94) | (2.09) | (4.43) | (2.56) | (1.74) | (10.68) | (1.34) | (30.50) | (8.97) | (12.12) | (6.86) | (6.06) | (0.31) |
| SUR | – | −2.169 | −0.120 | 2.470 | 0.335 | −0.014 | 0.010 | 0.196 | 0.783 | −0.182 | 2.409 | 0.457 | 0.527 | −1.901 | −1.045 | 0.003 |
| | | (3.25) | (3.08) | (9.79) | (2.41) | (4.98) | (2.81) | (1.89) | (11.72) | (1.40) | (31.80) | (9.35) | (12.59) | (7.15) | (6.34) | (0.26) |
| OLS | $\beta_5 = 0$ | −1.923 | −0.130 | 2.256 | 0.295 | −0.002 | −0.001 | 0.217 | 0.708 | −0.281 | 2.424 | 0.463 | 0.538 | −1.921 | −1.035 | – |
| | | (2.62) | (2.99) | (7.83) | (1.94) | (4.63) | (0.21) | (1.90) | (9.54) | (1.96) | (75.12) | (9.64) | (14.85) | (7.11) | (6.06) | |
| SUR | $\beta_5 = 0$ | −1.912 | −0.127 | 2.284 | 0.312 | −0.002 | −0.000 | 0.212 | 0.703 | −0.265 | 2.424 | 0.463 | 0.538 | −1.920 | −1.036 | – |
| | | (2.86) | (3.20) | (8.45) | (2.25) | (6.01) | (0.12) | (2.05) | (10.42) | (2.03) | (77.60) | (9.96) | (15.34) | (7.34) | (6.27) | |
| OLS | $\beta_5 = 0$ | −1.935 | −0.128 | 2.226 | 0.317 | −0.002 | 0.002 | 0.185 | 0.728 | −0.249 | 2.424 | 0.463 | 0.538 | −1.921 | −1.036 | – |
| | $\alpha_4 = -\alpha_5$ | (2.64) | (2.97) | (7.69) | (2.10) | (5.40) | (5.40) | (1.82) | (10.22) | (1.86) | (75.12) | (9.64) | (14.85) | (7.11) | (6.06) | |
| SUR | $\beta_5 = 0$ | −1.966 | −0.126 | 2.317 | 0.344 | −0.003 | 0.003 | 0.188 | 0.723 | −0.237 | 2.424 | 0.463 | 0.538 | −1.920 | −1.038 | – |
| | $\alpha_4 = -\alpha_5$ | (2.93) | (3.18) | (8.32) | (2.49) | (5.42) | (5.42) | (2.02) | (11.07) | (1.93) | (77.64) | (0.97) | (15.34) | (7.35) | (6.28) | |

*Note:* [a] Estimation period 1970:I–1990:IV; $t$-values are given in parentheses.

The long-run sales or 'income' elasticity is remarkably constant and varies between 2.25 and 2.50. The elasticities of short-term demand for credit with respect to the interest rate variables implied by the restricted models have a size of $-0.15$ to $-0.20$. Perhaps this result is surprising, but nevertheless convincing in view of the estimates obtained in empirical literature and discussed briefly below. This literature includes Fourcans' (1975) estimate of $-0.15$ for France, Heremans, Sommariva, and Verheirstraeten's (1976) estimate of $-0.16$ for Belgium, or Korteweg and Loo's (1977) estimate of $-0.12$ for The Netherlands. Notwithstanding the differences in methodology and sample period, the present study shows similar estimates. As to this main result, it is rather difficult to assess whether they fall within the range of earlier results because most other studies fail to report elasticities (*cf.* Caligiuri, Fazio, and Padoa-Schioppa (1974), Korteweg (1973a), Goldfeld (1966), Krainer (1969), Mélitz (1975)).

For the equation of dynamic demand for credit the estimates are all significantly different from 0. Most interesting is the significant influence of the error-correction term and the explanatory variable $\Delta_4 \ln q_n$. This result indicates that discrepancies between actual and expected sales, which are reflected in changes in $q_n$, are important in describing the demand for short-term credit.

## 10.6 Statistical Evaluation

With respect to the statistical evaluation of the estimation results, two issues have been examined. The first is whether the residuals are a white noise process. Second, and perhaps more importantly, a cointegration analysis has been carried out to assess the assumption of the long-run relationship for the demand for short-term credit implied by the estimation results.

To test the hypothesis that the residuals are white noise, the Ljung–Box statistic has been calculated, based on the first $p$ autocorrelations of the residuals, with $p = 1, 4, 8, 12$. Under the null hypothesis, the statistics are $\chi^2(p)$ distributed. The results, summarized in Table 10.3, show that in all cases residual correlation is absent in the interest equation. The hypothesis that the residuals in the loan equation are white noise must be rejected for the general model, in which no restrictions are imposed on the parameters. Imposing the restrictions $\beta_5 = 0$ and $\alpha_4 = -\alpha_5$ improves the statistical outcome. For these restricted models, the test statistics yield insignificant values. Hence, the specification finally chosen meets the requirement that the residuals are not autocorrelated.

*Table 10.2: Long-run elasticities of demand for short-term credit*[a]

| Estimation method | Restriction | Sales or 'income' elasticity | Short-term loan rate | | Long-term loan rate | |
|---|---|---|---|---|---|---|
| | | | semi-elasticity | elasticity | semi-elasticity | elasticity |
| OLS | – | 2.447 | −0.115 | −1.099 | 0.078 | 0.637 |
| SUR | – | 2.470 | −0.116 | −1.112 | 0.079 | 0.647 |
| OLS | $\beta_5 = 0$ | 2.256 | −0.015 | −0.140 | −0.006 | −0.050 |
| SUR | $\beta_5 = 0$ | 2.284 | −0.017 | −0.159 | −0.003 | −0.026 |
| OLS | $\beta_5 = 0$, $\alpha_4 = -\alpha_5$ | 2.266 | −0.019 | −0.179 | 0.019 | 0.153 |
| SUR | $\beta_5 = 0$, $\alpha_4 = -\alpha_5$ | 2.317 | −0.020 | −0.191 | 0.020 | 0.163 |

*Note:* [a] Interest rate elasticities are calculated as the product of the semi-elasticities and the sample mean of the corresponding interest rate.

*Table 10.3: Results of Ljung–Box test on residual autocorrelation*

| Estimation method | Restriction | Number of residual autocorrelations | | | | | | | |
|---|---|---|---|---|---|---|---|---|---|
| | | credit equation | | | | interest rate equation | | | |
| | | no. of autocorrelations | | | | no. of autocorrelations | | | |
| | | 1 | 4 | 8 | 12 | 1 | 4 | 8 | 12 |
| OLS | – | 6.88* | 10.53* | 15.69* | 18.50* | 0.82 | 1.90 | 4.51 | 13.63 |
| SUR | – | 6.78* | 10.32* | 15.57* | 18.47* | 0.87 | 1.92 | 4.50 | 13.55 |
| OLS | $\beta_5 = 0$ | 1.39 | 6.41 | 11.00 | 13.26 | 0.68 | 1.83 | 4.69 | 13.70 |
| SUR | $\beta_5 = 0$ | 1.51 | 6.45 | 10.99 | 13.26 | 0.69 | 1.83 | 4.68 | 13.69 |
| OLS | $\beta_5 = 0$, $\alpha_4 = -\alpha_5$ | 1.22 | 6.42 | 11.14 | 13.64 | 0.68 | 1.83 | 4.69 | 13.70 |
| SUR | $\beta_5 = 0$, $\alpha_4 = -\alpha_5$ | 1.26 | 6.38 | 11.10 | 13.62 | 0.70 | 1.83 | 4.67 | 13.67 |

*Note:* * Significant at significance level of 0.05.

The long-run relationship for the demand for short-term credit has been examined by means of (co)integration tools. For this purpose, the long-run equilibrium loan demand equation has been tested for cointegration. Several testing procedures have been proposed in the literature. Engle and Granger (1987) have demonstrated that a test for cointegration involves estimation of a cointegration regression for the $I(1)$ variables, conducting a unit root test for the regression residual. The results of this unit root analysis of the individual residual variables using the Dickey–Fuller $t$-statistic, are set out in Table 10.4. The statistics show that the volume of short-term loans and of 'sales' as well as the two rates of interest are integrated of order 1. The interest rate differential is, however, stationary. Estimation of the cointegration regression yields

$$\ln(CL/P) = -10.84 + 1.89 \ln SA + e$$

and the ADF-test on the residuals $e$ yields the value $-1.71$. Hence, cointegration has to be rejected.

An alternative is to examine the long-run relationship implied by the dynamic model specified in the former section. However, because the data used are not seasonally adjusted, the testing procedure of Hylleberg, Engle, Granger, and Yoo (1990) is more appropriate and has been applied. The equation

$$\Delta_4 x_t = \delta_1 y_{1t-1} + \delta_2 y_{2t-1} + \delta_3 y_{3t-2} + \delta_4 y_{3t-1} + \epsilon_t \qquad (10.10)$$

with $x_t$ being the deviations from the equilibrium path defined by equation (10.1), $y_{1t} = (1 + L + L^2 + L^3)x_t$, $y_{2t} = -(1 - L)(1 + L^2)x_t$ and $y_{3t} = -(1 - L)(1 + L)x_t$ and $\epsilon_t$ a disturbance term, has been estimated. Lags of $\Delta_4 x_t$ have been added to eliminate possible autocorrelation of the residuals. The restriction $\delta_1 = 0$ corresponds with a unit root equal to 1. The restriction $\delta_2 = 0$ implies that there is a unit root $-1$. If $\delta_3$ and $\delta_4$ both equal 0, the unit roots $L = \pm i$ occur. Since these roots are each other's complex conjugates, both $\delta_3$ and $\delta_4$ must be equal to 0. These restrictions can be tested with the $t$-values of $\delta_i, i = 1, \ldots, 4$ and the $F$-test for the hypothesis $\delta_3 = \delta_4 = 0$. These statistics, however, do not have the standard distributions. By means of simulation experiments, Hylleberg *et al.* (1990) derive the critical values of the test statistics.

To test for cointegration, equation (10.10) has been estimated with seasonal dummies, a constant and the first four lags of $\Delta_4 x_t$ included as additional explanatory variables. Subsequently, the most insignificant of the lags of $\Delta_4 x_t$ is successively removed from the equation. The results of the $t$- and $F$-tests mentioned above for the equation finally obtained, are summarized in Table 10.5. These results show that cointegration has to be rejected again. In all cases there is evidence that the unit root $L = 1$

*Table 10.4: Results of unit root tests*[a]

| Variable | $\tau_t$ |
|---|---|
| $\ln(CL/P)$ | $-1.34$ |
| $\ln(SA)$ | $-2.37$ |
| $r_B$ | $-3.28$ |
| $r_L$ | $-2.81$ |
| $r_B - r_L$ | $-3.53^*$ |

*Notes:*
[a] $\tau_t$ is the $t$-ratio of $\rho$ in the estimated equation $\Delta x_t = \rho x_{t-1} + \text{constant} + \text{trend} + \text{lags of } \Delta x_t$.
* Significant at a significance level of 0.05, corresponding to a critical value of $-3.41$.

is present. Seasonal unit roots, however, are absent. The important question is whether these findings mean that the equilibrium relation does not exist and that the error-correction model is inappropriate in our case. Banerjee, Dolado, Hendry, and Smith (1986) have shown that the small sample results for the above tests are a rather weak base for rejecting cointegration in every case. Another way of looking at our results is to recognize that the estimates in Table 10.1 indicate significant estimates for the ECM. Kremers, Ericsson, and Dolado (1992) show that the $t$-ratio of the estimate of the coefficient of the error-correction term can be used to test for cointegration. This ECM-statistic has, under particular assumptions, a standardized normal distribution. However, if these assumptions are violated, the DF-critical values can be used. Comparing the $t$-ratios for $\hat{\alpha}_1$ in Table 10.1 with the DF-critical value for $\tau_\mu$ $(-2.86)$ yields supportive evidence for the cointegration hypothesis, namely that the existence of the equilibrium relation is warranted.

## 10.7 Implications for Monetary Policy

In this chapter we have argued two related points. The first is that the aggregate loan rate charged by commercial banks at a certain point in time is a range rather than a point and that this fact requires to be taken into account in the econometric modelling of the demand for bank credit. The second is that the interest rate elasticity of credit demand is significant. Thus we have obtained a fairly conclusive quantitative result which seems to confirm the intuitive feeling and the *a priori* assumption

*Table 10.5: Results of cointegration analysis*

| Estimation method | Restriction | $t(\delta_1)$ | $t(\delta_2)$ | $t(\delta_3)$ | $t(\delta_4)$ | $F(\delta_3, \delta_4)$ |
|---|---|---|---|---|---|---|
| OLS | – | −2.097 | −5.244* | −3.508* | −5.952* | 32.120* |
| SUR | – | −2.092 | −5.240* | −3.515* | −5.946* | 32.125* |
| OLS | $\beta_5 = 0$ | −0.854 | −4.893* | −5.284* | −4.206* | 31.151* |
| SUR | $\beta_5 = 0$ | −0.827 | −4.885* | −5.247* | −4.218* | 30.919* |
| OLS | $\beta_5 = 0,\ \alpha_4 = -\alpha_5$ | −0.712 | −5.009* | −5.103* | −3.795* | 26.397* |
| SUR | $\beta_5 = 0,\ \alpha_4 = -\alpha_5$ | −0.638 | −4.989* | −5.098* | −3.791* | 26.309* |

*Note:* * Significant at a significance level of 0.05.

with regard to the importance of the rate of interest for bank credit prevailing in the banking community. A more general implication of our finding for monetary policy is perhaps that it supports the present shift in many countries from monetary targeting to credit targeting with the loan rate as an effective tool of credit control. This question of *money* versus *credit* is an important and interesting issue which modern literature addresses occasionally (see *e.g.* Friedman (1983), Bernanke and Blinder (1988)). The question whether money or credit matters for economic activity is beyond the scope of this chapter. However, irrespective of the answer to this important question, it is clear that knowledge of the interest rate elasticity of credit demand is of strategic importance. That was the main focus of the chapter.

# 11. The Way we Pay with Money

## 11.1 Introduction

Apart from Mandell's (1972) interesting study on credit card use in the United States and the recent study by Avery, Elliehausen, Kernickell, and Spindt (1986) on the use of cash and transaction accounts by American families, surprisingly little is known about the way expenditure is paid for. This is the more remarkable since making payments is an everyday phenomenon that concerns almost everyone. Knowledge of the use of the various means of payment can provide insight into velocity of money, as well as the way it is affected by shifts in the money supply. Moreover, for the currency-issuing authorities it is important to know to what extent they succeed in meeting the need for currency efficiently.

The paucity of information on these issues is perhaps due to difficulties of measurement. For instance, statistics on debits are distorted by financial transactions, with tremendously high transaction velocities (Garvy and Blyn 1969). For cash payments, only rough indirect estimates are available, either on the basis of cash withdrawals on the assumption of a certain cash loop (Cramer (1986), Fisher (1909)) or on the basis of figures on the circulation of bank-notes and their life length (Boeschoten and Fase (1987), Laurent (1970)). At least part of the missing empirical knowledge on the use of means of payment can be obtained from budget surveys containing questions on purchases and the way they are paid for. This chapter reports on such a survey for The Netherlands, 1984–1986. The Dutch case serves as the statistical example, but the methodology of the study is of much greater general value.

The organization of the chapter is as follows. Section 11.2 discusses the samples used to obtain the data of the present analysis. Section 11.3 investigates the association between household expenditure and the manner of payment. Section 11.4 estimates the probability distribution

Reprinted with kind permission from *Journal of Business and Economic Statistics*, **7** (July 1989), M.M.G. Fase and W.C. Boeschoten, 'The way we pay with money', 319–326, of payments by households which appears to be stable over the years studied here. Section 11.5 applies the obtained empirical distributions to the currency and note distribution. Section 11.6 draws some conclusions from our analysis.

## 11.2 The Basic Observations

The data of the present analysis are taken from a series of sample surveys among households in The Netherlands conducted by AGB-Intomart, an Anglo-Dutch market-research firm, during 1984–1986. This sample survey is a continuous inquiry on family income, as well as on consumer purchases, modes of payment, and other financial transactions by households. The main object is to determine the pattern of expenditure and payment by households, as well as their attitude towards different financial instruments. The conception of this panel research owes much to a similar sample survey in England by AGB-Research held during five years. The series of surveys was preceded by a pilot study conducted in 1982.

The observations are obtained from a panel of 1 000 households, covering about 2 400 persons of 12 years of age and older. The information was collected monthly by asking each household in the sample to complete diaries and detailed questionnaires and by interviews. The survey covers individuals living in private households in The Netherlands who are additionally interviewed once a year.

The sample covers, on average, 1 000 households in each survey, and the sampling is designed to obtain representative samples that are homogenous over time. As a result, differences in the composition of the panel between months are negligible. Each household in the sample reports all payments for transactions in excess of 10 guilders (*f* 10). In addition, a small number of the sampled households was asked to record payments below *f* 10 as well. The size of this subset declined, however, from 122 in 1984 to 100 in 1985 to 62 in 1986. This small and declining number may influence the assessment of the overall pattern of payments, particularly because over 40% of payments is less than *f* 10 per transaction. Therefore, the results were adjusted for fluctuations in the sample by means of weighting to maintain the sample representative.

There are several ways to assess the quality of the survey results. We took the route of comparing particular sample results with similar information obtained from other independent sources. First, we compared the sample estimates for consumer expenditure with the official figures recorded by the Dutch Bureau of Statistics (CBS). Table 11.1 shows the results for total consumer expenditure and consumption per household, with the CBS figures based on the nominal accounts and the national budget survey, respectively.

The results for total consumer expenditure indicate a considerably lower figure for the AGB sample over the years, mainly as a consequence of different consumption concepts. The differences between the two samples for the average consumption per household, however, are fairly small and are mainly due to variations in the definition in the samples.

In The Netherlands, the use of credit cards is not widespread but guaranteed cheques made available by the banking system under different names are an important means of payment. A guaranteed cheque is one written by the client and guaranteed by his bank, depending on the type, up to *f* 300. Therefore, these guaranteed cheques operate as a substitute for notes.

For competitive reasons, the banking system provides three different types of cheques, known as bankcheques, Eurocheques, and postal cheques, guaranteed up to *f* 100, *f* 300, and *f* 200, respectively. The only difference, besides the amount up to which they are guaranteed, is that the bankcheques are only for domestic use, while the other two are also accepted abroad.

Table 11.2 sets out the distribution of guaranteed-cheques' payments in both amounts and numbers over the different types according to the reporting of the banking system and the sample considered here. The figures make clear that the sample results closely match the distribution within the population, suggesting again that the sample is representative. On the basis of these assessments, we conclude that the sample design warrants further statistical analysis of the sample outcomes.

## 11.3 Expenditure and Manner of Payment

On the basis of the sample survey, the number of payments in, for example, 1986 may be estimated at nearly 3.8 billion, corresponding to an average of two payments per household per day. At first sight, this would seem to be a strikingly low figure, even if allowance is made for some downward distortion resulting from the presumed under-reporting of payments below *f* 10. Leaving aside the major difference in the years of observation, this number represents a surprising result relative to comparable figures for countries like the US and the UK. For these countries, the number was estimated at about three payments per person per day for the early 1970s (Evans and Hailey (1974), Little (1975)). Part of the discrepancy is perhaps due to under-reporting of the smaller cash

*Table 11.1: Assessment of the sample according to consumer expenditure*

| | Total consumer expenditure (billions of guilders) | | | Average consumption per household (guilders) | | |
|---|---|---|---|---|---|---|
| | 1984 | 1985 | 1986 | 1984 | 1985 | 1986 |
| AGB sample | 194.5 | 202.6 | 206.5 | 37 833 | 38 546 | 38 440 |
| CBS sample | 236.8 | 247.7 | 256.3 | 36 694 | 35 596 | – |

payments.

As to the average amount of payment, the results in Table 11.3 show that in The Netherlands cash, guaranteed cheques, and transfers are by far the most important means of payment. The share in total payments of, for instance, the credit card and the postal money order is negligible and declining. As is evident from Table 11.3, the payment pattern is very stable over the years and in line with the earlier findings by Fase and Boeschoten (1985). Cash payments account for nearly 40% in terms of amount and for nearly 80% in terms of the number of payments. This finding is in fair agreement with those for other countries and also with the rule of thumb, often used in practice, that cash payments account for about 20% in terms of amount and for 80% in terms of number. Schimmelmann (1985) estimated the share of cash payments in Germany at 86% in terms of number. Percentages of 87 and 95, respectively, have been reported for the US and the UK for the early 1970s by Little (1975) and Evans and Hailey (1974), while, according to the survey results reported by Avery, Elliehausen, Kernickell, and Spindt (1986), in terms of amount American families pay 36% of their expenditure in cash. These percentages relate solely to payments by households and, therefore, do not include business payments. Including business payments, which average higher amounts and are relatively more often made by transfers, the share of cash payments, notably in terms of amount, will probably be substantially lower.

During the observation period, the increase in the amount of cash payments was one percentage point less than the expansion of the amount of currency in circulation. On the assumption that business cash payments showed a similar development, the transaction velocity of currency thus declined slightly between 1984 and 1986. Even allowing for the fact that business transactions have been left out of consideration, the resulting transaction velocity of 2.8 is a strikingly low figure, which contrasts sharply with the estimations of Laurent (1970) and Feige (1979) for the US, amounting to 25 and higher.

*Table 11.2: Assessment of the sample according to modes of payment*

| | Shares in total amount of cheque payments (%) | | | Share in total number of cheque payments (%) | | |
|---|---|---|---|---|---|---|
| | 1984 | 1985 | 1986 | 1984 | 1985 | 1986 |
| *Banking system* | | | | | | |
| Bankcheques | | 9 | 8 | | 14 | 13 |
| Eurocheques | 51 | 43 | 45 | 48 | 34 | 35 |
| Postal cheques | 49 | 48 | 47 | 52 | 52 | 52 |
| Total | 100 | 100 | 100 | 100 | 100 | 100 |
| Total amount/number | 29.4 | 31.5 | 32.3 | 293.1 | 308.0 | 313.5 |
| *Sample* | | | | | | |
| Bankcheques | | 12 | 10 | | 14 | 13 |
| Eurocheques | 43 | 33 | 36 | 43 | 31 | 34 |
| Postal cheques | 57 | 55 | 54 | 57 | 55 | 53 |
| Total | 100 | 100 | 100 | 100 | 100 | 100 |
| Total amount/number | 26.0 | 29.1 | 29.8 | 277.5 | 296.4 | 299.0 |

*Note:* Amounts are in billions of guilders, numbers are in millions.

*Table 11.3: Expenditure by manner of payment*

| | Year | | |
|---|---|---|---|
| | 1984 | 1985 | 1986 |
| *In terms of amount (%)* | | | |
| Cash | 38 | 38 | 39 |
| Cheque | 14 | 14 | 14 |
| Transfer | 48 | 48 | 47 |
| *In terms of number (%)* | | | |
| Cash | 78 | 78 | 78 |
| Cheque | 8 | 8 | 8 |
| Transfer | 14 | 14 | 14 |
| *In terms of value (guilders)* | | | |
| Cash | 27 | 27 | 27 |
| Cheque | 94 | 98 | 100 |
| Transfer | 199 | 196 | 184 |

The share of guaranteed cheque in the total amount of household payments of 14% on average shows a slight increase from 1984 to 1986, resulting from a 6% rise in the average amount paid. This shift probably reflects the tendency for higher amounts in particular to be paid more often by cheque than by cash. Likewise, the average amount of transfers shows a 7% decline as a result of the substitution of cash and cheque payments by transfer payments.

Figure 11.1 illustrates that the manner of payment is strongly correlated to the amount paid. At amounts below *f* 50, nearly 90% of all expenditure is paid in cash. The share of cash payments declines to less than 15% at amounts of about *f* 300, at which level most payments – approximately 70% – are made by transfers. From about *f* 1 000 upward, cash regains importance as a means of payment. In 1986, 23% of the 15 million payments higher than *f* 1 000 was paid by cash. This share appears to be rising over time, amounting to 19% in 1984 and 21% in 1985.

Apart from the factor represented by the amount involved, the payment pattern depends on personal characteristics. The share of cash payments declines with age, income, education, and the number of checking accounts. Furthermore, women appear to pay more in cash than men do, and those persons who have guaranteed cheques at their disposal pay less in cash than those who have not. Each of these correlations is statistically significant at a 5% significance level, with a degree of association – expressed in Cramer's measure of association $V$ ranging from 0 to 1 (see Goodman and Kruskal (1979)) – of nearly 0.2. Since the personal characteristics may well be mutually dependent, the relationships established may be related as well, requiring a multivariate approach with, for example, the probit model. For the sake of simplicity and because it is not our intention here, this has been disregarded. Our present findings are, however, in fair agreement with those reported by Avery, Elliehausen, Kernickell, and Spindt (1986) for American families.

## 11.4 The Distribution of Payments

The data from the budget survey allow the establishment of the frequency distributions of amounts paid. This is a novelty because this distribution was hitherto unknown. Figures 11.2, 11.3 and 11.4 give the distributions with different class intervals in 1986 for cash, cheques, and transfer payments, respectively, each covering at least 95% of the payments concerned. The class interval of *f* 1 refers to amounts of *f* 0.46 up to and including *f* 1.45, *f* 1.46 up to and including *f* 2.45, and so forth.

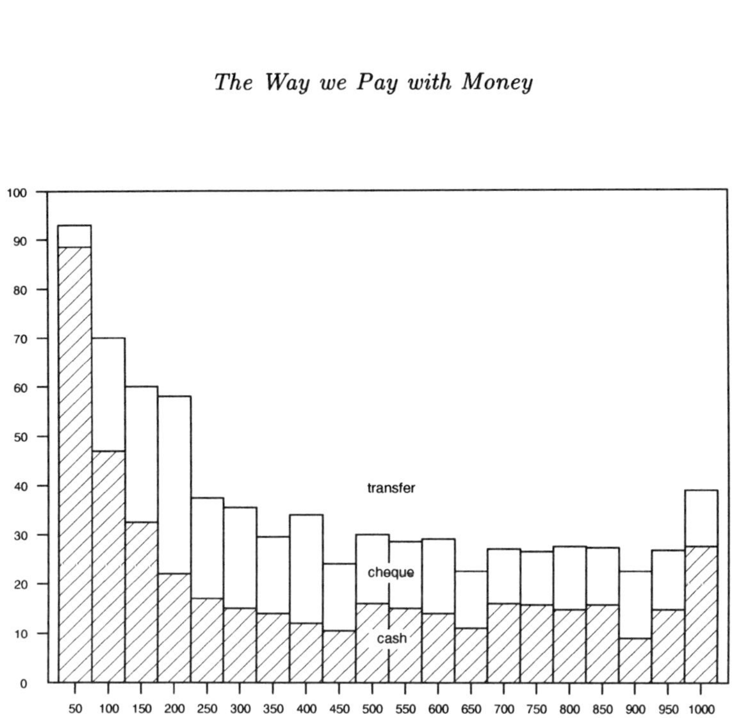


*Figure 11.1: Relationship between amount paid (in guilders) and manner of payment*

Likewise the class interval of *f* 5 refers to amounts of *f* 4.46 up to and including *f* 9.45, and so forth, and the class interval of *f* 10 to amounts of *f* 9.46 up to and including *f* 19.45 and so forth. The distribution of the cash payments, which account for nearly 85% of all payments for amounts up to and including *f* 100, shows marked peaks at multiples of *f* 5. Similar peaks can be observed in the distributions of cheques and transfer payments at a class interval of *f* 1 which for the sake of brevity are not shown here.

For payments in excess of *f* 100, notable peaks for all three means of payment occur at multiples of *f* 100. At least in the case of cash payments, the clustering of expenses at amounts of multiples of *f* 5 and *f* 100, respectively, could be due to reporting error. The distribution of cheque and transfer payments, which are administered, show, however, the same clustering. Moreover, less than 25% of the reported payments is rounded at full guilder amounts, which also seems to indicate that the extent to which the respondents may have resorted to rounding is limited. The distribution of the amounts of combined purchases of more than a single item do not show similar peaks at multiples of *f* 5 and *f* 100. Therefore, it seems unlikely that consumers arrange their combined purchases to attain totals of these amounts.

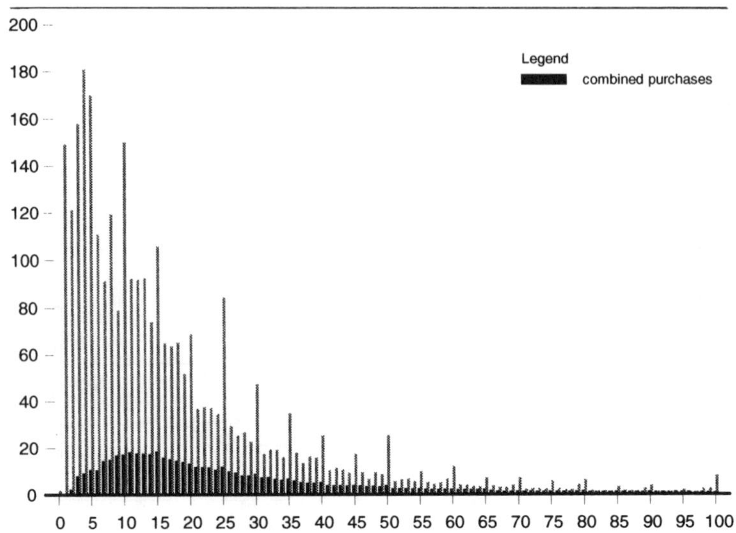


*Figure 11.2: Cash payments in 1986 up to and including f 100 at a class interval of f 1; amount in guilders*

The question arises of which probability distribution fits the observed frequency distributions satisfactorily. Besides the gamma distribution, which was assumed by Manski and Goldin (1987), we fitted the lognormal distribution defined by

$$f(x;\mu;\sigma) = \frac{1}{x\sigma\sqrt{2\pi}} \exp\left\{-\frac{1}{2}((\ln x - \mu)/\sigma)^2\right\},$$
$$x, \sigma \geq 0, \qquad -\infty \leq \mu \leq \infty. \tag{11.1}$$

According to the test statistic developed by Cox (1962), at a 5% significance level for all of the three years observed the lognormal distribution (Tables 11.4, 11.5, and 11.6) has to be preferred to the gamma distribution. As yet this empirical preference lacks a theoretical foundation. The case in question does not show clear similarity with the various applications of the lognormal distribution as described by Aitchison and Brown (1957), among others. The fitted distributions turn out to be fairly stable over time. The parameters estimated for 1986 differ by an average of 1% and by a maximum of 4% from those found for 1984 and for 1985.

With a class interval of *f* 1 or more, the frequency distributions shown in Figures 11.2, 11.3, and 11.4 do not afford insight into the rounding-

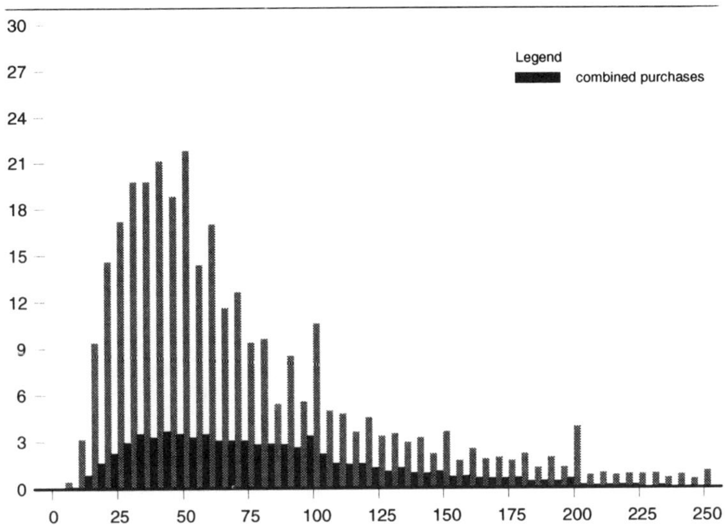


*Figure 11.3: Payments by means of guaranteed cheques in 1986 up to and including f 250 at a class interval of f 5; amount in guilders*

*Table 11.4: Estimation results for lognormal distribution for 1984*

| Manner of payment | $\mu$ | $\sigma$ | $\ln L$ $\times 1000$ | Standard deviation of residuals | $\chi^2$ $\times 1000$ | $\nu$ |
|---|---|---|---|---|---|---|
| Cash | 2.538 (.002) | 1.147 (.001) | −2 114 | 25.2 | 64 | 985 |
| Cheques | 4.117 (.004) | .853 (.003) | −284 | 8.6 | 432 | 847 |
| Transfers | 4.341 (.004) | 1.322 (.003) | −529 | 13.4 | 26 | 1 691 |
| Total | 2.905 (.002) | 1.350 (.001) | −3 038 | 25.1 | 67 | 1 937 |

*Notes:*
Standard deviations are in parentheses.
$L$ is the value of the likelihood function.
$\nu$ indicates degrees of freedom.

*Table 11.5: Estimation results for lognormal distribution for 1985*

| Manner of payment | $\mu$ | $\sigma$ | $\ln L$ $\times 1000$ | Standard deviation of residuals | $\chi^2$ $\times 1000$ | $\nu$ |
|---|---|---|---|---|---|---|
| Cash | 2.503 | 1.140 | −2 145 | 25.4 | 74 | 1 024 |
| | (.002) | (.001) | | | | |
| Cheques | 4.149 | .855 | −297 | 8.3 | 8 | 899 |
| | (.004) | (.003) | | | | |
| Transfers | 4.298 | 1.345 | −541 | 13.5 | 25 | 1 707 |
| | (.004) | (.003) | | | | |
| Total | 2.876 | 1.354 | −3 101 | 26.6 | 68 | 1 993 |
| | (.002) | (.001) | | | | |

*Note:* See Table 11.4.

*Table 11.6: Estimation results for lognormal distribution for 1986*

| Manner of payment | $\mu$ | $\sigma$ | $\ln L$ $\times 1000$ | Standard deviation of residuals | $\chi^2$ $\times 1000$ | $\nu$ |
|---|---|---|---|---|---|---|
| Cash | 2.496 | 1.157 | −2 153 | 31.9 | 79 | 1 049 |
| | (.002) | (.001) | | | | |
| Cheques | 4.153 | .859 | −293 | 8.1 | 8 | 933 |
| | (.004) | (.003) | | | | |
| Transfers | 4.258 | 1.313 | −557 | 13.5 | 24 | 1 727 |
| | (.004) | (.003) | | | | |
| Total | 2.871 | 1.360 | −3 119 | 30.3 | 64 | 2 029 |
| | (.002) | (.001) | | | | |

*Note:* See Table 11.4.

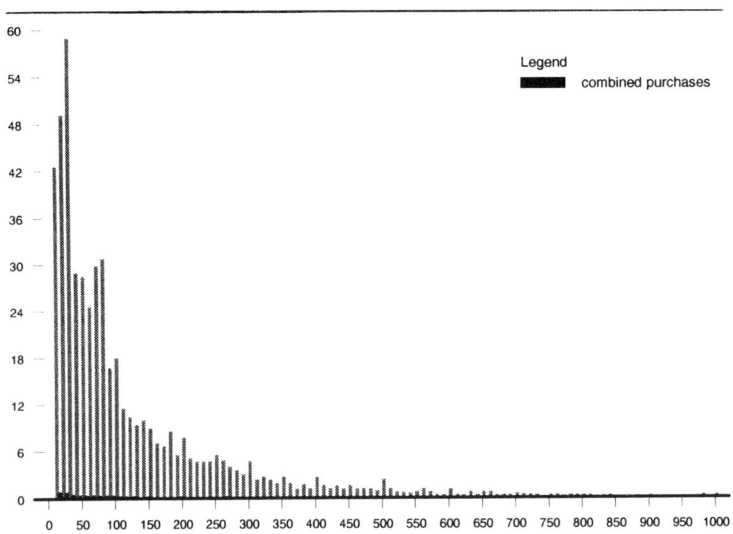


*Figure 11.4: Payments by means of transfers in 1986 up to and including f 1000 at a class interval of f 10; amount in guilders*

off practices of the amounts paid. It appears that nearly 25% of all cash payments concern full-guilder amounts and 12% are rounded at 50 cents. The results of our analysis suggest that rounding-off increases significantly with the amount paid. In excess of *f* 1 000 the majority – that is, more than 80% – of the amount is in full guilders or without rounding-off.

## 11.5 Application on the Use of Denominations

The observed probability distribution of cash payments allows the assessment of the households' need for currency for use in payments. For the currency-issuing authorities, it is important to know to what extent they succeed in meeting the need for currency efficiently by the denominational mix. Moreover, insight into the use of currency as a means of payment and as a means of hoarding is an essential element of forecasting the need for currency.

Following Cramer (1983), the frequency distribution enabled us to simulate the theoretically most efficient manner of payment, each payment involving a minimum of notes and coins. In addition, by way of sensitivity analysis, the computations were repeated by assuming, successively, payment with the exact amount – that is, efficient but without change – payment with the next higher denomination, change being returned in an efficient way; and a combination of these two payment forms in which for each amount the minimum number of notes and coins is taken.

According to the results obtained, set out in Table 11.7, efficient payment would have meant that in 1986 households needed for their 2.9 billion cash payments 9.5 billion notes and coins, or on average 3.3 notes and coins per payment. In the case of exact payment and in the case of payment with the next higher denomination, these numbers would be 35% and 70% higher, respectively. The payment pattern appears to affect the need for coins in particular. Payment with the next higher denomination involves nearly twice as many coins, but only 30% more notes than efficient payment. The share of the denominations in the number of notes and coins needed differ rather strongly, depending on the assumed manner of payment. As expected, in case of exact payment, the share of the lower and, in case of payment with the next higher denomination, the share of the higher denomination is relatively higher. In the case of efficient payment, the shares are somewhere in between.

In all of simulated payment patterns, the actual shares of the higher denominations are considerably higher and those of the lower denominations considerably lower than the computed shares. This means that the higher denominations are actually used much less frequently than the lower denominations. The physical velocity – that is, the number of times a note changes hands in a year – increases from 1 for *f* 1 000 notes to about 20 for *f* 10 and *f* 5 notes, with a coefficient of correlation between the face value of the denominations and their physical velocity of −0.65. To the extent that this physical velocity is a measure of the intensity with which a denomination is used in payments, this confirms the presumption formulated earlier that especially higher denominations are used not only as a means of payment, but also as a means of hoarding (see Fase (1985a)). From the discrepancy between the computed use of denominations and the actual circulation, the shares of the circulation of *f* 100 and *f* 1 000 notes that are hoarded is estimated at more than 80% and 90%, respectively. For the recently introduced *f* 250 note this percentage is estimated at 50%. These figures, however, perhaps overstate reality because business cash payments, which involve relatively many *f* 100 and *f* 1 000 notes, have not been taken into account. Besides, these notes are also used in the shadow economy. Moreover, the simulations of the payment pattern neglect the fact that when withdrawing cash people prefer the higher denominations regardless of the expenditure

*Table 11.7: Currency circulation and households' computed need for currency in 1986*

| Description | Currency (end of year) | Manner of payment: Efficient (1) | Efficient without change (2) | With the next higher denomination (3) | Minimum of alternatives (2) and (3) (4) |
|---|---|---|---|---|---|
| | | Composition (%) | | | |
| Notes | | | | | |
| *f* 1 000 | 3.6 | .4 | 0.3 | 0.3 | 0.2 |
| *f* 250 | 2.0 | 1.1 | 0.7 | 2.0 | 0.7 |
| *f* 100 | 35.4 | 3.6 | 2.3 | 5.3 | 3.6 |
| *f* 50 | 5.4 | 8.4 | 6.0 | 10.5 | 7.6 |
| *f* 25 | 19.0 | 22.1 | 16.0 | 24.9 | 20.3 |
| *f* 10 | 18.8 | 38.2 | 44.2 | 35.2 | 38.7 |
| *f* 5 | 15.8 | 26.2 | 30.5 | 21.8 | 28.9 |
| Total | 100 | 100 | 100 | 100 | 100 |
| Coins | | | | | |
| *f* 2.50 | 5.7 | 15.1 | 12.4 | 9.6 | 11.6 |
| *f* 1.00 | 19.0 | 34.1 | 32.7 | 30.5 | 34.9 |
| *f* 0.25 | 15.7 | 21.5 | 28.8 | 24.0 | 27.9 |
| *f* 0.10 | 23.2 | 15.9 | 18.8 | 29.7 | 16.6 |
| *f* 0.05 | 36.4 | 13.4 | 7.3 | 6.2 | 9.0 |
| Total | 100 | 100 | 100 | 100 | 100 |
| | | Number (millions) | | | |
| Notes | 350 | 3 620 | 3 641 | 4 596 | 3 680 |
| Coins | 3 211 | 5 917 | 9 092 | 11 446 | 7 677 |
| Total | 3 561 | 9 537 | 12 733 | 16 042 | 11 357 |
| | | Value (millions of guilders) | | | |
| Notes | 30 341 | 90 957 | 73 182 | 134 632 | 81 191 |
| Coins | 1 561 | 4 701 | 6 642 | 7 975 | 5 596 |
| Total | 31 902 | 95 658 | 79 824 | 142 607 | 86 787 |

they intend to make. Nevertheless, the results indicate a substantial degree of hoarding, which implies that even after a widespread adoption of electronic payment systems there will remain a considerable need for cash.

Contrary to expectations, the physical velocity of coins is considerably lower than the velocity of notes. According to the assumed payment pattern, they change hands one to three times a year. Moreover, this velocity declines with the coin value, as opposed to that of bank-notes, with a surprisingly high coefficient of correlation of 0.97. This is possibly caused by the disappearance from circulation of the low denominations in particular as a result of loss, destruction, and collecting (see Goldin (1985), Laurent (1974)).

*Table 11.8: Computed need for bank-notes at various bank-note ranges*

| | Need for bank-notes at bank-note range as at 1986 | Need for bank-notes at bank-note range as at 1986 | | | | |
|---|---|---|---|---|---|---|
| | | Excl. *f* 250 | Excl. *f* 50 | *f* 500 instead of *f* 250 | *f* 200 instead of *f* 250 | *f* 20 and *f* 200 instead of *f* 25 and *f* 250 |
| Number[a] | 3 620 | 3 658 | 3 856 | 3 633 | 3 615 | 3 570 |
| Value[b] | 90 957 | 89 646 | 93 411 | 89 691 | 89 952 | 90 534 |

*Notes:*
The bank-note range as at 1986 corresponds with the bank-note range in Table 11.3.
[a] Millions.
[b] Millions of guilders.

As is evident from the bottom rows of Table 11.8, the amounts of notes and coins needed for payments do not necessarily run parallel with their number. In the case of efficient exact payment, the required amount of currency is lowest and equals the total amount of cash payments. The total number of notes and coins is, however, 25% higher. This finding means that the manner of payment that is optimal from the point of view of the required number of notes and coins is not necessarily optimal from the economic viewpoint based on opportunity costs.

A similar conclusion holds in the case of a change in the bank-note range. The simulation results, which are based on the assumption of an efficient payment pattern, show that a reduction in the number of notes needed for cash payments is not necessarily accompanied by a decline in their total value. At least theoretically, the introduction of the denominations of *f* 50 and *f* 250 in 1984 and 1986, respectively, permitted reductions in the number of notes by 6% and 1%, respectively. Only in the case of the *f* 50 denomination, however, is this accompanied by a reduction in the value of the bank-note circulation of 2.6%. In the case of the *f* 250 denomination, the value increases slightly, by 1.5%. These results indicate that, contrary to Chen's (1976) assumption, the demand for currency does not necessarily decline with a more efficient denominational mix. Furthermore, the present bank-note range appears to meet the payment needs of households rather effectively. Only a changeover from the 5–10–25 range to a more normal 5–10–20 range would yield some material advantages. The 1.4% reduction in the number of notes is for the greater part undone by an increase in the number of coins. Alternatives tested for the remainder involve an equal of higher demand for notes.

In our analysis, the frequency distribution of cash payments was assumed to be independent of the available set of bank-notes and coins. It is reasonable to assume, however, that this is not entirely true and that the observed distribution is a reflection of the available set of bank-notes and coins. If so, the simulation results to some extent underestimate the decrease in the demand for notes resulting from the changes in the bank-note range and are consequently somewhat flattened.

## 11.6 Conclusions

Budget surveys can provide an insight into the use of means of payment. According to such a survey, the payment pattern of Dutch households was fairly stable in the years 1984–1986, cash payments accounting for nearly 80% of total payments in terms of numbers and for 40% in terms of value. The latter figure is in fair agreement with the 36% share reported for American households, in spite of the considerable differences between the payment systems in The Netherlands and the US. The payment pattern appears to be significantly dependent on the amount paid as well as on various personal characteristics of the payer, such as age, income, sex and education. The frequency distributions of the payments are described statistically in a satisfactory way by a lognormal distribution. The observed frequency peaks of amounts representing multiples of 5 and 100 guilders are mainly caused by the price tags of the separate items rather than by the buyer purchasing several goods at the same time to attain such amounts.

The need for currency and especially the need for coins is very sensitive to the way people pay cash. Inefficient payment can easily cause a 40% higher demand. On average, bank-notes change hands at least 10 to 15 times a year, the low figures for the higher denominations indicating a high degree of hoarding of these denominations. Moreover, from the simulations it appears that the total amount of currency is not invariant in respect to the denominational mix, and that a more efficient mix does not necessarily mean a lower demand for currency.

# 12. The Demand for Large Bank-notes

In many countries the high share of the largest bank-note denomination in the total currency circulation contrasts sharply with their limited use in payment transfers. This somewhat puzzling phenomenon has been discussed more than once for the US \$100 bill, which has a value share of nearly 50% (see Anderson (1977) and Kimball (1981) and Porter and Bayer (1984)). However, the phenomenon is the more remarkable for countries like Switzerland, Germany and The Netherlands, that issue a domination at the upper end of the bank-note range whose face value is 5 to 15 times as high as the \$100 note. In The Netherlands this is the *f* 1 000 note with a face value at end-1990 of more than \$500.[1] The circulation of this *f* 1 000 note has grown dramatically (see Table 12.1). At year-end 1987, *f* 1 000 notes accounted for almost 45% of the value of bank-notes in circulation, and this was thus the most important denomination in terms of value. At that time, there were approximately 15 million *f* 1 000 notes in circulation. This works out at an average of one of these notes per head of the population and over 2.5 notes per household, compared with less than one note per household just 10 years earlier. Nevertheless, *f* 1 000 notes are seldom encountered in the course of everyday payment transactions.

Analysis of the development of macroeconomic variables reveals that the remarkable increase in the importance of the *f* 1 000 note since 1980 cannot be solely attributed to an increased transaction demand including inflation, but that there was apparently a demand shift (Fase (1985a)). This means that the *f* 1 000 note is presumably being used to an increasing extent as a means of hoarding in addition to being a means of payment. The sharp rise in the average time in circulation for the *f* 1 000 note, i.e., the time elapsed between the moment of note issue

'The demand for large bank notes' by W.C. Boeschoten and M.M.G. Fase, *Journal of Money, Credit and Banking*, **24**(3) (August 1992), 319–337, is reprinted by permission. 

[1] See Table 12.A in the appendix for a comparative overview of the highest denominations in a number of OECD countries.

*Table 12.1: Development in the circulation of ƒ 1 000 notes*

| Year-end | Circulation | | Number of notes per capita | Percentage of value of total bank-note circulation |
|---|---|---|---|---|
| | Value in billions of guilders | % of national income | | |
| 1955 | 0.7 | 2.3 | 0.06 | 16.9 |
| 1960 | 0.8 | 1.9 | 0.07 | 15.7 |
| 1965 | 1.3 | 2.0 | 0.11 | 16.9 |
| 1970 | 2.0 | 1.8 | 0.15 | 20.5 |
| 1975 | 3.8 | 1.9 | 0.28 | 26.0 |
| 1980 | 6.4 | 2.1 | 0.45 | 29.4 |
| 1985 | 12.1 | 3.2 | 0.84 | 41.4 |
| 1986 | 12.6 | 3.3 | 0.87 | 41.6 |
| 1987 | 14.9 | 3.8 | 1.02 | 44.2 |

by the bank and the date on which it returns, supports this hypothesis. Between 1980 and 1989 this average circulation time has increased from 0.6 to more than 1.3 years.

In order to check whether these conclusions are borne out by micro-economic evidence a specially designed non-standard survey was carried out in 1986 in The Netherlands. The main purpose was to provide quantitative micro-based insight into the use of higher denominations. As these form the major part of the currency circulation the outcomes should have policy implications for the interpretation of money and particularly currency-holdings. The present chapter describes the design of the survey and its principal results. Further it analyses our own findings in view of economic theory against the background of statistical evidence obtained from other sources of information.

## 12.1 Survey Design

In view of the delicate nature of the enquiries on note-holding, the textbook sample approach seemed to be inappropriate to carry out the survey. Apart from a high non-response rate, direct questioning about possession and usage of ƒ 1 000 notes would, in all probability, have led to a considerable response bias. To illustrate this hypothesis, in the 1963 survey of Consumer Finances sponsored by the Federal Reserve, American consumers were not even asked about their cash-holdings because it was felt that accurate responses would be very unlikely. As it was, checking accounts and saving accounts, which were surveyed, were under-reported by about 50% (Anderson (1977)). Our second illustration concerns The Netherlands. A survey of money demand in

The Netherlands, conducted in 1971, and largely based on a written questionnaire, Cramer and Reekers (1972, 1976) could account for only 22% of the *f* 1 000 notes in circulation. Likewise, in the US, Avery, Elliehausen, Kernickell, and Spindt (1986) could trace even less with their survey among US households, only 11 to 12% of notes and coin in circulation outside banks. In view of these experiences we decided to adopt a more qualitative survey, comprising elements of a Delphi approach, extended to sectors usually not covered to any great extent by surveys, if at all.

The methodology underlying our survey within the various sectors distinguishes balances, either kept for payments, or as a store of value. Information on the cash balances is obtained by indirect questioning on:

1. the proportion of turnover in a sector paid by cash, say: *pcash*;
2. the proportion of cash turnover paid by *f* 1 000 notes, say: *p*1000;
3. the number of days that notes are kept before they are used for payments or deposited at banks, say: *t*.

The value of the holdings of *f* 1 000 notes, denoted by $V1000_i$, for transaction purposes in sector $i$ equals

$$V1000_i = (pcash_i * p1000_i * PT_i * t_i)/365$$

with $PT_i$ the value of incoming and outgoing transactions per sector, obtained from national accounts. This approach has the advantage that the respondents are indirectly questioned on the use of cash in general and *f* 1 000 bank-notes in particular within their sector. For the more permanent holdings of *f* 1 000 notes no such indirect approach was available. The respondents were asked therefore directly about those holdings. However, in certain sectors, like drug trade, no clear distinction could be made between the two types of cash-holdings.

The survey was carried out in three phases.[2] In the *first phase*, eight exploratory interviews were conducted among specialists in the field of cash payments or in certain strongly cash oriented branches of the Dutch economy. For the relevant individual sectors which these discussions helped to identify, the size of the payment flows and the number of units were derived from various public sources of information, principally The Netherlands Central Bureau of Statistics. Brief telephone interviews

[2] The subsequent results and the number of respondents per sector are summarized in Table 12.A in the appendix, which also contains the figures on the turnover and the number of units by sector.

were subsequently conducted among 130 respondents taken from the various sectors in order to obtain rough estimates of the proportion of cash payments within the payment flows, the share accounted for by *ƒ* 1 000 notes within each cash payment flow and the average length of time for which these notes were held. The respondents were not asked directly about their own dealings but were asked to make estimates of the averages for these variables in their particular sector. The number of respondents per sector were chosen on the basis of turnover figures and the degree of sector homogeneity. Within homogeneous subsectors the respondents were chosen at random. On the basis of an earlier orientation for drug trade and gambling sector it was preferred to interview experts in the relevant field. On the basis of the information thus obtained, along with the data concerning the number of units and the total payment flow per sector, an initial estimate was calculated of the numbers of *ƒ* 1 000 notes held in each sector. This estimate localizes more than 70% of the circulation of *ƒ* 1 000 notes (Table 12.A in the appendix).

In the *second phase* of the survey, this initial estimate was checked in greater detail by means of 190 telephone interviews. On this occasion the respondents were asked not so much for their own estimates but whether they thought the estimates derived from the initial survey were plausible, or if not, what they should be. To avoid biased answers and non-response, the questions were carefully worded. In each case so the questions were unambiguously related to the trade as a whole and not to the company or personal situation of the respondents themselves. In a number of sectors, including the 'other retail outlets' sector, the results were so varied that a further sub-division of the sectors concerned became necessary. Again, the degree of heterogeneity within the sectors and the size of the turnover were the main criteria for the sample size per sector, while per subsector the sample was chosen at random. This phase led to a considerable downward adjustment of the initial estimates. The results and the reported standard deviations show even for the various subsectors a high degree of heterogeneity. In addition to the 190 interviews, because of the high non-response rate in the household sector in the first phase, in an omnibus survey 2 000 households were asked on the use of *ƒ* 1 000 notes, as a means of payment and as a means of hoarding. The results affirmed the findings for the 20 respondents from the first phase. The original estimates for those sectors not included in this second telephone survey, namely industry, other services, households, the drug trade and the gambling community, were left unchanged.

In the *third phase* the holdings in a number of sectors, not considered so far, were traced by means of interviewing insiders in the relevant fields. These sectors included foreigners and caravan dwellers as well as car dealers and car breaking yards. As for some sectors in the first rounds, especially for the sectors covering 'grey' or even illegal activities, expert interviews are to be preferred to surveying a great number of respondents. Moreover, the *f* 1 000 notes kept by the banking sector were estimated from the figures on their till money. Thus, the number of non-located *f* 1 000 notes in circulation was reduced by nearly 12 percentage points compared with the estimate in the second phase.

## 12.2 The Main Results

With the above sampling strategy it was possible to trace almost 60% of the *f* 1 000 notes in circulation (Table 12.2). According to the estimates, almost 25% of the *f* 1 000 notes are to be found in the drug trade and the partly legal, but mainly 'underground', gambling community. A further 9% of *f* 1 000 notes are in the hands of private households. This works out at an average of 0.2 notes per household. Other sectors which stand out are the motor trade (including scrap yards) and caravan dwellers. According to our survey, these sectors hold more than 6% and 3%, respectively, of the total number of the issued *f* 1 000 notes, being equivalent to an average of 86 and 50 *f* 1 000 notes per household in these latter sectors, respectively. The latter information was obtained by persons who were well acquainted with the two sectors concerned and had no difficulty in conducting the necessary confidential interviews relating to use of *f* 1 000 notes.

Not only in absolute terms but also in relation to the estimated amount of cash changing hands, the drug trade and gambling community stand out as regards use of *f* 1 000 notes. Then, following at some distance, comes the motor trade, other services and agriculture and fisheries. According to the results, there is a clear relationship between the number of *f* 1 000 notes kept and the degree to which illegal transactions and transactions not declared to the tax authorities are likely to occur. The only clear exception is construction. Although this is traditionally a sector where a high number of illegal transactions and tax evasion take place, our estimates indicate a remarkably low holding of high denomination notes. The average number of notes per household, incidentally, shows a picture which is broadly in line with the frequency of use per sector. For a number of sectors, together accounting for approximately 40% of the *f* 1 000 notes in circulation, it was possible to make a very rough distinction between cash-holdings for transaction purposes and for hoarding purposes. According to the initial estimates, roughly 70% of the *f* 1 000 notes in circulation are hoarded. According to the later estimates presented in this chapter, the proportion is more like 60%. As said before, the distinction between means of transaction and means of hoarding is, however, fairly arbitrary. Thus for a number of sectors including the drug trade and caravan dwellers, it is not possible to draw a precise line between the two. In these sectors, *f* 1 000 notes commonly serve the function of a means of payment and a means of hoarding at one and the same time.

## 12.3 A Closer Look at the Results

In order to analyse the results obtained from the survey, we consider three aspects which are of particular interest to the issuer of bank-notes. These concern the holding of notes by sector, the holding and use of notes by households and the extent to which the *f* 1 000 note is used for hoarding purposes.

### 12.3.1 The Distribution of Holdings

Owing to the qualitative nature of the survey method employed, a fairly large degree of uncertainty is attached to the results. The number of respondents per sector very often is rather small, the sub-division into sectors is not exhaustive and, in a few of sectors, there is a certain amount of overlapping. Owing to the latter situation, the estimated proportion of the notes in circulation is perhaps upwards biased.

The picture we were able to construct, however, is in a number of respects remarkably similar to the findings of Cramer and Reekers (1972), which were based on logged counts by financial institutions, major companies and a large part of the retail trade as well as on a survey conducted among over 1500 small companies and households. The estimated percentages of notes held by the sectors industry, construction, the wholesale and distributive trade, hotel, catering and licensed trade, other services and banks are of a comparable order of magnitude despite the intervening years (Table 12.2).

For the sectors agriculture and fisheries, the motor trade, real estate and households, however, the estimates produced by the present survey are considerably higher. This is at least partly due to the more indirect qualitative approach. The combined share of the first 11 sectors in Table 12.2, which are covered by both studies, totals 38% in the case of the present survey compared with 19% in the case of the Cramer and Reekers's survey. On top of that, according to our survey, 20% of the

*Table 12.2: Estimated distribution of holdings of f 1 000 notes*

| Sector | | Present study for 1986[a] | | Cramer and Reekers' estimate for 1971[b] |
|---|---|---|---|---|
| | | % of notes held | total value (mln. of guilders) | % of notes held |
| 1 | Agriculture and fisheries | 4.6 | 557 | 0.9 |
| 2 | Industry | 1.7 | 206 | 1.0 |
| 3 | Construction | 2.0 | 242 | 1.0 |
| 4 | Motor trade | 6.7 | 811 | 0.6 |
| 5 | Retail trade | 2.8 | 339 | 1.3 |
| 6 | Wholesale and distributive trade | 1.2 | 145 | 0.9 |
| 7 | Hotel, catering, and licensed trade | 0.2 | 24 | 0.2 |
| 8 | Real estate | 1.8 | 218 | 0.1 |
| 9 | Other services | 1.4 | 169 | 1.0 |
| 10 | Households | 9.3 | 1.125 | 6.8 |
| 11 | Banks and government | 6.4 | 774 | 4.9 |
| 12 | Foreigners | 2.7 | 327 | – |
| 13 | Caravan dwellers | 2.9 | 353 | – |
| 14 | Drug trade | 10.1 | 1.211 | – |
| 15 | Gambling community | 3.7 | 488 | – |
| Sub-total | | 57.5 | 6.949 | 18.7 |
| 16 | Financial institutions | 1.0[c] | 121 | 1.0 |
| 17 | Transport | 1.4[c] | 169 | 1.4 |
| 18 | Other institutions | 0.2[c] | 24 | 0.2 |
| 19 | Abroad | 1.0 | 85 | 1.0 |
| Known holdings | | 61.1 | 7.348 | 22.3 |
| Unknown holdings | | 38.9 | 4.752 | 77.7 |
| Total | | 100 | 12.100 | 100 |

*Notes:*

[a] Percentages expressed in terms of average number of notes in circulation in first half of 1986.

[b] Cramer and Reekers (1972); percentages of number of notes in circulation on 31 March 1971.

[c] Additions to original survey estimates on basis of percentages estimated by Cramer and Reekers (1972).

*f* 1 000 notes are held by foreigners working in the Netherlands, caravan dwellers, the drug trade and the gambling community.

Despite the inclusion of these last four sectors, and the use of a survey method which made allowances for the delicate nature of the subject, initially over 40% of the holdings of *f* 1 000 notes could not be accounted for. Some of the untraced notes are bound to be held in sectors not included in the study. According to the estimates of Cramer and Reekers, for instance, a total of over 2.5% of *f* 1 000 notes can be traced to the currency-holdings of financial institutions (excluding banks), to the transport sector and to social institutions, churches, associations, educational establishments and local authorities. The existence of another 1% or so of the *f* 1 000 notes can be explained by the flow of payments abroad using these notes, which amounted to some *f* 2 billion in 1985. In addition, it is possible that some *f* 1 000 notes are held abroad for speculative reasons. All told, however, only some 5% of the notes in circulation which are still unaccounted for can be explained in this way (Table 12.2).

Presumably, therefore, the holdings of notes may have been underestimated in a number of sectors. One possible reason for this is that the possession and use of *f* 1 000 notes is very unevenly distributed within the sectors, with many holdings of a small number of notes and a relatively small number of holdings of large or very large numbers of notes. This possibility is confirmed, at least in the case of households, by the results of the supplementary omnibus survey, which we shall discuss later. If there is in fact a skewed distribution of this kind, then the respondents will have underestimated the true average to the extent that their answers reflect the modal value rather than the mean.

Since the respondents were asked to give an average figure for their particular sector as a whole – and not for their own situation – it is not possible to determine what shape the distribution actually has. This means that it is also impossible to determine the relationship between modal and mean values. A rough sensitivity analysis, however, indicates that between a quarter and a third of the non-identified holdings of notes could be explained by a distortion of this kind. If we assume, for the sake of simplicity, that the holdings of *f* 1 000 notes follow a (negative) exponential distribution, which is in defiance of the discrete character of the distribution, but not of the data (generally the mean equals the standard deviation), the actual mean amounts to 1.44 ($= 1/\ln 2$) times the median. By correcting the estimates in this way the unexplained proportion of the circulation of *f* 1 000 notes diminishes with some 12 percentage points, or one third. If it is assumed that not the median but the modus is reported, when holdings are estimated at 0, the correction would be even considerably larger. Moreover, if the skewness of the distribution curve for the holdings of *f* 1 000 notes differs from one sector to another, this could also distort the figures for the percentage of notes held by the various sectors.

A second important reason for the high proportion of unexplained holdings is presumably the tendency of respondents to understate the numbers and amounts involved as far as possession and use of *f* 1 000 notes is concerned. The results of our telephone survey confirm this conjecture. For instance, a number of respondents mentioned the existence of the hoarding of *f* 1 000 notes, but denied their use in transactions, which appears rather inconsistent. Contrary to the above mentioned understatement arising from the skewness of the distribution, this source of understatement cannot be tackled by enlarging the sample, but requires additional qualitative research. For a number of sectors, including agriculture and fisheries, construction and the hotel, catering and licensed trade, additional information obtained from insiders would possibly lead to an upward revision of the figures, as has already been the case with the motor trade, for example. The other sectors, however, are too large and too heterogeneous for this approach.

### 12.3.2 Households' Holdings of *f* 1 000 Notes

In the same way as for most of the other sectors, an attempt was made in the second phase of the survey to improve the initial estimates of the numbers of *f* 1 000 notes held by households. Since the questions asked necessarily related fairly directly to hoards of notes or, in some sense, inefficient cash management, the non-response rate was very high by usual standards and the reliability of the answers was too low for the results to be considered as providing any significant improvement. Finally, a random survey technique was resorted to in the case of households. To this end, a number of questions relating to familiarity with and possession and use of *f* 1 000 notes were included at our request in the omnibus survey conducted by the Centre of Marketing Analyses and Social Scientific Research in May 1986.

Almost 95% of the 2 000 respondents aged 15 and over had seen a *f* 1 000 note at some time. Despite this high level of familiarity, however, use of these notes is not very widespread according to the survey results. A quarter of the population never uses them and a quarter only uses a *f* 1 000 note once a year. On the other hand, there are also people who spend and receive these notes very frequently. The results show that the possession and use of *f* 1 000 notes exhibits a highly skewed distribution.

On average, the respondent in the random sample came into the possession of one or more *f* 1 000 notes, either withdrawn from an account or received in some other way, 2.0 times a year and spent one or more of these notes 1.4 times a year. The fact that *f* 1 000 notes are received more often than they are spent cannot be solely explained by hoarding.[3] Presumably, people spend more notes at once than they receive or withdraw. Assuming that two notes are withdrawn or received on average on each occasion and that they are held for an average of five days, the transaction requirement for *f* 1 000 notes can be estimated at 0.6 million notes, or 5% of the notes in circulation at year-end 1985.[4]

In addition, it was found that, according to the survey, 1.8% of the respondents held *f* 1 000 notes as a means of saving. People aged 50 and older tend to do this more than the younger generation. On average they have savings of three notes. This information, applied to the Dutch population as a whole, also gives a figure of around 0.6 million *f* 1 000 notes held by way of savings. The total number of *f* 1 000 notes held by households for transaction and hoarding purposes combined therefore works out on the basis of the omnibus survey results at 9.3% of the notes in circulation in 1985. This figure is not significantly different from the 9.2% arrived at in the initial phase of the survey.

The present estimate of holdings for transaction purposes also agrees closely with the findings of other surveys on the use of *f* 1 000 notes. For instance, on the basis of results of a survey on behalf of the bank in 1983, the turnover of *f* 1 000 notes for that year is estimated at *f* 10 billion. The necessary holdings of notes for this volume of transactions was estimated at around *f* 400 million or 5% of the notes then in circulation.

A comparable figure can be arrived at from the information concerning cash payments by households derived from a survey of spending behaviour in which the bank participated in the years 1984–1986 (Boeschoten and Fase 1989). According to this study, in value terms, households make almost 40% of their payments in cash. In 1986, this represented a sum of around *f* 80 billion. Over 15% of this sum is made up of payments of *f* 1 000 or more. In paying these amounts, it is estimated that 12 million *f* 1 000 notes were used. Even assuming a rather low turnover rate of 25 for cash transactions balances (Cramer and Reekers (1976) and Avery, Elliehausen, Kernickell, and Spindt (1986)),

---

[3] If the difference between issues and withdrawals and receipts of *f* 1 000 notes is attributed exclusively to hoarding, this gives an estimate of at least seven million notes for the number of *f* 1 000 notes held in hoards in 1985, while the actual number of notes in circulation increases by only one million.

[4] According to the results of a survey conducted on behalf of De Nederlandsche Bank in 1983, an average of around 11 days elapses between two consecutive cash withdrawals. Partly on the basis of this figure, the average retention time of a *f* 1 000 note has been taken as five days for the present purpose.

a circulation of *f* 1 000 notes of just over *f* 500 million should have been enough to meet the transaction requirements of households. According to all three studies referred to, the holdings of households for transaction purposes therefore amount to around 5% of the total number of *f* 1 000 notes in circulation. The closeness of agreement is remarkable. It is even more remarkable when one considers that the three random surveys were quite different in design and approach. Moreover, in two of the three surveys, respondents were not asked direct questions about their own particular use of *f* 1 000 notes, so the amount of distortion in the estimates is therefore presumably small.

As far as the use of *f* 1 000 notes by households for hoarding purposes is concerned, we only have the results of the omnibus survey to go on. A considerably greater degree of uncertainty is therefore attached to this estimate, particularly since it is based on direct questions relating to a rather tricky subject. Suspicion of financial institutions and the desire for secrecy are important reasons for holding financial assets in this non-interest-bearing form. Thus there are plenty of reasons for assuming that people will tend to quote figures which are on the low side rather than on the high side and that therefore the share of *f* 1 000 notes in circulation held in hoards by households is in fact higher than the estimated 5%.

### 12.3.3 The *f* 1 000 Note as a Means of Hoarding

According to the survey, 60 to 70% of the *f* 1 000 notes are used as a means of hoarding. This estimate is in fact based solely on the findings for just some of the sectors covered by the study and is therefore no more than an indication. Other estimates, however, give comparable or higher percentages. An earlier tentative estimate on the basis of information from a continuous budget survey among 1, 000 households on spending patterns arrived at a figure of 90% (Boeschoten and Fase (1989)). This percentage, which was derived from the difference between the estimated requirement of households for *f* 1 000 notes for transaction purposes and the actual number of notes in circulation, presumably results in an overestimate of the numbers of these notes in hoards.[5]

Even estimates arrived at by more direct methods, however, point to very substantial hoards of notes. As we have seen, a holding of *f* 1 000

[5] This analysis was necessarily restricted to households. Business transactions, in which relatively more *f* 1 000 notes are presumably involved, are therefore not included. In addition, the fact that the cash withdrawals are generally made in notes of larger denominations, and that these notes are therefore represented more frequently in cash-holdings for transaction purposes than one would assume on the basis of the amounts paid, also leads to an overestimate of the number of *f* 1 000 notes held in hoards.

notes for transaction purposes of around 0.6 million should presumably be enough to fund the *f* 12 billion in transactions which households pay in *f* 1 000 notes out of their total cash payments of *f* 80 billion each year. No estimates are available concerning the volume of business transactions paid for in cash. Using the results of the survey, however, a figure of *f* 60 billion[6] can be put on these transactions for 1985 as a very rough estimate, of which *f* 20 million is paid for with *f* 1 000 notes. For a turnover rate of 25, around 0.9 million *f* 1 000 notes would therefore be needed for these transactions. This means that a total of 1.5 million *f* 1 000 notes, or less than 15% of the notes in circulation, would suffice for the payments made by households and the business community together. On this basis, therefore, the remaining 85% of notes must fulfil a hoarding function.

A more general method of estimating the volume of notes held in hoards is based on the development in the return rate of bank-notes. This is the number of times that a note of a certain denomination returns on average to the bank each year.[7] The underlying thinking is that the return rate of a note of a particular denomination reflects the intensity of its use as a means of payment. If the actual numbers of notes of a particular denomination received turn out lower than the return rate which might be expected on the basis of use for payment transactions alone, this can be attributed to hoarding.

In Table 12.3, the proportion of hoarded *f* 1 000 notes in circulation has been estimated for the period 1965–1987 using this method. If we take the lowest value for the return rate of *f* 1 000 notes over the observation period as the normal return rate in the absence of hoarding, then we get an estimate of 77% for 1987. Even if we take the return rate for *f* 25 notes which are pre-eminently used as a means of payment, as the norm in view of the possible variations of the return rate over time, we arrive at a comparable figure of 76%. However, this method gives implausible negative percentages for the years up to 1970 since the return rate of *f* 25 notes was greater than that of *f* 1 000 notes in these years. It is therefore not always possible to take the return rate as a measure of intensity of use. Notes which are being intensively used in a particular payment system, may continue circulating in this system without regularly returning to the bank. Even so, the sharp

6 This is roughly a third of the total volume of cash payments. This result is based on the fact that cash withdrawals from business accounts are estimated to represent a third of all cash payments.

7 This figure is calculated as the quotient of the number of notes received by the bank each year and the average number of notes in circulation for the denomination concerned. The relevant key figure can be found in the Annual Report of De Nederlandsche Bank.

increase in the number of *f* 1 000 notes in circulation in response to the announcement in 1987 of the automatic reporting by the banks to the tax authorities of interest payments, which came into operation on 1 January 1988, is not reflected in the estimates given in Table 12.3. This is because this increase was coupled with a very substantial additional flight of capital abroad in the form of bank-notes. The consequent increase in the return rate is wrongly interpreted by the estimating method used in Table 12.4 as an increase in the intensity of use. After correction for this distortion, more than 80% of the *f* 1 000 notes in circulation in 1987, according to the estimates, serve as a means of hoarding.

The above problems are partly overcome by taking, like Anderson (1977), the average life of a particular denomination of bank-note as a measure of intensity of use instead of the return rate. If the actual number of rejects turns out lower than one would expect on the basis of the average life of the notes if used exclusively as a means of payment, this can be attributed to the fact that some of the notes in circulation are held in hoards and are therefore not subject to the usual wear and tear. Although the estimates arrived at in this way differ slightly from those based on return rates, as far as change with time is concerned, among other things, they all indicate that a very substantial proportion of the *f* 1 000 notes in circulation, maybe as high as 85%, is used as a means of hoarding.

The outcomes on the hoarding of the *f* 1 000 note are in fair agreement with the estimates of Anderson (1977) and Whitehead (1982) for the US. According to the estimates of Whitehead, which hardly differ from the results found earlier by Anderson, in 1980 more than 80% of the $50 bills and 90% of the $100 bills was hoarded. For total currency the estimated share of currency in hoards as a percentage of currency outstanding rises from 56% in 1960 to nearly 70% in 1980. The considerable growth of the use of currency as a means of hoarding is confirmed by the estimates of Kimball (1981) on the basis of the changing composition of currency flows to and from Federal Reserve Banks and by the slow-down of the turnover rate of currency, measured by Laurent (1981). Likewise the survey results of Avery *et al.* (1986) indicate that less than 15% of the stock of currency in the US (adjusted for vault cash and known losses) is held for transaction purposes by the sampled population of individuals. All these outcomes suggest that the hoarding of larger bank-notes is not only connected to a high face value in absolute terms but also to their position at the top end of the bank-note range. This would imply that the highest bank-notes in other countries, as shown in Table 12.B in the appendix, are probably also hoarded to a considerable extent.

*Table 12.3: Estimate of the number of f 1 000 notes in hoards*

| Year | Circulation (yearly average in millions) | Percentages of notes in hoards | | | |
|---|---|---|---|---|---|
| | | on the basis of return rate | | on the basis of life of notes | |
| | | highest rate for f 1 000 note[a] | rate for f 25 note | shortest life of f 1 000 note[a] | life of f 25 note |
| 1965 | 1.2 | 18 | −63 | 37 | 25 |
| 1970 | 1.8 | 48 | −7 | 38 | 46 |
| 1975 | 3.5 | 52 | 35 | 64 | 73 |
| 1980 | 6.0 | 60 | 54 | 75 | 85 |
| 1985 | 11.4 | 77 | 74 | 68 | 81 |
| 1986 | 12.1 | 78 | 76 | 71 | 86 |
| 1987 | 13.1 | 77 | 76 | 72 | 85 |

*Note:* [a] On the basis of three-yearly averages 1958–1960.

*Table 12.4: Circulation in eleven industrial countries at end-1987*

| Country | Circulation per capita (in $) | | Circulation as percentage of GNP | |
|---|---|---|---|---|
| | all bank-notes | highest denomination | all bank-notes | highest denomination |
| Belgium | 1.294 | 896 | 8.1 | 5.6 |
| Canada | 583 | 32 | 3.6 | 0.2 |
| France | 770 | 368 | 4.3 | 2.1 |
| Germany | 1.298 | 313 | 6.5 | 1.6 |
| Italy | 811 | 536 | 5.6 | 3.7 |
| Japan | 1.936 | 1.659 | 8.4 | 7.2 |
| The Netherlands | 1.297 | 573 | 7.8 | 3.5 |
| Sweden | 1.143 | 65 | 5.6 | 0.3 |
| Switzerland | 3.286 | 1.501 | 10.3 | 4.7 |
| United Kingdom | 449 | 60 | 3.2 | 0.4 |
| United States | 871 | 411 | 4.7 | 2.2 |

## 12.4 The Use of Cash Revisited

The astonishing large per capita demand for currency and especially larger bank-notes is a rather general phenomenon (Table 12.4), that has frequently been discussed in the literature (see, for instance, Cagan (1958) and Porter and Bayer (1984)). An interesting question is whether this phenomenon fits into any theoretical framework.

In the literature the demand for currency is hitherto mostly explained from the transactions motive only, building on the Baumol (1952) and Tobin (1956) inventory transactions approach, extended with a stochastic element by Whalen (1966) and Miller and Orr (1968). The basic assumption for a positive demand for currency is merely that some payments are cheaper when using currency than when using demand deposits. The simple version of the inventory-theoretic approach, based on the minimization of the transaction and opportunity costs of holding cash results in the well-known square root law

$$M = \sqrt{\alpha Y/2r} \tag{12.1}$$

with $M$ the average money-holding, $Y$ the predetermined value of transactions, $r$ the interest rate and a constant transaction cost $\alpha$. This simple version holds only under very strict assumptions with respect to, for instance, the spacing of withdrawals (see Akerlof and Milbourne (1978)) and the limitation to one alternative means of exchange, but suffices in this context by way of illustration. The demand for money rises with transactions and diminishes with rising opportunity costs, the elasticities – in this simple case – being 0.5 and −0.5, respectively.

As pointed out by, for example, Sprenkle (1969) and Akerlof and Milbourne (1978) the transactions model appears to underpredict actual cash balances. In explaining the growth of the demand for currency the transaction approach is relatively more successful (see Kimball (1981)). This may however be the result of a parallel movement of the additional explaining factors with total transactions. The outcomes of this study confirm, at least for the Netherlands, the inadequacy of the transaction motive as the sole explaining factor of the amount of cash-holdings. The finding that only about 15% of the actual circulation of the largest Dutch bank-note would suffice for transaction purposes, implies that at least 35% of the total bank-note circulation is used for other purposes. As there are strong indications that the same phenomenon, be it to a lesser extent, also holds for the next lower denominations (see Boeschoten and Fase (1989)), this percentage can be even 50% or more.

Many authors consider the large currency circulation and especially its growth relative to the outstanding demand deposits despite the widespread use of currency substitutes like credit cards and cheques, as an indication of a growing underground economy (Cagan (1958), Gutmann (1977), Feige (1979) and (Tanzi 1982)). Because currency transactions are less easily traced than transactions carried out by cheque, currency has a decided advantage over cheques for those who wish to avoid taxes. The higher probability of detection lowers the expected yields of alternative means of payment, thus causing, according to the square root formula, a higher demand for currency. The results shown in Table 12.3 indicate indeed that a considerable share of the holdings of the highest denomination in the Netherlands is located in illegal sectors like the drug trade and in sectors where tax evasion is the most likely to occur. The cash transactions in the underground economy alone can, however, not explain the high currency figure. Even if the underground economy would amount to 10% of GNP, and all relevant transactions totalling about *f* 150 billion (Boeschoten and Fase (1984)) were paid in cash, at a turnover rate of cash of 25, a currency circulation of less than *f* 6 billion would suffice. If all underground transactions were paid with *f* 1 000 bills – which is not the case – they would require at most 50% of the *f* 1 000 notes outstanding, while according to the findings in Section 12.3 there is an excess of about 85%. As the turnover rate of transaction cash balances is probably higher than 25 (see Avery, Elliehausen, Kernickell, and Spindt (1986)) and black market transactions are paid partly by cheque (Feige 1979), the need for cash for the underground economy is, however, much lower. Therefore, as has also been concluded by Kimball (1981) and Porter and Bayer (1984) for the US, the use of cash for transactions in the underground economy can at most explain part of the high per capita currency circulation in The Netherlands.

A second, and perhaps more important explanation for the high currency figures is hoarding. Akerlof and Milbourne (1978) point out the hoarding of currency as a major complication in explaining the size of cash-holdings. Moreover, several studies mentioned earlier give, mainly on the basis of currency figures, indirect evidence for a considerable size of currency hoarding. The present study affirms, at least for the Netherlands, this hypothesis.

The question arises why households would hoard such large amounts in the form of bank-notes with the nominal interest as opportunity costs and with the risk of loss, theft or destruction. The answer seems to be the unique combination of liquidity, security and privacy of this financial asset (Kimball 1981). The lack of one or more of these qualities may cause lower yields of alternative assets and, according to the inventory model result in higher currency-holdings. Bank-notes are extremely liquid in the sense that they can be used and changed directly and in any amount without loss of value. Thus, besides an outstanding means of payment for transactions, they can also be an attractive means for precautionary balances. By this we mean the need for liquid resources to deal with unforeseen contingencies as well as with large disbursements which are known in advance. As far as the gains in transfer costs, that is, the costs of transferring alternative assets in means of exchange, exceed the opportunity costs with respect to foregone interest or other yields, it can be economically preferable to hold precautionary balances in cash.

The liquidity of bank-notes and of currency in general is connected with its security. Insofar as the risk perception regarding the loss of value of other assets, be it financial or real, exceeds their yields, individuals can prefer to hold wealth in the form of currency. The well-known rise of currency-holdings in wartime illustrates this security aspect.

The third, and in combination with the two other features probably most important, quality of currency as a means of hoarding is the privacy it provides. The lack of bank statements and records allows holders of currency to conceal the existence of such hoards. As pointed out by Anderson (1977), the desire for privacy can be based on solely legitimate motives. Some may simply not want anyone to know how much they have in savings. Others may be shy and feel uncomfortable in the white-collar atmosphere of banks or they may dislike the prying that is involved in opening a deposit account. Still others may be classical misers.

Holding wealth in the form of currency in order to conceal accumulated earnings or wealth for tax authorities can, however, have purely economic reasons. Reportedly, the large tax evader or drug dealer frequently accumulates sizeable amounts of currency in the larger denominations. These cash balances may be maintained, despite high interest rates, to avoid arousing suspicion in converting this currency into other assets. When it becomes profitable to do so, the holder may purchase a legitimate business or launder the illegal gains.

Assuming a constant expected before tax interest rate $r_i$ on asset $i$, the expected value of unreported earnings $W_o^u$ after $t$ years in case of tax evasion follows from

$$W_t^u = (1 + r_i - p_i\beta)^t W_o^u \tag{12.2}$$

where $p_i$ is the probability of detection in the case of holding $W_o^u$ in the form of asset $i$, and $\beta$ is the fraction of the amount outstanding that has to be paid to the tax authorities in case of detection. From (12.2) it appears that keeping unreported or illegal income in the form of an interest-bearing asset $i$ instead of in a cash hoard is worth while only if

$$(r_i - p_i\beta) + p_c\beta = r_i - (p_i - p_c)\beta > 0 \tag{12.3}$$

with subscript $c$ indicating currency. Generally speaking the probability of detection for interest-bearing financial assets is considerably higher than for currency. Thus especially for illegally acquired income, where $\beta$ may be even higher than 1, the interest earnings do not outweigh the losses expected due to the higher probability of detection.

But also in the case of legally acquired, but unreported earnings, the high value of $p_i$ – especially since the introduction of automatic reporting by the banks to the Dutch tax authorities of interest payments for several financial assets – keeping unreported earnings in the form of interest-bearing assets does not make sense. Thus, leaving apart moral feelings, for holding unreported earnings, especially if they have been illegally acquired, currency has to be preferred as a store of value to interest-bearing assets.

Illegally acquired or black income, as described before, must by definition stay unreported. With regard to legally acquired income individuals can, however, outweigh tax evasion in combination with keeping earnings in a cash hoard against reporting the income and hold it in the form of interest-bearing assets. In case of reporting and holding $W_o$ in the form of financial asset $i$ at a constant expected marginal income tax rate $\tau$, the resulting value after $t$ years follows from

$$W_t^r = (1 + (1 - \tau)r_i)^t (1 - \tau) W_o. \tag{12.4}$$

Whenever $W_t^u$ exceeds $W_t^r$ it is preferable to keep $W_o$ unreported. We assume for the sake of simplicity a probability of detection of 0 for cash hoards. The break-even time horizon $t_o$ (in years), from when on it is preferable to report income and to hold $W_o$ in the form of an interest-bearing asset $i$, then follows from

$$t_o = -\ln(1 - \tau) / \ln(1 + (1 - \tau)r_i). \tag{12.5}$$

The time horizon indicates the attractiveness of keeping earnings concealed and hoarding it in the form of currency. According to (12.5) tax evasion combined with hoarding is the more attractive, as the tax rate is higher and the interest rate is lower. For instance, at a 6% interest rate, an individual in the 40% tax bracket would be as well off only after about 15 years by paying his income tax and earning 5% before tax on the remaining income (Table 12.5). This illustrates that at least in the case of tax evasion there can be strong incentives for hoarding currency, especially for shorter periods. Besides the evasion of income tax there can, however, especially for older people, be other economic motives to hoard currency such as evading inheritance duties or, at least in the Netherlands, bypassing the regulation that individuals with a wealth of more than $f$ 8 000 have to contribute to their stay in homes for the elderly, while others do not.

*Table 12.5: Break-even time horizons for hoarding (in years)*

| Tax bracket | Interest rate | | | | | | |
|---|---|---|---|---|---|---|---|
| | 2% | 4% | 6% | 8% | 10% | 12% | 14% |
| 20% | 14.1 | 7.1 | 4.8 | 3.6 | 2.9 | 2.4 | 2.1 |
| 30% | 25.7 | 12.9 | 8.7 | 6.5 | 5.3 | 4.4 | 3.8 |
| 40% | 42.8 | 21.5 | 14.4 | 10.9 | 8.8 | 7.3 | 6.3 |
| 50% | 69.7 | 35.0 | 23.4 | 17.7 | 14.2 | 11.9 | 10.3 |
| 60% | 115.0 | 57.7 | 38.6 | 29.1 | 23.4 | 19.5 | 16.8 |
| 70% | 201.3 | 100.9 | 67.5 | 50.8 | 40.7 | 34.0 | 29.3 |

*Note:* The figures, computed with formula (12.5) give the time horizons within which it is economically more lucrative to keep earnings concealed in hoards rather than to receive interest payments but pay tax.

Some rather convincing indirect evidence for the importance of these motives, is the apparent sensitivity of the bank-note circulation to fiscal disturbances. Thus the publicity of a raid by the Dutch fiscal authorities on a major bank in 1983 caused an autonomous and permanent rise of the bank-note circulation of about 10%, mainly located in *f* 1 000 notes. The announcement of the introduction of the automatic reporting on interest payments by banks to the tax authorities in 1987 had a similar effect. Likewise the German announcement of a 10% withholding tax on interest payments at the end of 1987 resulted in an autonomous rise of the German bank-note circulation of between 5 and 10%. Such shifts from saving deposits into currency are economically meaningful only as far as tax evasion is at issue. Otherwise neither automatic reporting nor withholding tax has any influence on the yields from financial assets.

## 12.5 Summary and Conclusions

Using a qualitative sample design this chapter shows that it is possible to account for 60% of the *f* 1 000 notes in circulation in The Netherlands. More than a third of the notes traced in this way are held by the drug trade, gambling community and motor trade sectors. A large proportion of these notes presumably represents money which people want to keep hidden from the authorities because of the way in which it was acquired. Households and the currency-holdings of banks account for the largest share in the other sectors. The nearly 40% of notes unaccounted for can presumably be put down to underestimating the holdings in the various sectors. As far as they go, however, the results of the study indicate that around 10% of the *f* 1 000 notes are held by households, half for the purpose of transactions and half for the purpose of hoarding. The markedly similar results of the qualitative approach and the additionally applied conventional survey indicate that conventional survey methods may be equivalent or even more appropriate in sectors such as households and certain industries. In sectors such as caravan dwellers and drug trade, however, the applied qualitative approach contributed significantly to the estimates, where the more conventional survey methods appeared inappropriate.

The results of the study also suggest that 60 to 70% of the *f* 1 000 notes in circulation are used as a means of hoarding. The findings of studies based on information relating to payments and the payment system and on circulation figures, even indicate that around 80% of the *f* 1 000 notes in circulation are used as a means of hoarding. At year-end 1987, this would represent *f* 12 billion or almost 35% of the total currency circulation. The estimated degree of hoarding of *f* 1 000 notes, as well as its considerable growth show a remarkable similarity with the figures estimated for the $50 and $100 bills in the US. Hoarding in the form of currency can be meaningful from an economic point of view, especially where illegal or unreported income and wealth are concerned. This phenomenon probably explains to a considerable extent the high demand for large bank-notes in particular.

The findings imply that even in the case of a strongly diminishing transaction demand for cash as a consequence of financial innovations and electronic payment systems, there still remains, at least in terms of value, a considerable demand for cash as a means of hoarding. Moreover the findings have consequences for the interpretation of M1: as the narrow money aggregate appears to contain a sizeable component that is not used for transactions but is held for some other purpose, the concept of M1 as used principally for transactions is distorted.

## Appendix 12.A Key data on survey estimation of holding *f* 1 000 notes

| Sector | Number of units (thousands) | Turnover (bln. guilders per year) | Survey results: number of respondents | | | share of cash in turnover (%) | | | share of *f* 1 000 in cash turnover (%) | | |
|---|---|---|---|---|---|---|---|---|---|---|---|
| Phase: | | | 1 | 2 | 3 | 1 | 2 | (*S*) | 1 | 2 | (*S*) |
| Agriculture/fisheries | 136.6 | 42.4 | 16 | | | 40.2 | | | 77.6 | | |
| farmers | | | | 19 | | | 16.7 | (20.9) | | 24.1 | (17.4) |
| casual work | | | | 12 | | | 2.6 | (6.2) | | 5.0 | (5.4) |
| cattle-breeding | | | | 12 | | | 31.7 | (27.1) | | 32.6 | (16.9) |
| nursery-gardens | | | | 11 | | | 15.6 | (19.7) | | 10.0 | (10.0) |
| Industry | 46.5 | 552.0 | 16 | 15 | | 0.8 | | | 37.7 | | |
| Construction | 41.8 | 48.2 | 15 | 18 | | 11.8 | 11.4 | (17.6) | 58.4 | 27.7 | (21.1) |
| Motor trade | 9.4 | 22.0 | 11 | 19 | 2 | 48.5 | 48.0 | (34.8) | 30.0 | 37.1 | (20.2) |
| Retail trade | 131.4 | 103.0 | 15 | | 1 | 32.4 | | | 1.9 | | |
| butchers' shops | | | | 7 | | | 37.1 | (21.1) | | 13.0 | (6.2) |
| supermarkets | | | | 5 | | | 22.3 | (3.8) | | 4.2 | (3.7) |
| clothes shops | | | | 6 | | | 22.0 | (19.7) | | 4.8 | (2.8) |
| furniture shops | | | | 11 | | | 19.1 | (13.5) | | 14.6 | (14.2) |
| radio, TV and hifi | | | | 7 | | | 19.1 | (19.3) | | 2.4 | (0.9) |
| antique trade | | | | 11 | | | 41.5 | (25.2) | | 16.1 | (11.0) |
| Wholesale/distributive trade | 62.3 | 246.0 | 10 | 13 | | 2.7 | 3.3 | (9.4) | 70.6 | 17.7 | (20.2) |
| Licensed trade | 43.0 | 13.6 | 10 | 18 | | 14.4 | 23.9 | (21.2) | 4.7 | 11.8 | (3.8) |
| Real estate | 29.0 | 36.5 | 10 | 15 | | 5.4 | 5.5 | (5.3) | 77.3 | 46.9 | (10.3) |
| Other services | 29.1 | 6.8 | 10 | | | | | | | | |
| Households | 5558.0 | 283.0 | 20 | 2000 | | | | | | | |
| Cash banks | 8.3 | | 2 | | | | | | | | |
| Foreigners | 140.0 | | | | 2 | | | | | | |
| Caravan dwellers | 7.1 | | | | 2 | | | | | | |
| Drug trade | – | 4.5 | 1 | | | | | | | | |
| Gambling community | – | 1.5 | 1 | | | | | | | | |
| Unknown holdings | | | | | | | | | | | |
| Total | | 1373.6 | 138 | 190 | 7 | | | | | | |

| Sector | Survey results | | | | | | | | | | | |
|---|---|---|---|---|---|---|---|---|---|---|---|---|
| | number of days notes are kept | | | notes stored per unit | | | number of $f$ 1 000 notes per unit | | | composition of ciculation $f$ 1 000 | | |
| Phase: | 1 | 2 | ($S$) | 1 | 2 | ($S$) | 1 | 2 | ($S$) | 1 | 2 | ($S$) |
| Agriculture/fisheries | 12.5 | | | 8.5 | | | 14.3 | 14.3 | 4 | 16.2 | 4.6 | 4.6 |
| farmers | | 14.9 | (10.1) | | 2.1 | (2.7) | | | | | | |
| casual work | | 1.2 | (1.3) | | 0.3 | (0.6) | | | | | | |
| cattle-breeding | | 5.4 | (8.1) | | 1.4 | (1.8) | | | | | | |
| nursery-gardens | | 1.4 | (3.5) | | 0.3 | (0.7) | | | | | | |
| Industry | 4 | | | 3 | | | 3.7 | 3.7 | 3.7 | 1.7 | 1.7 | 1.7 |
| Construction | 5.5 | 4.8 | (3.8) | 14 | 3.8 | (4.3) | 16.8 | 5.7 | 5.7 | 5.8 | 2.0 | 2.0 |
| Motor trade | 7.5 | 5.9 | (15.3) | 14 | 2.1 | (2.1) | 38.1 | 10.0 | 88 | 4.9 | 0.7 | 6.7 |
| Retail trade | 5 | | | 5 | | | 5.1 | 2.6 | 2.6 | 5.6 | 2.8 | 2.8 |
| butchers' shops | | 4.8 | (2.1) | | 1.6 | (1.8) | | | | | | |
| supermarkets | | 1.9 | (0.7) | | – | (0.0) | | | | | | |
| clothes shops | | 3.4 | (3.4) | | 2.3 | (2.3) | | | | | | |
| furniture shops | | 1.8 | (1.4) | | 4.5 | (10.3) | | | | | | |
| radio, TV and hifi | | 3.5 | (3.6) | | 0.4 | (0.9) | | | | | | |
| antique trade | | 6.3 | (3.0) | | 1.9 | (2.4) | | | | | | |
| Wholesale/distributive trade | 5 | 2.3 | (2.2) | 10 | 2.1 | (1.6) | 10.8 | 2.3 | 2.3 | 5.6 | 1.2 | 1.2 |
| Licensed trade | 10 | 4.1 | (4.4) | 4.7 | 0.5 | (1.3) | 5.9 | 0.6 | 0.6 | 2.2 | 0.2 | 0.2 |
| Real estate | 9 | | | 15 | 4.4 | (5.9) | 18.4 | 7.4 | 7.4 | 4.5 | 1.8 | 1.8 |
| Other services | 5 | | | 5 | | | 5.8 | 5.8 | 5.8 | 1.4 | 1.4 | 1.4 |
| Households | | | | 0.1 | | | 0.2 | 0.2 | 0.2 | 9.2 | 9.2 | 9.3 |
| Cash banks | | | | | | | | | | 6.4 | 6.4 | 6.4 |
| Foreigners | | | | | | | | | 2.4 | | | 2.7 |
| Caravan dwellers | | | | | | | | | 50 | | | 2.9 |
| Drug trade | | | | | | | | | | 10.1 | 10.1 | 10.1 |
| Gambling community | | | | | | | | | | 3.7 | 3.7 | 3.7 |
| Unknown holdings | | | | | | | | | | 29.1 | 54.2 | 42.5 |
| Total | | | | | | | | | | 100 | 100 | 100 |

*Notes:* The symbol $S$ denotes standard deviation. In phase 2 a number of turnover figures were slightly adapted; moreover the trade in new and second-hand cars was combined. Changes in phase 3 are based on seven expert interviews, apart from the omnibus survey for the households sector. The figures in the motor trade in phase 3 also include approximately 1 000 car-breaking yards.

Appendix 12.B The highest denomination in each of a number of OECD countries in 1987 (end-of-year figures)

| | Currency | Highest denomi-nation | Value in US$ | Share in value of total bank-note circulation (%) |
|---|---|---|---|---|
| Australia | Aus $ | 100 | 72 | 30.6 |
| Austria | Sh | 1 000 | 89 | 77.1 |
| Belgium | Bfr | 5 000 | 151 | 69.3 |
| Canada | Can $ | 1 000 | 769 | 5.5 |
| Denmark | DKr | 1 000 | 164 | 50.6 |
| West Germany | DM | 1 000 | 632 | 24.1 |
| Finland | FIM | 1 000 | 253 | 18.9 |
| France | Ffr | 500 | 94 | 47.8 |
| Greece | Drachma | 5 000 | 40 | 61.8 |
| Iceland | IKr | 5 000 | 140 | 43.5 |
| Ireland | IR£ | 100 | 168 | 0.8 |
| Italy | Lire | 100 000 | 86 | 66.2 |
| The Netherlands | *f* | 1 000 | 563 | 44.2 |
| Norway | NKr | 1 000 | 160 | 64.8 |
| Portugal | Esc | 5 000 | 39 | 70.5 |
| Spain | Pts | 10 000 | 92 | 10.7 |
| Sweden | SEK | 10 000 | 1,710 | 5.6 |
| Switzerland | Sfr | 1 000 | 782 | 45.7 |
| Turkey | TLira | 10 000 | 10 | 84.9 |
| United Kingdom | £ | 50 | 94 | 13.3 |
| United States | $ | 100 | 100 | 47.2 |

# 13. Forecasting the Demand for Bank-notes: Some Empirical Results for The Netherlands

## 13.1 INTRODUCTION

Forecasting is partly an art and partly a science. No doubt this is true for many human activities, it certainly needs little emphasis among an audience which is in some way or another engaged in the design, production or processing of bank-notes. The art aspect is present in a feeling of new developments hanging in the air, the imagination of engineers and the vision of central bankers. The contribution of science comes from the systematic examination of the available information and the modelling of historical data along with the development of new methodologies. The distinction between art and science is, we believe, important in order to make people aware of the fact that forecasting is a complex activity which cannot be derived from abstract reasoning alone: it requires inputs from a variety of sources.

Forecasting is a substantial element of decision-making by the management of any organization. Therefore, forecasting is not an end in itself, but mainly a means of facilitating and improving decision-making. Obviously, forecasts become more beneficial as uncertainty in the external world increases unless forecast errors increase with uncertainty. As pointed out by e.g. Makridakis and Wheelwright (1978) forecasting may play a role in different areas. Some of these are:

1. scheduling of existing resources (in the case of bank-notes it may facilitate the planning of production, transportation and scheduling of personnel);
2. acquiring additional resources (raw material, new personnel, add-

Reprinted from *European Journal of Operational Research*, **6**(3) (March 1981), M.M.G. Fase, 'Forecasting the demand for bank-notes: Some empirical results for The Netherlands', 269–278, ©1981 with kind permission from Elsevier Science-NL, Sara Burgherhartstraat 25, 1055 KV Amsterdam, The Netherlands.

itional equipment);

3. determining desired resources in the long-run (new technology, changing preferences and institutions, fixed capital investment, environmental developments, the introduction of new denominations).

The above three areas are typical of short-, medium- and long-term forecasting, respectively. As an example of the first category we may regard the use of sorting machines or the routing of trucks in the case of a central bank which has its own transportation network. This may encourage forecasting needs for periods covering a week or a month. As for the second area, one may need forecasts by individual items to foresee the demand and to schedule production and inventories. The third area mainly involves new developments which may have an impact on investment decisions in the paper mill, printing works or handling of notes. Such developments may range from the desire for new denominations and coins among the public to the appearance of new technologies and payment habits.

The desired production of bank-notes is the product of the demand for bank-notes at any particular time, and the average lifetime. While the latter might be relatively constant, the first shows a steady increase over time. Various techniques are available to generate forecasts of bank-note demand. They have in common that they are extrapolative methods which assume that the future may be derived from the pattern of the past. One major class of forecasting methods of this type are time series models, which are particularly useful in a limited information environment. Causal or regression models provide another class of forecasting methods and are particularly valuable for annual or medium-term prediction, and in cases where explanatory variables are controlled by the policy maker. Contrary to these quantitative models, qualitative forecasting methods do not require as many data but are sometimes very beneficial in guiding intuitive thinking about future developments.

This chapter presents some examples of forecasting models studied at De Nederlandsche Bank as well as some results obtained from qualitative research undertaken in the recent past. In writing this chapter we have relied heavily on statistical research done at the bank, which is mentioned in the list of references (see Broekhuis and Nieuwkerk (1979), Fase (1978a), Fase and Nieuwkerk (1976, 1977), and Fase, Hoeven, and Nieuwkerk (1979)).

## 13.2 Demand for Bank-notes: A Regression Approach

One way of looking at the demand for bank-notes is to view it as part of the demand for money. The explanatory variables can therefore be derived from that part of monetary theory dealing with the demand for money. Consequently, we assume the demand for bank-notes to be dependent on the size of transactions in each period, which is measured by national income $Y_t$. In addition, special events which bring about a change in payment habits have to be taken into account. In view of earlier results (see Fase and Nieuwkerk (1977)) we have deliberately omitted the rate of interest as an explanatory variable. Therefore, for each denomination the following regression cquation has been postulated:

$$B_{it} = \alpha_{i1} + \alpha_{i2}Y_t + \alpha_{i3}d_t + \alpha_{i4}d_tY_t, \qquad (13.1)$$

with $B_{it}$ the 13 four-week averages of the circulation for denomination $i$ in year $t$, and $Y_t$ nominal national income in year $t$ with $Y_t$ a proxy for the volume of transaction to be measured. Although there may be a problem with this assumption (see *e.g.* Jonker (1973)) we ignore it here because of a lack of data. The dummy variable $d_t$ has been used to take into account the most striking change in payment habits, *viz.* the introduction of the guaranteed cheque in 1967. For the dummy variable, therefore, we have $d_t = 0$ before 1967 and $d_t = 1$ from 1967 onwards. As the *f* 5 note was only introduced in the course of 1966, we have ignored the dummy variable in the corresponding equation.

The choice of a linear rather than a logarithmic-linear specification has been motivated by results of earlier work (see Fase and Nieuwkerk (1977)). To begin with we tested the null hypothesis that the errors of the regression equation are homoskedastic and serially uncorrelated, using the test procedures developed by Breusch and Pagan (1979) and Godfrey (1978), which are equivalent to the likelihood ratio test. As a result we applied generalized least-squares to obtain estimates of the coefficients of equations (13.1), assuming the variance of the error term to be proportional to $Y_t$ for the denominations of *f* 100 and *f* 1000 and first order autocorrelation for all equations. The estimation results, using annual data from the sample period 1955–1978 are reported in Table 13.1. The results in Table 13.1 indicate, in accordance with our expectation, that the introduction of the guaranteed cheque in 1967 mainly affected the *f* 100 denomination while it reduced the income coefficient of the *f* 10 note – derived from $(\alpha_{i2} + \alpha_{i4})$ – to almost 0.

With the exception of the smallest denomination the income elasticities, evaluated at the means of the relevant sub-period and reported

*Table 13.1: Estimation results for equations (13.1)*[a]

| Denomination | $\alpha_{i1}$ | $\alpha_{i2}$ | $\alpha_{i3}$ | $\alpha_{i4}$ | $\bar{R}^2$ |
|---|---|---|---|---|---|
| *f* 5 | 44.29 | 0.0006 | | | 0.99 |
| | (12.7) | (30.1) | | | |
| *f* 10 | 495.28 | 0.0022 | 118.80 | −0.0022 | 0.21 |
| | (7.2) | (2.2) | (1.6) | (2.1) | |
| *f* 25 | 1069.34 | 0.0017 | −148.30 | 0.0012 | 0.85 |
| | (9.6) | (1.0) | (1.2) | (0.7) | |
| *f* 100 | −382.86 | 0.0715 | 2979.98 | −0.0429 | 0.96 |
| | (2.3) | (18.6) | (8.8) | (8.9) | |
| *f* 1000 | 121.57 | 0.0166 | −100.51 | 0.0011 | 0.62 |
| | (2.0) | (0.6) | (0.8) | (0.6) | |

*Note:* [a] The figures in parentheses are *t*-values.

in Table 13.2, increase with the size of the denomination. Thus we may predict the percentage share of the larger denominations to increase with income.

Another use of equations (13.1) is to predict future demand. This assumes the equations to be reasonably stable over time. To assess this assumption we present in Table 13.3 our prediction in accordance with equations (13.1) for 1979, while Table 13.4 sets out our long-term forecasts assuming three different percentages of growth of $Y_t$.

The results of Table 13.3 show that, at least for 1979, the predictive power of equations (13.1) is fairly good, with an error not exceeding 4.8% although our equations seem to underpredict actual development, particularly when heteroskedasticy occurs. Bearing this in mind we have attempted to forecast the demand for bank-notes up to the year 2000. The results have been set out in Table 13.4.

The results in Table 13.4, which are aggregated totals of our forecasts per denomination, show the importance of the assumed growth rate of nominal national income. This is dependent on both real growth and the rate of inflation which are not easy to forecast in the long-run. Therefore, the forecasts presented in Table 13.4, should be considered as indicative of future development given the underlying assumptions.

*Table 13.2: Income elasticities for each denomination*

| Denomination | Before 1967 | From 1967 onwards |
|---|---|---|
| *f* 5 | | 0.73 |
| *f* 10 | 0.17 | 0.00 |
| *f* 25 | 0.07 | 0.33 |
| *f* 100 | 1.17 | 0.68 |
| *f* 1000 | 0.85 | 0.99 |

*Table 13.3: Predicted and actual average bank-note circulation in 1979 (millions of guilders)*

| Denomination | Predicted | Actual | Prediction error (millions of guilders) | % |
|---|---|---|---|---|
| *f* 5 | 202.1 | 209.2 | −7.1 | 3.4 |
| *f* 10 | 633.2 | 642.6 | −9.4 | 1.5 |
| *f* 25 | 1 750.9 | 1 777.7 | −26.8 | 1.5 |
| *f* 100 | 10 845.9 | 11 347.6 | −501.7 | 4.4 |
| *f* 1000 | 4 924.1 | 5 172.6 | −248.5 | 4.8 |

*Table 13.4: Predicted total bank-note circulation (millions of guilders) with three alternative growth rates of nominal income*

| Year | Assumed annual growth rate | | |
|---|---|---|---|
| | 5% | 7½% | 10% |
| 1980 | 19 000 (6.5)[a] | 19 000 (6.5) | 19 000 (6.5) |
| 1985 | 22 900 (6.1) | 25 200 (6.0) | 27 700 (5.9) |
| 1990 | 28 000 (5.9) | 34 300 (5.7) | 42 100 (5.5) |
| 1995 | 34 600 (5.7) | 47 500 (5.5) | 65 300 (5.3) |

## 13.3 Demand for Bank-notes: A Time Series Approach

Forecasting with a regression or causal model as set out in Section 13.2 requires knowledge of the related (economic) variables which serve as the explanatory variables in the equation. Thus, equation (13.1) requires data on national income. Very often the required data become available with considerable lag or are not reported at all. Under such circumstances conventional econometric approaches do not provide an appropriate forecasting device, but a useful alternative is provided by the time series approach. In this section we present an autoregressive integrated moving average or ARIMA time series model to forecast for each denomination separately the end-of-week and the end-of-month demand for bank-notes.

The employed ARIMA model has the following mathematical form

$$\phi_p(L)\Phi_P(L^S)\nabla^d\nabla_S^D \ln B_{it} = \theta_0 + \theta_q(L)\Theta_Q(L^S)a_t, \tag{13.2}$$

where $\phi_p(L)$ and $\theta_q(L)$ are scalar polynomials of order $p$ and $q$, respectively in the backward shift operator $L$, with $L^k x_t = x_{t-k}$, $B_{it}$ the number of bank-notes of denomination $i$ in circulation at the end of period $t$, and $a_t$ a serially independent random shock with 0 mean and constant variance (or zero-mean white noise as called by process engineers). The difference operator is defined by $\nabla = 1-L$, $\nabla_S = 1-L^S$, with $d$ and $D$ integers. The polynomials $\Phi_P(L^S)$ and $\Theta_Q(L^S)$ take into account seasonal variation with period $S$ so that $S = 12$ for monthly and $S = 52$ for weekly data. The $\theta_0$ is a constant term. The seasonal differencing operator $\nabla_S$ converts a series, which has a non-stationary seasonal component, into a stationary series.

In fitting our ARIMA model (13.2) to the data an iterative approach is adopted which encompasses three stages (see Box and Jenkins (1970)). To begin with the postulated model is identified, i.e., appropriate values for $p$, $d$, $q$, $P$, $D$ and $Q$ are chosen according to cross-correlation and partial autocorrelations derived from the data. In the second stage the tentatively entertained model is fitted to the data, i.e., its parameters are estimated. In the final stage diagnostic checks are applied to examine the adequacy of the model for describing the data. If any inadequacy is found the cycle is started again. It is beyond the scope of this chapter to go into the intricacies of the computational procedure at length. For details we refer to the work of Box and Jenkins (1970), as well as to Jenkins (1979), Morales (1977) or Nelson (1973). We proceed to our own estimates now, obtained by fitting model (13.2) to weekly and monthly data.

*Table 13.5: Estimation results for each denomination with weekly data 1976–1978 (end-of-week figures, numbers* $\times$ 1000*)*[a]

| Denomination | Fitted ARIMA models | Sample statistics | |
|---|---|---|---|
| $f$ 5 | $(1+0.22L^3)\nabla\nabla_{52}\ln B_5 = a_t$ | $\hat{\sigma}_a = 0.00375$ | |
| | (2.2) | | $\chi^2_{54} = 33.8$ |
| $f$ 10 | $\nabla\nabla_{52}\ln B_{10} = (1-0.27L-0.42L^2)a_t$ | $\hat{\sigma}_a = 0.00578$ | |
| | (3.0) (4.7) | | $\chi^2_{53} = 30.0$ |
| $f$ 25 | $(1-0.25L^{13})\nabla\nabla_{52}\ln B_{25} = (1-0.36L-0.34L^2)a_t$ | $\hat{\sigma}_a = 0.00989$ | |
| | (2.7) (3.4) (3.0) | | $\chi^2_{52} = 27.3$ |
| $f$ 100 | $(1-0.36L^{13})\nabla\nabla_{52}\ln B_{100} = (1-0.42L-0.34L^2)a_t$ | $\hat{\sigma}_a = 0.00928$ | |
| | (4.1) (4.4) (3.3) | | $\chi^2_{52} = 29.2$ |
| $f$ 1000 | $\nabla\nabla_{52}\ln B_{1000} = a_t$ | $\hat{\sigma}_a = 0.00813$ | |
| | | | $\chi^2_{54} = 36.9$ |

*Note:* [a] The figures in parentheses are $t$-values, $\hat{\sigma}_a$ is the standard deviation of the residuals, $\chi^2_n$ is the portmanteau test statistic with $n$ degrees of freedom.

Table 13.5 sets out the estimation results of the models fitted to end-of-week data covering 1976 to 1978, for each denomination separately. The models show a yearly seasonal pattern (52 weeks) while for the notes of *f* 25 and *f* 100 also a quarterly seasonal movement (13 weeks) is apparent. As the series have been differenced in order to obtain stationary series, no constant term has been estimated. The goodness of fit is indicated by the standard deviation of the residuals, while the $\chi^2$ statistics indicate that the hypothesis that residual noise is white noise indeed should not be rejected.

The estimated weekly models have been used to forecast the circulation of each denomination in 1979. The result is depicted in Figure 13.1 together with the original time series and the fitted model. As the realizations beyond the sample period are already known for 1979, we have computed inequality coefficients to evaluate the predictive power of our models. To measure this we use the inequality coefficient introduced by Beld (1965) which measures the accuracy of a forecast. This statistic is defined as

$$U = \left[ \frac{1}{n} \sum_t \left( \frac{\dot{P}_t - \dot{R}_t}{\bar{\dot{R}}} \right)^2 \right]^{1/2},$$

within the present case $\dot{P}_t$ the predicted $\nabla\nabla_S \ln B_i$ and $\dot{R}_t$ the actual $\nabla\nabla_S \ln B_i$ at time $t$ with $S = 12$ and 52 for monthly and weekly figures, respectively. $\bar{\dot{R}}_t = ((1/n) \sum \dot{R}_t^2)^{1/2}$. When the forecast is perfect $U = 0$, while $U = 1$ means that the naive forecast of no change would do. The results reported in column 2 of Table 13.6 reflect the systematic deviations between the predicted and observed time path in 1979 for the weekly forecasts with the inequality coefficients larger than one. The inequality coefficient for the total is obtained by adding up the forecasts of all denominations.

The estimation results for the monthly models fitted to data of the sample period 1970–1978 are presented in Table 13.7 and displayed in Figure 13.2. Similar to the weekly models the monthly models do not include a constant term. We note that the estimated ARIMA models are somewhat more complicated than the models fitted to weekly data. Again the predictive performance is not entirely satisfactory for the same reason as with the weekly model. Again the inequality coefficient is large as shown in column three of Table 13.6, but, unlike the weekly forecasts, the predicted time profile does not show a systematic pattern.

To assess the numbers presented in Table 13.6, it should be kept in mind, however, that the values are greatly affected by the fact that they are computed as the differences $\nabla\nabla_S \ln B_{it}$. If we compare levels, the computed inequality coefficients for totals fell to 0.01 for weekly and 0.09

*Table 13.6: Inequality coefficients of the weekly and monthly forecasts for 1979*

| Denomination | Weekly forecasts | Monthly forecasts |
|---|---|---|
| *f* 5 | 1.64 | 1.33 |
| *f* 10 | 1.61 | 1.16 |
| *f* 25 | 1.62 | 1.10 |
| *f* 100 | 1.45 | 1.71 |
| *f* 1000 | 1.47 | 1.49 |
| Total | 1.46 | 1.51 |

for monthly figures, which is certainly due to the non-stationarity of thc series.

## 13.4 Comparison of Two Monthly Models

It would be argued that the monthly ARIMA model estimated in the previous section should be extended to a multivariate model which includes some measure of economic activity as a causal element. This may improve the forecasting power while the estimation results become comparable with those of the regression equations of Section 13.2. Monthly data on national income are unfortunately not available in The Netherlands, but there are monthly data for industrial production. To examine this extension of our ARIMA model, we postulated a transfer model for the relationship between the end-of-month bank-note circulation $B_{it}$ and the monthly flow of industrial production $IP_t$. This model has the following mathematical form:

$$\nabla^d \nabla_S^D \ln B_{it} = \theta_0 + \frac{\omega_S(L)}{\delta_r(L)} \nabla^d \nabla_S^D \ln IP_t + \frac{\theta_q(L)}{\phi_p(L)} a_t, \tag{13.3}$$

with $\omega_s(L)$, $\delta_r(L)$, $\theta_q(L)$ and $\phi_p(L)$ scalar polynomials of the order $s$, $r$, $q$ and $p$, respectively, in the backshift operator $L$; $\nabla = 1 - L$; $\nabla_S^D = 1 - L^D$ with $S = 12$ because monthly data are considered here; $D$, $d$, $p$, $q$, $r$ and $S$ are integers $> 0$ and the $a_t$ are, as before, white noise. Again $\theta_0$ is a constant term. We fitted model (13.3) to end-of-month data covering, as before, the period 1970–1978. The estimated models, obtained by iteration of fitting and checking are displayed in Table 13.8, with $t$-values in parentheses. The results show that the estimates of the constant are more often than not insignificant, while the noise part resembles the noise structure of the univariate model set out in Table 13.7. However, the transfer function part is significant. The residual variance is never smaller than the residual variance of the univariate model, indicating that the inclusion of industrial production as explanatory variable hardly improved the earlier results shown in Table 13.7. To examine this more closely we brought together in Table 13.9 the standard errors of the residuals in the two models.

The table reveals that the goodness of fit showed no improvement at all. A similar conclusion can be drawn from the inequality coefficients, not reported here, which are invariably worse than for the ARIMA models. Looking at the cross-correlations we found that all but one denomination showed significant peaks at leadtime of between 2 and 25 months. This seems highly implausible. Therefore, we may conclude that for monthly figures the univariate model is at least as good as the causal or single-input single-output model.

## 13.5 Future Bank-notes: Some Results From a Survey

In view of continuing inflation one has to consider the desirability to adjust the assortment of bank-notes periodically. Of course for such a decision it may be useful to know the preferences of the public. To investigate the preferences of the public on this matter De Nederlandsche Bank conducted a national survey among 1859 households in March 1978, which was preceded by a pilot survey among the personnel of the bank. In this section we report some of the results, as this survey may be viewed as an example of qualitative forecasting.

As to the satisfaction with the existing bank-notes the survey shows that about 80% would not like to see any of the notes withdrawn; 15% does not consider the bank-note of *f* 1000 indispensable and 6% believes they could do without the *f* 5 note. With regard to the desired extension of the existing series, it is noteworthy that 6% is in favour of the introduction of a *f* 2.50 note, 6% favours a *f* 50 note and 3% would like to see a *f* 500 note introduced. I would like to note, in passing, that those who favour the now historical *f* 20 note – quantitatively of no great importance, namely 2% – combine their wish with a withdrawal of *f* 10 and/or *f* 25 and/or *f* 100 notes.

The percentage that would not miss the *f* 5 note, is, as we have seen above, 6, and does not show a noteworthy difference among the sexes. To the question whether a *f* 5 coin or a *f* 5 note is to be preferred, 68% answered that they were satisfied with a note, 11% preferred a coin and

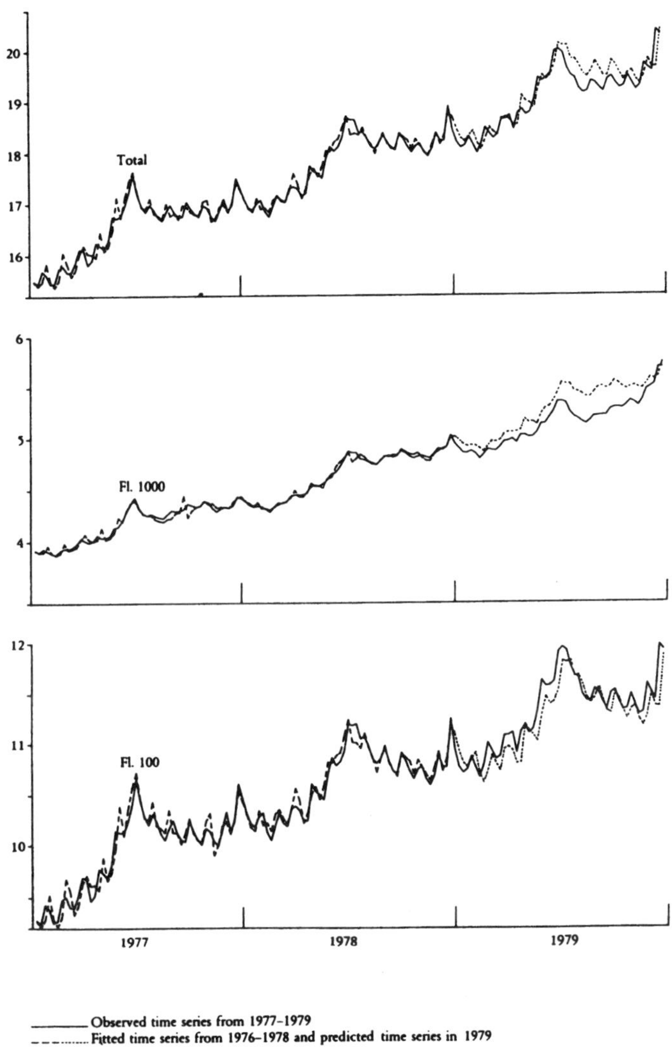


*Figure 13.1: Fitted model for weekly bank-note series 1977–1978 and forecasts 1979 (end-of-the-week figures in billions of guilders)*

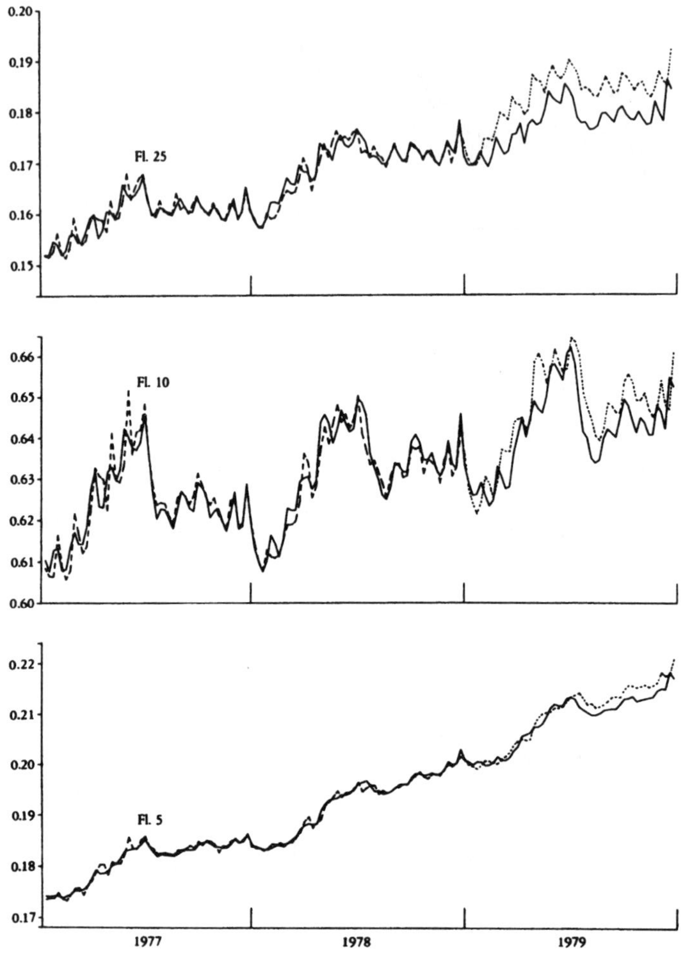


*Figure 13.1: (continued)*

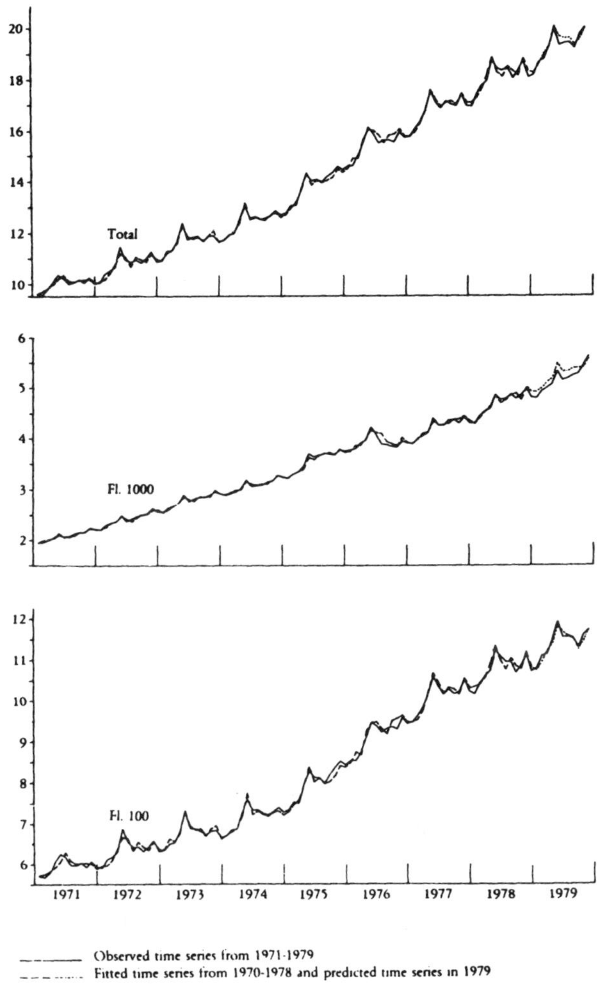


*Figure 13.2: Fitted model for monthly bank-note series 1971–1978 and forecasts 1979 (end-of-the-month figures in billions of guilders)*

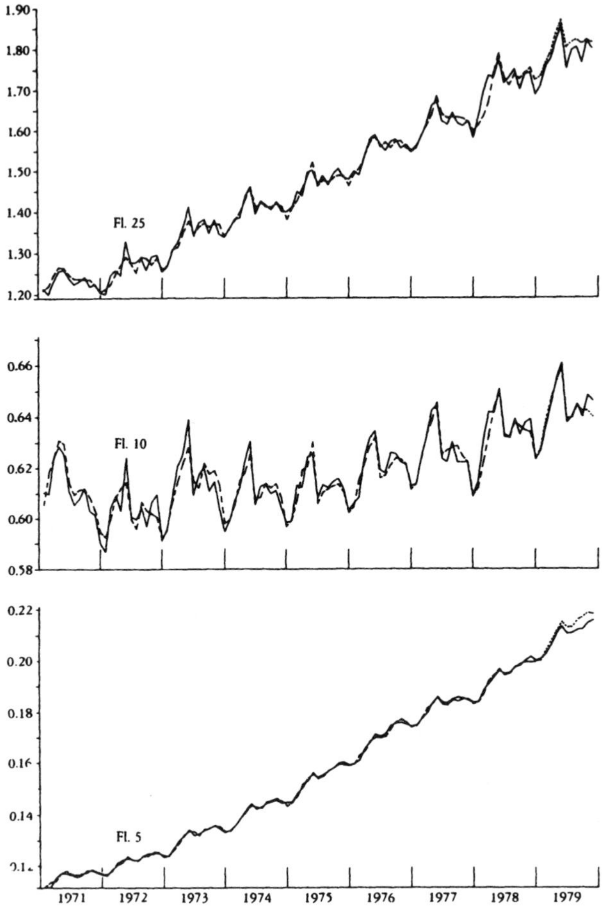


*Figure 13.2: (continued)*

*Table 13.7: Estimation results for each denomination with monthly data 1970–1978 (end-of-month figures, numbers × 1000)*

| Denomination | Fitted ARIMA models | Sample statistics | |
|---|---|---|---|
| $f$ 5 | $(1-0.28L^3)\nabla\nabla_{12}\ln B_5 = (1-0.19L)(1-0.87L^{12})a_t$ | $\hat{\sigma}_a = 0.00558$ | |
| | (2.8) (1.8) (26.5) | | $\chi^2_{33} = 37.2$ |
| $f$ 10 | $(1+0.68L+0.48L^2)\nabla\nabla_{12}\ln B_{10} = (1+0.19L^5)(1-0.90L^{12})a_t$ | $\hat{\sigma}_a = 0.00701$ | |
| | (7.3) (5.0) (1.8) (24.2) | | $\chi^2_{32} = 38.6$ |
| $f$ 25 | $(1+0.74L+0.45L^2)\nabla\nabla_{12}\ln B_{25} = (1+0.40L^9)(1-0.87L^{12})a_t$ | $\hat{\sigma}_a = 0.01145$ | |
| | (7.9) (4.8) (4.0) (20.4) | | $\chi^2_{32} = 31.4$ |
| $f$ 100 | $(1+0.52L+0.32L^2-0.20L^3)\nabla\nabla_{12}\ln B_{100} = (1+0.18L^5+0.27L^9)a_t$ | $\hat{\sigma}_a = 0.01265$ | |
| | (5.0) (2.8) (2.0) (1.8) (3.0) | | $\chi^2_{31} = 25.9$ |
| $f$ 1000 | $\nabla\nabla_{12}\ln B_{1000} = (1-0.28L^4)(1-0.86L^{12})a_t$ | $\hat{\sigma} = 0.01163$ | |
| | (2.8) (25.1) | | $\chi^2_{34} = 25.8$ |

*Note:* The figures in parentheses are $t$-values, $\hat{\sigma}_a$ is the standard deviation of the residuals, $\chi^2_n$ is the portmanteau test statistic with $n$ degrees of freedom.

*Table 13.8: Estimation results for the single-input single-output transfer model for each denomination with monthly data 1970–1978*

| Denomination | Fitted transfer models | Sample statistics |
|---|---|---|
| *f* 5 | $\nabla\nabla_{12}\ln B_5 = \underset{(0.2)}{-0.00009} + \underset{(2.0)}{0.06}\nabla\nabla_{12}\ln IP + \dfrac{(1-\underset{(1.8)}{0.19}L)(1-\underset{(4.8)}{0.47}L^{12})}{(1-\underset{(2.5)}{0.26}L^3)}a_t$ | $\chi^2_{35} = 21.8$<br>$\tilde{\chi}^2_{33} = 28.5$<br>$\hat{\sigma}_a = 0.00698$ |
| *f* 10 | $\nabla\nabla_{12}\ln B_{10} = \underset{(0.8)}{0.00037} + \dfrac{\underset{(3.5)}{0.11}}{(1+\underset{(3.1)}{0.57}L)}\nabla\nabla_{12}\ln IP + (1-\underset{(7.8)}{0.57}L+\underset{(6.2)}{0.50}L^3)(1-\underset{(4.6)}{0.47}L^{12})a_t$ | $\chi^2_{34} = 16.7$<br>$\tilde{\chi}^2_{33} = 39.3$<br>$\hat{\sigma}_a = 0.00807$ |
| *f* 25 | $\nabla\nabla_{12}\ln B_{25} = \underset{(2.2)}{0.00055} + \dfrac{\underset{(4.4)}{0.19}}{(1+\underset{(3.4)}{0.62}L)}\nabla\nabla_{12}\ln IP + (1-\underset{(9.2)}{0.69}L+\underset{(2.5)}{0.19}L^3-\underset{(4.6)}{0.35}L^7)a_t$ | $\chi^2_{34} = 29.1$<br>$\tilde{\chi}^2_{33} = 50.3$<br>$\hat{\sigma}_a = 0.01335$ |
| *f* 100 | $\nabla\nabla_{12}\ln B_{100} = \underset{(0.2)}{0.00023} + \dfrac{\underset{(4.4)}{0.22}}{(1+\underset{(2.4)}{0.46}L)}\nabla\nabla_{12}\ln IP + (1-\underset{(6.8)}{0.57}L+\underset{(3.7)}{0.31}L^3)a_t$ | $\chi^2_{34} = 35.1$<br>$\tilde{\chi}^2_{34} = 41.5$<br>$\hat{\sigma}_a = 0.01278$ |
| *f* 1000 | $\nabla\nabla_{12}\ln B_{1000} = \underset{(0.2)}{-0.00014} + (\underset{(2.1)}{0.12}L-\underset{(3.0)}{0.17}L^3)\nabla\nabla_{12}\ln IP + (1-\underset{(2.7)}{0.30}L^4)(1-\underset{(3.4)}{0.38}L^{12})a_t$ | $\chi^2_{34} = 29.4$<br>$\tilde{\chi}^2_{34} = 26.9$<br>$\hat{\sigma}_a = 0.01305$ |

*Note:* The figures in parentheses are *t*-values, $\hat{\sigma}_a$ is the standard error of residuals, $\chi^2_n$ and $\tilde{\chi}^2_n$ are the statistics with $n$ degrees of freedom for cross-correlation and autocorrelation respectively.

*Table 13.9: Sample statistics of the two monthly models*

| Denomination | ARIMA model $\hat{\sigma}_a \times 10^{-5}$ | transfer model $\hat{\sigma}_a \times 10^{-5}$ | Gain % | Significant peaks in cross-correlation function[a] | |
|---|---|---|---|---|---|
| | | | | lag | lead |
| ƒ 5 | 556 | 698 | −25 | 0 | |
| ƒ 10 | 701 | 807 | −15 | 0,1 | 3, 22, 25 |
| ƒ 25 | 1 145 | 1 335 | −17 | 0,1 | 2, 3, 25 |
| ƒ 100 | 1 265 | 1 278 | −1 | 0 | 3, 18, 22, 25 |
| ƒ 1000 | 1 163 | 1 305 | −12 | 1,3 | 9, 15, 25 |

*Note:* [a] Among $\nabla\nabla_{12} \ln B_{it}$ and $\nabla\nabla_{12} \ln IP_t$.

5% wished for both; 15% had no preference.

About 50% of the population makes use of guaranteed cheques. When a distinction is made as to income group, this percentage rises with the income. Only 8% pays an amount over *f* 100 in cash, a percentage which hardly varies with the income. It must also be noted that smaller amounts are paid in cash only to a limited extent. It goes without saying that no conclusions can be drawn as to whether non-cash payments are made by giro or by means of guaranteed cheques. The results of the survey indicate that users of guaranteed cheques are more prepared to accept the withdrawal of a bank-note than those who never make use of this way of payment. Likewise, the need for expansion – notably for notes of *f* 50 and *f* 500 – is greater among users of guaranteed cheques.

When the answers of the survey are grouped according to age it appears that there is no connection between preference and age. A breakdown according to profession also offers little new information: the degree of satisfaction of, for example, self-employed and that of others hardly differs. Only the *f* 5 note seemed to score better with the small self-employed.

The national survey confirms the picture that was presented by an internal survey of December 1977. It offers some empirical evidence for the view that the present bank-note series may be supplemented with a *f* 50 and a *f* 500 note (see Fase (1978a)). A surprising outcome is the demand for a *f* 2.50 note. As for withdrawals, it appears that, contrary to the results of the internal survey, a considerably larger percentage of people are prepared to give up the *f* 1000 note (15% against less than 3% in the internal survey). With regard to the *f* 5 note the percentages are more or less the same.[1]

## 13.6 Summary and Conclusion

This chapter presents three types of forecasts employed for different purposes at the bank. They have in common their focus on the denominations separately, but differ in methodology and time horizon. The causal or regression models explain the demand for bank-notes by national income. We have used this type of relationship for medium and long-run forecasts up to 1995. A notable problem with this method is that it requires additional forecasts on real income and the rate of inflation. Our general experience until now is that we have underestimated future development to some extent.

[1] Since this was written, notes of *f* 50 and *f* 500 and a coin of *f* 5 were introduced in the 1980s.

The ARIMA models, presented in Section 13.3, provide an alternative method of forecasting the bank-note circulation without requiring data on related variables. Forecasts of seasonal fluctuations are reasonably accurate. Extending the ARIMA model to a transfer model, however, does not improve the goodness of fit. The survey results reported in Section 13.5 indicate possible modifications of the supply of different denominations if the bank feels it necessary to respond to the preferences of the public. Of course this is typically a long-term problem, but one of which producers of bank-notes should be aware.

Forecasts of the time profile of the future bank-note circulation tells the management of the central bank what may happen if no action is taken. Therefore, the exercises of this chapter should be viewed in the wider perspective of integrating forecasting, decision-taking and the action system with the overall management activity. Thus the forecasting models in this chapter serve a management system that starts with predictions. To translate these into production plans requires additional information as on the life of bank-notes, which is to some extent a control variable (see Gillieson (1977) or Koeze (1979)).

# 14. Forecasting the Need for Coins: A Case Study for The Netherlands

## 14.1 Introduction

This chapter attempts to examine the future need for coins in The Netherlands. Conceptually, there is no difference between bank-notes and coins. The differences are mainly practical. First, unlike bank-notes, coins hardly return spontaneously to the issuer. This means that any addition demand for coins must be treated as equal to the growth in the need for coins. Thus, not only the growth of demand must be taken into account but also replacement of existing notes.

The second difference concerns the volume of the two types of currency. At the end of 1979, the share of coins in the total value of the currency in circulation was well over 5%. In terms of numbers, however, it was nearly 95%. From the point of view of production, total numbers are more significant than total value.

## 14.2 Coins and Bank-notes in The Netherlands

Figure 14.1 illustrates the circulation of coins in The Netherlands during the last 20 years. It shows that circulation of the low-denomination coins has fairly gradually increased in this period, with the 1-cent coin leveling off after 1971. This was entirely because of its being rationed from that time, which in 1975 resulted in a fixed supply of 15 million new 1-cent pieces a year, leading sometimes to its commanding a premium. The 1-guilder and the 2½-guilder graphs initially show a rather erratic movement, ending in a smoother path, however, after the first

Reprinted with permission from *Technological Forecasting and Social Change*, **19**(2) (March 1981), M.M.G. Fase, 'Forecasting the need for coins: A case study for The Netherlands', 147–159, ©1981 Elsevier Science Inc., 655 Ave. of the Americas, New York, N.Y. 10010-517.

few months of 1975. The jumps before 1975 express the changes that occurred during those years in respect of the two coins.

A somewhat different view is offered by the percentage composition of coins in circulation, as shown in Table 14.1.

First, Table 14.1 indicates that coins fitting in the decimal structure (i.e., the 1-cent and 10-cent pieces and the guilders) are relatively more important than the other coins. It is interesting to see that this picture has been maintained over the years and, moreover, deviates from that for bank-notes. In 1950 the lowest denomination note counted for the largest share of the total number of bank-notes, while the share of the other denominations steadily declined with increasing size. In 1979, this picture had disappeared entirely and the *f* 100 note had become the most dominant one. Apparently and unlike for coins, the relative order of importance of different denominations is no invariable principle over time.

Second, Table 14.1 implies a declining average nominal value since World War II. In 1950, the calculated average value per coin or currency note was nearly *f* 0.25. In 1979, this was almost *f* 0.20, showing a decline of 20%. This is quite in contrast to the movement of the average value of bank-notes outstanding, which over 30 years doubled from over *f* 32 in 1950, to *f* 66 at the end of 1979. Over that period, however, the index of consumer prices went up fourfold. In principle, the explanation of this diverging movement is the same: the shift in structure. Bank-notes offer a fairly large opportunity to introduce substantially higher denominations. In this connection, the movements in national income, standing as a proxy for the flow of transactions, is of great importance, as reflected in the diverging income elasticities measured with notes.[1]

Coins are properly called fractional currency or small change. This implies, among other things, that the frequency distribution of the size of transactions and of the number of transactions around the mean is probably more important than their absolute size. There is little ground to assume that the frequency distribution of the transactions around the mean has changed radically over time. As to coins, the decline of average value, therefore, has less to do with inflation or the trend of income than with the fact that only the two larger pieces – the 1-guilder and 2½-guilder coins – have lost significance as a means of payment. After all, this is the same phenomenon as observed for bank-notes. Incidentally, the picture is sensitive including, or not, the 1-cent coin, as shown in Table 14.2.

If we leave the 1-cent coin out of account, then, unlike bank-notes, their average value and distribution over the various denominations ap-

1 See Fase (1981).

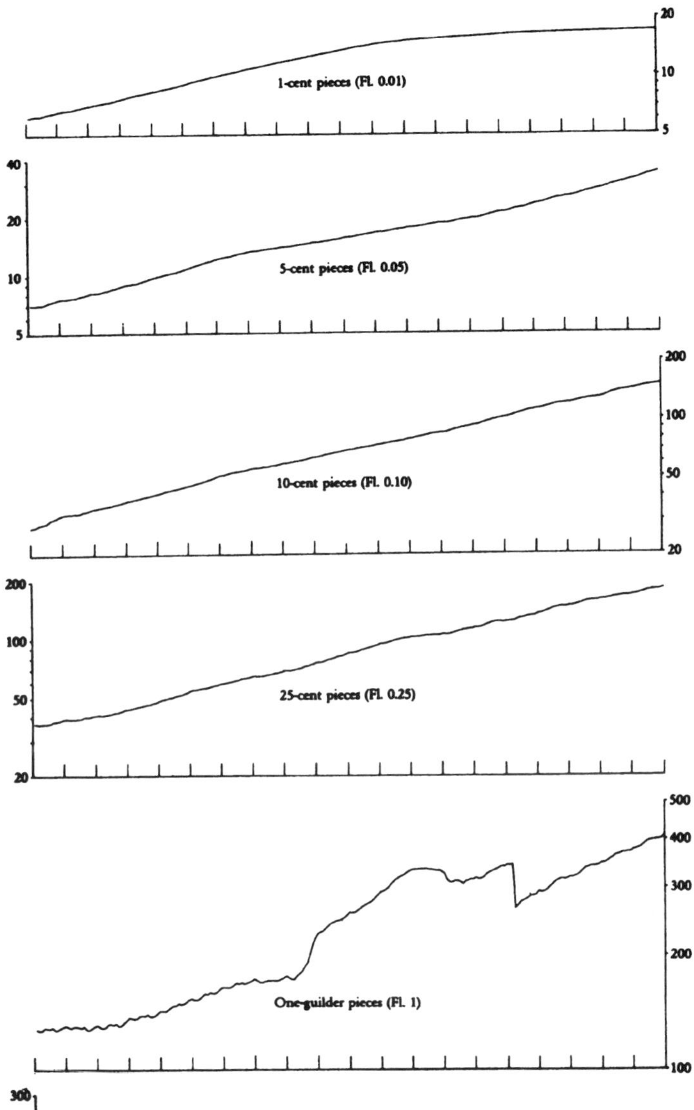


*Figure 14.1: Coin circulation 1960–1979 (end-of-the-month figures in millions of guilders)*

*Table 14.1: Percentage composition of coins in circulation*

| Type of coin | 1950 | 1960 | 1970 | 1975 | 1979 |
|---|---|---|---|---|---|
| *f* 0.01 | 53.3 | 45.8 | 45.3 | 40.9 | 33.9 |
| *f* 0.05 | 2.8 | 10.3 | 10.3 | 11.3 | 13.6 |
| *f* 0.10 | 24.3 | 21.8 | 22.4 | 26.7 | 28.7 |
| *f* 0.25 | 4.9 | 10.5 | 11.5 | 13.0 | 14.2 |
| *f* 1.00 | 10.9 | 8.8 | 8.8 | 7.0 | 7.9 |
| *f* 2.50 | 3.8 | 2.8 | 1.7 | 1.1 | 1.7 |
| Total % | 100 | 100 | 100 | 100 | 100 |
| Total number (million) | 1 383.9 | 1 481.0 | 3 293.5 | 4 180.2 | 5 212.7 |

*Notes:* The data on the 1-guilder and the 2½-guilder pieces include currency notes of the same denomination. Although their number was important in the 1950s, it is quantitatively neglibible now. In 1979, the percentage shares were 0.09 and 0.06, respectively.

pears to be fairly robust for inflation.

As far as the annual growth rates of coins are concerned, Table 14.3 more or less confirms the picture emerging from Table 14.1: fairly constant growth rates for the 5-, 10- and 25-cent pieces and heavily fluctuation growth rates for the higher value coins. The sharp deceleration shown for the 1-cent coin is entirely due to the alteration in production policy from demand oriented to supply determined. It is striking that the average growth rate of the *f* 5 note is almost identical with that of the 5-, 10-, and 25-cent pieces.

*Table 14.2: Average value of coins and notes in circulation*

| | 1950 | 1960 | 1970 | 1975 | 1979 |
|---|---|---|---|---|---|
| All coins | 0.25 | 0.22 | 0.19 | 0.17 | 0.20 |
| All coins except 1-cent pieces | 0.52 | 0.40 | 0.34 | 0.27 | 0.29 |
| Bank-notes | 32.40 | 38.60 | 50.60 | 60.30 | 66.20 |
| Consumer price index (1975 = 100) | 32 | 66 | 66 | 100 | 126 |

*Table 14.3: Average annual percentage growth rate of the number of coins and notes in circulation*

| Denomination | 1959–1969 | 1959–1979 | 1969–1979 |
|---|---|---|---|
| *f* 0.01 | 5.2 | 8.1 | 2.4 |
| *f* 0.05 | 8.4 | 8.4 | 8.4 |
| *f* 0.10 | 8.8 | 9.4 | 8.1 |
| *f* 0.25 | 8.4 | 8.7 | 8.1 |
| *f* 1.00 | 5.9 | 7.1 | 4.8 |
| *f* 2.50 | 4.3 | 2.9 | 5.7 |
| *f* 5.00 | - | - | 8.2 |
| *f* 10.00 | 0.7 | 1.0 | 0.0 |

## 14.3 General Reflection on Forecasting

Although this chapter is intended to be nontechnical, it might be useful to present here a brief review of the available forecasting techniques from which forecaster and manager must choose. These methods differ in complexity and the level of sophistication as well as in the amount of statistical expertise required.

A first classification is obtained by contrasting subjective with objective forecasting methods. Subjective methods are methods using procedures which are not well specified and depend entirely on the transformation of inputs into forecasts in the forcaster's mind. Intentions data and responses in opinion surveys are cases in point. Obviously, this type of prediction does not meet the criterion of unambiguousness, which requires that it must be clear, under which observable circumstances the prediction is fulfilled or not.[2] Objective methods employ a well-specified procedure to generate forecasts in such a way that, ideally, other researchers can reproduce the analysis and obtain the same result. Subjective methods are likely to be predominant in long-term predictions and objective methods are apt to be used to support or check existing ideas.

Within the class of objective methods, a further distinction can be drawn between causal and noncausal or historical methods. Methods in the latter class rely on the projection into the future of patterns observed within past data on the variable to be forecast. Causal methods take account of the likely impact of one or more external variables based on

[2] See e.g. Dantzig (1952), Theil (1958), and Cramer (1978).

the projection into the future of a relationship observed in recorded data.

It should be noted that both approaches rely on historical stability. Noncausal methods look for stability in the internal structure of the data, while causal methods look for stability in relationships involving two or more sets of data. The principal advantage of causal methods is that they enable account to be taken of likely changes in the trend while historical methods rest on the present information content of the data and are unable to do so. Furthermore, with causal models various alternative possibilities for the future can be examined by varying the assumed path for the external variable.

This suggests that historical methods are probably more useful in shorter time spans. As far as historical methods are concerned, exponential smoothing and deseasonalizing (moving averaging) models are the best known. A more general approach, which is becoming quite popular now, is the univariate Box–Jenkins model.[3] If we are to assign a ranking to the above-mentioned forecasting methods, we believe the Box–Jenkins approach scores low in terms of cost and intelligibility, but perhaps high in short-run prediction accuracy.

The causal methods are the classical econometric approach and the extensions of the Box–Jenkins approach to the transfer function. Application of these methods requires a good insight into the causal relationship and the availability of data on appropriate explanatory variables. An obvious advantage of the econometric methods is that they are relatively easy to apply. However, the number of simplifying assumptions required by the econometric method may reduce its practicability as the sole instrument of forecasting the circulation of coins in the long-run.

## 14.4 The Circulation of Coins in the Short-run

There are various ways of generating a forecast. One method is to estimate the demand for each denomination and to use the estimation equation as a predictor. The total circulation of coins will then be obtained as the total of all single denominations. A possible drawback of this method is that a fall in the number of coins of one particular denomination will not easily be predicted when that of the others is rising. A second method explains the total value of coins in circulation and attempts to allocate this total to the available denominations. Although explanation of the total seems an attractive approach, it is not simple to find a satisfactory solution for the allocation over the various denomina-

[3] See Box and Jenkins (1970). An application on forecasting the demand for bank-notes is presented in Fase (1981). See also Cave and Fase (1980).

tions. Considering the steadily growing quantity of coins in circulation, as shown in Table 14.1, the objection against estimating single equations should not be given too much weight. Table 14.1 furthermore suggests a clear underlying trend with small fluctuations around it. It justifies a time series model for short-term forecasting. This is of particular importance for scheduling the demand to be met from stocks and the planning of production when the physical capacity of the mint is by and large fixed. In long-term forecasting new machinery may be installed and the structure of the coin and note circulation may be radically changed. In that case, forecasts based on the present and immediate past seem to be inappropriate and causal methods appear more useful than historical ones.

It is generally agreed that it is desirable to forecast demand a year in advance. To do so for the demand for coins, we postulate an autoregressive moving average or ARIMA model of the following mathematical form

$$\phi_p(L)\Phi_p(L^S)\nabla^d\nabla_S^D \ln C_{it} = \theta_0 + \theta_q(L)\Theta_Q(L^S)a_t, \tag{14.1}$$

where $\phi_p(L)$ and $\theta_q(L)$ are scalar polynomials of order $p$ and $q$, respectively in the backward shift operator $L$, with $L^k x_t = x_{t-k}, C_{it}$ the number of coins of denomination $i$ in circulation at the end of period $t$, and $a_t$ a serially independent random shock with zero mean and constant variance (or zero-mean white noise, as called by process engineers). The difference operator is defined by $\nabla = 1 - L, \nabla_S = 1 - L^S$, with $d$ and $D$ integers. The polynomials $\Phi_p(L^S)$ and $\Theta_Q(L^S)$ take into account seasonal variation with period $S$ so that $S = 12$ for monthly data. The $\theta_0$ is a constant term. The seasonal differencing operator $\nabla_S$ converts a series, which has a nonstationary seasonal component, into a stationary series.

We have used monthly data to estimate the ARIMA model. In fitting model (14.1) to the data, an iterative approach is adopted which encompasses three stages. To begin, the postulated model is identified, i.e., appropriate values for $p$, $d$, $q$, $P$, $D$, and $Q$ are chosen according to cross-correlation and partial autocorrelations derived from the data. In the second stage, the tentatively entertained model is fitted to the data, i.e., its parameters are estimated. In the final stage, diagnostic checks are applied to examine the adequacy of the model to describe the data. If any inadequacy is found, the cycle is started again. It is beyond the scope of this chapter to go at length into the intricacies of the computational procedure. For details we refer to the work of Box and Jenkins. We proceed to our estimates now, obtained by fitting model (14.1).

Table 14.4 sets out the estimation results of model (14.1) fitted to end-of-month data covering 1970–1978 for the 5-, 10- and 25-cent pieces

*Table 14.4: Estimation results for each denomination with monthly data (end-of-month figures)*

| Type of coin | Sample period | Fitted model | Sample statistics | |
|---|---|---|---|---|
| 5-cent | 1970:1–1978:12 | $(1-0.46L)(1-0.57L^{12})\nabla \ln C_t = 0.0015 + (1-0.18L^4)a_t$ | $\chi^2_{21} = 25.1$ | $\hat{\sigma}_a = 0.0025$ |
| | | (5.09) (6.72) (3.77) (1.77) | | |
| 10-cent | 1970:1–1978:12 | $(1-0.33L)(1-0.72L^{12})\nabla \ln C_t = 0.0012 + (1+0.17L^4)a_t$ | $\chi^2_{21} = 17.8$ | $\hat{\sigma}_a = 0.0022$ |
| | | (3.50) (9.47) (3.07) (1.76) | | |
| 25-cent | 1970:1–1978:12 | $(1-0.41L)\nabla_{12}\nabla \ln C_t = (1+0.40L^3)(1-\ 0.84L^{12})a_t$ | $\chi^2_{21} = 20.8$ | $\hat{\sigma}_a = 0.0028$ |
| | | (4.25) (4.06) (20.69) | | |
| 1-guilder | 1975:3–1979:6 | $\nabla_{12}\nabla \ln C_t = (1+\ 0.81L^{11})a_t$ | $\chi^2_{23} = 16.6$ | $\sigma_a = 0.0034$ |
| | | (10.95) | | |
| 2½-guilder | 1975:3–1979:6 | $(1-0.40L)\nabla_{12}\nabla \ln C_t = (1+0.36L^6)a_t$ | $\chi^2_{22} = 11.1$ | $\sigma_a = 0.0070$ |
| | | (2.63) (2.30) | | |

*Note:* The figures in parentheses are $t$-values, $\hat{\sigma}_a$ is the standard deviation of the residuals, $\chi^2_n$ is the portmanteau test statistic with $n$ degrees of freedom.

and 1975:3–1979:6 for the two largest coins of 1- and 2½-guilder.[4] As the supply of the 1-cent pieces is fixed by the mint rather than by public demand, we did not estimate an ARIMA model for the smallest coin. The fitted models suggest two sets of similar models: one for the 5- and 10-cent pieces, another for the other denominations. The series have been differenced to obtain stationarity. The fact that the $\chi^2$ statistic falls outside the critical region with a probability of at least 20% indicates that the hypothesis of model adequacy should not be rejected.

The estimated models have been used to forecast the circulation of coins. To illustrate the forecasting procedure, we consider the equation for 10-cent pieces as an example. The $l$-period-ahead forecast $\hat{C}_{t+l}$ may be written as a weighted sum of actual and predicted values. That is,

$$\begin{aligned}\ln \hat{C}_{t+l} = {} & 0.0012 + 1.33 \ln C_{t+l-1} - 0.33 \ln C_{t+l-2} \\ & + 0.72 \ln C_{t+l-12} - 0.96 \ln C_{t+l-13} + 0.24 \ln C_{t+l-14} \\ & + 0.17 a_{t+l-3}. \end{aligned} \tag{14.2}$$

Similar equations may be derived for the other denominations. Using these equations, we compute the *ex post* forecast values for lead times up to 12 months. The forecasts, given in Appendix 14.A, indicate a fairly good predictive power with a slight tendency to overpredict the time profile of the number of 5-cent, 25-cent, 1- and 2½-guilder pieces. For the 10-cent pieces the forecast is systematically too low.

It is interesting to compare the forecasts generated by the ARIMA models with the naive forecasts obtained by extrapolating the average annual growth rate over the period 1969–1979 for the small coins and the 1976–1979 growth rate for the 1- and 2½-guilder pieces. We focus on the accuracy of these simple forecasts relative to the predictions over the same period derived from the ARIMA model. To evaluate the forecast quality we have used the inequality coefficient $U$, where

$$U = \left( \frac{\sum_1^T (\hat{y}_t - y_t)^2}{\sum_T^2 y_t^2} \right)^{\frac{1}{2}}$$

with $\hat{y}_t$ the predicted value, $y_t$ the realized value, and $T$ the number of observations. $U$ measures the relative success of the model. Obviously, $U = 0$ implies perfect forecasts. Table 14.5 presents the computed values of the $U$ statistic for both the forecasts generated with the ARIMA models and with the simple extrapolative model. The results of Table 14.5

[4] The 10-guilder coins have been ignored because of their commemorative character.

indicate that the ARIMA model serves better for the 5-cent, 25-cent and $2^1/_2$-guilder pieces, but worse for the 10-cent and 1-guilder pieces. However, this result does not necessarily mean that the simple prediction model is to be preferred for the two denominations because the result is very sensitive to the selected growth rate.

## 14.5 The Circulation of Coins in the Long-run

It seems absurd to consider detailed forecasts of the circulation of coins beyond a period of five years. But, because of the fact that the denominational set-up may be considered a decision variable as the production of coins requires investment decisions, there are important reasons to give some thought to the long-run evolution of the circulation of coins. It seems best to start with the observation that in The Netherlands the proportion of coins in the note circulation is approximately stable and that the frequency distribution of different denominations has not changed either way over the last few years. These two assumptions that seem quite reasonable offer a framework to determine the circulation of coins, provided a forecast of the note circulation is made. For this we may draw on the forecast for the demand for bank-notes to the year 1995.[5] The basis of these forecasts is the assumed stability of the relationship between the value in circulation and nominal national income (or a similar variable, like consumption). The prediction results are displayed in Table 14.6, for three different hypothetical growth rates of nominal national income.

The results in Table 14.6, which are aggregated totals of our forecasts per denomination, show the importance of the assumed growth rate of nominal national income. This is dependent on both real growth and the rate of inflation, which are not easy to forecast for the long-run. Therefore, the forecasts presented in Table 14.6 should be considered to be indicative of future development given the underlying assumptions. The boundary between notes and coins is mainly determined by tradition but might be subject to change and, as political decisions may be involved, might at times be not closely predictable. However, to be able to forecast, we assume the future breakdown between notes and coins to be constant and equal to the average percentage in 1975–1979 of 5.5%. As a result, the predicted circulation of coins follows immediately from Table 14.6 and is shown in Table 14.7.

From the production point of view, the number of coins is more relevant than the total value of circulation. This means that we have

---

[5] See Fase (1981).

*Table 14.5: Inequality coefficients of two forecasting models for coins*

| Type of coin | ARIMA prediction | Simple prediction[a] | Forecasting period |
|---|---|---|---|
| 5-cent | 0.00815 | 0.03065 | 1979:1–1979:12 |
| 10-cent | 0.01947 | 0.01246 | 1979:1–1979:12 |
| 25-cent | 0.00910 | 0.00948 | 1979:1–1979:12 |
| 1-guilder | 0.00916 | 0.00690 | 1979:7–1980:3 |
| 2 1/2-guilder | 0.01849 | 0.06407 | 1979:7–1980:3 |

*Note:* [a] The employed growth rates are 8.10%, 8.08%, 8.39% (annual averages over 1969–1979) for the small coins and 17.54% and 24.80% (annual averages over 1976–1979) for the two largest denominations.

*Table 14.6: Predicted total bank-note circulation with three alternative growth rates of nominal national income*

| Year | Assumed growth rate | | | | | |
|---|---|---|---|---|---|---|
| | 5% | | 7 1/2% | | 10% | |
| 1980 | 19 000 | (6.5) | 19 000 | (6.5) | 19 000 | (6.5) |
| 1985 | 22 900 | (6.1) | 25 200 | (6.0) | 27 700 | (5.9) |
| 1990 | 28 000 | (5.9) | 34 300 | (5.7) | 42 100 | (5.5) |
| 1995 | 34 600 | (5.7) | 47 500 | (5.5) | 65 300 | (5.3) |

*Notes:* The figures in parentheses are the predicted currency ratios (% of nominal national income).

*Table 14.7: Predicted circulation of coins with three different growth rates of nominal national income (millions of guilders)*

| Year | 5% | 7 1/2% | 10% |
|---|---|---|---|
| 1985 | 1 260 | 1 390 | 1 520 |
| 1990 | 1 540 | 1 890 | 2 320 |
| 1995 | 1 900 | 2 100 | 3 590 |

to design a reasonable method to transform the total values shown in Table 14.7 into numbers of coins of different denominations. Our discussion of coins and bank-notes in The Netherlands has shown that the percentage breakdown of coins in circulation, unlike that of notes, is fairly stable. Thus, there is sufficient inertia in the system to make a reasonable forecast. Ignoring currency notes and the silver *f* 10 coins, we postulate in Table 14.8 the breakdown of the value of coins to hold for the future. With the exception of the *f* 2.50 piece, these figures are averages over the period 1975–1979. As the share of the *f* 2.50 coin increased drastically in recent years, we took 1979 as the forecasting base for this denomination. The resulting number of coins has been relegated to Appendix 14.B. Our exercises show that the percentage increase in the number of coins is slightly lower than the assumed increase of nominal income, corresponding to an elasticity of about 0.7 (for bank-notes, about 0.75).

Some comments may be made on the method used above. The method is based on an estimate of the bank-note ratio, various assumptions concerning the growth of nominal national income, and the assumed constancy of the ratio of coins to bank-notes. This constancy is open to question. For example, our extrapolation does not take into account the possibility of the abolishment of the 1-cent piece. Likewise, no attention has been given to the introduction of new coins or to the replacement of bank-notes by coins of the same denomination. Such replacement seems to become more likely in view of the sharp fall in the average real value of bank-notes.

*Table 14.8: Percentage composition of the total value of coins*

| Denomination | Percentage share |
|---|---|
| *f* 0.01 | 1.90 |
| *f* 0.05 | 3.38 |
| *f* 0.10 | 14.98 |
| *f* 0.25 | 18.56 |
| *f* 1.00 | 39.66 |
| *f* 2.50 | 21.52 |
| | 100.00 |

## 14.6 Concluding Remarks

This chapter intended to provide information on the methodology and results of short- and long-term forecasting of the circulation of coins, keeping in mind the results obtained for bank-notes. It does not cover new ground, but attempts to establish a possible framework for different time spans. Forecasting is an important element in the decision-making process. Managers are not normally interested in the ins and outs of sophisticated forecasting techniques, but rather in their potential usefulness to operate their organization more effectively and efficiently. It is here that forecasting has to make its greatest contribution.

The ARIMA models presented in this chapter are considered an appropriate forecasting method for the short-run. The forecasts are reasonably accurate. For the very long-run, we use a mixture of causal models and simple allocation procedures to generate forecasts up to the year 1995. A long-run forecast tells the management of a mint, for example, what will happen if no action is taken. As we already know from the Bible, a forecast becomes self-denying as soon as action is taken. This illustrates very well the major purpose of any long-run forecasting exercise, i.e., to get an idea of what lies ahead, thus enabling managers to anticipate critical situations which could otherwise take us by surprise. 'Facing the future is mastering the probable and managing the unpredictable' is also a valuable message to producers of coins.

Appendix 14.A Monthly ARIMA predictions for 1979–1980, different denominations (thousands of guilders)

| | 1979 | | | | | | | | | | | | 1980 | | |
|---|---|---|---|---|---|---|---|---|---|---|---|---|---|---|---|
| | Jan. | Feb. | Mar. | Apr. | May | June | July | Aug. | Sept. | Oct. | Nov. | Dec. | Jan. | Feb. | Mar. |
| *f* 0.05 | | | | | | | | | | | | | | | |
| I actual | 31 839 | 32 078 | 32 336 | 32 638 | 33 086 | 33 456 | 33 834 | 34 128 | 34 401 | 34 718 | 34 999 | 35 407 | | | |
| II prediction | 31 863 | 32 102 | 32 374 | 32 647 | 32 995 | 33 283 | 33 547 | 33 843 | 34 088 | 34 334 | 34 551 | 34 909 | | | |
| III prediction error (%) | −0.1 | −0.1 | −0.1 | −0.0 | 0.3 | 0.5 | 0.8 | 0.8 | 0.9 | 1.1 | 1.3 | 1.4 | | | |
| *f* 0.10 | | | | | | | | | | | | | | | |
| I | 140 989 | 141 939 | 142 944 | 143 679 | 144 809 | 145 945 | 146 487 | 147 180 | 147 631 | 148 266 | 148 551 | 149 694 | | | |
| II | 140 885 | 142 003 | 143 487 | 145 103 | 147 046 | 148 257 | 149 194 | 150 467 | 151 373 | 152 284 | 152 848 | 153 829 | | | |
| III | 0.1 | −0.0 | −0.4 | −1.0 | −1.5 | −1.6 | −1.8 | −2.2 | −2.5 | −2.7 | −2.9 | −2.8 | | | |
| *f* 0.25 | | | | | | | | | | | | | | | |
| I | 171 580 | 172 718 | 174 265 | 175 770 | 177 717 | 179 642 | 179 947 | 181 012 | 181 815 | 182 235 | 182 684 | 184 883 | | | |
| II | 170 706 | 171 253 | 172 301 | 173 876 | 175 800 | 177 283 | 178 456 | 179 764 | 180 521 | 180 864 | 181 190 | 183 285 | | | |
| III | 0.5 | 0.8 | 1.1 | 1.1 | 1.1 | 1.3 | 0.8 | 0.7 | 0.7 | 0.8 | 0.8 | 0.9 | | | |
| *f* 1.00[a] | | | | | | | | | | | | | | | |
| I | | | | | | | 398 118 | 398 838 | 399 724 | 400 088 | 401 890 | 409 958 | 410 710 | 414 360 | 420 957 |
| II | | | | | | | 398 834 | 400 873 | 401 913 | 401 756 | 402 037 | 407 746 | 407 054 | 409 853 | 412 834 |
| III | | | | | | | −0.1 | −0.5 | −0.3 | −0.4 | −0.0 | 0.5 | 0.9 | 1.3 | 1.9 |
| *f* 2.50[a] | | | | | | | | | | | | | | | |
| I | | | | | | | 204 162 | 207 457 | 210 254 | 210 543 | 217 729 | 223 185 | 228 458 | 233 466 | 240 107 |
| II | | | | | | | 203 292 | 205 459 | 207 130 | 209 379 | 210 934 | 221 062 | 224 673 | 229 005 | 233 188 |
| III | | | | | | | 0.4 | 1.0 | 1.5 | 0.6 | 3.1 | 1.0 | 1.7 | 1.9 | 2.9 |

*Note:* [a] Coins and currency notes.

Appendix 14.B Predicted number of coins with different rates of expansion of nominal income

| | 1979 | 1985 | | | 1990 | | | 1995 | | |
|---|---|---|---|---|---|---|---|---|---|---|
| | | 5% | 7½% | 10% | 5% | 7½% | 10% | 5% | 7½% | 10% |
| Currency notes (millions) | | | | | | | | | | |
| *f* 1.00 | 4.9 | | | | | | | | | |
| *f* 2.50 | 3.3 | | | | | | | | | |
| Coins | | | | | | | | | | |
| *f* 10.00 | 10.6 | | | | | | | | | |
| Subtotal | 18.8 | 20 | 20 | 20 | 20 | 20 | 20 | 20 | 20 | 20 |
| *f* 0.01 | 1 768.9 | 2 170 | 2 410 | 2 670 | 2 700 | 3 360 | 4 170 | 3 390 | 4 740 | 6 600 |
| *f* 0.05 | 708.1 | 770 | 860 | 950 | 960 | 1 190 | 1 480 | 1 210 | 1 690 | 2 350 |
| *f* 0.10 | 1 497.0 | 1 710 | 1 900 | 2 100 | 2 130 | 2 650 | 3 290 | 2 670 | 3 730 | 5 200 |
| *f* 0.25 | 739.5 | 850 | 940 | 1 040 | 1 050 | 1 310 | 1 630 | 1 320 | 1 850 | 2 580 |
| *f* 1.00 | 405.0 | 450 | 500 | 560 | 560 | 700 | 870 | 710 | 990 | 1 380 |
| *f* 2.50 | 86.0 | 100 | 110 | 120 | 120 | 150 | 190 | 150 | 210 | 300 |
| Subtotal | 5 204.5 | 6 050 | 6 720 | 7 440 | 7 520 | 9 360 | 11 630 | 9 450 | 13 210 | 18 410 |
| Total | 5 223.3 | 6 070 | 6 740 | 7 460 | 7 540 | 9 380 | 11 650 | 9 470 | 13 230 | 18 430 |

# Bibliography

Adekunle, J.O. (1968), 'The demand for money: Evidence from developed and less developed economies', *IMF Staff Papers*, **15**, 220–266.

Aigner, D.J. and A.S. Goldberger (1977), *Latent Variables in Socio-economic Models*, Amsterdam: North-Holland.

Aigner, D.J. and J.L. Simon (1970), 'A specification bias interpretation of cross-section vs. time series parameter estimates', *Western Economic Journal*, **8**, 144–161.

Aitchison, J. and J.A.C. Brown (1957), *The Lognormal Distribution*, Cambridge, U.K: Cambridge University Press.

Akerlof, G.A. and R.D. Milbourne (1978), 'New calculation of income and interest elasticities in Tobin's model of the transactions demand for money', *The Review of Economics and Statistics*, **60**, 541–546.

Akhtar, M.A. and B.H. Putnam (1980), 'Money demand and foreign exchange risk: The German case, 1972–1976', *Journal of Finance*, **35**, 787–794.

Al-Khuri, S. and S.M. Nsouli (1978), 'The speed of adjustment of the actual to the desired money stock', *European Economic Review*, **11**, 181–206.

Anderson, P.S. (1977), 'Currency in use and in hoards', *New England Economic Review* **8**(2), 21–30.

Anderson, W.H.L. (1964), *Corporate Finance and Fixed Investment: An Econometric Study*, Boston, Mass.: Harvard University Press.

Angeloni, I., C. Cottarelli, and A. Levy (1991), 'Cross-border deposits and monetary aggregates in the transition to EMU', Working Paper 91/114, IMF.

Arango, S. and M.I. Nadiri (1981), 'Demand for money in open economies', *Journal of Monetary Economics*, **7**, 69–83.

Artis, M.J., R.C. Bladen-Hovell, and W. Zhang (1993), 'A European money demand function', Technical Report, University of Manchester.

Artis, M.J. and M.K. Lewis (1984), 'How unstable is the demand for money in the United Kingdom?', *Economica*, **51**, 473–476.

Atkinson, P., A. Blundell-Wignall, M. Rondoni, and H. Ziegelschmidt (1984), 'The efficacy of monetary targeting: The stability of demand for money in major OECD countries', *OECD Economic Studies*, no. 3, 145–176.

Avery, R.B., F.E. Elliehausen, A.B. Kernickell, and P.A. Spindt (1986), 'The use of cash and transaction accounts by American families', *Federal Reserve Bulletin*, **72**, 87–108.

Baade, R.A. and N. Nazmi (1989), 'Currency substitution and money demand in the United States, West Germany and Japan', *Kredit und Kapital*, **22**, 363–374.

Baba, Y., D.F. Hendry, and R.M. Starr (1987), 'US money demand, 1960–1984', Discussion Paper 88-8, University of California.

Bakhoven, A.F. (1971), 'De verklaring van het renteniveau in Nederland', *Maandschrift Economie*, **35**, 577–588.

Banerjee, A.F., J.J. Dolado, D.F. Hendry, and G.W. Smith (1986), 'Exploring equilibrium relationships in econometrics through static models: Some Monte Carlo evidence', *Oxford Bulletin of Economics and Statistics*, **48**, 253–277.

Banerjee, B. (1973), 'The demand for money in India: A theoretical and empirical analysis', Departmental Memorandum 73, IMF.

Barnett, W.A. (1978), 'The user cost of money', *Economics Letters*, **1**, 145–149.

Barnett, W.A. (1980), 'Economic monetary aggregates: An application of index number and aggregation theory', *Journal of Econometrics*, **14**, 11–48.

Barnett, W.A. (1997), 'Which road leads to stable money demand?', *The Economic Journal*, **107**, 1171–1185.

Barnett, W.A., D. Fisher, and A. Serletis (1992), 'Consumer theory and the demand for money', *Journal of Economic Literature*, **30**, 2086–2119.

Barr, D. (1992), 'The demand for money in Europe – comment on Kremers and Lane', *IMF Staff Papers*, **39**, 718–729.

Barrett, R.J., M.R. Gray, and J.M. Parkin (1975), 'The demand for financial assets by the personal sector of the UK economy', in G.A. Renton (ed.), *Modelling the Economy*, London: Heinemann, pp. 500–532.

Baumol, W.J. (1952), 'The transactions demand for cash: An inventory theoretic approach', *Quarterly Journal of Economics*, **66**, 545–556.

Bekx, P. and G. Tullio (1989), 'A note on the European monetary system and the determination of the DM–dollar exchange rate', *Cahiers Économiques de Bruxelles*, no. 123, 329–343.

Beld, C.A. van den (1965), *Voorspelling en realisatie: De voorspellingen van het Centraal Planbureau in de jaren 1953–1963*, 's-Gravenhage: Staatsuitgeverij.

Beld, C.A. van den (1968), 'An experimental medium-term macro-model for the Dutch economy', in M.G. Kendall (ed.), *Mathematical Model Building in Economics and Industry*, London: C. Griffin, pp. 31–48.

Belongia, M.T. and K.A. Chrystal (1991), 'An admissible monetary aggregate for The United Kingdom', *The Review of Economics and Statistics*, **73**, 497–503.

Bennett, A. (1987), 'Wealth, expenditure and the demand for money: The case of France', Working Paper WP/87/26, IMF.

Bernanke, B.S. and A.S. Blinder (1988), 'Is it money or credit, or both, or neither?', *American Economic Review*, **78**, 435–451.

Bethenod, J.M. (1988), 'La stabilité de la demande de monnaie en france, 1964–1985: l'apport d'une reformulation du revenu permanent', *Revue d'Economie Politique*, **98**, 508–529.

Bierwag, G.O. and M.A. Grove (1968), 'Slutsky equations for assets', *Journal of Political Economy*, **76**, 114–127.

Blaug, M. *et al.* (1995), *The Quantity Theory of Money: From Locke to Keynes and Friedman*, Aldershot: Edward Elgar.

Blomgren-Hansen, N. (1974), *An Econometric Study of the Financial Sector in Denmark*, Ph. D. thesis, University of Pennsylvania, Philadephia.

Blommestein, H.J. and F.C. Palm (1982), 'Econometric specification analysis – an application to the aggregate demand for money in the Netherlands', in *Games, Economic Dynamics and Time Series analysis*, Wien-Würzburg: Physica, pp. 201–230.

Boeschoten, W.C., G.J. de Bondt, and J.A. Bikker (1995), 'EUROMON: Een macro-economisch model voor de Europese Unie', WO&E Research Memorandum 436, De Nederlandsche Bank.

Boeschoten, W.C. and M.M.G. Fase (1984), *The Volume of Payments and the Informal Economy in the Netherlands 1965–1982*, Dordrecht: Martinus Nijhoff Publishers.

Boeschoten, W.C. and M.M.G. Fase (1987), 'Betaalgedrag in Nederland (Dutch)', *Economisch-Statistische Berichten*, **72**, 780–786, 794.

Boeschoten, W.C. and M.M.G. Fase (1989), 'The way we pay with money', *Journal of Business and Economic Statistics*, **7**, 319–326, reprinted as Chapter 11 in this volume.

Bofinger, P., J. Reischle, and A. Schächter (1996), *Geldpolitik: Ziele, Institutionen, Strategien und Instrumente*, München: Vahlen.

Boissieu, C. de (1978), 'Pouvoirs et régulations monétaires', *Économies et Socieétés*, **1**.

Bomhoff, E.J. (1991), 'Stability of velocity in the major industrial countries: A Kalman Filter approach', *IMF Staff Papers*, **38**, 626–642.

Boorman, J.T. (1972), 'The evidence on the demand for money: Theoretical formulations and empirical results', in J.T. Boorman and T.M. Havrilesky (eds), *Money Supply, Money Demand, and Macroeconomic Models*, Boston, Mass.: Allyn and Bacon, pp. 248–291.

Boot, J.C.G., W. Feibes, and J.H.C. Lisman (1967), 'Further methods of derivation of quarterly figures from annual data', *Applied Statistics*, **16**, 65–75.

Bordes, C. and M.O. Strauss-Kahn (1989), 'Cointegration et demande de monnaie en france', *Cahiers Economiques et Monétaires, Banque de France*, **34**, 161–197.

Bordo, M.D. and E.U. Choudhri (1982), 'Currency substitution and the demand for money: Some evidence for Canada', *Journal of Money, Credit and Banking*, **14**, 48–57.

Boughton, J.M. (1979), 'Demand, for money in major OECD ccountries', *OECD Economic Outlook Occasional Studies*, no. 1, 35–57.

Boughton, J.M. (1981), 'Recent instability of the demand for money: An international perspective', *Southern Economic Journal*, **47**, 579–597.

Boughton, J.M. (1991), 'Long-run money demand in large industrial countries', *IMF Staff Papers*, **38**, 1–32.

Boughton, J.M. (1992), 'International comparisons of money demand: A review essay', *Open Economies Review*, **3**, 323–343.

Boughton, J.M. and G.S. Tavlas (1990), 'Modeling money demand in large industrial countries: Buffer stock and error correction approaches', *Journal of Policy Modeling*, **12**, 433–467.

Boughton, J.M. and G.S. Tavlas (1991), 'What have we learned about estimating the demand for money? A multicountry evaluation of some new approaches', Working Paper WP/91/16, IMF.

Box, G.E.P. and G.M. Jenkins (1970), *Time Series Analysis: Forecasting and Control*, San Francisco: Holden-Day.

Brainard, W.C. and J. Tobin (1968), 'Pitfalls in financial model building', *American Economic Review*, **58**, 99–122.

Breusch, B.T. and A.R. Pagan (1979), 'A simple test for heteroscedasticity and random coefficient variation', *Econometrica*, **47**, 1287–1294.

Brissimis, S.N. and J.A. Leventakis (1981), 'Inflationary expectations and the demand for money: The Greek experience', *Kredit und Kapital*, **14**, 561–573.

Broekhuis, J. and M. van Nieuwkerk (1979), 'Korte-termijn fluctuaties in de bankbiljettencirculatie van Nederland', *Revue Belge de Statistique, d'Informatique et de Recherche Operationelle* **19**(1), 58–68.

Brown, A.J. (1938), 'The liquidity preference schedules of the London clearing banks', *Oxford Economic Papers*, **1**, 49–82.

Brown, A.J. (1939), 'Interest, prices and the demand schedule for idle money', *Oxford Economic Papers*, **2**, 46–69.

Browne, F.X. (1986), 'Multilateral currency substitution and capital flows as sources of instability in the sole demand for money function: A case study', *Empirical Economics*, **11**, 181–196.

Brunner, K. (1971), 'A survey of selected issues in monetary theory', *Schweizerische Zeitschrift für Volkswirtschaft und Statistik*, **107**, 1–146.

Brunner, K. and A.H. Meltzer (1964), 'Some further investigations of demand and supply functions for money', *Journal of Finance*, **19**, 240–283.

Brunner, K. and A.H. Meltzer (1966), 'A credit market theory of the money supply and an explanation of two puzzles in U.S. monetary policy', in T. Bagiotti (ed.), *Essays in Honor of Marco Fanno, II*, Padova: Cedam, pp. 151–176.

Brunner, K. and A.H. Meltzer (1968), 'Liquidity traps for money, bank credit, and interest rates', *Journal of Political Economy*, **76**, 1–37.

Buscher, H.S. (1984), 'The stability of the West-German demand for money', *Weltwirtschaftliches Archiv*, **120**, 256–278.

Buscher, H.S. (1985), 'Zur Stabilität der Geldnachfrage: Eine empirische Betrachtung', *Kredit und Kapital*, **17**, 507–539.

Buscher, H.S. and W. Schröder (1983), 'Instabilität der Geldhaltung stellt Geldmengenregel in Frage', *Wirtschaftdienst*, **63**, 309–312.

Butter, F.A.G. den and M.M.G. Fase (1981), 'The demand for money in EEC countries', *Journal of Monetary Economics*, **8**, 201–230, reprinted as Chapter 2 in this volume.

Butter, F.A.G. den and J.B. Kuné (1976), 'De functionele vorm van de geldvraagvergelijking in Nederland 1952:I–1971:IV', *Tijdschrift voor Economie en Management*, **21**, 169–177.

Cagan, P. (1958), 'The demand for currency relative to total money supply', *Journal of Political Economy*, **66**, 303–328.

Caligiuri, G.F., A. Fazio, and T. Padoa-Schioppa (1974), 'Demand and supply of bank credit in Italy', *Journal of Money, Credit and Banking*, **6**, 455–479.

Canarella, G. and R.M. Roseman (1978), 'The demand for money: Some evidence from Western Europe', *Schweizerische Zeitschrift für Volkswirtschaft und Statistik*, **114**, 9–18.

Caramazza, F. (1989), 'Technical note: The demand for M2 and M2+ in Canada', *Bank of Canada Review* **19**(12), 3–20.

Carr, J. and M.R. Darby (1981), 'The role of money supply shocks in the short-run demand for money', *Journal of Monetary Economics*, **8**, 183–199.

Cave, C.J. and M.M.G. Fase (1980), 'General reflections on forecasting the note issue', Technical Report, paper presented at the Banknote Printers' Conference Statistics Committee, Rome, 27 March 1980.

Cesar, H., J. de Haan, and J. Jacobs (1990), 'Monetary targeting in the Netherlands: An application of cointegration tests', *Applied Economics*, **22**, 1537–1548.

Chen, C. (1976), 'Currency denominations and the price level', *Journal of Political Economy*, **84**, 179–183.

Chow, G.C. (1966), 'On the long-run and short-run demand for money', *Journal of Political Economy*, **74**, 111–131.

Christ, C.F. (1963), 'Interest rates and portfolio selection among liquid assets in the US', in C.F. Christ *et al.* (eds), *Measurement in Economics: Studies in Mathematical Economics and Econometrics and Econometrics in Memory of Yehuda Grunfeld*, Stanford: University Press, pp. 201–218.

Christ, C.F. (1993), 'Assessing applied econometric results', *Federal Reserve Bank of St. Louis Review*, **75**, 71–94.

Clinton, K. (1973), 'The demand for money in Canada, 1955–70: Some single-equation estimates and stability tests', *Canadian Journal of Economics*, **6**, 53–61.

Cooley, T.F. and S.F. LeRoy (1981), 'Identification and estimation of money demand', *American Economic Review*, **71**, 825–844.

Corker, R. (1990), 'Wealth, financial liberalization, and the demand for money in Japan', *IMF Staff Papers*, **37**, 418–432.

Cotula, F. (1970), 'La demanda di moneta', Rome: Banca d'Italia.

Cox, D.R. (1962), 'Further results on tests of separate families of hypothesis', *Journal of the Royal Statistical Society, Series B*, **24**, 406–424.

Cramer, J.S. (1978), 'On prediction', in *Proceedings of the Bicentennial Congress of the Wiskundig Genootschap*, Amsterdam.

Cramer, J.S. (1983), 'Currency by denomination', *Economics Letters*, **12**, 299–303.

Cramer, J.S. (1986), 'The volume of transactions and the circulation of money in the United States, 1950–1979', *Journal of Business and Economic Statistics*, **4**, 225–232.

Cramer, J.S. and G.M. Reekers (1972), *Het houderschap van liquiditeiten in Nederland*, Amsterdam: NIBE.

Cramer, J.S. and G.M. Reekers (1976), 'Money demand by sector', *Journal of Monetary Economics*, **2**, 99–112.

Crouch, R.L. (1967), 'A model of the United Kingdom's monetary sector', *Econometrica*, **35**, 398–418.

Cuthbertson, K. (1988), 'The demand for M1: A forward-looking buffer stock model,', *Oxford Economic Papers*, **40**, 110–131.

Cuthbertson, K. and M.P. Taylor (1987a), 'The demand for money: A dynamic rational expectations model', *The Economic Journal*, **97**, 65–76.

Cuthbertson, K. and M.P. Taylor (1987b), 'Monetary anticipations and the demand for money: Some evidence for the UK', *Weltwirtschaftliches Archiv*, **123**, 509–520.

Cuthbertson, K. and M.P. Taylor (1990), 'Money demand, expectations, and the forward-looking model', *Journal of Policy Modeling*, **12**, 289–315.

Dantzig, D. van (1952), 'Voorspelling en Profetie', *Statistica Neerlandica*, **6**, 196–203.

De Nederlandsche Bank (1985), *MORKMON, A Quarterly Model of the Netherlands Economy for Macroeconomic Policy and Analysis*, number 2 in Monetary Monographs, Amsterdam: De Nederlandsche Bank.

Deutsche Bundesbank (1995, Juli), 'Überprüfung des Geldmengenziels und Neuordnung der Mindestreserve', *Monatsberichte*.

Dhrymes, P.J. (1971), *Distributed Lags: Problems of Estimation and Formulation*, number 8 in Mathematical Economics Texts, San Francisco: Holden-Day.

Dierick, A.M. (1967), 'De liquiditeitsquote als variabele factor', *Maandschrift Economie*, **32**, 130–157.

Divisia, F. (1925), 'L'indice monétaire et la théorie de la monnaie', *Revue d'Economie Politique*, **39**, 842–861, 980–1008, 1121–1151.

Divisia, F. (1926), 'L'indice monétaire et la théorie de la monnaie', *Revue d'Economie Politique*, **40**, 49–87.

Dolado, J.J. and J.L. Escriva (1992), 'La demanda de dinero en españa: Definiciones amplias de liquidez', *Moneda-y-credito*, no. 195, 69–99.

Domowitz, I. and C.S. Hakkio (1990), 'Interpreting an error correction model: Partial adjustment, forward-looking behaviour, and dynamic international money demand', *Journal of Applied Econometrics*, **5**, 29–46.

Dooley, M.P. and F. Spinelli (1985), 'Financial innovation, deregulation, and money demand in France, Italy and Japan', Working Paper DM/86/15, IMF.

Driehuis, W. (1972), *Fluctuations and Growth in a Near Full Employment Economy: A Quarterly Econometric Analysis of the Netherlands*, Rotterdam: University Press.

Ebrill, L.P. (1988), 'Money demand in the United States', Working Paper WP/88/86, IMF.

Engle, R.F. and C.W.J. Granger (1987), 'Cointegration and error correction: Representation, estimation and testing', *Econometrica*, **55**, 251–276.

Epps, T.W. (1975), 'Wealth effects and Slutsky equations for assets', *Econometrica*, **43**, 301–303.

Evans, S.A. and M.J. Hailey (1974), 'A cashless society', in *Transactions of the Manchester Statistical Society, Session 1973–1974*, London, Manchester Statistical Society, pp. 1–28.

Fair, R.C. (1987), 'International evidence on the demand for money', *The Review of Economics and Statistics*, **69**, 473–480.

Fase, M.M.G. (1972), 'Bond yields and expected inflation: A quantitative analysis of the Dutch experience', *Economic Quarterly Review AMRO-bank*, no. 30, 5–10.

Fase, M.M.G. (1973), 'A principal components analysis of market interest rates in the Netherlands 1962–1970', *European Economic Review*, **4**, 107–134.

Fase, M.M.G. (1976), 'The interdependence of short-term interest rates in the major financial centres of the world: Some evidence for 1961–1972', *Kyklos*, **29**, 63–96.

Fase, M.M.G. (1977), 'Savings deposits, time deposits and interest rate differentials: An econometric analysis', *De Nederlandsche Bank Quarterly Statistics*, **1977**/2, 78–88.

Fase, M.M.G. (1978a), 'De bankbiljetten en hun gebruikers', *De Florijn*, **1**, 9–10.

Fase, M.M.G. (1978b), 'Een verdeelmodel voor liquide activa: de overheveling als voorbeeld van toegepaste economie', *Economisch-Statistische Berichten*, **63**, 215–218.

Fase, M.M.G. (1979), 'The demand for financial assets: Time series evidence for the Netherlands: 1963:II–1975:IV', *European Economic Review*, **12**, 381–394, reprinted as Chapter 9 in this volume.

Fase, M.M.G. (1981), 'Forecasting the demand for banknotes: Some empirical results for the Netherlands', *European Journal of Operational Research*, **6**, 269–278, reprinted as Chapter 13 in this volume.

Fase, M.M.G. (1985a), 'The f 1,000 bank note: Means of payment or means of hoarding', *De Nederlandsche Bank Quarterly Bulletin*, **1984**/4, 31–38.

Fase, M.M.G. (1985b), 'Monetary control: The Dutch experience – some reflections on the liquidity ratio', in C. van Ewijk and J.J. Klant (eds), *Monetary Conditions for Economic Recovery*, Dordrecht/Boston: M. Nijhoff, pp. 95–125.

Fase, M.M.G. (1993), 'The stability of the demand for money in the G7 and EC countries: A survey', WO&E Research Memorandum 9321, De Nederlandsche Bank, and CEPS Working Document no. 81.

Fase, M.M.G. (1994), 'In search for stability: An empirical appraisal of the demand for money in G7 and EC countries', *De Economist*, **142**, 421–454, reprinted as Chapter 5 in this volume.

Fase, M.M.G. and W.C. Boeschoten (1985), 'The distribution of payments and the use of bank notes', *De Nederlandsche Bank Quarterly Bulletin*, **1985**/2, 43–53.

Fase, M.M.G., D. van der Hoeven, and M. van Nieuwkerk (1979), 'A numerical planning model for a central bank's bank notes operations', *Statistica Neerlandica*, **33**, 7–18.

Fase, M.M.G., P. Kramer, and W.C. Boeschoten (1992), 'MORKMON II: The Nederlandsche Bank's quarterly model of the Netherlands economy', *Economic Modelling*, **9**, 146–204.

Fase, M.M.G. and J.B. Kuné (1974a), 'De vraag naar liquiditeiten in Nederland, 1952–1971', *De Economist*, **122**, 326–356.

Fase, M.M.G. and J.B. Kuné (1974b), 'Price and income expectations in the demand for money', paper presented at ESEM'74, Grenoble. Reprinted as Chapter 1 in this volume.

Fase, M.M.G. and J.B. Kuné (1975), 'The demand for money in thirteen European and non-European countries: A tabular survey', *Kredit und Kapital*, **8**, 410–419.

Fase, M.M.G. and M. van Nieuwkerk (1975), 'Anticipated inflation and interest rates in an open economy: A study of the Gibson paradox for the Netherlands', in F. Masera *et al.* (eds), *Econometric Research in European Central Banks*, Rome: Banca d'Italia, pp. 297–321.

Fase, M.M.G. and M. van Nieuwkerk (1976), 'The bank note circulation in the Netherlands since 1900', *De Nederlandsche Bank Quarterly Statistics*, **1976**/1, 80–87.

Fase, M.M.G. and M. van Nieuwkerk (1977), 'The demand for bank notes in four countries', *De Nederlandsche Bank Quarterly Statistics*, **1977**/1, 84–98.

Fase, M.M.G. and M.E.J. Schuit (1992), 'Monetaire aggregatie en de Divisia-index', *Maandschrift Economie*, **56**, 434–449.

Fase, M.M.G. and C.C.A. Winder (1989), 'De vraag naar geld in Nederland opnieuw bezien', WO&E Research Memorandum 8917, De Nederlandsche Bank.

Fase, M.M.G. and C.C.A. Winder (1990), 'The demand for money in the Netherlands revisited', *De Economist*, **138**, 276–301, reprinted as Chapter 3 in this volume.

Fase, M.M.G. and C.C.A. Winder (1992), 'The demand for money in the Netherlands and the other EC countries', WO&E Research Memorandum 9214, De Nederlandsche Bank, Centre for European Policy Studies, Working Document Series no. 72.

Fase, M.M.G. and C.C.A. Winder (1993), 'The demand for money in the Netherlands and other EC countries', *De Economist*, **141**, 471–496, reprinted as Chapter 4 in this volume.

Fase, M.M.G. and C.C.A. Winder (1994), 'Money demand within EMU: An analysis with the Divisia measure', *De Nederlandsche Bank Quarterly Bulletin*, **1994**/2, 25–55, reprinted as Chapter 7 in this volume.

Fase, M.M.G. and C.C.A. Winder (1997), 'Wealth and the demand for money in the European Union', DNB-Staff Reports 6, De Nederlandsche Bank.

Fazio, A. (1995), 'La tutela del risparmio', Bolletino Economico 24, Banca d'Italia.

Feige, E.L. (1964), *The Demand for Liquid Assets: A Temporal Cross-section Analysis*, Englewood Cliffs: Prentice-Hall.

Feige, E.L. (1967), 'Expectations and adjustments in the monetary sector', *American Economic Review*, **57**, 462–473.

Feige, E.L. (1974), 'Temporal cross-section specifications of the demand for demand deposits', *Journal of Finance*, **29**, 923–940.

Feige, E.L. (1979), 'How big is the irregular economy?', *Challenge*, **22**, 5–13.

Feige, E.L. and D.K. Pearce (1972), 'A methodological survey of the time series evidence on the demand for money and money substitutes', Paper 7221, Social Systems Research Institute, University of Wisconsin.

Feige, E.L. and D.K. Pearce (1977), 'The substitutability of money and near-monies: A survey of the time series evidence', *Journal of Economic Literature*, **15**, 439–469.

Feige, E.L. and P.A.V.B. Swamy (1974), 'A random coefficient model of the demand for liquid assets', *Journal of Money, Credit and Banking*, **6**, 241–252.

Fischer, S. (1972), 'Assets, contingent commodities and the Slutsky equations', *Econometrica*, **40**, 371–385.

Fisher, D. (1968), 'The demand for money in Britain, quarterly results 1951 to 1967', *The Manchester School of Economic and Social Studies*, **36**, 329–343.

Fisher, I. (1909), 'A new method of estimating the velocity of circulation of money', *Journal of the Royal Statistical Society*, **72**, 604–618.

Fisher, P., S. Hudson, and M. Pradhan (1993), 'Divisia measures of money', *Bank of England Quarterly Bulletin*, **33**, 240–255.

Fourcans, A. (1975), 'Bank credit and interest rate in France: A theoretical and empirical analysis', in B. Jacquillat (ed.), *European Finance Association 1974 proceedings*, Amsterdam: North-Holland, pp. 149–182.

Frazer, W.J. (1967), *The Demand for Money*, Cleveland: World Publishing.

Friedman, B.M. (1981), 'The relative stability of money and credit velocities in the United States: Evidence and some speculations', Working Paper 645, NBER, Cambridge, Mass.

Friedman, B.M. (1983), 'The roles of money and credit in macroeconomic analysis', in J. Tobin (ed.), *Macroeconomics, Prices and Quantities: Essays in Memory of Arthur M. Okun*, Oxford: Blackwell, pp. 161–199.

Friedman, M. (1956), 'The quantity theory of money: A restatement', in M. Friedman (ed.), *Studies in the Quantity Theory of Money*, Chicago: University of Chicago Press, pp. 3–21.

Friedman, M. (1959), 'The demand for money: Some theoretical and empirical results', *Journal of Political Economy*, **67**, 327–351.

Friedman, M. (1969), *The Optimum Quantity of Money and Other Essays*, Chicago: Aldine Publishing Company.

Friedman, M. (1971), *A Theoretical Framework for Monetary Analysis*, New York: Colombia University Press.

Friedman, M. and A.J. Schwartz (1963), *A Monetary History of the United States, 1867–1960*, Princeton, N.J.: University Press.

Friedman, M. and A.J. Schwartz (1970), *Monetary Statistics of the United States – Estimates, Sources, Methods*, New York: Colombia University Press.

Fröchen, P. and S. Roubine (1979), 'La demande de monnaie: Quelques résultats économétriques', *Bulletin trimestriel, Banque de France*, **31**, 21–28.

Fröchen, P. and P. Voisin (1986), 'La stabilité des équations de demande de monnaie: Le cas de France de 1970 à 1984', *Cahiers Economiques et Monétaires, Banque de France*, **21**, 5–48.

Fürst, E., F. Schebeck, and J. Schulz (1970), 'Die Geldnachfrage in Österreich', *Zeitschrift für Nationalökonomie*, **30**, 159–196.

Garvy, G. and M.R. Blyn (1969), *The Velocity of Money*, New York: Federal Reserve Bank.

Ghosh, S.K. (1989), 'Currency substitution and demand for money in Canada: Further evidence', *Journal of Macroeconomics*, **11**, 81–93.

Gilbert, J.C. (1953), 'The demand for money: The development of an economic concept', *Journal of Political Economy*, **61**, 144–159.

Gillieson, A.H. (1977), 'Research into the extension of the life of bank notes: Results of 1973, 1975 and 1976 field trials', Technical Report 10, Bank of Canada.

Godfrey, L.G. (1978), 'Testing for multiplicative heteroskedasticity', *Journal of Econometrics*, **8**, 227–236.

Goldberger, A.S. (1964), *Econometric Theory*, New York: Wiley.

Goldberger, A.S. (1972), 'Maximum-likelihood estimation of regressions containing unobservable independent variables', *International Economic Review*, **13**, 1–15.

Goldberger, A.S. (1974), 'Unobservable variables in econometrics', in P. Zarembka (ed.), *Frontiers in Econometrics*, New York: Academic Press, pp. 193–213.

Goldfeld, S.M. (1966), *Commercial Bank Behavior and Economic Activity: A structural study of monetary policy in the postwar United States*, Amsterdam: North-Holland.

Goldfeld, S.M. (1973), 'The demand for money revisited', *Brookings Papers on Economic Activity*, **1973**, 577–638.

Goldfeld, S.M. (1976), 'The case of the missing money', *Brookings Papers on Economic Activity*, **1976**, 683–730.

Goldfeld, S.M. and D.E. Sichel (1987), 'Money demand: The effects of inflation and alternative adjustment mechanisms', *The Review of Economics and Statistics*, **69**, 511–515.

Goldfeld, S.M. and D.E. Sichel (1990), 'The demand for money', in B.M. Friedman and F.H. Hahn (eds), *Handbook of Monetary Economics*, Volume I, Amsterdam: Elsevier, pp. 299–356.

Goldin, E. (1985), 'Statistical analysis of coins lost in circulation', *Journal of Business and Economic Statistics*, **3**, 36–42.

Goodhart, C.A.E. (1970), 'The importance of money', *Bank of England Quarterly Bulletin*, **10**, 159–198.

Goodhart, C.A.E. (1975), *Money, Information and Uncertainty*, London: Macmillan.

Goodhart, C.A.E. (1989), *Money, Information and Uncertainty* (2nd ed.), London: Macmillan.

Goodman, L.A. and W.H. Kruskal (1979), *Measures of Association for Cross Classifications*, New York: Springer.

Gouriéroux, C., A. Montfort, and A. Trognon (1985), 'Moindres carrés asymptotiques', *Annales de l'INSEE*, **58**, 91–122.

Gramlich, E.M. and D.T. Hullett (1972), 'The demand for and supply of savings deposits', in E.M. Gramlich and D.M. Jaffee (eds), *Savings Deposits, Mortgages and Housing: Studies for the Federal Reserve-Mit-Penn Economic Model*, Lexington: Heath and Company, pp. 13–62.

Gramlich, E.M. and J.H. Kalchbrenner (1970), 'A constrained estimation approach to the demand for liquid assets', Special Studies Paper 3, Federal Reserve Board, Washington, DC.

Grandmont, J.M. (1973), 'On the short-run and long-run demand for money', *European Economic Review*, **4**, 265–287.

Gray, M.R. and J.M. Parkin (1973), 'Portfolio diversification as optimal precautionary behaviour', in M. Morishima *et al.* (eds), *Theory of Demand: Real and Monetary*, Oxford: Clarendon Press, pp. 301–350.

Gray, M.R., R. Ward, and G. Zis (1976), 'The world demand for money function: Some preliminary results', in M. Parkin and G. Zis (eds), *Inflation in the World Economy*, Manchester: University Press, pp. 151–181.

Gutmann, P.M. (1977), 'The subterranean economy', *Financial Analysts Journal*, **33**, 26–28.

Hacche, G. (1974), 'The demand for money in the United Kingdom: Experience since 1971', *Bank of England Quarterly Bulletin*, **14**, 284–305.

Hafer, R.W. and S.E. Hein (1979), 'Evidence of the temporal stability of the demand for money relationship in the US', *Federal Reserve Bank of St. Louis Review* **61**(12), 3–14.

Hafer, R.W. and D.W. Jansen (1991), 'The demand for money in the United States: Evidence from cointegration tests', *Journal of Money, Credit and Banking*, **23**, 155–168.

Hall, S.G., S.G.B. Henry, and J.B. Wilcox (1989), 'The long run determination of the UK monetary aggregates', Discussion Paper 41, Bank of England.

Hamada, K. and F. Hayashi (1985), 'Monetary policy in postwar Japan', in A. Ando, H. Eguchi, R. Farmer, and Y. Suzuki (eds), *Monetary Policy in Our Times*, Cambridge, Mass.: MIT Press, pp. 83–121.

Hamburger, M.J. (1973), 'The demand for money in an open economy: Germany and the United Kingdom', paper presented at the Fourth Konstanzer Seminar on Monetary Theory and Monetary Policy. New York: Federal Reserve Bank (1974).

Hamburger, M.J. (1977), 'The demand for money in an open economy: Germany and the United Kingdom', *Journal of Monetary Economics*, **3**, 25–40.

Haulman, C.A. (1972), 'A structural model of the Canadian monetary sector', *Southern Economic Journal*, **38**, 336–349.

Hawtrey, R.G. (1928), *Trade and Credit*, London: Longmans.

Heller, H.R. and M.S. Khan (1979), 'The demand for money and the term structure of interest rates', *Journal of Political Economy*, **87**, 109–129.

Helliwell, J.F., H.T. Shapiro, G.R. Sparks, I.A. Stewart, F.W. Gorbet, and D.R. Stephenson (1971), 'The structure of RDX2 part I', Staff Research Studies, Bank of Canada.

Hendershott, P.H. (1971), 'A flow-of-funds model: Estimates for the non-bank finance sector', *Journal of Money, Credit and Banking*, **3**, 815–832.

Hendry, D.F. (1979), 'Predictive failure and econometric modelling in macroeconomics: The transactions demand for money', in P.A. Ormerod (ed.), *Economic Modelling: Current Issues and Problems in Macroeconomic Modelling in the UK and the US*, London: Heinemann, pp. 217–242.

Hendry, D.F. (1985), 'Monetary economic myth and econometric reality', *Oxford Review of Economic Policy*, **1**, 72–48.

Hendry, D.F. and N.R. Ericsson (1991a), 'An econometric analysis of U.K. money demand in "Monetary trends in the United States and the United Kingdom" by Milton Friedman and Anna J. Schwartz', *American Economic Review*, **81**, 8–38.

Hendry, D.F. and N.R. Ericsson (1991b), 'Modelling the demand for narrow money in the United Kingdom and the United States', *European Economic Review*, **35**, 833–886.

Hendry, D.F. and G.E. Mizon (1978), 'Serial correlation as a convenient simplification, not a nuisance: A comment on a study of the demand for money by the Bank of England', *The Economic Journal*, **88**, 549–563.

Hendry, D.F. and R.M. Starr (1993), 'The demand for M1 in the USA: A reply to James M. Boughton', *The Economic Journal*, **103**, 1158–1169.

Heremans, D., A. Sommariva, and A. Verheirstraeten (1976), 'A money and bank credit model for an open economie: The Belgian experience 1960–1073', *Kredit und Kapital*, Beihefte **3**, 155–208.

Heri, E.W. (1985), 'The short-run demand for money in Germany: Some caveats for empirical work', *Weltwirtschaftliches Archiv*, **121**, 524–540.

Herz, B. and W. Röger (1990), 'Evaluating conflicting stability results in German money demand regressions', *Weltwirtschaftliches Archiv*, **126**, 691–708.

Hester, D.D. and J.L. Pierce (1975), *Bank Management and Portfolio Behavior*, New Haven: Yale University Press.

Himarios, D. (1986), 'Administered interest rates and the demand for money in Greece under rational expectations', *Weltwirtschaftliches Archiv*, **122**, 173–188.

Himarios, D. (1987), 'Has there been a shift in the Greek money demand function?', *Kredit und Kapital*, **20**, 106–115.

Hoffman, D.L. and R.H. Rasche (1991), 'Long-run income and interest elasticities of money demand in the United States', *The Review of Economics and Statistics*, **73**, 665–674.

Holtrop, M.W. (1928), *De omloopsnelheid van het geld*, Amsterdam: H.J. Paris.

Huijser, A.P. (1987), 'De vraag naar geld – enige recente ontwikkelingen', WO&E Research Memorandum 8703, De Nederlandsche Bank.

Hunt, B.F. and P.A. Volker (1981), 'A simplified portfolio analysis of the long-run demand for money in Australia', *Journal of Monetary Economics*, **8**, 395–404.

Hylleberg, S., R.F. Engle, C.W.J. Granger, and B.S. Yoo (1990), 'Seasonal integration and cointegration', *Journal of Econometrics*, **44**, 215–238.

Issing, O., K.H. Tödter, H. Herrmann, and H.E. Reimers (1993), 'Zinsgewichtete Geldmengenaggregate und M3: ein Vergleich', *Kredit und Kapital*, **26**, 1–21.

Jaffee, D.M. (1971), *Credit Rationing and the Commercial Loan Market: An Econometric Study of the Structure of the Commercial Loan Market*, New York: Wiley.

Jeanfils, P. (1992), 'La demande de monnaie', Technical Report, Banque Nationale de Belgique.

Jenkins, G.M. (1979), *Practical Experiences with Modelling and Forecasting Time Series*, St. Helier: Jenkins.

Johansen, S. (1991), 'Estimation and hypothesis testing of cointegration vectors in Gaussian vector autoregressive models', *Econometrica*, **59**, 1551–1580.

Johansen, S. and K. Juselius (1990), 'Maximum likelihood estimation and inference on cointegration – with applications to the demand for money', *Oxford Bulletin of Economics and Statistics*, **52**, 169–210.

Jonker, R. (1973), 'Raming van de transacties in Nederland', *Economisch-Statistische Berichten*, **58**, 675–676.

Judd, J.P. and J.L. Scadding (1982a), 'Dynamic adjustment in the demand for money: Tests of alternative hypotheses', *Economic Review, Federal Reserve Bank of San Francisco* **8**(4), 19–30.

Judd, J.P. and J.L. Scadding (1982b), 'The search for a stable money demand function: A survey of the post-1973 literature', *Journal of Economic Literature*, **20**, 993–1023.

Judd, J.P. and B. Trehan (1987), 'Portfolio substitution and the reliability of M1, M2 and M3 as monetary policy indicators', *Economic Review, Federal Reserve Bank of San Francisco* **13**(3), 5–29.

Juselius, K. (1987), 'Cointegration and identification in a vector time series model – an application to the demand for money in Denmark', Research Memorandum, University of Copenhagen.

Juselius, K. (1991), 'Stationary equilibrium error processes in the Danish money market - an application of ML cointegration', Research Memorandum, University of Copenhagen.

Juselius, K. (1992), 'On the duality between long-run relations and common trends in the I(1) versus I(2) model – an application to aggregate money holdings', Research Memorandum, University of Copenhagen.

Jüttner, D.J.P. and R.H. Tuckwell (1974), 'Partial adjustment, multiple expectations and the demand for money in Australia', *Kredit und Kapital*, **7**, 48–68.

Kessler, G.A. (1958), *Monetair evenwicht en betalingsbalansevenwicht*, Leiden: Stenfert Kroese.

Kimball, R.C. (1981), 'Trends in the use of currency', *New England Economic Review, Federal Reserve Bank of Boston* **13**(5), 43–53.

Kiviet, J.F. (1980), 'Effects of ARMA errors en tests for regression coefficients: Comments on Vinod's article; improved and additional results', *Journal of the American Statistical Association*, **75**, 353–358.

Kiviet, J.F. (1985), 'Model selection test procedures in a single linear equation of a dynamic simultaneous system and their defects in small samples', *Journal of Econometrics*, **28**, 327–362.

Klevmarken, N.A. (1975), 'On the small sample properties of Aitken-type estimators and test-statistics applied to seemingly unrelated regressions', in *Proceedings of the American Statistical Association (Business and Economic Statistics Section)*, pp. 362–367.

Knoop, H.S. van der and F.C. Hooijmans (1985), 'De evenwichtigheid van de huidige liquiditeitsquote', *Maandschrift Economie*, **49**, 389–409.

Kodde, D.A., F.C. Palm, and G.A. Pfann (1990), 'Asymptotic least squares estimation: Efficiency considerations and applications', *Journal of Applied Econometrics*, **5**, 229–243.

Koeze, P. (1979), 'An accurate statistical estimation of the life-length of Dfl. 100 banknotes: A circulation trial with two qualities of currency paper', *International Statistical Review*, **47**, 283–297.

König, H. (1968), 'Einkommenskreislaufgeschwindigkeit des Geldes und Zinssatzveränderungen: Eine ökonometrische Studie über die Geldnachfrage in der BRD', *Zeitschrift für die gesamte Staatswissenschaft*, **124**, 70–90.

Kopcke, R.W. (1977), 'United States household sector demand for liquid financial assets, 1959–1970', *Journal of Monetary Economics*, **3**, 409–441.

Korteweg, P. (1973a), 'Over de beheersbaarheid van de geldhoeveelheid in Nederland', *De Economist*, **121**, 273–299.

Korteweg, P. (1973b), 'The supply and controllability of money in an open economy: The Dutch experience 1953–1971', paper presented at the Fourth Konstanzer Seminar on Monetary Theory and Monetary Policy. New York: Federal Reserve Bank (1974).

Korteweg, P. and P.D. van Loo (1977), *The Market for Money and the Market for Credit: Theory, Evidence and Implications for Dutch Monetary Policy*, Leiden: Martinus Nijhoff.

Krainer, R.E. (1969), 'Structural estimates of supply and demand in the USA short-term bank loan market', *Bulletin of the Oxford University Institute of Economics and Statistics*, **31**, 39–46.

Kremers, J.J.M., N.R. Ericsson, and J.J. Dolado (1992), 'The power of cointegration tests', *Oxford Bulletin of Economics and Statistics*, **54**, 325–348.

Kremers, J.J.M. and T.D. Lane (1990), 'Economic and monetary integration and the aggregate demand for money in the EMS', *IMF Staff Papers*, **37**, 777–805.

Kuipers, S.K. and B. Boertje (1988), 'On the causes of the rise in the liquidity ratio in the Netherlands during the early eighties', *De Economist*, **136**, 50–90.

Laidler, D.E.W. (1969), *The Demand for Money: Theories and Evidence*, Scranton: International Textbook.

Laidler, D.E.W. (1977), *The Demand for Money: Theories and Evidence* (2nd ed.), London: Intertext Books.

Laidler, D.E.W. (1980), 'The demand for money in the United States – yet again', in K. Brunner and A.H. Meltzer (eds), *On the State of Macro-economics*, Volume 12 of *Carnegie-Rochester Conference Series on Public Policy*, Amsterdam: North-Holland, pp. 219–271.

Laidler, D.E.W. (1982), *Monetarist Perspectives*, Oxford: Philip Allen.

Laidler, D.E.W. (1991), 'Karl Brunner's monetary economics: An appreciation', *Journal of Money, Credit and Banking*, **23**, 633–658.

Laidler, D.E.W. and M. Parkin (1970), 'The demand for money in the United Kingdom 1956–1967: Preliminary estimates', *The Manchester School of Economic and Social Studies*, **38**, 187–208.

Langfeldt, E. and H. Lehment (1980), 'Welche Bedeutung haben "Sonderfaktoren" für die Erklärung der Geldnachfrage in der Bundesrepublik Deutschland?', *Weltwirtschaftliches Archiv*, **116**, 669–684.

Latané, H.A. (1954), 'Cash balances and interest rates: A pragmatic approach', *The Review of Economics and Statistics*, **36**, 456–460.

Laurent, R.D. (1970), *Currency Transfer by Denomination*, Ph. D. thesis, University of Chicago, Dept. of Economics.

Laurent, R.D. (1974), 'Currency and the real value of notes', *Journal of Money, Credit and Banking*, **6**, 213–226.

Laurent, R.D. (1981), 'Currency and the subterranean economy', *Economic Perspectives, Federal Reserve Bank of Chicago* **5**(2), 3–6.

Lecarpentier, S. (1993), 'Quel type de pondérations pour les indices monétaires?', *Revue d'Économie Politique*, **103**, 865–887.

Leponiemi, A. (1966), *On the Demand and Supply of Money: The Evidence from the Quarterly Time Series in the United States, the United Kingdom and Finland 1949–1962*, number 27 in Economic studies, Helsinki: The Finnish Economic Association.

Lieberman, C. (1977), 'The transactions demand for money and technological change', *The Review of Economics and Statistics*, **59**, 307–317.

Little, A.D. (1975), 'The consequences of electronic funds transfer', Technical Report, National Science Foundation, Cambridge, Mass.

Lovell, M.C. (1963), 'Seasonal adjustment of economic time series and multiple regression analysis', *Journal of the American Statistical Association*, **58**, 993–1010.

MacCallum, B.T. and M.S. Goodfriend (1988), 'Theoretical analysis of the demand for money', *Economic Review, Federal Reserve Bank of Richmond*, **76**, 16–24.

Makridakis, S. and S.C. Wheelwright (1978), *Forecasting Methods and Applications*, New York: Wiley.

Mandell, L. (1972), 'Credit card use in the United States', Technical Report, Institute for Social Research, University of Michigan, Ann Arbor.

Mankiw, N.G. and L.H. Summers (1986), 'Money demand and the effects of fiscal policies', *Journal of Money, Credit and Banking*, **18**, 415–429.

Manski, C.F. and E. Goldin (1987), 'The denomination-specific demand for currency in a high-inflation setting: The Israeli experience', in R.D.H. Heijmans and H. Neudecker (eds), *The Practice of Econometrics: Studies in Demand, Forecasting Money and Income*, Dordrecht: Kluwer, pp. 99–120.

Marques, C.R. and L.H. Lopes (1992), 'Money demand in Portugal: A cointegration approach', Working document, Bank of Portugal.

Mattfeldt, H. (1974), 'Untersuchungen zur Stock-Adjustment Hypothese', *Konjunkturpolitik*, **20**, 113–127.

Mehra, Y.P. (1989), 'Some further results on the source of shift in M1 demand in the 1980s', *Economic Review, Federal Reserve Bank of Richmond*, **75**, 3–13.

Mélitz, J. (1972), 'La demande de monnaie en France: Tentative d'explication', *Statistiques et Ètudes Financières*, **11**, 21–48, Direction de la Prévision, Ministère de l'Economie et des Finances, La Série Orange.

Mélitz, J. (1975), 'Une étude économétrique de la demande de crédit bancaire en France', *Revue d'Economie Politique*, **16**, 84–116.

Mélitz, J. and M.H. Pardue (1973), 'The demand and supply of commercial bank loans', *Journal of Money, Credit and Banking*, **5**, 669–692.

Miller, M.H. and D. Orr (1968), 'Demand for money by firms: Extensions of analytic results', *Journal of Finance*, **23**, 735–759.

Miller, S.M. (1989), 'Monetary demand instability: Has it ended?', *Economics Letters*, **30**, 345–349.

Miller, S.M. (1991), 'Monetary dynamics: An application of cointegration and error-correction modeling', *Journal of Money, Credit and Banking*, **23**, 139–154.

Modigliani, F. (1972), 'The dynamics of portfolio adjustment and the flow of savings through financial intermediaries', in E.M. Gramlich and D.M. Jaffee (eds), *Savings Deposits, Mortgages and Housing*, Lexington: Heath and Company, pp. 63–102.

Monti, M. (1972), 'Deposit, credit and interest rate determination under alternative bank objective function', in G.P. Szegö and K. Shell (eds), *Mathematical Methods in Investment and Finance*, Amsterdam: North-Holland, pp. 430–454.

Monticelli, C. and M. Strauss-Kahn (1992), 'European integration and the demand for broad money', Working Paper 18, BIS.

Morales, R. (1977), *Etudes et Analyse des Modèles ARIMA de Box-Jenkins en vue de leur Utilisation en Économétrie*, Bern: Peter Lang.

Muscatelli, V.A. (1989), 'A comparison of the "rational expectations" and "general-to-specific" approaches to modelling the demand for M1', *Oxford Bulletin of Economics and Statistics*, **51**, 353–375.

Muscatelli, V.A. and L. Papi (1990), 'Cointegration, financial innovation and modelling the demand for money in Italy', *The Manchester School of Economic and Social Studies*, **3**, 242–259.

Nelson, C.R. (1973), *Applied Time Series Analyses for Managerial Forecasting*, San Francisco: Holden-Day.

Neumann, M.J.M. (1983), 'Stabilität von Geldnachfrage und Geldpolitik', *Wirtschaftsdienst*, **63**, 415–420.

Nieuwenburg, C.K.F. (1969), *Het liquiditeitsbezit van gezinshuishoudingen in Nederland*, Deventer: A.E. Kluwer.

Nieuwenburg, C.K.F. and M.F. Koeman (1969), 'Actuele en berekende kapitaalmarktrente', *Maandschrift Economie*, **33**, 185–189.

OECD (1977), *Main Economic Indicators: Sources and Methods*, Paris: OECD.

Palm, F.C. (1983), 'Structural econometric modeling and time series analysis: An integrated approach', in *Applied Time Series Analysis of Econometric Data*, Washington D.C.: U.S. Department of Commerce, Bureau of the Census, pp. 199–233.

Papers, I.S. (1974), 'Belgium–Luxemburg recent economic developments', Rapport SM/74/110, IMF.

Parkin, J.M. (1970), 'Discount house portfolio and debt selection', *The Review of Economics and Statistics*, **27**, 469–497.

Parkin, J.M., M.R. Gray, and R.J. Barrett (1970), 'The portfolio behaviour of commercial banks', in K. Hilton and D.F. Heathfield (eds), *The Econometric Study of the United Kingdom*, London: Macmillan, pp. 229–251.

Patterson, K.D. (1987), 'The specification and stability of the demand for money in the United Kingdom', *Economica*, **54**, 41–55.

Plosser, C.F. and G.W. Schwert (1978), 'Money, income and sunspots: Measuring economic relationships and the effects of differencing', *Journal of Monetary Economics*, **4**, 637–660.

Porter, R.D. and A.S. Bayer (1984), 'A monetary perspective on underground economic activity in the United States', *Federal Reserve Bulletin*, **70**, 177–190.

Price, L.D.D. (1972), 'The demand for money in the United Kingdom: A further investigation', *Bank of England Quarterly Bulletin*, **12**, 43–55.

Quintijn, M. (1986), *De uitvoerbaarheid van een geldgroei beleid: algemene theoretische analyse en toepassing op de Belgische economie*, Ph. D. thesis, State University of Gent.

Quintijn, M. (1988), 'Money demand in Belgium – one step ahead in search of its stability', *Cahiers Économiques de Bruxelles*, **117**, 37–65.

Rasche, R.H. (1990), 'Equilibrium income and interest elasticities of the demand for M1 in Japan', *Monetary and Economic Studies, Bank of Japan*, **8**, 31–56.

Riet, A.G. van (1993), 'Studies of EC money demand: Survey and assessment', *De Nederlandsche Bank Quarterly Bulletin*, **1992**/4, 63–75.

Rose, A.K. (1985), 'An alternative approach to the American demand for money', *Journal of Money, Credit and Banking*, **17**, 439–455.

Roskamp, K.W. and G.S. Laumas (1969), 'The rate of interest and the demand for money: Some empirical evidence from the West-German economy 1953–1965', *Weltwirtschaftliches Archiv*, **102**, 150–155.

Saito, M. (1977), 'Household flow-of-funds equation: Specification and estimation', *Journal of Money, Credit and Banking*, **9**, 1–20.

Schelbert-Syfrig, H. (1967), *Empirische Untersuchungen über die Geldnachfrage in der Schweiz*, number 12 in Zürcher volkswirtschaftliche Forschungen, Neue Folge, Zürich: Polygraphischer Verlag.

Schimmelmann, W. von (1985), 'EFT developments in Germany', in *Texts of the Presentations at the Seventh European Financial Management and Marketing Association Convention*, Paris, European Financial Management and Marketing Association, pp. 41–46.

Schumpeter, J. (1912), *Theorie der wirtschaflichen Entwicklung*, Leipzig: Duncker und Humblot.

Selden, R.T. (1975), 'A critique of Dutch monetarism', *Journal of Monetary Economics*, **1**, 221–232.

Silveira, A.M. (1973), 'The demand for money: The evidence from the Brazilian economy', *Journal of Money, Credit and Banking*, **5**, 113–140.

Smith, L.B. and J.W.L. Winder (1971), 'Price and interest expectations and the demand for money in Canada', *Journal of Finance*, **26**, 671–682.

Sparks, G.R. (1974), 'Econometric estimation of constrained demand functions for assets', Technical Report, Bank of Canada, Montreal.

Sprenkle, C.M. (1969), 'The uselessness of transactions demand models', *Journal of Finance*, **24**, 835–847.

Sterken, E. (1992), 'The financial transactions motive in the Dutch money demand function', *Kredit und Kapital*, **25**, 386–405.

Stevers, T.A. (1963), *Renteverschillen en renteniveau: een onderzoek naar de oorzaken van de rendementverschillen tussen staatsobligaties en daarmede samenhangend, van het renteniveau, over de periode 1969 t/m 1960 in Nederland*, Rotterdam: Nijgh & Van Ditmar.

Suzuki, Y. (1984), 'Financial innovation and monetary policy in Japan', *Monetary and Economic Studies, Bank of Japan*, **2**, 1–47.

Tanzi, V. (1982), 'Underground economy and tax evasion in the United States: Estimates and implications', in V. Tanzi (ed.), *The Underground Economy in United States and Abroad*, Lexington Books: Lexington, pp. 69–92.

Taylor, M.P. (1986), 'From the general to the specific: The demand for M2 in three European countries', *Empirical Economics*, **11**, 243–261.

Teigen, R.L. (1964), 'Demand and supply functions for money in the United States: Some structural estimates', *Econometrica*, **32**, 476–509.

Teigen, R.L. (1970), 'The demand and supply of money', in W.L. Smith and R.L. Teigen (eds), *Readings in Money, National Income, and Stabilization Policy* (rev. ed.), Homewood Ill.: Irwin, pp. 74–112.

Teigen, R.L. (1971), 'The demand for money in Norway, 1959–1969', *Statsökonomisk Tidskrift*, **85**, 65–99.

Theil, H. (1958), *Economic Forecasts and Policy*, Amsterdam: North-Holland.

Thomas, J.J. and K.F. Wallis (1971), 'Seasonal variation in regression analysis', *Journal of the Royal Statistical Society, Series A*, **134**, 57–72.

Tinbergen, J. (1934), 'De vraag naar korte kredieten en de rentestand', *De Nederlandsche Conjunctuur*, no. 3, 18–31.

Tinbergen, J. (1937), 'Het verband tusschen de vraag naar korte kredieten en den rentestand in Nederland en Engeland', *De Nederlandsche Conjunctuur*, no. 4, 118–126.

Tinbergen, J. (1942), *Econometrics*, Gorinchem: J. Noorduyn & Zoon.

Tobin, J. (1956), 'The interest-elasticity of transactions demand for cash', *The Review of Economics and Statistics*, **38**, 241–247.

Tobin, J. (1969), 'A general equilibrium approach to monetary theory', *Journal of Money, Credit and Banking*, **1**, 15–29.

Traa, B.M. (1991), 'Money demand in the Netherlands', Working Paper WP/91/57.

Trehan, B. (1988), 'The practice of monetary targeting: A case study of the West German experience', *Economic Review, Federal Reserve Bank of San Francisco* **14**(2), 30–44.

Verrijn Stuart, G.M. (1953), *Geld en crediet* (8th ed.), 's-Gravenhage: Delwel.

Villanueva, D.P. (1971a), 'The adaptive expectation model of the demand for money: Some further results', *IMF Staff Papers*, **18**, 183–188.

Villanueva, D.P. (1971b), 'Simple demand-for-money functions in Belgium: Parameter estimates and stability tests', Departmental Memorandum 33, IMF.

Villanueva, D.P. (1972), 'Permanent income and partial adjustment in the monetary sector: The case of Japan', Departmental Memorandum 32, IMF.

Walters, A.A. (1970), 'The Radcliffe report – ten years after, a survey of empirical evidence', in D.R. Croome and H.G. Johnson (eds), *Money in Britain 1959–1969*, London: Oxford University Press, pp. 39–68.

Waud, R.N. (1968), 'Misspecification in the "partial adjustment" and "adaptive expectations models"', *International Economic Review*, **9**, 204–217.

Wenniger, J. (1988), 'Money demand – some long-run properties', *Federal Reserve Bank of New York Quarterly Review* **13**(1), 23–40.

Westphal, U. (1970), *Theoretische und empirische Untersuchungen zur Geldnachfrage und zum Geldangebot*, Tübingen: J.C.B. Mohr (Paul Siebeck).

Whalen, D.D. (1966), 'A rationalization of the precautionary demand for cash', *Quarterly Journal of Economics* **80**(2), 314–324.

White, W.H. (1976), 'The demand for money in Canada and the control of monetary aggregates: Evidence from the monthly data', Staff Research Studies 12, Bank of Canada, Montreal.

White, W.H. (1978), 'Improving the demand-for-money function in moderate inflation', *IMF Staff Papers*, **25**, 564–607.

Whitehead, D.D. (1982), 'Explaining the cash explosion', *Economic Review, Federal Reserve Bank of Atlanta*, **67**, 14–18.

Wood, J.H. (1975), *Commercial Bank Loan and Investment Behaviour*, London: Wiley.

Yoshida, T. and R.H. Rasche (1990), 'The M2 demand in Japan: Shifted and unstable?', *Monetary and Economic Studies, Bank of Japan* **8**(2), 9–30.

Zarembka, P. (1968), 'Functional form in the demand for money', *Journal of the American Statistical Association*, **63**, 502–511.

Zellner, A. (1962), 'An efficient method of estimating seemingly unrelated regressions and tests for aggregation bias', *Journal of the American Statistical Association*, **57**, 348–368.

Zellner, A. (1970), 'Estimation of regression relationships containing unobservable independent variables', *International Economic Review*, **11**, 441–454.

Zwick, B. (1971), 'The adjustment of the economy to monetary changes', *Journal of Political Economy*, **79**, 77–96.

# Name Index

# Subject Index